MICRO ECONOMICS

——— *by Graham Walker* ———

THE ESSENTIAL CONCEPTS

© CHECKMATE PUBLICATIONS 1992

Published in Great Britain 1992 by Checkmate Publications
P.O. Box 585, Chester, CH3 7TF.

British Library Cataloguing in Publication Data
Walker, Graham
Micro Economics — The Essential Concepts
1. Title
330

ISBN 1 85313 052 4

All rights reserved. No part of this publication may be reproduced, stored in a retrieval system, or transmitted in any form or by any means, electronic, photocopying, recording, or otherwise without prior written permission of Checkmate Publications, PO Box 585, Chester, CH3 7TF. This book may not be lent, resold, hired out or otherwise disposed of by way of trade in any form of binding or cover other than that in which it is published, without the prior written consent of the publishers.

Text set in 10/12 pt Times
by Merseyside Graphics Ltd., 130 The Parade, Meols, Wirral L47 5AZ
Printed in Great Britain by Redwood Press, Melksham, Wiltshire

Cover design by Merseyside Graphics Ltd.

CONTENTS

Preface and Acknowledgements   *iv*
Answering Data Response Questions   *v*
Answering Essay and Data Response Questions   *ix*

Chapter		Page
1	Basic Concepts I	1
2	Basic Concepts II	11
3	Business Organisations	34
4	Market Analysis: How Price is Determined	60
5	Elasticity	85
6	Cost, Revenue & The Output of the Firm	102
7	Competitive Markets & Business Behaviour	117
8	The Economic Behaviour of the Monopolist	123
9	Oligopolistic Markets	137
10	Alternative Theories of the Firm	148
11	Factor Incomes — Wage Determinations	152
12	Labour & Land Markets — Industrial Application	170
13	Capital: Nature & Analysis	181
14	Governments & Markets — Micro Economic Policy	193
15	Governments & Markets — Monopolies — Mergers	207
16	Optimising Behaviour — Decision Theory	227
17	Basic Mathematical & Statistical Concepts	243
18	Basic Mathematical Concepts: Use in Economics	262

Appendices
i. Multiple Choice Questions   *273*
ii. Essay Questions   *290*
iii. Bibliography   *293*
iv. Glossary   *295*
Index   *304*

PREFACE AND ACKNOWLEDGEMENTS

This book is designed to meet the needs of undergraduate students following a first course in economics as part of an economics, business studies, management or modular programme. It also covers thoroughly the requirements of students studying GCE 'A' and 'AS' level in schools and colleges at home and overseas. It will also be essential reading for a variety of students preparing for professional examinations in economics such as: the Chartered Institute of Management Accountants, Chartered Association of Certified Accountants, Chartered Institute of Marketing, Institute of Chartered Secretaries and Administrators, Institute of Purchasing and Supply and other professional bodies having an introductory examination in economics. BTEC and SCOTVEC Higher students will also find this book provides them with a grasp of the essential concepts.

The book contains a complete glossary of terms, a comprehensive index, clear headings, many diagrams, tables and charts to help economic understanding and a variety of questions designed to test knowledge, skill and understanding in important examination areas. Questions are divided into Data Response, Essay/Research and Multiple Choice. Each Chapter begins with a statement of aims and key concepts that are explained within the chapter so that the reader can focus upon the essential concepts they need to know.

Micro Economics the essential concepts has a companion volume *Macro Economics the essential concepts*, also published by Checkmate.

Acknowledgements

The author would like to thank the following who have kindly given permission to use published material as listed:- Dr. N. Barr, The Economic Review, Vanderbilt University, C.S.O., U.N.(F.A.O.), Midland Bank Review, Lloyds Bank Review.

The author also thanks London University School Examination Board for permission to use past 'A' level examination questions. The specimen answers are the work of the author and do not represent the Board's opinions, model answers or marking scheme. The University of London Schools Examination Board accept no responsibility for the accuracy or method of working in the answers given. Lastly I would like to thank my wife, Rosemary, who typed the manuscript and without whose assistance this project would never have been completed and Lesley and Giles who helped her. As for any mistakes, those are my responsibility.

ANSWERING DATA RESPONSE QUESTIONS

Why Data Response?

Data Response questions are increasingly used as a form of assessment in Economics examinations. They are now established as a reliable form of assessment because they enable economic theories to be applied to real world situations and in so doing students are able to relate their knowledge to current economic problems and events, i.e. Economics has some practical value. This means the data response approach to economics allows for the new activity centred philosophy to learning stressed in the new educational assessment initiatives, e.g. G.C.S.E. At the same time educational research has shown how data response scores are a more reliable indicator of overall examination performance than either the essay or multiple choice form. In short the data response approach allows the candidate and student to apply economic theory, and in so doing they are able to select relevant principles and hence discriminate between arguments and policies. Economic theories are also being applied and evaluated so the candidate must know and be able to use a range of economic and numerical skills before getting down to writing a structured and cogent response. Data response balances the theoretical academic deductive approach, which was the hallmark of the earlier forms of assessment, with the more inductive or empirical real world approach. This means that whilst the deductive or theoretical aspect stresses an analytic framework, often using unrealistic assumptions, data response with its emphasis on evidence and observation allows the student to question principles and develop a more sensible and pragmatic grasp of the economic environment. Whatever the educational philosophy underlying data response questions, Advanced level Exam. Boards, the new G.C.S.E. syllabus, B.T.E.C. and other professional and degree awarding institutions have all incorporated this form of assessment within their overall testing packages. Educationally Data Response questions test the candidate in the higher order of skills, namely the ability to analyse, synthesise, evaluate and apply principles. These skills account for around 30% of the total examination marks, though individual examination boards vary in the actual marks awarded for the Data Response questions.

Data Response Questions

There is no standard format or type of data response question. Questions are often structured from simple definitions or calculations to a discussion and evaluation of principles involved. On the other hand, questions can be unstructured. For example "Discuss the economic significance of the above information" etc. Furthermore, the type of question can range from the hypothetical to the factual and prose comprehension though currently there is no common practice amongst the main Advanced level Examination Boards. The A.E.B., London, and S.U.J.B.

tend to offer a choice and structure their questions over all three types of questions. The Cambridge Board and Cambridge and Oxford Boards use numerical or statistical data together with short response questions. Oxford Delegacy incorporate the data response question within the Essay paper and the J.M.B. tend to go for one large passage, e.g. a newspaper article, often with a table, and structured questions. Nevertheless, for all this disparity it may be useful to briefly outline the three main question types and provide simple guidance points.

a)   *Hypothetical Type*
A favourite with London, A.E.B. and S.U.J.B. whereby hypothetical data are presented usually on the firm, supply or demand, National Income, etc. The question can incorporate definitions, calculations and a discussion on the economic principles involved and candidates are left in no doubt regarding which economic ideas are being tested. These questions are similar to multiple choice questions and so the answers should follow the structure of the question and candidates should show all calculations or workings. In the main, be brief and to the point in your answer and relate and explain your ideas to the Data. It is useful with this type of question to make a rough plan of your answer beforehand.

b)   *Factual Type*
These questions use real data in the form of a table, chart, diagram or newscutting, etc. They are selected from the Press, Government publications, Treasury Report, Bank Review etc. The data are not specifically designed for examination purposes so the student should carefully read, often more than once, to grasp its economic significance and relevance. Underline any important points or statistical information, and you may have to discriminate and disregard much of the passage. This does not matter and in itself is a test of your ability to select only that material relevant to the question. Examiners' Reports regularly stress that the failing of students with this type of question is their inability to understand the statistical presentation, technique or concept. This means, for example, candidates should be able to understand time and cross sectional data. They should also be able to understand:- index numbers, "real" and current prices, trends and seasonal variations, logarithmic and normal scales. Also they should recognise a simple equation, a pie chart or histogram etc., and generally understand the significance and relationship between a passage and the accompanying table, chart or diagram. This means those who have studied mathematics or statistics will be able to cope better than those from a non-numerate background. See the Statistical Chapters.

c)   *Prose Comprehension Type*
These are specifically selected textual passages again from a newspaper, book or Government publication etc. The questions are structured to incorporate definitions and interpretation of basic economic principles. The more difficult questions concern the usefulness, or evaluation, of the theories with regard to the

data. These questions are often difficult because there is usually more than one answer and the passage can cover a wide range of principles and syllabus areas. In this type of question, search for the likely major principles being tested and note how they are being applied. There may be other minor ideas which can be used but the importance of these can often be seen by the way the question is structured.

Sometimes a passage relates to only one economic problem but there are usually underlying assumptions which have to be made explicit and discussed. The source of the passage can often be a clue as to why it was selected. To gain practice for this question type get into the habit of continually reading good quality newspapers and try to relate economic ideas you are familiar with to the relevant financial or economic article. This enables you to develop a critical approach and encourages sensible comment and evaluation of the main arguments.

Some Summary Points to Remember

(i)   Know and understand basic economic theory thoroughly.

(ii)   Continually practice relating economic theory to the real world by looking at suitable tables, passages etc. in newspapers and other sources.

(iii) Obtain past Examination Reports and Questions and practice doing the Data Response problems within the time allowed. Note the marks allowed where these are printed and allocate time accordingly.

(iv) Develop a good background knowledge of current commercial, economic and political events.

(v)   Know and be able to work with basic statistical concepts and key economic formula (see Statistical Chapters).

(vi) Appreciate why examiners use Data Response questions. Are you able to apply theory to real or hypothetical data?

(vii) Check instructions regarding the Data Response questions and allocate time on the basis of the number of questions to be attempted and the marks awarded. Structure your answer on the basis of the question and appreciate that the latter parts of a question often use the answer you obtained in the first part of the question.

(viii) Write legibly, logically and try to be neat when drawing up a chart, table or diagram. Slang must be avoided — write in textbook English.

(ix) In conclusion, Examiners Reports stress the following "Data Response questions are frequently open-ended, permitting a variety of approaches and material. In assessing answers, examiners, whilst requiring theoretical and factual correctness, take answers on their merits. Each exposes the candidate's intellectual and educational standard, as well as technical grasp and skill. Examination centres would do well to consider how far their study of economics is part of an educational process: the former being an instrument of the latter. Above all, Data

Response questions can be so varied that a questioning approach to the subject is important. The relevant theory to provide a structure needs to be selected and applied. Its appropriateness to the situation needs to be considered and a reasoned discussion presented. In the ideal case, applied economics requires the selective use of theory and a synthesis with the facts of the situation. In this respect they discriminate in favour of those who have been *educated* in their subject."

Source: London, 1982 'A' Economics Examiners Report.

(ANSWERING ESSAYS & DATA RESPONSE QUESTIONS — Some Points to Remember in Essay and Examination Preparation)

Candidates Checklist

A *Before the Exam*

1. Obtain a copy of the latest detailed syllabus of the examining body. This will give a comprehensive outline of the principles, content, range and application, etc. which the student will be expected to know, i.e. what the examiners will be looking for. Some syllabuses are general and not detailed so careful examination of Examiners reports is essential.

2. Obtain a set of past examination questions (covering the up-to-date syllabus) in order to get an idea of the range of difficulty, coverage, etc. You may also be able to detect if any questions appear regularly. Often this happens if the question was badly answered in previous years. At the same time send for a copy of the Examiners Report to see where the previous candidates went wrong. This often gives a good idea of the overall problems encountered by all candidates. Poorly answered questions have a habit of appearing in the next year's exam.

3. Buy at least one of the main textbooks recommended either by the exam board or by someone you know has had experience of preparing candidates for the exam.

4. Cover all the syllabus and do not try to pass knowing only half the subject. Increasingly these days, questions require answers which draw on many parts of the syllabus.

5. Essay papers are the form of assessing your economic knowledge because they enable the candidate to analyse problems, express arguments, reason methodically and demonstrate his grasp of the English language. This does not mean that candidates are penalised for poor spelling, but they do have to present arguments in a logical and grammatical manner.

6. Obtaining a pass or a good grade means you have to practise essay writing. Being good at data response or multiple choice questions does not mean you can assume you will find the essay paper easy. Students should try to do the previous exam paper within the time allotted, without any help. This will enable you to allocate time so that all five questions are adequately attempted.

B *In the Exam Room*

1. Look carefully at the instructions. What does the question mean? Which principles of economics are being tested, e.g. marginal revenue product, the multiplier, diminishing returns?

2. Look at key words. These indicate the treatment required and the principles, concepts and coverage the examiner is trying to assess. Look carefully at each word of the question as the type of answer sought depends upon them. Some examples to illustrate.

- a) *Discuss..* Explain then give the pros and cons, implications, likely effects, e.g. "Comparative cost analysis adequately explains international trade." Discuss.
- b) *Compare/Contrast...* Point out similarities and differences between, e.g. Compare and contrast the efficiency of fixed and flexible exchange rate systems.
- c) *Evaluate...* Outline the system, principle, etc. then compare the main feature of the question to the principle, i.e. use the principle as the criteria, e.g. Evaluate the contribution made by marginal productivity theory in explaining wage differentials.
- d) *Explain...* Again ensure you outline briefly the facts or principles, showing the "why" and "how" in order to explain the answer, e.g. Explain why some economists question the ability of Incomes Policies to control the level of inflation.

3. Before you start writing, try to put into three or four sentences what the question is about. This will clarify your ideas about the subject and ensures that the essay keeps to the point. A brief essay plan with key words, phrases and overall essay structure outlined is useful so that you do not stray from the question.

4. Do not forget the time element. Allow yourself an equal amount of time per question and no more. Each question carries equal marks so set yourself about 36 minutes, i.e. 3 hours divided by 5 questions, and spend about 5 to 6 minutes thinking it out, planning and deciding diagrams. Always answer 5 questions if instructed to do so. When using an answer plan tick off each point as you go.

5. Use the first paragraph to show the Examiner that you do understand the question by rewriting it, if you like in your own words, describing how the question will be answered or by explaining the key words etc. There is a danger of writing an answer to the question you would like rather than the question you have been given.

6. It is sometimes a good idea to start with the question you are best able to answer since this will help your confidence and prepare you for the next one.

7. In the main part of the answer make sure you keep to the question. Try not to use platitudes, dogma or political bias. Support all arguments with examples, illustrations or facts.

8. When appropriate use a diagram. In particular, market analysis or Keynesian analysis questions can all be profitably answered using a correctly drawn and labelled diagram, adequately explained by the text of course.

9. Use the last paragraph to sum up your ideas, particularly if you feel you have deviated from the question.

10. Try to use correct English grammar, etc. Write legibly and remember that presentation is important. Examiners have to mark hundreds of scripts so do not put them in a bad mood by writing illegibly. Do not ramble; padding fools no one and do not worry about the occasional misspelt word. That has never been a reason for failing or for not obtaining a good grade.

11. Far too many candidates try to impress the Examiner by showing how up-to-date they are with the latest theories or that they have read the latest text book, etc., without demonstrating a firm grasp of economic principles or attempting to answer the question. Of course it is perfectly legitimate to outline Friedman's theory of inflation but if you do not demonstrate that you understand exactly what inflation is then the Examiner will draw his own conclusions. Remember that you are trying to pass an intermediate level economics exam and not a degree in economics. There is no substitute for a good grasp of basic principles, so know your subject thoroughly.

12. Many of the individual words used in the answer need to be chosen carefully. In general it is better to use moderate rather than conclusive words. Slang must also be avoided — write in textbook English.

13. When you have attempted all five questions, go back and try to complete any which you have left unfinished, if time allows. If time is getting short on the last question, as a last resort write answers in note form.

14. Finally, try to arrive at the examination hall in good time, calm and collected, even if a little nervous. Check the night before that you have a pen that writes, ink, pencil, ruler and rubber. Poorly drawn diagrams and scruffy presentation are penalised. Remember all the candidates are as concerned and worried as you are. This may be some consolation!

BASIC CONCEPTS I

AIMS: To define, explain and discuss
- The Method of Economics
- Economic Systems: Free Enterprise and Command
- Problems of Economics: What, How, Who
- Private and Public Goods: The Role of The Government

KEY CONCEPTS
Positive, Normative Statements
Economic Man, Economic Models
Consumer, Perishable, Capital Goods
Free Enterprise, Collectivist, Mixed Economy
Private, Collective, Public Goods, Cost, Rivalry
Merit/Demerit Goods, Externalities

Economics and Methodology

J.M. Keynes described the value of studying economics in terms of the thought process or method it developed when analysing a problem. Today the view is that economics uses a scientific method in so far as it employs theories whose predictions can be tested by empirical evidence. If the evidence disproves or refutes these predictions a new theory has to be developed. This approach is referred to as positive economics to distinguish it from normative economics which uses value judgements. An example illustrates. A positive statement is "a lower tea price causes more tea to be bought" whilst a normative statement would be "tea should be subsidised in order to encourage tea drinking". The former statement can be tested by statistical evidence whilst the latter is a matter of opinion.

What is the scientific method which characterises physics or chemistry and how far can it be said to exist in economics? The theories of physics and chemistry can be tested under controlled laboratory conditions but economics is a social science concerned with predicting human behaviour in the market place. This means it is often difficult to hold conditions constant in the real world in order to test economic theories accurately. Human behaviour is sometimes irrational and it is often impossible to pin down the main factor at work in an economic situation since so many may be influencing events. Nevertheless, overall statistical (econometric analysis) can be useful in explaining trends to both government and business sectors. What are the elements of the economic method? Economics constructs a simulation or abstraction of the real world in the form of an economic model or hypotheses which links the behavioural cause to the predicted effect using certain basic assumptions. In market analysis a most important assumption is the "ceterus paribus" clause meaning other things remain constant. This enables specified market influences to be held constant in order to concentrate on one specific influence, e.g. price. These assumptions may not always be realistic but they do enable the economist to deduce or work out testable predictions and therefore they show a systematic method of reasoning. The other approach is the inductive method which builds up explanatory theories on the basis of observation. Economists seem to use both methods. When Giffen observed the behaviour of Irish peasants buying more bread even when bread prices rose, he formulated the inductive idea of a Giffen good. On the other hand the neoclassical theory of the firm which allegedly uses unrealistic assumptions about business behaviour has developed a more deductive theory with respect to business price, output and profit. A summary of the scientific method in economic research is shown in Fig. 1.1.

FIG. 1.1
THE STAGES OF SCIENTIFIC METHOD IN ECONOMICS

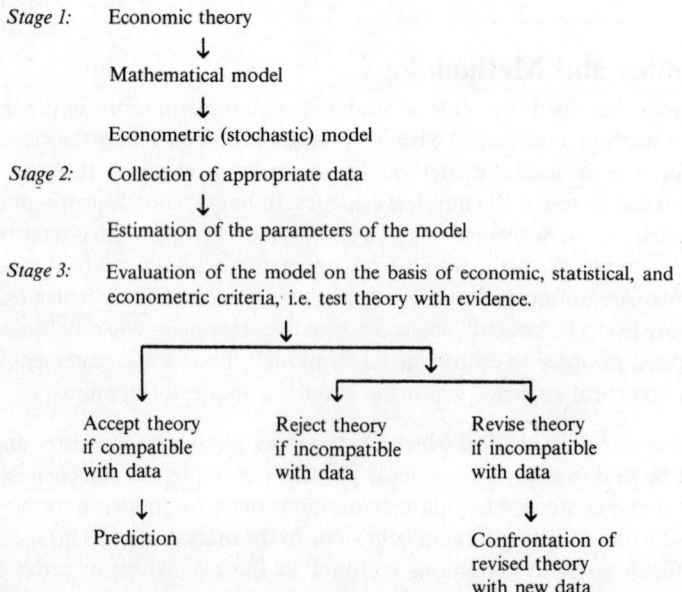

Economic Man and Arguments in Economics

Much of economics is concerned with decisions taken by the consumer, producer or income earner. In this it is assumed there is such a person as an economic man who, as an individual unit, is well informed, rational and guided by material self interest. Furthermore, this person makes unrestrained decisions based upon his own preferences for goals. These assumptions lie at the heart of much economic theory. However, in many areas of business individuals behave in a social manner so that, it is alleged, people try to maximise the welfare of others before their own. Furthermore, uncertainty means that decisions are often non-scientific in nature and only recently has economics attempted to analyse economic behaviour under conditions of risk. The above helps to explain why economists often disagree. Economics is not an exact science and even simple definitions are open to argument. The classification of those persons unemployed has changed many times over the last few years. There are many disagreements about how realistic assumptions should be and also whether people are really guided by social or individualistic motives. Lastly, economists are bound to have their own political viewpoint which will colour their views on economic policy. Much of economics is concerned with inconclusive evidence so there is bound to be argument over policy decisions.

Micro and Macro Economics

Modern treatment divides the subject into micro and macro economics. Micro is concerned with the behaviour of the individual decision maker as well as a specific market and institutional operation. This is the subject matter of this book. Macro economics is concerned with overall problems affecting the economy such as inflation, unemployment, growth, etc. These problems are covered in a separate accompanying volume "Essential Concepts in Macro Economics" by N. Proctor. A detailed syllabus for micro and macro economics is at the end of this book together with a selected book list.

The Economic System: Defining Economics

A selection of definitions of Economics

1. "A study of mankind in the ordinary business of life" (Marshall)
2. "A study of human behaviour as a relationship between ends and scarce means which have alternative uses" (Robbins)
3. "That part of human behaviour which relates to the production, exchange, and use of goods and services" (Begg)
4. "The study of how people and society choose to employ scarce resources that could have alternative uses" (Samuelson)

4 Basic Concepts I

The central theme of the above definitions is that economics is concerned with the study of human behaviour with respect to resource allocation and use. Economic problems arise because there are limited resources but unlimited wants. This scarcity of resources means that a choice has to be made about what to produce. Human wants should not be confused with needs. Individuals have basic needs such as the need for shelter, clothing and food, etc. and these needs, in a developed economy are often the first to be provided. However people are not satisfied with fulfilling these basic needs, they also want other goods and services which satisfy their yearning for social status and prestige, e.g. positional goods. Thus new wants both individual and social in nature are always developing and they are fulfilled by producers using scarce resources such as land, labour, capital and enterprise. These are also called factors of production and they are owned by the same individuals supplying the initial wants. The connection between wants and resources is made by the producer who brings together in the business organisation the factors in order to produce goods and services. These goods and services provide the satisfaction or utility to the consumer.

Economic goods and services have a scarcity value and can be classified as follows. Consumer Perishables are consumed or used up immediately, e.g. food, newspapers, etc. Consumer Durables provide utility or satisfaction over a longer time period, e.g. T.V., motor car, video, etc. Personal Services provide utility directly to the consumer in the form of hair cuts, entertainment, holidays. Commercial Services help the individual obtain these goods by providing credit, insurance or retailing or wholesaling outlet, etc. Capital Goods also called producer or intermediate goods, provide utility indirectly by making the consumer goods used in final consumption. These capital goods are used by householders, companies and the state in the form of houses, motor cars, plant and equipment, factories, roads, hospitals, schools, etc. This means that a motor car is a consumer durable to an individual but to a company it could be classified as a fixed capital asset, i.e. helping indirectly in the production of final goods. When there is an abundance of a good, for example fresh air or sand in the desert, there will be no scarcity value and these are defined as free goods.

In producing the goods and services the producer in western economies combines factors of production in the best way (lowest cost) in order to achieve the objective of profit. Military, religious or other objectives can be persued by other political systems. Nevertheless the problem of scarcity always exists. In some parts of Africa this scarcity is extreme and poverty exists, whilst in affluent western economies choice of scarcity is between one or two holidays a year. The universal economic problem of scarcity can be subdivided into the following problems: 1) what goods and services are to be produced with the available resources? 2) how are these resources best used in order to produce these goods and services? 3) who will receive these goods and services once they have been produced? Two subsidiary problems associated with the above are 4) where will production take place and 5) when will production take place? Now or later?

Different economic systems have evolved to allocate scarce resources ranging from the Free Market to the Command or Collectivist system. The Mixed Economy lies between the extreme systems. The *Free Market or free enterprise system* is prevalent in the U.S.A., Japan, the U.K. and other western democracies and generally exhibits the following features:-

(i) *Individual capital or property.* Individuals are allowed to own wealth in the form of land, houses, shares and also they own their own companies, etc.

(ii) *Free Enterprise depends upon individual self interest.* Individuals can freely choose to consume or produce what they wish, guided by the motives of maximising satisfaction or profit. Individual factors of production will also seek the highest income.

(iii) *Competition within the market.* Competition is the overriding condition which affects both the consumer and the producer. Competition between buyers and sellers takes place within the market and this establishes the price for goods, services and factors of production (Income). Ideally competition through the market serves to ensure prices are the correct signals to the consumer and producer and this information limits the powers of seller and buyer and automatically regulates the system.

(iv) *Prices and profits.* The information for decision making comes from the prices and profits which arise in both product and factor markets. In order to ensure this market system works properly, consumers, producers and income earners must know how prices and profits change so that they can then adapt their buying and selling patterns to these price changes. An example, using Fig. 1.2, serves to illustrate how the above features (i) to (iv) work in order to answer the scarcity problems outlined. The computer market is taken as the example.

Example: More Computers!

Fig. 1.2 shows how the free enterprise system reacts to a sudden increase in the demand for computers by consumers. The computer product market will experience a rise in price and profits and producers see this and decide to move resources into producing more computers at the expense of other goods which now make relatively lower profits, or even losses. The producers now hire more factors of production from factor markets and this will push up incomes to those in the computer factor market. Householders who ultimately own resources will now be attracted into the higher paid occupations in the computer sector. Furthermore, since they now earn high incomes they will also have a greater claim over the goods and services produced. Capital, land resources, and entrepreneurial skills will all move to produce more computers so their incomes will also increase. Thus the free enterprise unit (sole trader, partnership or limited company) motivated by self interest, (profit) and guided by the market will help to

6 Basic Concepts I

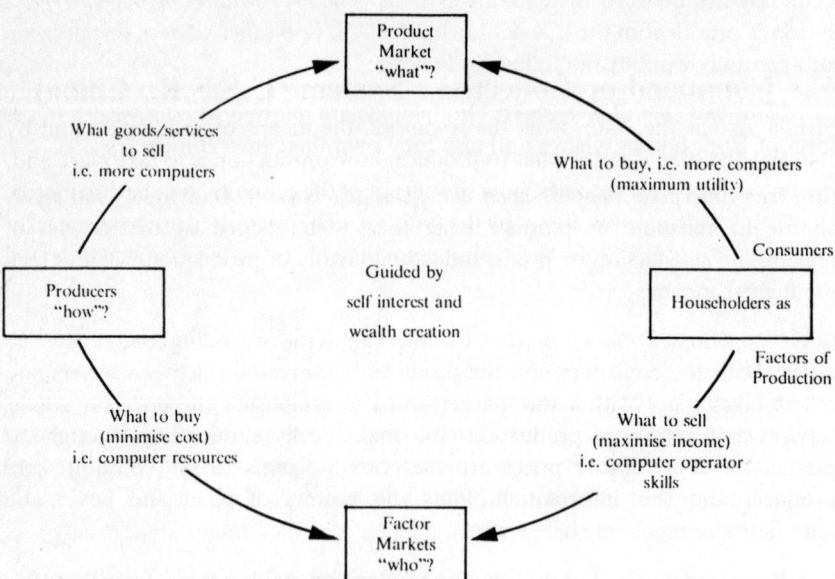

**FIG. 1.2
THE FREE ENTERPRISE SYSTEM — MORE COMPUTERS**

solve the problem of i) what to produce? — more computers, ii) how to produce? — lowest cost, highest profit, and iii) for whom? — those owning scarce computer resources who now earn higher incomes. In order to make the right decisions both producers and consumers will compare the extra benefits or revenues against the extra costs or risks before taking any action to produce extra products or before moving their resources into a particular factor market. The above computer example also serves to illustrate the advantages of the free enterprise system which are:

1) goods and services are produced in line with free consumers choice and wants.

2) the price signals automatically and quickly inform consumers, producers and income earners how the market is changing.

3) competition encourages the lowest price for both product and factor markets so resources are quickly and efficiently used and not wasted.

Even so there are *disadvantages of the free market system*. These are:

1) inequalities of income and wealth will develop so that some may enjoy the luxuries of life before others have been properly fed or clothed.

2) if competition does not exist due to monopolistic markets, then inefficiency and excessive profits can result.

3) consumers are not always able to make a fully informed choice so resources may be used inefficiently.

4) important goods such as defence, law and order, health or education may not be provided in sufficient quantity through the market to guarantee a caring, civilised society.

The Command or Collectivist System (U.S.S.R., China)

In this system the state owns the resources, the means of production and by essential planning decides what to produce, how production is to take place and, by controlling factor incomes, how the output of the economy is to be distributed. Under this system prices are set by the state, i.e. 'fiat' prices, and not by the market and hence the needs of the state are put above the individual wants of the consumer.

The Advantages of the Collectivist System

1) In theory basic needs can be provided for all before individual wants or luxuries are catered for. 2) Social costs and benefits can be identified and valued so that resources can be allocated to improve the environment, or to reduce monopoly power or to provide adequate health services, etc.

3) By owning the means of production, the state ensures continuous production of essentials and so helps to reduce the problems of unemployed resources which often result with the free market system.

Disadvantages of the Collectivist System

1) In practice food shortages arise and consumer wants are usually ignored.

2) There is a lack of incentive to provide goods because there is no profit motive and furthermore costs are often allowed to escalate because of a lack of accountability.

3) Bureaucratic self-interest replaces the profit motive, waste increases and coordinating production decisions is often made difficult due to the absence of price signals and profits.

4) Inequality of incomes does not disappear. The bureaucratic and state officials become the high income earners rather than the entrepreneur.

The Mixed Economy

In this system, illustrated by the economies of the U.K., Sweden, France, etc. the private entrepreneur and the state coexist to produce goods and services the consumer wants and needs. In the U.K. the private sector produces around 70% of output with the state providing the rest. The state has a variety of roles.

1) Public and merit goods. Public goods, e.g. defence, roads, road signs, are provided by taxation because it is alleged that otherwise they would not be

provided in sufficient quantity if left to the market. Merit goods, e.g. education and health, are those which the state provides because they are thought to be good for the community. These are discussed in more detail below.

2) Industrial policy. The state has always attempted to regulate both factor and product markets. Factor markets, wage controls and trade union legislation have sought to achieve social and economic objectives. In product markets price controls and anti-monopolistic legislation have a long history in the U.K. The nationalisation of certain key industries, for example electricity, gas, coal, rail, was pursued after the second world war. Since the 1979 Thatcher government, the role of the state in this area has been subject to critical review, and policy has been designed to privatise nationalised industries, encourage private provision in health and education and generally deregulate the controlled sectors.

3) After the second world war Keynesian demand management policies were used to reduce unemployment and generate economic growth, although since the 1980's a monetarist stance has been assumed which relies upon free market sources determining levels of inflation and unemployment. Generally the role of the state has reduced over the last few years and has now to be seen in the context of the state's aim to achieve greater economic and social equality against the free enterprise search for profit and efficiency. These topics are discussed more fully under the micro-economic policy and economic efficiency chapters in this book.

Classification of public, collective and private goods

In order to understand the state versus free enterprise argument it is useful to classify the types of goods and services provided in a mixed economy. The matrix in Table 1.1 identifies four groups of goods according to the criteria of rivalry and excludability. Examples of these goods are given for each type along with an explanatory note.

TABLE 1.1
PRIVATE, COLLECTIVE AND PUBLIC GOODS

	RIVALROUS OR POSITIVE COST IN CONSUMPTION	NON-RIVALROUS OR COSTLESS IN CONSUMPTION
EXCLUDABLE FROM NON-PAYER	**PRIVATE GOODS** e.g. CARS, FOOD	**TOLL GOODS** e.g. BRIDGES, ROADS!
NOT EXCLUDABLE FROM NON-PAYER	**COMMON GOODS** e.g. FISHING	**PUBLIC GOODS** e.g. ROAD SIGNS, DEFENSE, FIREWORKS, LIGHTHOUSE

Notes

a) Rivalry in consumption means that if one person consumes a good then that good cannot be consumed by another, i.e. it has a positive opportunity cost. If it is non-rivalrous in consumption then the enjoyment of the good by one person does not prevent other people from consuming and enjoying the same good, i.e. one person's use of a bridge, under normal circumstances, would not stop another person using it at the same time. In fact the use of road signs by others provides positive benefits to everyone.

b) Excludability means it is possible to provide the good on a one to one basis, for example one person uses one pair of shoes. Thus a non-excludable good is one where it is not possible to exclude others from consuming even if they haven't paid, e.g. a private firework function which is overlooked by others. From the Table private goods are those which are both excludable and rivalrous whilst the other three categories are generally classified as collective goods since they either are non-excludable, non-rivalrous or both. In these three cases of goods which are called collective goods the state often finances, by taxation, the operation and provision of the goods or services.

Merit/Demerit Goods

Merit goods, e.g. health/education, are thought by the state to be good for the community, so their consumption is actively encouraged by free state provision or some sort of subsidy, etc. Demerit goods, e.g. smoking, alcohol, drugs, etc., are not thought by the state to be good for the individual so the production and consumption of these goods is discouraged by taxation or other regulations, etc.

Externalities and Social Costs

External social benefits and costs are those extra costs and benefits that fall outside of the market decision by either buyer or seller. They are ignored because the market only values benefits and costs to the buyer and private seller. These external benefits and costs are nevertheless enjoyed or borne by the community. External social costs would be the extra pollution or congestion which society has to pay for whilst social benefits would be the fruits of a healthy and well-educated society. It is alleged that the free market ignores these costs and benefits so the state has to play a role ensuring that they are appreciated. This is discussed in further detail in Chapters 14 and 15.

CHAPTER 1 Research

1. *Using current data such as newspapers, etc., collect statements which you consider are positive/normative economic ideas.*

2. *Use real world sources and identify one example of each, with suitable reasons for your choice, a capital good, a free enterprise society, a merit good, an externality.*

 **BASIC CONCEPTS II**

AIMS: To define, explain and discuss
- *Diminishing Returns and Economic Efficiency*
- *Costs, Opportunity Costs, Fixed, Variable Factors*
- *Factors of Production*
- *Industry Interdependence*
- *Specialisation and Trade*
- *Population and Economic Welfare*

KEY CONCEPTS

Opportunity Cost, Diminishing Returns, Optimum Output, Allocative Efficiency, Per Capita Income, Labour, Land, Capital, Value Added, Input-Output Analysis, Absolute and Comparative Advantage, Optimum Population; Birth, Death and Migration Rate

Diminishing Returns, Opportunity Cost and Economic Efficiency

Since there are limited resources available and different bundles of output possible, society has to choose which goods it prefers to consume. This choice could be, for example, more guns or less butter or more books and fewer cars, etc. In producing more goods, in the short run, the law of diminishing returns applies and in choosing between the alternative bundles the cost of choosing one good rather than another reflects its opportunity cost. These two concepts are examined and illustrated in Table 2.1 and accompanying figure.

Diminishing Returns and Opportunity Cost

As more cars or books are produced, see Table 2.1, proportionately more labour, the variable input, is required given technology and capital. To produce each one million extra units of books requires proportionately more labour, i.e. 1, 3, 6, 10 thousand employees. At the same time each two thousand car workers employed increases car output, but at a falling rate, i.e. 20,000, 14,000, 10,000, etc. These

TABLE 2.1
PRODUCTION POSSIBILITIES IN A HYPOTHETICAL ECONOMY

Alternate Bundles of Output	Output of Books (millions)	Employment in Books (th)	Output of Cars (th)	Employment in Cars (th)	Opportunity Cost of:- Books in terms of Cars	Cars in terms of Books
A	0	0	50	8		
B	1	1	44	6	6	1/6
C	2	3	34	4	10	1/10
D	3	6	20	2	14	1/14
E	4	10	0	0	20	1/20

TABLE 2.2
A SIMPLE ECONOMY AND CONSTANT RETURNS

Alternate Bundles	Output of Beaver	Employment to catch Beaver	Output of Deer	Employment to catch Deer
L	3	3	0	0
M	2	2	1	1
N	1	1	2	2
O	0	0	3	3

FIG. 2.1
TECHNICAL (E–A) EFFICIENCY AND ALLOCATIVE EFFICIENCY (D)

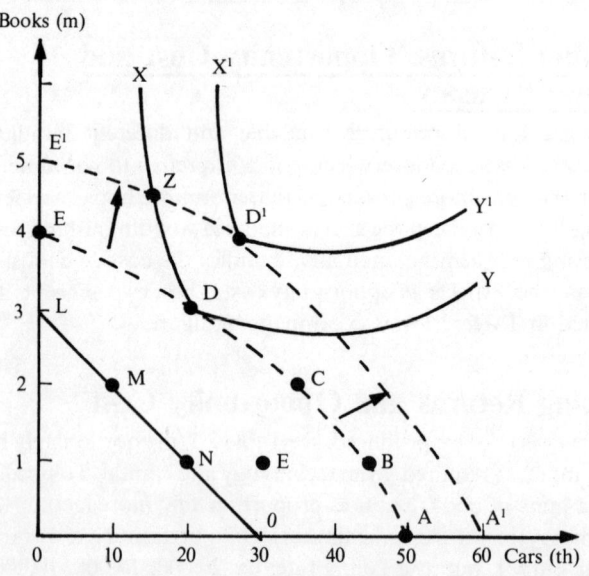

calculations are obtained by subtracting the difference between total car production as it increases from zero to 20,000, 34,000, etc. This phenomena is known as the law of diminishing returns and it is discussed fully later in the chapter. In moving from one bundle of goods to another we see that in each case more books or cars have to be given up in order to consume more of the other good. In moving from alternative A to B, one million books can only be consumed by giving up 6,000 cars or from E to D 20,000 extra cars costs one million books, in terms of what has to be given up. This concept illustrates the idea of opportunity cost which is the cost of the foregone alternative. The opportunity cost rate of books for cars or cars for books, is given in the last two columns of Table 2.1 and this trade off for one good or another varies showing how opportunity cost increases and decreases.

Technical and Allocative Efficiency

By plotting the alternative bundles of goods A to E on Fig. 2.1 we obtain the production possibility curve for an economy. This defines the maximum output of goods possible given resources and technology. Any point inside the curve, e.g. E, means that resources could be used more efficiently so E is inefficient since the economy could produce another 20th cars from E to B. At the same time more economic growth could increase overall output at each level and so the economy could move to $E^1 A^1$. This would mean, for a given population, that there is now a higher per capita income, i.e. $\frac{\text{output}}{\text{population}}$ = output per head. Although points along A–E define technical efficiency there will only be one combination of output which maximises consumer preferences. The curve XY defines the combination of cars and books which maximises this preference, see Fig. 2.1, i.e. satisfaction or utility is at a maximum as we move further away from the origin, O. Given the production possibilities in A to E, there will only be one point, D, where technical and allocative efficiency is maximised. As this cannot be improved upon it is defined as the Pareto optimum — see Chapter 14 for more discussion of this. If economic growth shifts the curve AE to $A^1 E^1$ society will be able to consume more and hence move to a higher preference curve $X^1 Y^1$ with a new optimum of D^1. Even if the economy moved to a point Z on the new output curve $A^1 E^1$ it would still be on the old preference schedule XY. By moving down $E^1 A^1$ to D^1 the economy could become better off, i.e. it could improve its overall efficiency.

A Simple Economy and Constant Costs   See Table 2.2

In a simple economy where only labour is used, so no land or capital is employed, the output and employment of labour is shown in terms of the beaver and deer caught. For every beaver or deer caught one unit (hour) of labour is used so implying a constant return to labour in terms of labour output given up.

14 Basic Concepts II

Furthermore the trade off of beaver for deer is always the same so implying a constant opportunity cost. This is shown as a straight line L–N in Fig.2.1, i.e. if this had been applied to the books and cars case it would have been one million to ten thousand, etc.

The Law of Diminishing Returns

Initially the law of diminishing returns was derived from observing the behaviour of farm output when successive units of labour or capital were applied. It was later applied to other business unit behaviour, e.g. firms. Simply put it says that if successive units of a variable factor are added to the fixed factor, e.g. land, then the output of the variable factor will initially rise but then decline.

Assumptions/Definitions

(i) All variable factor inputs are equally efficient.

(ii) The fixed factor cannot be increased or decreased in the short term.

(iii) Techniques of production are given.

(iv) The marginal product is the change in the total product resulting from each unit of variable (labour) factor employed, i.e. $MP_n = TP_n - TP_{n-1}$.

(vi) The average product or per capita income for a population is equal to
$$\frac{\text{Total Product}}{\text{quantity of variable factor}} = \frac{TP}{n}$$

Table 2.3 shows how, given land as the fixed factor, a variable factor, labour, increases total product, see Fig. 2.3. Average and marginal products are also derived and are plotted in Fig. 2.2.

Diminished Returns Illustrated

As the Table 2.3 shows the marginal product of the variable factor, labour, at first increases but then declines along with the average product. In fact MP cuts AP at the highest point on the AP curve. This is because as more labour is employed on the land the proportions between the fixed and variable factors eventually become less favourable and inefficiencies develop between the labour and land. Any attempt to increase total output on an overall basis would have to come about by changing the scale of the operation, i.e. by employing more of the fixed factor (land) which could be done by amalgamating adjoining farms. In Fig. 2.2. and 2.3. the employment of more labour increases total output but then diminishing returns lead to falling MP and AP. In fact as MP falls it pulls down AP and vice versa. The maximum output per man, known as the optimum employment level, is when five are employed. Between one and five workers the farm experiences increasing returns and from five workers on it experiences diminishing returns; it

TABLE 2.3
TOTAL, AVERAGE AND MARGINAL PRODUCT AS LABOUR (VARIABLE INPUT) CHANGES

INPUT OF			OUTPUT (Wheat)	
Labour	Land	Total product	Average product (iii)/(i)	Marginal product
(i)	(ii)	(iii)	(iv)	(v)
1	10	40	40	40
2	10	100	50	60
3	10	210	70	110
4	10	400	100	190
5	10	550	110	150
6	10	600	100	50
7	10	630	90	30
8	10	640	80	10
9	10	630	70	−10

over employs labour. This concept of optimum population was applied by Malthus, see Section on Population.

Return to the Variable Factor as Scale Changes

In the long run all factors can be varied in proportion. As mentioned the farm can be enlarged by the amalgamation of adjoining farms. The employment of more labour, under these conditions of varying factor inputs, could lead to constant increasing or decreasing returns to scale, see Figs. 2.4(i)–(iii). Even though the size of the farm may double and increasing returns are experienced, see Fig. 2.4(ii), diminishing returns at l_1 still apply to the variable factor in the short run before the increase in scale, i.e. l_1 to l_2. This can be further illustrated in Table 2.4 which shows a matrix of output as land and labour vary.

TABLE 2.4
OUTPUT CHANGES AS LAND AND LABOUR VARIES

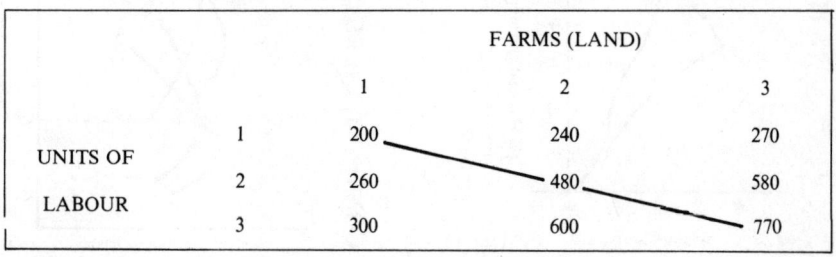

16 Basic Concepts II

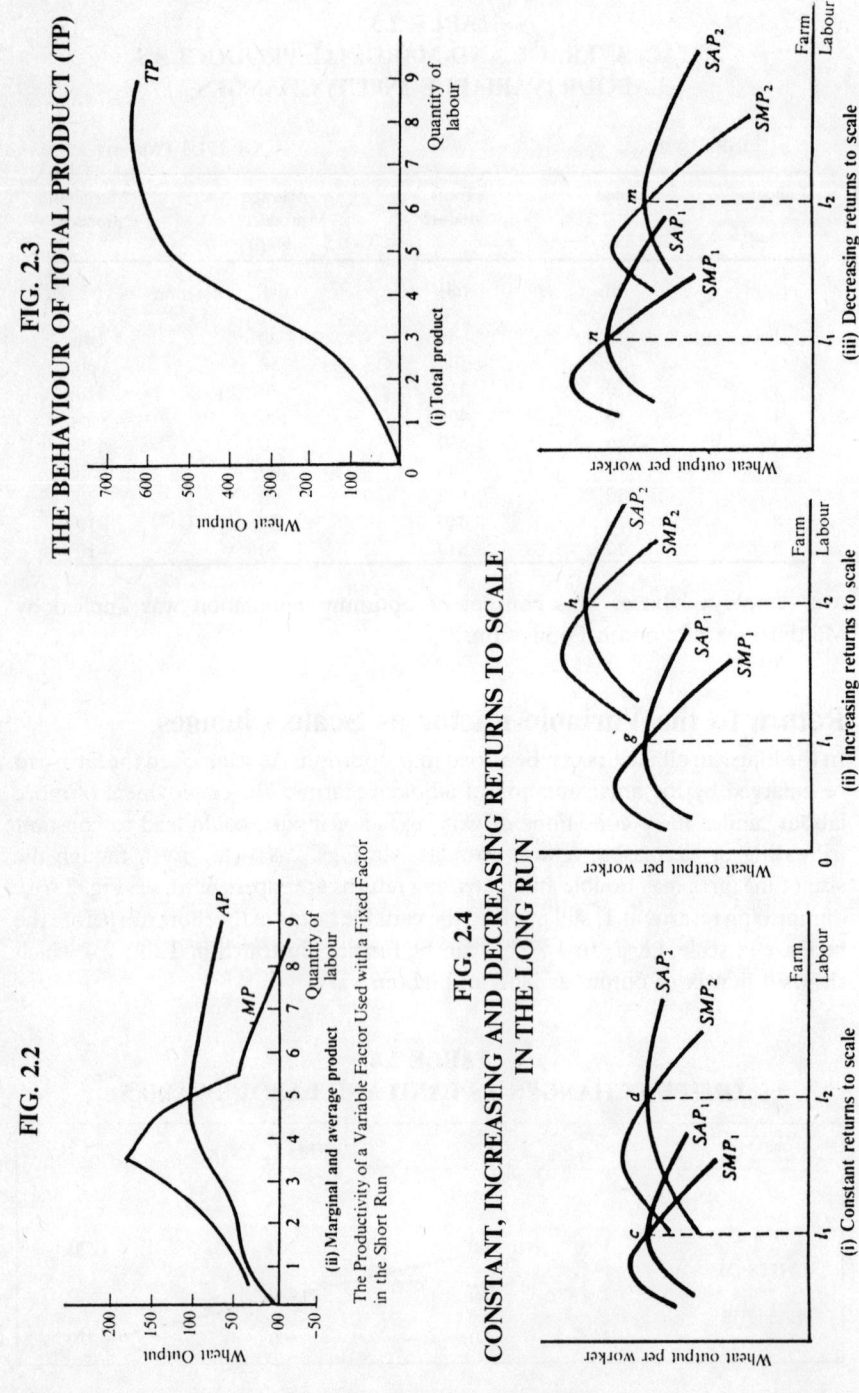

With land the fixed factor, i.e. one farm, and as labour increases from 1 to 2 to 3, representing a 100%, 50% increases in labour input, output increases disproportionately less, i.e. by 30% and 15%. If labour is the fixed factor, then as more land is used diminishing returns still applies, i.e. there is still only 20% and 12½% increase in output as land increases. However, as scale increases and both labour and land are varied, the diagonal figures show how output increases from 200 to 480 to 770 which show disproportionate percentage rises in output as factors are increased by 100% and 50%, i.e. increasing returns to scale.

Factors of Production and their Uses (Summary)

Land

Land includes all the scarce natural resources both on and under the earth. This includes the land used for locating offices, roads, houses, factories and also the land used for providing raw materials such as coal, iron ore, chemicals and even food stuffs. Land also provides a means of transport, e.g. roads, rivers, canals, etc. Land is fixed in supply but can be used for different purposes. This means land located close to markets often has a high site value. The more uses available to land the scarcer it becomes and hence higher in value. Land is paid a rent which, when capitalised up, indicates the sale value of a piece of land.

Manpower

Entrepreneurs hire labour in return for an income, i.e. wages. The quantity of labour available in the market depends upon the birth rate, death rate and migration rate of the population as well as the participation rate of different groups of workers, i.e. if more women returned to work then the participation rate and hence labour supply into the market would increase. The willingness and ability of labour to move between jobs (occupational mobility) and between regions (geographical mobility) is also important, and the degree to which labour will and can move influences how quickly industry is able to adapt to changing market conditions. Governments have attempted to reduce immobility and this is seen as important in improving overall labour efficiency. Manpower is only scarce if it can be used to supply output in demand. A coal miner in the north of England, working in an inefficient pit, is not considered as economically scarce as, say, a surgeon faced with a long waiting list of patients waiting for an operation.

Capital

Capital is not required for its own sake, but because it is able to provide for future output and satisfaction. Capital goods are often referred to as producer or intermediate products. The business unit uses capital which is categorised in the balance sheet as fixed and current capital assets. Fixed capital assets, e.g. plant and machinery, are used to provide profit over a long term and they are costed over this term. This is referred to as depreciation. The total of all capital goods produced is gross investment and after allowance has been made for depreciation, the result is the net investment. Current assets, often referred to as working capital is the flow of cash to work in progress, to stock, to sales, which generates the profit in the business. The speed with which this process is maintained affects overall profitability of the business. The state owns capital in the form of hospitals, roads and schools, etc. and this is identified as infrastructure whilst the private sector's capital stocks is mainly in the form of houses, cars, caravans, etc. See Chapter 13 for further discussion on capital.

The Entrepreneur

The enterprise culture of the U.K. in the 1980's highlighted the role of the entrepreneur. The entrepreneur is the businessman who takes the risk of investing in producing a new product. This entails the bringing together of factor inputs in order to produce a market product for a profit. The dynamism and risk-taking associated with this process, whilst not tangible, are nevertheless seen as essential in the development of a capitalistic system. An example illustrates. The entrepreneur, given the current state of technology has to choose between technique A or B in order to produce a given level of output. The entrepreneur will cost factor inputs in such a way as to minimise investment cost and maximise profits in the long term. Table 2.5 illustrates.

TABLE 2.5
THE LEAST COST ALTERNATIVE

	Unit Input Of		Cost £ Per Unit Of				= Total Cost of (£)
	Capital	Labour	Capital	Labour	Capital	Labour	
Technique A	4	4	320	300	1280 +	1200 =	2480
Technique B	2	6	320	300	640 +	1800 =	2440

From the Table it is seen that the least cost combination of labour and capital is given by technique B which is £40 cheaper than technique A. If output and revenue levels are the same in both cases, the entrepreneur will choose technique B, which maximises profit in the long run and employs more labour and less capital than technique A.

Industry Interdependence; Value Added and Input/Output

Industry is classified into three broad categories — primary, secondary and tertiary production. Primary or extractive industries are those involved in extracting basic raw materials, e.g. iron ore, oil, grain, etc. The business unit in this sector is the farmer, the fisherman, miner, forester, etc. These producers provide inputs for the secondary or manufacturing sectors. Business units in secondary manufacturing industries make or assemble components, T.V.s, cars, clothes, food, chemicals, etc. The last sector, the tertiary or service sector, ensures that the goods reach the consumer. This sector covers retailing, wholesaling as well as insurance, banking and other financial and personal services which are needed by the consumer. An affluent economy such as the U.S.A. or U.K. is characterised by a growing tertiary or service sector, often accompanied by a relative decline in importance of the other two; in terms of output and employment. The significance of both U.K. manufacturing and service sectors are illustrated in Table 2.6.

TABLE 2.6
U.K. EMPLOYMENT 1979-88

	1979	1986	1988
Index of Manufacturing Output (1980 = 100)	109.5	104.7	118.7
Share of Manufacturing in Total Output (%)	27.3	23.0	23.9
Employment in Manufacturing (thousands)	7259	5239	5152
Share of Manufacturing in Total Employment (%)	31.3	24.3	22.7
Employment in Services (thousands)	13556	14495	15319
Share of Services in Total Employment (%)	58.5	67.1	69.5
Balance of Trade in Manufactures (£ million)	+2698	−8055	−15770
UK Import Penetration in Manufactures (%)	26	33	38

(Sources: CSO National Income and Expenditure; Employment Gazette; British Business)

Industrial Interdependence: Value Added/GDP

Industries depend upon each other. The primary sector supplies the manufacturing sector which in turn supplies the tertiary or service sectors and hence the final consumer, i.e. one industry's output is another industry's input. At each stage of production these inputs are worked upon by labour and capital and value is added before this output becomes an input at the raw material, semi-finished or finished good stage. The Table 2.7 shows how flour becomes a loaf of bread in the supermarket. Value added is the difference between bought in cost and sales price, and this is then paid to the factor inputs of labour, land, capital, etc. in proportion to the relative size of factor inputs.

TABLE 2.7
VALUE ADDED & OUTPUT

Production Stage	Cost £	- Sales £	=	Value Added (OUTPUT)	Labour	Land	Capital	Profit	=	Total Income
I PRIMARY (WHEAT)	0	– INPUT 10	=	10	5	3	1	1	=	10
II MANUFACTURE (BREAD)	10	– INPUT 20	=	10	3	1	5	1	=	10
III TERTIARY (SALES)	20	– 25	=	5	1	1	2	1	=	5
					9	5	8	3		25

Gross Domestic Product = 25 less 3 (Depn) = 22 Net Domestic Product

The land can be assumed to be costless (0) and the farmer grows wheat and hence adds value which is the output of the farm sector and input of the miller, etc. At the same time the value added by the factors is returned in the form of income which reflects the value of factor inputs, e.g. land gets the largest share of income at the primary stage. In the second stage the return to capital in the form of interest is 60% of the total income. The final output, i.e. Gross Domestic Product, is £25 but capital wear and tear (depreciation) reduces this to a net Domestic Output figure of £22. Also, labour's share of the GDP is the largest, 9:25's or 36%. Table 2.8 shows the concept of industrial value added and GDP for the U.K. over the period 1979-88 for the main sectors of economic activity.

TABLE 2.8
THE OUTPUT OF THE U.K. ECONOMY 1979–88

Main sectors of economic activity	Value added £ billion 1988	Volume change in output % pa 1979-88	% share of gdp at current factor cost 1988
Agriculture, forestry, and fishing	5.8	2.6	1.5
Energy and water supply	21.9	3.6	5.5
Manufacturing	95.8	0.7	24.3
Construction	27.9	2.2	7.1
Distribution, hotels and catering	56.4	2.8	14.3
Transport and communications	28.7	3.0	7.3
Financial services	76.9	7.5	19.5
Ownership of dwellings	21.4	1.1	5.4
Education and health	35.2	1.6	8.9
Public administration	27.0	0.1	6.8
Other services	25.8	3.9	6.5
Adjustment and residual	-28.0		
Gdp at factor cost	394.8	2.2	100

Source: Lloyds Bank Profile of U.K. 1990.

Input/Output Analysis (IOA)

IOA shows the degree of interdependence between industries. In the real world this would be complex but in Table 2.9 a simplified model illustrates the basic concept of IOA. The agricultural sector actually supplies itself with 30% of its own input $\left(\frac{600}{2000} \times \frac{100}{1}\right)$ in the form of livestock, feed, etc. Twenty percent comes from manufacturing (tractors, etc.) and ten percent from services (finance). Forty percent comes from primary input services (land, etc.). Adding up the value of inputs to all sectors gives 2000 + 2300 + 1500 = 5800. This figure is equal to the sum of total production since total inputs equal output, i.e. profits are included as a factor input (enterprise). The final demand for services is equal to the sales from the various sectors less total production, i.e. 1500 less (200 + 230 + 450) equals 620. Reading across, agricultural outputs of 600 + 1380 + 225 totals 2205 which exceeds total inputs by 205 which must indicate net imports into the agricultural sector of 205. Using this Table it is also possible to calculate the direct input requirement percentages and this would thus indicate the current input mix for each industry — see brackets for agriculture. The Table can also be used to trace the effects of inflation through the system and also indicate the unemployment impact through the whole economy in the event of one sector experiencing a downturn in demand.

TABLE 2.9
INPUT/OUTPUT TABLE OF A HYPOTHETICAL ECONOMY

	Agri-culture	Manu-facture	Services	Final demand	Total production
Agriculture	600(.3)	1380	225		1000
Manufacturing	400(.2)	460	225		2300
Services	200(.1)	230	450	620	1500
Primary inputs	800(.4)	230	600		
Total value of inputs	2000	2300	1500		5800

(OUTPUT OF / INPUT TO (Type of purchaser))

Specialisation and Trade

Originally primitive societies were only able to produce enough output for self-sufficiency or autarky. This meant little or no excess output was available to trade and so individuals were prevented from specialising in what they were good at doing, e.g. hunting or fishing, since they had to do everything for themselves. Therefore societies were unable to exploit their natural resources. These resources could have taken the form of an abundance of land, mineral wealth or an ability to farm the land, etc. The development of free political democratic societies, markets, money and free enterprise systems, enabled individuals and regions to concentrate on producing and then trading those goods where costs were lowest. This enabled them to exploit their natural resources and also meant that others could, by trade, enjoy these advantages. Industries developed which were able to concentrate on producing a narrow range of products efficiently and, in the simplest form, led to the breaking down of complex tasks into simple repetitive jobs, i.e. division of labour. Adam Smith quotes the famous pin factory example where the making of one pin was broken down into 18 different operations. The output of the pin factory was far higher per head by this process of specialisation than would have been the case if one man had produced the whole pin. This specialisation process eventually led to a variety of craft and professional occupations as well as specialist firms and industries and a concentration of specialist production facilities in regions and countries. Mass production technologies were developed to exploit this and by this standardisation of components and products, efficiency increased further. Specialisation led to excess production and hence trade, which increases overall output, income and economic welfare. At the simplest level, individuals perform a specialist task for an income which they then trade for the goods and services they are no longer able to produce. This is also the basis for trade between countries. The following example illustrates how specialisation and then trade can benefit both individuals and hence countries, so long as the terms on which trade takes place are mutually beneficial.

Example 1 — Absolute Advantage

Suppose that two people, A and B, are able to produce wine and cheese. A takes one hour of labour to produce one pound of cheese and two hours of labour to produce one gallon of wine. B, on the other hand, takes two hours and one hour to produce one pound of cheese and one gallon of wine. This means that A has an absolute advantage in producing cheese and B has an absolute advantage in producing wine because each is able to produce these products using less labour than the other. If they were to specialise in what they are best or more efficient at producing, they could then trade any surplus and still end up better off than under self-sufficiency. Table 2.10 shows the matrices (i) self-sufficiency and (ii) after trade, to illustrate. Exchange is on the basis of one gallon of wine for one pound of cheese, i.e. these rates are the terms of trade of cheese for wine.

Basic Concepts // 23

TABLE 2.10

$$\begin{pmatrix} \text{(i)} & \textbf{HOURS REQUIRED} \\ & \textbf{TO MAKE} \\ & \text{1lb Cheese} \quad \text{1 gall Wine} \\ A & 1 \quad\quad\quad\quad 2 \\ B & 2 \quad\quad\quad\quad 1 \end{pmatrix} \begin{pmatrix} \text{(ii)} & \textbf{HOURS REQUIRED} \\ & \textbf{AFTER TRADE} \\ & \text{1lb Cheese} \quad \text{1 gall Wine} \\ A & 1 \quad\quad\quad\quad 1 \\ B & 1 \quad\quad\quad\quad 1 \end{pmatrix}$$

Note: Terms of Trade 1.1.

Person A can specialise in cheese and sell one pound of cheese for one gallon of wine, i.e. the opportunity cost now of one pound of cheese is now one gallon of wine, whereas before, to produce one pound of cheese meant that he had to give us two pounds of cheese. The same applies to B with respect to cheese for wine. Their effort now enables them to obtain more of the product they had to work two hours each for.

Example 2 — Comparative Advantage

Even if A were more efficient in time of hours worked in producing both wine and cheese, it would still pay A as an individual or as a country to specialise and trade. Suppose now it takes A one hour of labour to make a pound of cheese and two hours of labour to make a gallon of wine. In B it takes 6 hours to make a pound of cheese and 3 hours to make a gallon of wine, i.e. A is more efficient in both goods but more so in cheese. If the price or terms of trade is still one to one, then it is still worthwhile specialising and then trading. In A, more efficient in making both goods, an hour of labour can produce one unit of cheese or two units of wine. However, as 1lb of cheese can be traded for one gallon of wine, it makes sense for A to specialise in cheese and trade some cheese for wine. So A can consume as much cheese as before but twice as much wine. B is less efficient than A in producing both wine and cheese. An hour of B's labour can make 1/6th of a pound of cheese and 1/3rd of a gallon of wine; which is worth 1/3rd of a 1lb of cheese in the market. So B specialises in wine and trades wine for cheese. This means that B can consume as much wine as before and twice as much cheese. These situations are shown in matrices (i) and (ii) in Table 2.11.

TABLE 2.11

	(i) BEFORE SPECIALISATION HOURS REQ'D TO MAKE			(ii) HOURS REQUIRED AFTER TRADE	
	1lb Cheese	1 gall Wine		1lb Cheese	1 gall Wine
A	1	2	A	1	1
B	6	3	B	3	3

Note: Terms of Trade 1.1.

In this case B, through trade, has an opportunity to produce at lowest cost the good in which it has a comparative advantage. This analysis explains why both individuals and countries specialise and trade. However, the above does assume that both A and B are perfectly able to move between producing wine or cheese (there is perfect mobility). Also, it assumes that there is a constancy in terms of hours required to produce more of each good, i.e. constant returns. Finally, the terms of trade of wine for cheese are always mutually beneficial. In the real world these conditions may not always apply, e.g. cheese or wine can be heavily taxed so A or B might find themselves once more better off producing their own wine or cheese. These ideas are developed in the International Trade Section of "Essential Concepts in Macro-economics" by N. Proctor.

The Advantages of Specialisation

1. Specialisation enables mass production and hence mass consumption of those goods in which individuals and countries have absolute and comparative advantage.

2. Specialisation leads to uniform and identical products and components which are interchangeable and universally recognised and purchased.

3. Specialisation enables labour, land and capital to improve their productivity as they become more task specific. This improves individual skills and talents, allows capital to become specialised which reduces costs and releases resources for use elsewhere.

4. Specialisation enables consumers to benefit from the natural advantages of their neighbours in terms of lower cost products, i.e. economic welfare and efficiency is increased.

However, *specialisation* has certain drawbacks:-

1. Specialisation leads factors of production and countries to overdependence upon a particular task or product which is exported. If demand for their product is hit in a slump, then the factors of production will be unemployment and the country will be badly affected.

2. Specialisation can lead to capital, labour and land becoming too job specific and so unadaptable to a change in demand.

3. Specialisation leads to increasing interdependence between industries, occupations and countries which may suffer if any one part or link in the chain breaks down.

Population

General Facts

The population of the UK was 57.2m in 1989, the 15th largest in the world. That is comparable closely with Italy (57m) and France (56m), the Philippines (59m) and Vietnam (62m). In the UK, 19 per cent of the population is under 15, 65 per cent is aged between 15 and 64 and 16 per cent is 65 or over. Females outnumber males by 29.3m to 27.9m. The population grew steadily up to 1971, but has grown more slowly since then. However, the age structure has changed, with a lower proportion of children aged under 15 and a higher proportion aged 65 and over. The population is projected to increase slowly, to 61m by 2031, when the composition would be 19 per cent under 15, 61 per cent aged between 15 and 64 and 20 per cent over 64.

FIG. 2.5
AGE OF POPULATION — U.K.

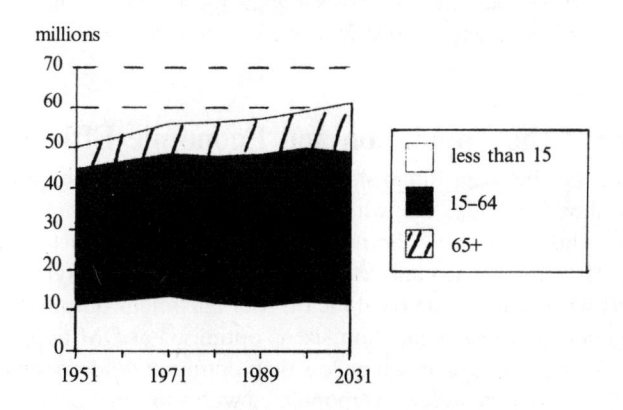

Source: Lloyds Bank profile of the UK 1990.

Determinants of the Population

The overall growth of the population depends upon the following factors:-

1. The birth rate per thousand. In the U.K. from 1971–88, it changed from 16.1 to 13.8 per thousand.
2. Death rate per thousand. In the U.K. from 1971–88, it changed from 11.5 to 11.4 per thousand.
3. Net migration rate, i.e. emigration less immigration rates.

The U.K. Population

In the U.K. the death rate for males and females stabilised with life expectancy at 72 and 78 respectively. Infant mortality is 9.1 per thousand live births. The most common causes of death in 1989 were heart disease (204,331), cancer (163,536), respiratory disease (78,266) and road accidents (5,547). The 1960's were characterised by a rise in the birth rate which created the population bulge and this ultimately led to the rise in demand for school places in the 1970's. By the 1980's this had also created a demand for houses as this led to a growth in the number of young married couples looking for first time homes. Figure 2.5 shows the U.K. age structure from 1951 to the year 2031 and this indicates that the U.K. is becoming an ageing population. This can be illustrated using the concept of the dependency ratio. This is the ratio of those aged between 0 and 16 plus those over 65 expressed over the total number in the workforce. This ratio is around 30% in the U.K. at the present, 1990. As this ratio increases it means that the productivity of the working population must also increase so that the real value of pensions and the provision of health care and schooling for the young does not suffer. The overall age structure of the population is illustrated in a population pyramid, see Chapter on Statistics, which shows both age and sex distribution of the U.K. population. The distribution of the population between jobs (occupational distribution) and between regions (geographical distribution) is also of economic importance.

The Size of the Population and Economic Efficiency

The relationship between diminishing returns, population size, and per capita income is shown in Fig. 2.6 which illustrates the concept of the optimum population. This shows how the marginal and average product of the variable input, population, rises then falls as diminishing returns apply (given capital and technology) when land is the fixed factor. The maximum output per head (per capita income) for some population size is optimised at OM population. Thus from O to M the population will be less than optimum (underpopulated) whilst beyond OM the country will be overpopulated with a low per capita income. This could be at a poverty income level. Malthus used the idea of an economy being overpopulated in his essay "The Principles of Population" in 1798. In particular

Malthus stressed that in an agrarian economy food could only be increased at an arithmetic rate, i.e. 1, 2, 3, whilst population grew geometrically, i.e. 2, 4, 8. The result of having too many mouths to feed would be poverty, pestilence and plague unless moral restraint was exercised, i.e. a lower birth rate. The increase in the U.K. population and overall living standards in 19th century Britain could not have been foreseen by Malthus. The increase in living standards was due to a rise in the capital stock, improved technology and international trade which kept incomes rising above population levels, i.e. AP rose to AP_1 and AP_2 as shown in Fig. 2.6. Furthermore life expectancy and overall living standards also improved due to increased prosperity, improved diets, municipal public health provision, the water cistern and better housing standards.

FIG. 2.6
MALTHUS AND POPULATION

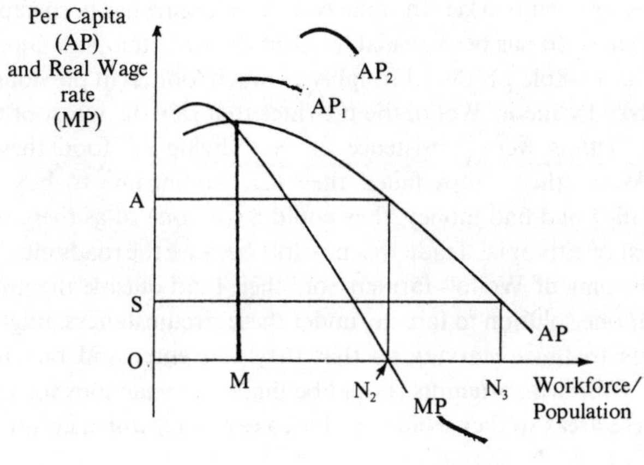

Poverty and Malthus in the 20th Century

In many parts of Africa, South America, and Asia poverty still exists. Neo-Malthusians and others have tried to explain this phenomena —

(a) *Neo-Malthusians* attempt to explain poverty in terms of over population together with the method of wage payment used in a rural economy. In simple rural economies, peasant farmers are largely self-employed and so they are able to pay themselves the value of their average product. In terms of the economy this could lead to a population size ON_3 in Fig. 2.6 which may imply a subsistence wage of OS. This means that the whole of the output in the agricultural sector is absorbed by wages so nothing is available for capital or other factors. This could lead to a reduction in productivity. Furthermore, at population level ON_3 the marginal product, MP, is negative so the total output of food is falling and therefore inefficient. If the workforce were reduced to ON_2, by the population exercising birth control, the real per capita income would increase to OA. The theory of wages in a market system implies that a wage equivalent to MP not AP is paid. See Chapter 11. If this could be applied to the underdeveloped economy in Fig. 2.6 it would imply that no more than ON_2 workers are employed on the land and this would boost per capita income to OA. In practice everyone could receive an identical share in output equal to $ON_2 \times OA \div ON_3$ which is greater than the subsistence (poverty wage) of OS. The labour $ON_3 - ON_2$ taken off the land would not necessarily be worse off because they were unemployed. They could receive cash benefits and therefore the overall level of welfare is improved in this simple rural economy.

(b) *Poverty and Entitlements*

Economists such as Professors Sen/Drèze* have stressed that poverty may not always be the result of overpopulation but rather because of a poorly working labour market or food market. In some countries famine has been experienced at the same time as food has been available. Consider the Ethiopian famine of 1973. The country as a whole produced roughly as much food as in previous years, but there was a big decline in Wollo, the province that saw the worst of the famine. Most of the victims were subsistence farmers, living off food they produced themselves. When their crops failed they had no income to buy food from elsewhere. If they had had money, they could have done so as there was enough food in the rest of Ethiopia. Trade was possible because the roads into Wollo were open. Indeed, some of Wollo's farmers sold their food outside the province. It is suggested that one solution to famine, under these circumstances, might be to give cash handouts to those starving so that they can enter and buy food in the marketplace. Otherwise attempts should be made to create jobs for unemployed farmers in these areas so they would be able to earn an income, i.e. an entitlement to buy food.

*"Hunger and Public Action" by Jean Drèze and Amartya Sen, Clarendon Press, Oxford. 1990.

CHAPTER 2 Research

1. *Obtain comparative figures for miles per gallons for motor cars and use it to discuss economic efficiency, diminishing returns and opportunity cost.*

2. *Identify from current newspapers, journals or other media where the following factors of production are traded; labour, land, capital, enterprise.*

3. *Trace the link between population and poverty.*

DATA RESPONSE QUESTIONS

Question 1 — Comparative Economic Statistics

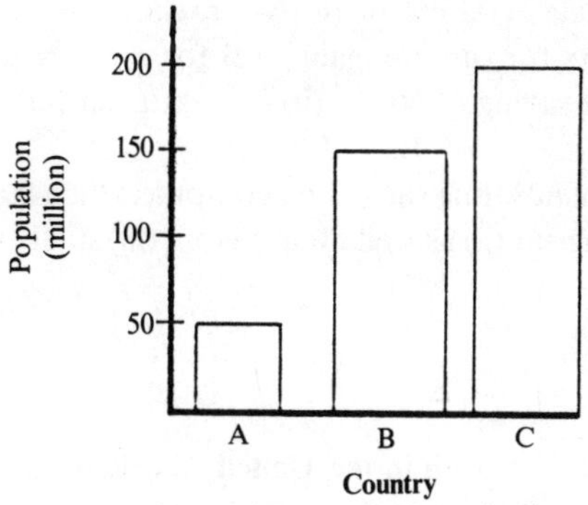
Population (million)
200
150
100
50
A
B
C
Country

1. Calculate per capita income for each country and comment on your findings.
2. Comment upon variations in factor endowments between countries A, B and C.
3. Using your findings in Q1, discuss the idea of optimum population viz B & C.

Land area, population and GNP in three different countries (A, B, C)

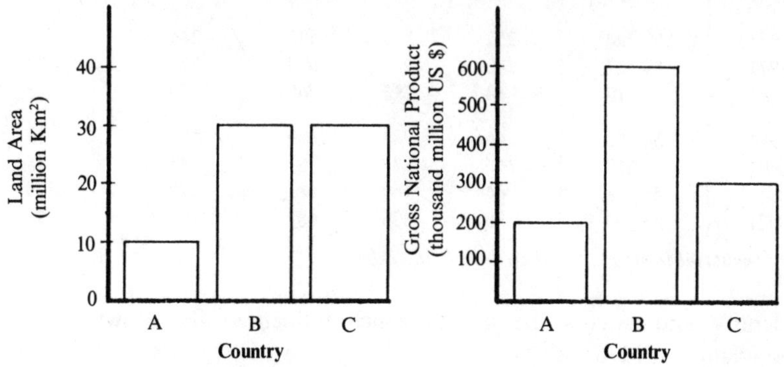
Land Area (million Km²)
40
30
20
10
0
A
B
C
Country
Gross National Product (thousand million US $)
600
500
400
300
200
100
A
B
C
Country

Question 2 — Specialisation

Country A and B can produce the following output with given labour units

	Hours needed to produce		
	1 car	and	1 computer
country A	10		20
country B	50		30

1. Identify the country which has absolute and comparative advantage in cars and computers?
2. Which country will specialise in cars and which in computers?
3. If the terms of trade are one car to one computer then the gain to A will be the equivalent of, (i) one extra car or (ii) two extra computers, after trade?
4. If B exports computers for cars the gain to B for each car imported is the equivalent of (i) a cost saving of $66\frac{2}{3}\%$ (ii) one extra car (iii) 30 hours saved (iv) none of these.
5. If the terms of trade are now one car to two computers then B is now (i) worse off than when self sufficient (ii) as well off as before (iii) still better off by 20%.

Question 3

Population growth in the United Kingdom
(figures in thousands)

	Population at beginning of period	Total increase	Births	Deaths	Excess of births over deaths	Net civilian migration and other adjustments
1931-1951	46,038	212	734	603	190	+22
1951-1961	50,290	252	839	593	246	+6
1961-1971	52,807	280	962	638	324	-20
1971-1981	55,610	64	793	666	70	-5
1981-1991	56,252	66	788	679	109	-43
1991-2001	56,912	106	832	691	141	-35
2001-2011	57,968	44	760	681	79	-35
2011-2021	58,403	90	806	681	125	-35

Average annual change

Source: *Annual Abstract of Statistics*, H.M.S.O., 1984.

1. Identify and discuss the factors which influenced the growth of UK population 1931-81.
2. Discuss the problems of making projections with respect to population changes. Use the above figures to illustrate.

Question 4 — Marginal Utility

Given below are the daily utility functions for three cold drinks for a man arriving at a desert oasis with a budget of £28.

Price	Drink A £2	Drink B £4	Drink C £6
Quantity	Total utility	Total utility	Total utility
1	8	8	14
2	14	13¼	27
3	18	18¼	39
4	21	23	49
5	22	27½	55
6	24	31¾	60
7	25	35¾	62

Assuming that holding money has no utility for him and that he seeks to maximize his satisfaction, answer the following:
1. On his first visit the only drink for sale is B. How many drinks does he buy and why?
2. In the circumstances of (1); calculate the consumer's surplus.
3. On a return visit, with another £28, all the drinks are available. How will he allocate his budget between the three drinks?
4. What is unlikely about the total utility figures for drink A?

(London, June 1980)

Question 5 —
Diminishing Returns and Marginal Revenue Product

You are given the following information:

Cost per tonne of fertiliser = £140
Fixed cost of land = £3,000
(Assume that no further costs are incurred.)
Selling price of wheat = £2 per unit.

32 Basic Concepts II

Tonnes of fertiliser applied to a fixed area of land	Total production (units)
0	1,100
1	1,100
2	1,250
3	1,500
4	1,900
5	2,150
6	2,275
7	2,350
8	2,380
9	2,330

1. With reference to the above data, comment on the relationship between the application of fertiliser and the production of wheat.
2. What level of fertiliser would a profit-maximising farmer choose to apply? Show the amount of wheat produced and the profit earned. Justify your answer. *(London Economics, June 1983)*

Question 6

Comparative Agricultural Productivity

(a) cereal output per agricultural worker (b) yield per hectare, cereals

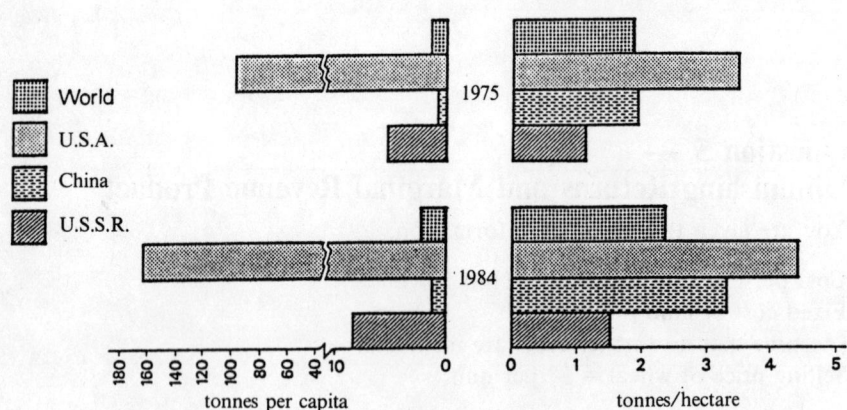

- World
- U.S.A.
- China
- U.S.S.R.

tonnes per capita / tonnes/hectare

Source: Food and Agricultural Organisation, United Nations 1985.

1. Carefully distinguish between measure (a) and (b).
2. Compare the relative productivity of labour and land, in the U.S.A., between 1975 and 1984.

3. Analyse how agricultural productivity has changed between 1975 and 1984 for (i) China (ii) U.S.S.R.
4. Use your findings in Q3 for China and discuss the law of diminishing marginal returns.

Question 7 — Data

The relationship between inputs of labour and capital and output is shown in the Table 1.

Table 1

		Units of land		
		1	2	3
Units of Labour	1	100	120	135
	2	130	220	290
	3	150	300	335

1. What happens to the marginal product of labour, land, when (i) one unit of land and (ii) one unit of labour is used.
2. What are the returns to scale in the long run when both labour and land are variable?

Answers to many of these questions can be found in "Data Response for Economics" by G. Walker, published by Checkmate.

3 BUSINESS ORGANISATIONS

AIMS: *To define, explain and discuss*
- *Business Units – Organisational Forms*
- *Corporate Finance : Forms and Capital Structure*
- *Financial Performance Ratios*
- *Size and Growth of Business Units*
- *Location of Industry*
- *Business Risk and Uncertainty*

KEY CONCEPTS

Sole Proprietor, Partnership, Joint Stock Companies Public Corporations, Balance Sheet, Profit and Loss Account, Profitability and Profit, Ratios, Gearing Ratios, Debt, Equity, Concentration Ratio, Integration, Small Business Units, External Economies, Regional Aid, Adverse Selection, Moral Hazard, Location Quotient

Organisation/Main Types

Table 3.1 identifies the main forms of commercial organisation in the U.K. together with their main business features and characteristics.

A. *Sole Proprietor*

This is the form of business unit used by a single individual, e.g. a plumber, who provides the capital, runs the business himself, and takes all the risks and hence the profit. There are drawbacks to being a sole proprietor. The major one is unlimited liability for the owner in the event of financial problems. This means that an individual can lose all personal assets in settlement of the debt. The sole proprietor bears all the risk, runs the business without the help of a partner and is often hampered by lack of finance.

B. *Partnerships*
There are two main types:-

A. Ordinary Partnerships as set up by the Partnership Act of 1890 and
B. Limited Partnerships as controlled by the Limited Partnership Act of 1907.

The latter form of partnership is unusual since the benefit of limited liability can be obtained as a private company. A limited partnership arises when a partner, i.e. a sleeping partner, invests in a business but takes no part in its operation or management. In ordinary partnerships all partners take part in the management and running of the business and as such all partners are jointly and severally liable for any debts incurred by the partnership. The usual advantage of this partnership type is that more than one person shares in the decision-making so each person can specialise in different management functions. On the other hand there are disadvantages. If one partner disagrees with the others and leaves, the partnership must be dissolved. Partnerships generally suffer from a lack of adequate finance and furthermore the partnership cannot sue or be sued in its own name but only in the name of a partner or partners. Also, a partner can act as a representative of the business and bind his fellow partners in a contract. Finally, a partner may not transfer his shares of the business without the consent of fellow partners.

C. and D. *Private and Public Joint Stock Companies*
Joint Stock Companies exist as a separate legal entity from the shareholders who own the business, so the business is able to sue or be sued. These bodies are also known as corporations. Joint Stock Companies are able to raise capital by issuing ordinary shares which, by the end of the 19th century, carried the privilege of limited liability for shareholders. This means that shareholders cannot lose any more money than the nominal share issue or stock in which they have invested. These corporations grow by takeovers and are now referred to as conglomorates or multinationals. As well as being a separate legal entity a company is unaffected by a change of membership of the Board of Directors or shareholders, i.e. there is continuity.

The main differences between a private and a public company.

a. A private company, unlike a public company, cannot trade its shares on the Stock Exchange.

b. a private company cannot sell shares and debentures to the public, unlike a public company.

c. shares of a public company are freely transferable whereas the shareholder of a private company has first to obtain the other members permission to trade shares.

d. a private company trades once it has registered whereas a public company must also have a Trading Certificate.

However, both public and private companies are regulated by:-

a. Memorandum of Association.

This sets out the company objectives, types of business operation and its legal identity.

b. The Articles of Association.

These outline the internal rules of the company, the powers, rights and obligations of its members, etc.

c. The Companies Act 1985 which sets out for private and public companies the legal framework for running and liquidating a company.

The above regulations, etc., mean there can be a difference between those who own the business (shareholders) and those who manage (Board of Directors). This is discussed in more detail in Chapter 10 — Alternative Theories of the Firm.

TABLE 3.1
TYPES OF BUSINESS ORGANISATION

	Type of business (Legal Forms)	No. involved in ownership	Examples	Sources of finance (Major)	Who is Liable for debts	Profit to	Authority and control of business
A.	Sole proprietor	1	hairdresser plumber	Bank loans and/or personal savings, HP finance, credit, etc.	Owner is fully liable for all debts incurred	Owner keeps all profits	Full control by proprietor
B.	Partnership	2 to 20	doctors, solicitors, dentists, surveyors	Bank loans and/or personal savings, HP finance, mortgages, etc.	At least one partner is fully liable for all debts	Profits shared according to deed of partnership	All partners have equal power (except sleeping-partners) See 1907 Act.
C.	Private joint-stock company	2 or more	small local builder or Little-woods	All the above the issue of shares to agreed members	Limited liability for debts. Each shareholder only risks the amount put in to buy shares	Distributed between all shareholders – dividends being paid per share	Normally directed by shareholders (in proportion to the number of shares held)
D.	Public joint-stock company	2 or more	ICI, Shell, Sainsbury Marks & Spencer	All the above. But the ownership of shares is open to all via the stock exchange. e.g. Public Issue	As for private joint-stock company. But annual general report must be available to the public and accounts publicized in the national press. (A minimum amount of share capital is another prerequisite.)		Shareholders appoint a board of directors to act on their behalf. (These directors are voted in/out at the AGM.)

Note:

(1) All the above types of business organization are owned and controlled by private individuals, that is, they form part of the private sector. In contrast government-funded and -organized firms (not detailed above) constitute the public sector, e.g. British Rail.

(2) Since the 1980 Companies Act, a private joint-stock company must include the word 'limited' in its title, and a public joint-stock company must have the words 'public limited company' at the end of its name, e.g. Marks & Spencer plc.

Table 3.1 adapted from "Economics Explained" by Maunder et alia, Collins Educational 1990.

Public Corporations — Nationalised Industries
(see Note 1 in Table 3.1)

Public Corporations are owned by the state and take the form of nationalised industries, many of which were privatised in the 1980's by the Thatcher government. However, there are still a few nationalised industries, e.g. British Rail and the National Coal Board. These industries were established by Act of Parliament. They are run by a Chairman and a Board appointed by the appropriate Minister. The corporations are responsible for the day to day running of the industry and do not have shareholder control as in the form of an AGM as operated by corporations owned by shareholders.

Control of public corporations is exercised as follows:-

1. *Control by the Minister of State responsible.* The Minister is able to control by appointing the Chairman, the Board, and the Minister can also ask for specific industry information as well as by setting financial targets, e.g. break even, etc.

2. *Parliament.* Parliament can control the industry through the Public Accounts Committee and by the specific Nationalised Industry Committee which examines the annual financial reports of nationalised industries. This control can also come about because the board can be cross-examined by members of the Parliamentary Committee and furthermore any subsequent reports published can be used by the public to see how efficiently the industry is being managed.

3. *Consumers Councils.* These act as a method by which public opinion can be relayed to the appropriate industry. Disputes, grievances and overall impressions regarding the standard of public provision can be aired within these councils.

4. The *privatisation* process, together with the *deregulation* and competitive *tendering* within nationalised industries, has been used, in the 1980's, as a method by which competitive market pressures are used as an effective control of public corporations in so far as they set market standards of efficiency.

Corporate Finance — Statements and Structure

Financial Statements — Balance Sheet/ Profit and Loss Account

Financial statements are a means of providing up to date information to the market about corporate economic efficiency. The balance sheet shows the assets, what the company owns, against the liabilities, what the company owes. It is a snapshot of a company's financial position. A simple balance sheet is shown below with notes explaining the items.

TABLE 3.2

BALANCE SHEET OF XYZ CO. LTD. PLC.
/1/90 — 31/12/90

Assets	£		Liabilities	£
Fixed Assets (after depreciation)		Equity	Shares	200
			Reserves	300
Factory				
Plant	300	Debt	Loans/mortgages	100
Equipment			Debentures	
Investments				
in other companies	200		**Current Liabilities**	
Current Assets			Creditors	100
Stock	100		Overdraft	100
Goods	100 500		Tax/dividend owed	200
Debt	100			
Cash	200			
	1000			1000

Notes

1. The company has limited liability and since 1981 all public limited companies have to show this with the initials plc. after the company name. The balance sheet in Table 3.2 shows the assets and liabilities at the end of 1990. Companies would also show the assets and liabilities at the end of 1989 for comparison purposes.

2. *Debentures* are a source of long terms loans, secured on assets, they are known as mortgages. Interest on loans is a tax deductable expense.

3. *Equity or shareholders funds.* Shares are ordinary or preference with normally a vote for ordinary shares. Preference shares are paid a guarantee or stated dividend. EQUITY PLUS DEBT = CAPITAL EMPLOYED, e.g. £500 + £100 = £600.

4. *Current liabilities* or short term money owed to others.

5. *Fixed assets* are used up over a period of time and this costing procedure is known as depreciation which shows the net or book value of each asset.

6. *Investments.* These are shareholdings the company has acquired in other companies.

7. *Current assets.* These are bought and used by the company to provide ongoing profit, e.g. stock becomes goods sold which becomes sales and hence profit.

8. A balance sheet must balance because for every transaction there is a credit and debit entry.

Profit and loss statements or How Efficiently the Company is Trading

TABLE 3.3
PROFIT/LOSS A/C OF XYZ CO. LTD. PLC.
1/1/90 to 31/12/90

		Accountant	(£)	Economist	(£)
	Sales		100		100
(1)	− Cost of goods sold		60		70
(2)	= Profit/loss		40 (gross profit)		30 (abnormal profit)

Notes

1. The accountant and the economist's definition of costs, and hence profits, sometimes differ. This is because the economist would include within costs not only the purchase price but also a normal profit which includes an amount imputed into the costs which reflects how much these resources would earn in their next best use. In the £70 costs there may be a charge of £5 for the capital used, in the sense that this could have been earned elsewhere, and another £5 may be the wages the owner could have earned in another job. This makes the difference of £10 between the accountant's and the economist's cost figure. The residual £30 profit is called abnormal profits.

2. Profitability. Profit is measured against capital employed, i.e. equity plus debt, or sales, so that management can see how efficient they are in using the resources of the business. The two main profitability measures are (using the accountant's definition of profits):-

a) $\dfrac{\text{Profit}}{\text{Capital employed}} \times \dfrac{100}{1}$ or $\dfrac{£40}{£600} = 15\%$

b) $\dfrac{\text{Profit}}{\text{Sales}} \times \dfrac{100}{1}$ or $\dfrac{£40}{£100} = 40\%$

a) is also called the return on capital and it thus reflects the current cost of capital.

The Importance of Profit

Profit varies between firms in the same industry due to cost and efficiency differences, management practices, industrial location and degrees of competition. Profits also vary between different industries because of differences in demand, risk, and cost variations. Profit is the prime objective of company activity and its functions are to:-

1. Measure the efficiency of capital use by comparing profit to capital employed.
2. Motivate the company to make the best or most efficient use of its resources. In this it works as a signal to others to indicate how well or badly the company is performing.
3. It is itself a source of future investment funds.
4. It serves as a reward to risk taking, so usually the higher the risk the higher the return to capital.
5. Profitability serves as a standard method of comparison between firms and industries.

Other Financial Measures

Apart from profitability measures used by management other financial measures are required by investors, lenders, government and workers.

Investors

Those who buy shares are paid a dividend and receive capital growth on their investment. The following are some simple basic ratios.

(c) Dividend yield $= \dfrac{\text{par value} \times \text{dividend}(\%)}{\text{market price of share}}$

(d) Price/Earnings $= \dfrac{\text{current price of share}}{\text{earnings per share}}$

(e) Earnings yield $= \dfrac{\text{earnings per share}}{\text{price of share}} \times \dfrac{100}{1}$

Note, (d) and (e) are the inverse of each other.

Lenders

Those who lend (debt) to a company usually wish to know whether the company is able to repay the loan plus interest. The number of times the earnings cover interest plus debt repayment is a good indicator to the extent to which the company has incurred debt. Another indicator is the gearing ratio discussed below. The extent to which a company is liquid is also important and this is shown by the amount of liquid funds, e.g. cash plus saleable stock compared to the short-term liabilities of a company.

Government and Workers

The Government analyses financial statements in order to ascertain how healthy the economy is and also whether there is excessive profits due to monopolistic market conditions. Workers negotiating wage claims will be interested in

FIG. 3.1
COMPANY FINANCE: WHERE THE MONEY COMES FROM AND WHERE IT GOES

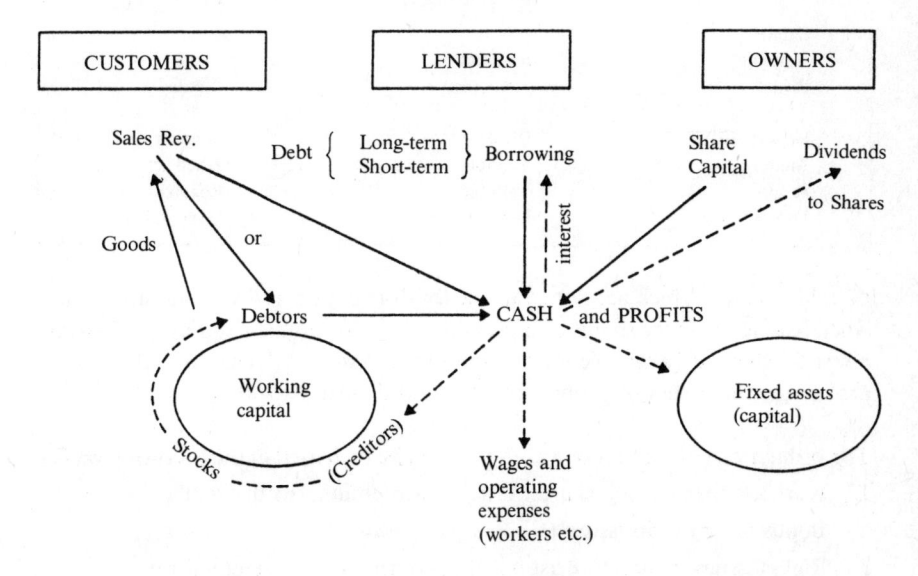

company sales and profits so they are able to calculate how much a company can afford to pay in respect to wages.

Company Funding Requirements — Flow of Funds

A summary of where corporate funds or money comes from and where it goes to is shown in Fig. 3.1. Customers, lenders, and shareholders supply funds for investment in stock, debt, and other fixed assets. These are turned into cash and profits which are then used to pay interest, dividends, tax and other expenses.

Capital Sources (see Balance Sheet in Table 3.2)

The main categories of capital employed are:-
1. Ordinary share capital and reserves (equity)
2. Preference share capital
3. Long-term loans (debt).

Capital is either debt or equity. From a company's point of view, debt is cheaper than equity but riskier. Other differences are summarised in Table 3.4.

TABLE 3.4
DIFFERENCES BETWEEN EQUITY AND DEBT — A SUMMARY

	Equity e.g. shares	Debt e.g. loan
Capital		
Amount	Residual	Fixed
Period	Permanent	Limited
Income	**Dividend**	**Interest**
Amount	Variable	Fixed
Period	Variable	Regular
Commitment	Discretionary	Legal liability

Capital reserves, which are not available for distribution as dividends, arise either when issuing ordinary shares at a premium or on revaluing fixed assets. *Revenue reserves*, which are available for distribution as dividends, arise through retained profits, i.e. the excess of profits after tax and dividends paid.

The ordinary share capital of a company can be increased in the following ways:-
1. Issue for cash: selling shares, often at a premium, to the public.
2. Bonus issue ('scrip issues').
3. Rights issues: issued to existing shareholders at a preferential rate.

Bonus issues involve capitalising reserves, which transfer amounts out of reserves and into share capital without causing an increase in total equity. Rights issues increase total equity. Preference share capital carries rights to a fixed dividend payable before any ordinary dividend and to a fixed money amount upon redemption or liquidation. Its characteristics are, on the whole, closer to those of debt capital than to equity. Preference dividends are paid out of after tax profits, unlike debt interest which can be charged before tax. Preference capital tends to be expensive compared with debt.

Other Long-term Sources of Capital Finance

1. *Profits or Retained Earnings.* These can be increased or decreased by running the company more or less efficiently.
2. *Asset Sales.* A company can sell a fixed asset, e.g. property and make a capital gain.
3. *Working Capital Management.* This means using current assets more efficiently. Thus the investment in stock and debtors is reduced but the turnover of these items is increased so there is less cash needed but more profit generated.
4. *Government Grants.* Discretionary capital grants, often made on a geographical basis, are available from relevant government departments. See Section on Location of Industry.

5. *Increased Current Liabilities.* By delaying payment to shareholders, the tax authority or suppliers, cash is released which reduces the borrowing requirement of a company. A long-term strategy aimed at improving the management of these liabilities increases long-term capital finance generated internally.

Gearing or Debt Burden

The larger the proportion of debt in a company's capital structure, the more highly geared it is said to be. The higher the gearing, the greater the risk for ordinary shareholders, but the greater the prospects of profit. In the example shown in Table 3.5, the highly geared company, Gold, with debt ratio of 50%, has a higher return on equity in year 1 than Silver with a debt ratio of 10%. In year 2, however, when earnings before interest and tax (EBIT) are low, there is less left for Gold's ordinary shareholders whilst Silver's, with a lower gearing ratio, received 3.3% return. Figure 3.2 illustrates how gearing affects a company's return on equity. When the return on capital employed is greater than 10%, the cost of interest on debt, Gold's return on equity is higher than Silver's. The reverse is true when the return on capital employed is less than 10%. The effect of gearing is to make the return on equity change more sharply than the return on capital employed. This operates in the other direction so that when profits are falling the opposite occurs. As the debt ratio increases new capital becomes more expensive as risk increases, both for the lenders of debt and for the subscribers of new share capital. When deciding whether the debt ratio is too high it must be appreciated that the nature of the business is of great importance. The more stable the nature of an industry, the higher the debt ratio can be, e.g. property sectors tend to be heavily geared. Other factors which influence the level of gearing are:-

a) The existing level of debt and hence the precommitments to pay existing interest charges.

b) The level of control on the business. If a company sells shares rather than debt then the issue of more shares could weaken the control of existing shareholders. On the other hand, by issuing more shares, it could make it more difficult or expensive for others to take over a company.

c) Current share price levels. If share prices are high then the current dividend payments to share prices may represent a small cost compared to current interest on debt capital.

d) Under certain conditions Miller and Modigliani outlined a theory which suggested that the average cost of capital is unaffected by the firm's debts: equity ratio, i.e. gearing.

Modigliani and Miller: "The Cost of Capital, Corporation Finance and the Theory of Investment". AER, June 1958.

FIG. 3.2
CAPITAL STRUCTURE

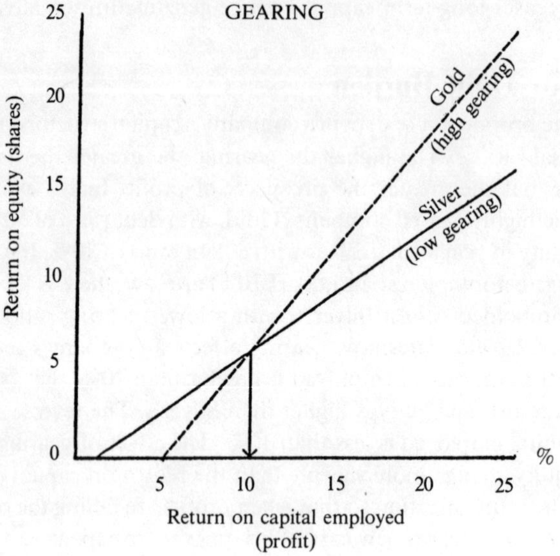

TABLE 3.5

	Low gearing *Silver Ltd.*	**High gearing** *Gold Ltd.*
Equity (shares)	90.00	50.00
Debt at 10%	10.00	50.00
Capital employed	£100.00	£100.00
Debt ratio:	10%	50%
Year 1, Return on capital employed: 20.0%	£	£
EBIT	20.00	20.00
Loan interest	1.00	5.00
Profit before tax	19.00	15.00
Tax at 40% (say)	7.60	6.00
Profit after tax	£11.40	£9.00
Return on equity:	12.7%	18.0%
Interest cover	20.0	4.0
Year 2, Return on capital employed: 6.0%	£	£
EBIT	60.00	60.00
Loan interest	10.00	50.00
Profit before tax	50.00	10.00
Tax at 40% (say)	20.00	4.00
Profit after tax	£30.00	£6.00
Return on equity:	3.3%	1.2%

Business Units — Size and Growth

1. *Measurement of Scale*

a) *Concentration Ratios (CR's)*

A typical concentration ratio is the five firm industry ratio which indicates how much output or market share the five largest firms or business units, in the industry, produce when compared to the whole industry's output. This is given by the formula:

$$CR_5 = \frac{\text{output of largest five firms}}{\text{output of whole industry}} \times \frac{100}{1}$$

In manufacturing industries such as brewing, cement, motor car production, etc. the CR_5 would be around 60–70% concentration.

b) *Minimum Scale of Efficiency (MSE)*

This defines the output level where the firms average cost curve becomes horizontal. This output level also identifies efficient levels of production and in U.K. manufacturing the MSE for any one organisation would represent significant market shares in the market for cigarettes, refrigerators, petrol refining, etc. See Chapter 6.

c) *Turnover or Capital Assets Employed*

This is a simple measure to identify the largest companies in an economy or an industry. Table 3.6 illustrates this measure with respect to the U.K. (turnover).

2. *Methods of Growth*

Business units become large by:

a) internal growth, i.e. by building new plant or outlets from internal profits or share issues, e.g. Marks and Spencers.

b) Mergers.

More usual is the process where two firms agree to merge by setting up a holding company.

c) Takeover.

This is where one firm buys up one or more other firms.

3. *Reasons for Merging and Takeovers*

a) To exploit economies of scale. This normally requires the complete reorganisation of all economic operations and is usually concentrated on particular economies, e.g. market economies, etc.

b) To dominate the market, i.e. this is where the growth in the size of the business is used to exploit monopoly power in particular industrial sectors.

c) To stabilise the market share of the business unit/or secure its sources of supply in terms of inputs and often to maintain its output.

d) Diversification. By buying up different businesses involved in a variety of consumer or industrial markets, the business is able to spread its risk. Increasingly this is the main reason today for conglomerate business growth.

e) Asset stripping. When a company's asset value is greater than its share price, then the acquirer can sell off the most valuable assets of a company in order to make capital gains.

Types of Integration

There are three types of integration, namely horizontal, vertical and lateral.

TABLE 3.6
THE 20 LARGEST UK INDUSTRIAL COMPANIES IN 1989*

	Turnover £ billion	Profits £ billion	Profits as % of turnover
British Petroleum *(Oil industry)*	33.1	3.3	10.0
British Telecom *(Telecommunication services)*	11.1	2.8	25.2
Shell Transport and Trading *(Oil industry)*	22.3	2.4	10.8
Imperial Chemical Industries *(Petrochemicals)*	11.7	1.8	15.4
B.A.T. Industries *(Tobacco, retailing, etc)*	11.4	1.7	14.9
Electricity Council** *(Electricity suppliers)*	11.4	1.6	14.0
British Gas Corporation *(Gas suppliers)*	7.4	1.5	20.3
Hanson *(Consumer products)*	7.4	1.2	16.2
Esso UK *(Oil industry)*	5.8	1.1	19.0
BTR *(Construction, energy, etc)*	5.5	0.9	16.4
RTZ Corporation *(Mining and industrial)*	3.9	0.9	23.1
Glaxo Holdings *(Pharmaceutical manufacturer)*	1.7	0.8	47.1
General Electric *(Electrical engineers)*	5.6	0.7	12.5
Shell UK *(Oil industry)*	6.6	0.7	10.6
Grand Metropolitan *(Hotels, milk products, brewers)*	6.0	0.6	10.0
Unilever *(Food, detergents, etc)*	6.4	0.6	9.4
Guinness *(Brewers)*	2.8	0.6	21.4
Allied Lyons *(Brewers, hotels, etc)*	4.5	0.6	13.3
Marks & Spencer *(General stores)*	5.1	0.6	11.8
IBM – UK Holdings *(Computer supplier, etc)*	3.9	0.5	12.8

*Ranked by pre-tax profits.
**Public corporation or nationalised industry.

Source: Lloyds Bank, Economic Profile of Britain 1990.

Each of these is illustrated in Table 3.7 which uses the brewing and leisure industries as examples.

TABLE 3.7

	Stage of Production	Brewing Units		Leisure (fast foods)	
I	Tertiary (Pubs/outlets)	x	x	x	x (Restaurants, Hotels, etc.)
II	Manufacturer (Brewery)	x	x		
III	Extractive (Hop farms)	x	x		

Table 3.7 shows initially six separate and independent business units in the brewing sector and two units in the leisure sector. This situation then changes by a process of:-

Horizontal integration

If the two brewers amalgamated at the same stage of production, this is referred to as horizontal integration; as would be the amalgamation of the pubs and/or the hop farms. The motives for horizontal integration are:- to gain economies of scale in e.g. marketing, to reduce competition or to gain control of the market by building up monopoly power. Currently around 70% of all mergers are horizontal.

Vertical — (forward/backwards)

Vertical integration is when a business unit takes over a producer in the same industry but at a different stage of production. Forward vertical integration is when e.g. the brewers take over the marketing outlets (pubs) at the tertiary or service stage of production. This is usually done in order to control the market price of the good or to control the distribution network and hence diversify into other retail sectors. Vertical backwards integration is when the brewers then proceed to take over the sources of their input supplies, e.g. hop farms. This form of integration is usually undertaken in order to control input prices, to ensure the certainty and continuity of good quality inputs and also to diversify into other market areas. Vertical integration accounts for 5% of all mergers.

Lateral integration

This is the creation of conglomerates or holding companies. In this case the conglomerate buys into business units which are unrelated to each other and to the original industries. Thus the brewers may buy into the leisure industry, e.g. fast food chains or health farms, etc. This is done in order to exploit managerial economies of scale and also to diversify and spread risk across a number of markets. One method of doing this financially is by using a holding or parent company which has a significant shareholding in other companies and hence it effectively can control their activities. Lateral integration is now commonplace in the U.K., e.g. Hanson Trust, BAT, Whitbread Trust, etc. This form of integration accounts for 25% of all mergers. Sears Holdings Ltd., for example, has interests in cutlery production, shipbuilding, footwear, engineering, department stores and insurance. In view of the pressures which lead to business units growing in scale, it is important to appreciate that the small scale firm still plays an important role in the U.K. industrial structure.

The Survival of the Small Firm

Definition of a Small Firm

The Bolton Committee which investigated the small firm in the U.K. suggested a variety of measures for defining a small business unit including sales turnover, number of employees, share of the total market, etc. None of these criteria provided an overall, realistic or consistent definition. The 1981 Companies Act defined a small firm as one with up to fifty employees, less than £700,000 worth of assets or with a sales turnover up to £1.4m per annum.

Main Areas of Activity

Despite the increase in the scale of production, illustrated by growing concentration ratios, small scale units still dominate in market areas such as road haulage, the motor trades, restaurants and catering, retailing, building and the hotel business. The reasons for the survival of the small firm are:-

1. *Small market size*

When demand is smallscale, personalised, irregular or seasonal in nature, then neither the product nor the service can be standardised. This means mass production methods and hence economies of scale cannot be exploited. This concept is illustrated by Adam Smith's maxim that "specialisation is limited by the extent of the market".

2. *Personalised or Bespoke service*

When personal attention and service is required a large unit would not be able to provide this individualistic service, e.g. personal tailor.

3. *The Business Owner*

Often the owner of the business does not wish to increase the size of the firm, rather preferring to remain in control. In retailing, by binding together in a cooperative organisation, e.g. Spar, smallscale retailers are able to buy in bulk. Furthermore, this type of operator can also maintain the goodwill of the customers.

4. *Stage of Growth*
The smallness of the business may be because the firm is at an early stage of industrial growth and may in due course become a large firm.

5. *Flexibility and Risk Aversion*
In the building industry the small contractor works for a major sub-contractor because of the flexibility this provides for both firms. The main sub-contractor finds that this arrangement reduces his financial risk because he is no longer responsible for employing a large workforce. This reduces the problems of man management and because of the uncertainty factor with respect to future work, it reduces the risk of heavy investment in machinery which would then lead to the growth of scale.

6. *The Political Climate*
The Conservative economic philosophy of the 1980's in the U.K. encouraged the growth of the small, self-employed unit by using a variety of tax concessions and other financial incentives. However, in times of recession bankrupcy is highest amongst this group.

The Location of Industry

Location economics seeks to explain where production takes place. Whether the business unit is small or large-scale, involved in primary, manufacturing or tertiary industry. Whether it is private enterprise or a government agency overall economic forces usually dictate where the unit locates.

Micro-economic Factors

Generally, the profit-maximising entrepreneur will seek to locate in order to maximise profit or minimise costs and maximise revenue.

Cost Factors

a) *Raw Materials*
Heavy industries locate where low cost raw material supplies are available and these attract other associated industries, e.g. steel and shipbuilding were attracted to coal fields in the north.

b) *Transport*
The maintenance of low transport costs was the main factor influencing location in the U.K. in the 19th century. Most heavy industries tended to locate near cheap sources of transport, e.g. rivers or canals. These days the availability of good and

efficient transport facilities such as roads or railways is still a major consideration. Weber analysed transport costs as the prime locational factor and classified goods into those with low and high value to weight ratios. Those with low value to weight ratios would locate close to the raw material source whilst those with high value to weight ratios, e.g. consumer goods, would locate near the market. In the case of the latter type of goods industries have now become footloose with respect to material costs and will often be influenced by the availability of labour.

c) *Labour*

Modern location economics emphasises that cheap labour is not as important as the availability of skilled labour. For most high tech industries the spread of automation in both factory and office has reduced the need for unskilled labour.

d) *Power*

Originally industries such as wool and cotton manufacturing were located near cheap sources of power but with the supply of electricity and the national grid system, many engineering firms can now locate in any region they choose, i.e. they are footloose.

e) *External Economies*

Many industries and business units congregate where other associated and complementary industries are established. This is done in order to exploit external economies of scale which improves efficiency and lowers unit costs. External economies are such things as the nearness to associated markets, a trained and available workforce, good communications, improved road or rail links. This explains why financial institutions gravitate towards the centre of London and why mechanical engineering firms move to the Midlands.

f) *Market Influences*

The growth of consumer goods industries providing personal goods and services, has meant that businesses tend to locate close to the market. For example, catering, retailing, education, health services, entertainment and professional services, are all to be found within major centres of population. In the London area there are many consumer goods industries attracted by the magnet of high incomes.

g) *Social factors, etc.*

A major new influence affecting the businessman is the environmental or social influences. These take the form of cheap housing, an attractive countryside and other social influences.

Government Policy Towards Location

A Brief history of U.K. policy

The 1930's to the late 1970's

The heavy unemployment experienced in the North in the 1930's, due to the decline of staple heavy industries, prompted governments to direct capital to these depressed areas. There was a policy of moving work to the workers. This was achieved by firstly identifying geographical areas of high unemployment, e.g. Development Areas and then providing financial carrots to attract industry. These carrots took the form of tax concessions, cheap loans, grants, low rents, etc. The decline of consumer goods industries in the 1970's saw the above policy extended to parts of the Midlands. Together with strict planning controls which operated in the South East there was a belief that this policy achieved the following:-

a) It reduced the impact of the regional income multiplier affecting depressed regions and directed capital to the worker.

b) It reduced the drift of population to the South East and so helped reduce congestion and pressure on house prices and other social services.

c) It meant that the infrastructure and social capital in the North was efficiently utilised.

d) It would be more effective than other policies because of the high degree of geographical immobility in the U.K.

However, the work to the workers policy was accused by free market economists of certain weaknesses. These were:-

a) The policy of planning controls, operated in the South, acted as a deterrent on new industries starting up and so these either did not invest in the U.K. or moved abroad to do so.

b) The generous capital grants available to business in the North was wasteful at the expense of the taxpayer, and was often given to firms who would have invested regardless.

c) Blanket assistance based upon geographical development area policy, did little to solve the problem of structural unemployment in the North. This policy also failed to analyse the cost effectiveness of these and other policies.

d) The policy tended to featherbed industries which led to union militancy, strikes and uncompetitive practices.

Economists nevertheless calculate that regional policy 1960–81 created 630,000 jobs in the assisted areas at a cost of £40,000 a job at 1982 prices.

1980 – 1990

The advent of the free-market Thatcher government in 1979 led to new policies being brought in. This has meant that the government relaxed planning controls in the South and adopted a more selective approach to financial assistance for those firms wishing to set up in the North. In particular, discretionary grants have been introduced together with a series of special regional and local initiatives such as Urban Development Corporations, Inner City Grants and Enterprise Zones, etc., see Fig. 3.3. This approach has allowed capital to move where it will get the best return and so workers now generally have to move to the work. In the main, capital seems to have moved not so much to low cost areas but to where income and market pull is strongest, i.e. the South East. The government has reduced not only geographically based grants but also the financial aid given to Nationalised Industries, many of which are located in the North. Local variations in income, as measured by GDP per head still show strong regional variations as Table 3.8 and the map "U.K. Aid 1990" show. Criticisms of the free market approach have grown in recent years. The rise in congestion and high house prices in the South have lead to the belief that the social costs are in excess of the private costs which a businessman decides upon when employing labour and capital in the South East.

TABLE 3.8
REGIONAL GROSS DOMESTIC PRODUCT (factor cost, current prices, £bn)*

	1988	1979–88 % change	Per head (£) 1988	1979–88 % change
UK	387.7	10.3	6.795	10.2
North	18.4	9.5	6.005	9.6
Yorkshire and Humberside	30.4	9.8	6.196	10.0
North West	40.4	9.4	6.347	9.7
East Midlands	25.6	10.7	6.438	9.9
West Midlands	32.2	9.4	6.190	9.5
East Anglia	13.4	11.5	6.604	10.2
South East	140.7	10.9	8.113	10.6
Greater London	58.6	9.9	8.699	10.2
South West	29.5	11.3	6.376	10.8
England	330.7	10.4	6.958	10.2
Wales	16.3	10.3	5.709	10.0
Scotland	32.5	9.9	6.387	10.1
Northern Ireland	8.2	10.4	5.173	10.0

Source: Lloyds Bank "An Economic Profile of Britain 1990".

Measures of Industrial Location and Concentration

There are two main measures:- (i) Location Quotient
(ii) Concentration Quotient

1. *Location Quotient (LQ)*. The LQ measures the degree to which a region specialises in a particular industry compared to the national average. It is given by the formula

$$LQ = \frac{\text{the percentage of a region's workers in industry Y}}{\text{the percentage of the national workforce in industry Y}}$$

"U.K. AID 1990"

Total Aid Budget:
1987/88 - £478m
1988/89 - £560m (estimate)
1989/90 - £513m (estimate)

Assisted Areas from 1.4.88

Development Areas
Regional Development Grants abolished 31.3.88.
New Regional Selective Assistance.
New Investment Grants for firms employing fewer than 25 people: 15% of capital expenditure (max. grant £15,000).
New Innovation Grants of 50% for firms employing fewer than 25 people (max. grant 25,000).
New Enterprise Initiatives (govt. grant towards 2/3 of cost of business consultancy schemes).

Intermediate Areas
New Regional Selective Assistance.
New Enterprise Initiatives.

Northern Ireland
Separately funded aid.

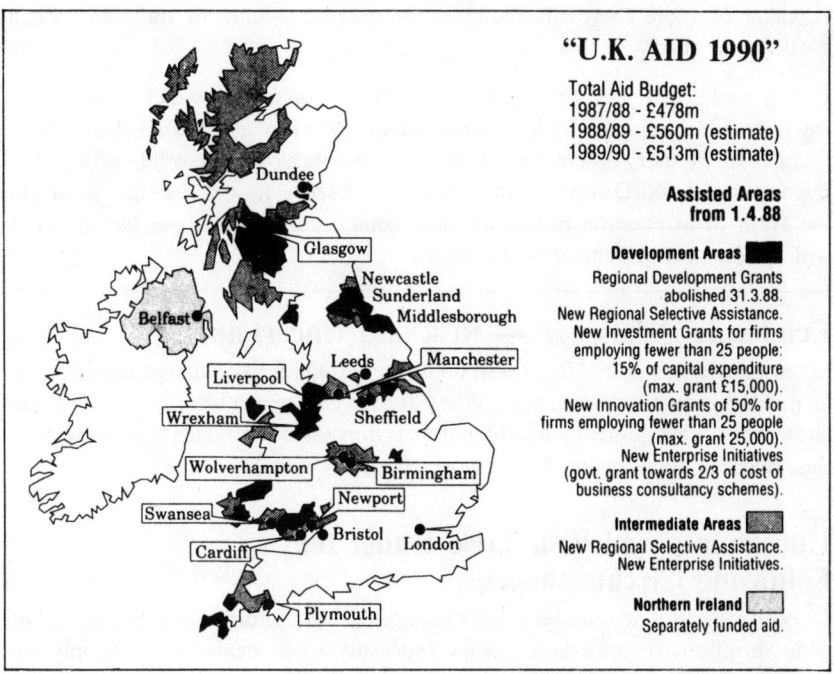

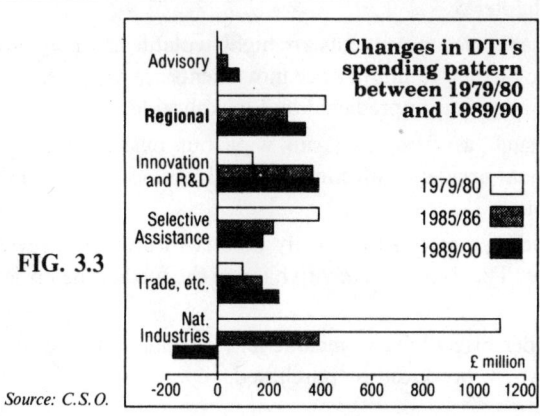

FIG. 3.3

Changes in DTI's spending pattern between 1979/80 and 1989/90

Source: C.S.O.

A value of more than one indicates a dependency of the region's workforce on a particular workforce.

2. *Concentration Quotient (CQ)*. The CQ measures the degree to which an industry is concentrated in an area compared to the national average. It is given by the formula

$$CQ = \frac{\text{the proportion of industry X in region Y}}{\text{the proportion of the nation's industry in region Y}}$$

A value of more than one indicates an overdependence of the region on a particular industry.

Both 1. and 2. can be combined into the coefficient of location which measures the extent to which an industry is regionalised and/or overconcentrated. Thus, in the event of an industry downturn both a region and its workforce will be affected. A region with a low LQ and/or a low CQ will, in a sense, have spread its risk and, in the event of a recession hitting one particular sector, there is less likelihood of widespread unemployment in the region.

Economic Behaviour — Risk and Uncertainty

Economic decisions are often taken under conditions of risk and uncertainty, both in product and factor markets. Whereas risk can be statistically assessed and allowed for, uncertainty by its very nature is impossible to predict and, because of this, markets may not be able to work efficiently.

Uncertainty and Risk Arise Under the Following Circumstances

1. Unforeseen demand and supply changes in agricultural markets can lead to wide variations in price and income especially when demand and supply are inelastic. See Chapter 5.
2. Ordinary share price movements are highly volatile and may change because of non-economic factors. Random price movements are recognised and have been reported. These are often unpredicted and inexplicable.
3. Accidents, such as fires, etc., can wipe out business stocks and profits overnight. Personal accidents affecting the workforce can also require expensive medical attention.
4. Investment decisions can incorrectly predict future costs, revenues, profits and interest rates. This is more likely to happen the further the project is planned into the future.
5. Current tender prices have to include and calculate future costs of materials which have yet to be produced or purchased.

Economic Behaviour

Businessmen and consumers are regarded by economists as risk averse. This means that people would prefer not to take on a fair bet, i.e. one with a 50/50 chance of winning, because the extra utility of a wealth gain is less than the extra utility of a wealth loss. This is especially true as the scale of the loss or gain increases. Thus both individuals and businessmen look for ways of reducing risk often by buying an insurance policy which offsets this risk. In the case of insurance, some have estimated that the premium is in fact around 30% more than the statistical probability of the event occurring. At the same time, with respect to the above example of a 50/50 bet, those who are indifferent about taking on the bet are said to be risk neutral whilst those keen to take on the bet are classified as risk lovers.

Methods and Markets to Offset Risk

1. *The Insurance Method*

This is a long established technique for reducing financial risk whereby individuals, for a premium, pay insurance companies to take over the risk on those events which can be statistically assessed. Although this puts up the fixed costs of a business it allows the business to provide for a larger, more certain scale of activity and hence tends to encourage competition. This means the number of potential competitors in an industry is increased which tends to be more efficient.

2. *Speculators* operate in financial, commodity and agricultural markets. Their role is to buy when prices are low and to sell in order to make a profit when prices are high. This has the effect of stabilising price movements and hence reduces the risk associated with volatile markets.

3. *Forward Traders*

In both commodity and financial markets forward traders provide the certainty of a predetermined forward price which reduces the risk to the businessman. It allows businessmen to hedge against unforeseen risk and so encourages these markets to operate and develop products and services which otherwise would not be produced.

4. *Portfolio Analysis*

This is a new technique of analysis by which overall risk is reduced in equity and investment markets. Essentially it leads to analysts investing in a broad range of shares. Some shares tend to move with the market, some against the market and some in an erratic, unpredicted fashion. By not putting all their financial eggs in one basket, this type of analysis encourages trade and hence investment in financial assets. Associated techniques such as probability and sensitivity analysis attempt to isolate the key significant variables most likely to affect the outcome in order that a measured and informed investment decision can be taken.

5. *Market Research and Good Management Practices*

Professional management attempts to reduce risk by thorough research of both product and factor markets, e.g. before recruiting or launching new products intensive research will be undertaken. Nevertheless there are two major problems in this, adverse selection and moral hazard.

Adverse Selection and Moral Hazard in Risk Markets

In insurance markets adverse selection means that high risk, i.e. high cost clients are more likely to take out insurance than the low or medium risk clients on whom the premiums have been assessed. In labour markets adverse selection means that those who apply for jobs are often the ones least suitable. However, the cost of reducing the business risk in the insurance market and the cost of correcting selection procedures in the labour market may lead to such a high price that the consumer is unable to afford it. One way of overcoming this is by sophisticated recruitment procedures in the labour market and by a system of weighting bad risk clients in the insurance market. Moral hazard refers to the concept whereby the insured policy holder may behave in such a way as to increase the likelihood of the undesired outcome actually occuring. This, in the case of car insurance, may lead to poor driving which increases accident claims and hence makes premiums expensive. Some even claim that seatbelts increase the likelihood of motor car accidents because the driver has less to fear by driving fast. These two problems can increase uncertainty and the cost of insurance and lead to risk or contingent markets either not working at all or working very inefficiently. In the public sector moral hazard is a problem with respect to unemployment insurance because it can affect people's attitude to work. It may reduce one's willingness to look for a job because the individual may be able to claim unemployment benefit too easily. In health markets where national insurance applies only an irrational person would behave in such a way as to claim medical insurance by having an accident in order to occupy a hospital bed.

Business Decisions, a General Overview

A business has to make a variety of decisions in order to produce the most profitable output using its resources. In this it has to decide the product, the quantity and quality of the product and also the business has to decide upon the pricing structure and stock holding quantities of the product range. Furthermore the business has to decide the factor input mix, e.g. capital or labour or land, and also where to locate and how best to raise the capital it uses for the technology it employs. In selling the product the business, subject to market structure, has to decide upon the channels of distribution, advertising policy and the best mix of home and overseas markets. A business unit can take on a number of different forms, e.g. a partnership, sole trader, or joint stock company and a decision will have to be made as to the most suitable type for a business unit. It has also to determine a policy with respect to the government which will impose a variety of regulations in produce and factor markets. Lastly a business has to decide upon the degree of acceptable risk and how best to reduce uncertainty in the markets. The following analysis in both product and factor markets assumes zero risk of uncertainty unless otherwise stated.

CHAPTER 3 Research

1. *Using your local high street or city centre, collect the names of businesses which you consider are: sole proprietors, partnerships, private and public joint stock companies.*

2. *Refer to the financial pages of the newspapers and select ten shares and monitor their price over the term. Try to explain why prices rise and fall for each one.*

3. *For the above shares, calculate the following: P/E ratio, dividend yield, gearing ratio, interest cover, etc.*

DATA RESPONSE QUESTIONS

Question 1

The planned 1990 operating budget for a company is given in Table 1 below together with the actual results.

Table 1

	£m Budget	£m Actual
Value of Sales	10.00	8.51
Direct costs	7.62	6.37
Indirect costs	2.00	2.03
Average fixed assets	0.57	0.57
Average nett current assets	1.70	1.58

a) Compute the seven financial ratios depicted in Table 2, for both planned and actual performance and comment.

Table 2

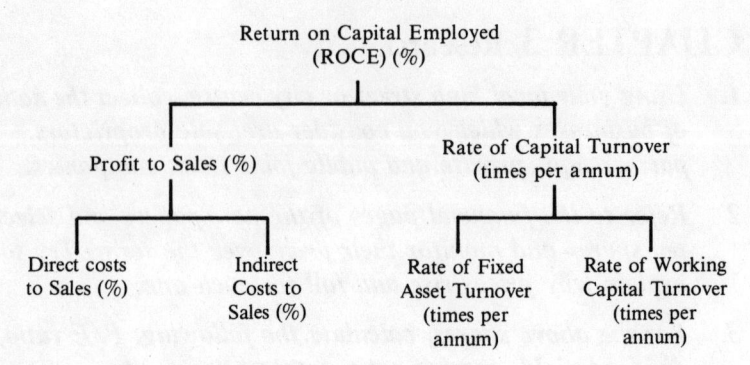

Return on Capital Employed (ROCE) (%)
├── Profit to Sales (%)
│   ├── Direct costs to Sales (%)
│   └── Indirect Costs to Sales (%)
└── Rate of Capital Turnover (times per annum)
    ├── Rate of Fixed Asset Turnover (times per annum)
    └── Rate of Working Capital Turnover (times per annum)

The top three tiers of the "ROCE Pyramid"

CAPITAL EMPLOYED = FIXED ASSETS + NETT CURRENT ASSETS

Question 2

The balance sheet of XYZ Retailers Ltd at 30 June was as follows:

	(£)		(£)
Share capital	10,000	Fixed assets	15,000
Retained profits	15,000	Current assets	10,000
	25,000		25,000

However, it had been forgotten that tax of £4,000 would have to be paid on the £6,000 profits for the year which had been added to retained profits, and that the shareholders were certain to approve a proposed dividend of £2,000 at the annual general meeting.

a) Make any necessary changes to the balance sheet.
b) Explain what has been done and why.

Risk Questions

Which of the following situations illustrate moral hazard and which adverse selection.

a) Fred never locks his car, knowing it is insured for theft.
b) George takes out life insurance, knowing that his work in mining has given him terminal lung cancer.
c) George takes out extra health insurance before going on a mountaineering holiday.

d) "Those who can't, teach and those who can't teach administer".

Data

Tom, Dick and Harry are each offered the opportunity of buying a second-hand car for £1,000. However, there is a 50:50 chance that the car's real value is double or half that. Tom refuses the deal, Dick decides by tossing a coin and Harry is keen to buy.

How would you describe each person's attitude to risk. Match the person to the characteristics.

a) Tom   (i) Risk averse
b) Dick   (ii) Risk neutral
c) Harry   (iii) Risk lower

Eric wishes to invest £100 in shares. Two industries, petrol and retailing, have shares on offer at £50 each. The returns from each are independent and in each case there is a 50% chance that returns will be good (£20) and a 50% chance that returns will be poor (£5).

a) If Eric buys petrol shares and times are (i) good (ii) bad, what will be the return in each case and on average.
b) If Eric buys retail shares and times are (i) good (ii) bad, what will be the return in each case and on average.
c) If you put your money into just one industry, what is the chance of a poor return.
d) What is the average return if Eric diversifies.
e) If Eric diversifies, compare the likelihood of a poor return compared to the likelihood of a poor return by not diversifying.

MARKET ANALYSIS
HOW PRICE IS DETERMINED

AIMS: To define, explain and discuss
- Markets and Functions
- Price Determination
- Marginal Utility
- Application and Evaluation of Market Analysis

KEY CONCEPTS

Demand, Supply, Equilibrium Price,
Marginal and Total Utility, Consumer Surplus,
Substitutes, Complements, Income,
Expectations, Price Controls, Perverse Demand,
Buffer Stocks, Market Failure, Product Factor goods,
Market Links

A market is a set of institutional arrangements which allows buyers and sellers to exchange goods and services for some agreed price.

Basic Characteristics of Markets

1. Markets are:- local, national and/or international in nature. They can exist in one place or be geographically dispersed and connected by telephone, etc. Markets exist in many forms, e.g. auctions, ring trading or most usually as a private contract, e.g. the second-hand car market.

2. Markets are regular or irregular in their frequency and exist for products, factors of production, personal or financial services, etc. They can be for a flow of new goods or for a stock of existing goods and assets, etc.

3. Markets range from those which are free and competitive to those dominated by the monopolistic buyer or seller. Within this range market structures can be oligopolistic with a few players, duopolistic with two producers or they can be competitively monopolistic which means there can be many producers selling a slightly different product, i.e. each has a small market share.

4. Most markets are, to some extent, influenced and possibly distorted by government intervention which takes a variety of forms such as price controls, rules and regulations, taxation and subsidies. In many cases the government may be the only buyer or seller. The reasons for government intervention are because markets do not always operate efficiently, quickly or smoothly and so governments try to improve the overall performance of markets.

5. Markets operate currently so the forces of supply and demand determine the day's spot price, or they can be used to determine future prices for commodities and currencies. Futures markets reduce uncertainty as discussed. Expectations play an important part in markets. Buyers and sellers adapt their behaviour about future prices based upon how prices have behaved in the past and how they expect prices to behave in the future. Many prices quoted in today's markets are based upon not only today's market forces but what is expected to happen to future demand and supply.

6. Markets determine the price of a good which is not the same as its value to an individual or a society. Price is the result of a demand for scarce resources in a market interacting with its supply whilst value is a subjective view which includes the idea of need. The concept of value is difficult to analyse because political and psychological factors influence how the value of a good is perceived. Market analysis is concerned with price in terms of how much can be afforded with respect to the supply in the market.

7. In the real world prices behave in a variety of ways. Price can fluctuate wildly, remain stable or be subject to slight increases or decreases over time. Market analysis sets out to build a simplified model of how market forces work, in terms of demand and supply, in order to explain and predict future movements in the market.

Demand as a Market Force

The market model of demand refers to effective demand which is the quantity of a good which will be demanded or bought at any given price over some time period, i.e. it is backed up by a consumer's purchasing power. In the example, see Fig. 4.1, market demand is the result of the addition of individual demand for the product, e.g. widgets, at different prices. The behaviour of the individual demand schedule is discussed later, see Section on individual demand. The initial assumptions about market demand are:-

1. The price of widgets is the only variable changing and other factors such as income, etc. are given, i.e. ceterus paribus, applies.

2. The price is the real price so inflation does not exist.

62 *Market Analysis: How Price is Determined*

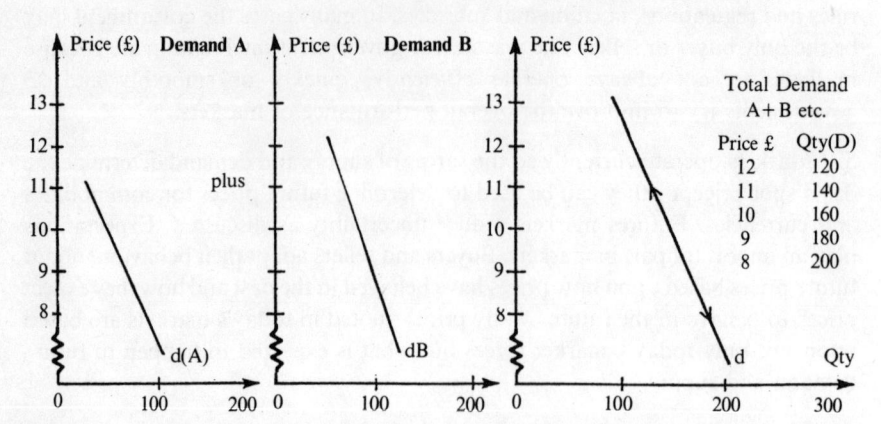

FIG. 4.1
INDIVIDUAL AND MARKET DEMAND FOR WIDGETS

Price £	Qty(D)
12	120
11	140
10	160
9	180
8	200

3. The rational consumer behaves consistently so the shape of the demand schedule reflects both an income and substitution effect. If the price of the good falls then real income or purchasing power of the consumer rises. This means if the price falls the consumer will buy more, i.e. substitute in favour of the relatively cheap good. Also because income rises even more of the good will be bought. In this case the good is a normal good and the income and substitution effect work to increase the amount of the good purchased; vice versa if the price of the good falls. See Chapter 16 for a more detailed analysis.

4. Individuals behave as if they were independent agents in determining their buying decisions, so demand is competitive and does not reflect collusion or monopolistic agreements.

Determining the Market Demand for Widgets

Fig. 4.1 shows how, by adding together A and B's demand for widgets, total demand is arrived at and this shows how much product is demanded at each price. As price falls more widgets are bought and vice versa as price rises. Demand contracts as price rises and expands as price falls, so there is an inverse relationship between demand and price.

Determining the Market Supply for Widgets

(the supply and demand curves referred to are shown as straight lines in order to facilitate the explanations).

The supply schedule, see Fig. 4.2 and curve for widgets shows the relationship between market price and the quantity each competitive (independent) supplier will put onto the market. Supply is a flow concept and shows the amount the supplier produces for the market over a period of time at different prices. The simple supply schedule is illustrated in Fig. 4.2 and this illustrates the idea that more will be supplied at a high price and less at the low price, i.e. there is a direct relationship between price and the quantity supplied. The supply curve reflects rising marginal costs for individual suppliers A and B and hence for the industry, which is the combined output of all producers' supply schedules. Although factor input prices are constant, diminishing returns means that unit output costs rise so requiring a higher price in the market to offset these costs. Movements along the supply curve reflect an expansion of supply as price rises and a contraction of supply as price falls.

FIG. 4.2
INDIVIDUAL AND MARKET SUPPLY OF WIDGETS

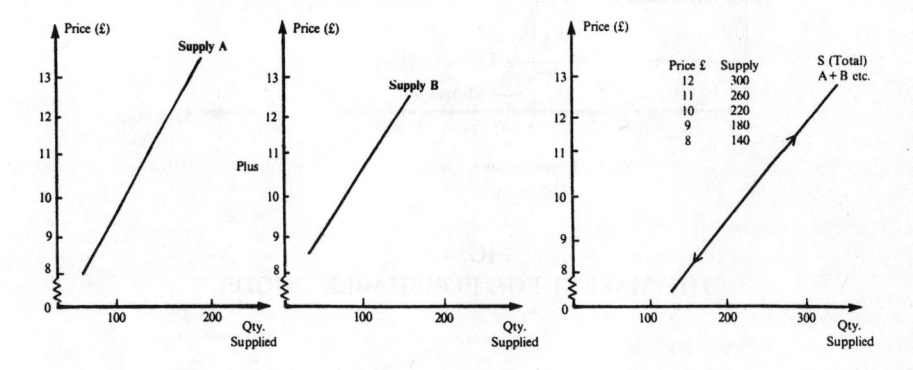

Price £	Supply
12	300
11	260
10	220
9	180
8	140

Supply and Demand and Market Price

If supply and demand for widgets are brought together, with respect to price, in the free market then there will only be one price where quantity demanded and supplied are equal. This is the equilibrium price in Fig. 4.3, at £9 and here demand and supply will be 180 units. If the price was temporarily at £8 then demand will exceed supply by 60 units and so there will be a shortage and price will be pushed up. If there was a temporary price of £10 in the market this will result in a surplus of 60 units so price will now be forced down. Thus market forces work to move the price to an equilibrium at £9 where there is stability.

The Market for Perishables and Equilibrium Price

If the product has a short life, e.g. perishable goods, and suppliers supply a non-equilibrium quantity of 200 units at a price of £9.50, see Fig. 4.4, then in order to clear the market the price will have to drop to £8. This price may appear to be the equilibrium price as well as the market price by suppliers. At this price, demand

FIG. 4.3
MARKET EQUILIBRIUM FOR WIDGETS

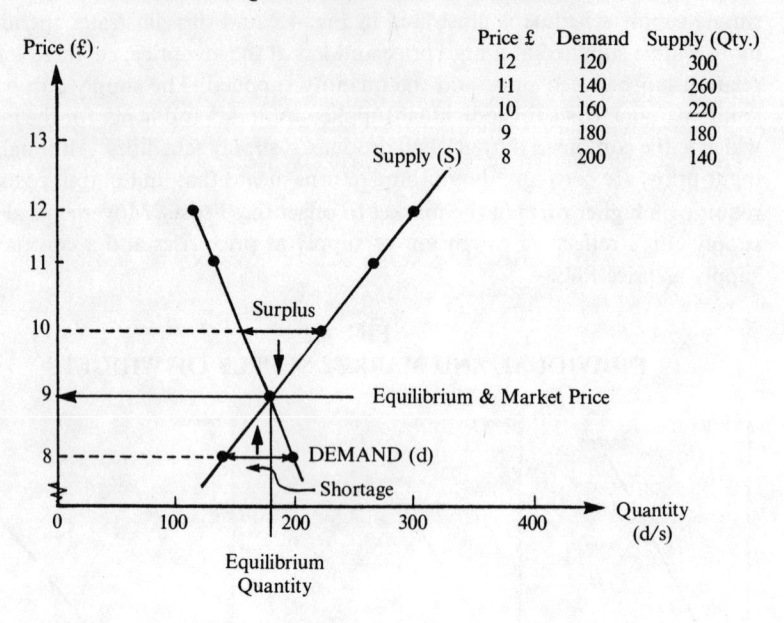

Price £	Demand	Supply (Qty.)
12	120	300
11	140	260
10	160	220
9	180	180
8	200	140

FIG. 4.4
THE MARKET FOR PERISHABLE GOODS

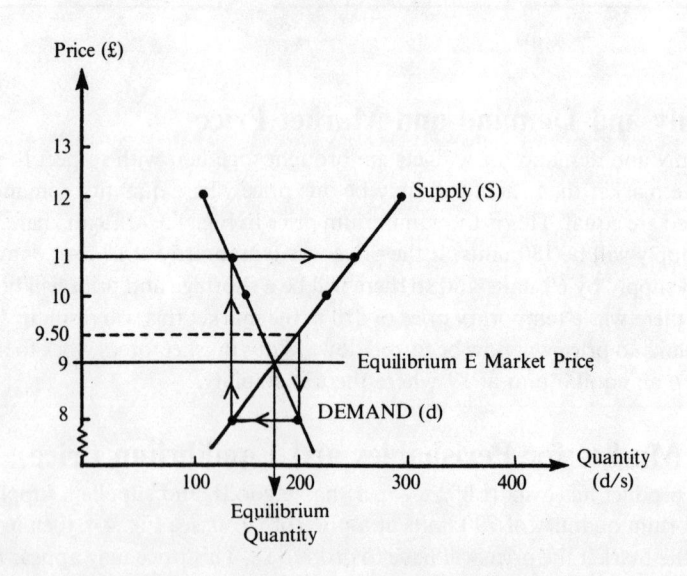

now exceeds the supply by 60 units and now price will be bid up to £11 because at £8 demand is 200 and supply is 140. This means the market will become unstable because of the nature of the good. However, when the product can be gradually increased or decreased in production, the equilibrium will be slowly reached as in Fig. 4.3. Because perishable goods have a short shelf-life, then there is a possibility of a non-stable market situation. This is also true when individual competitive suppliers are ignorant of all relevant supply and demand conditions. See Chapter 5 — the Cobweb Theory.

Individual Demand for Widgets

The explanation of why the individual demand schedule is downward sloping, uses the concept of marginal utility which means the extra satisfaction or utility derived from consuming one more good, e.g. a widget. As more of the good is bought and consumed, the individual gains utility but at a decreasing rate, so the total utility increases but not in proportion to the increase in the consumption of goods. Indeed, after a point the extra utility can become negative as the consumer becomes satiated with the product. Since marginal utility decreases as more widgets are bought, then the individual will be less willing to pay the previous price for each extra widget consumed. As Fig. 4.5(a) shows, the first widget provides a high level of extra or marginal utility and so the consumer is prepared to pay a relatively high price for this level of satisfaction gained. The second widget increases overall total utility but the extra utility is less than for the first unit consumed. The extra utility from the third, fourth and fifth widget consumed, also falls and so the consumer will not be prepared to pay the same price, i.e. as more are consumed a lower price will have to be paid to offset the reduction in marginal utility experienced. The line AB in Fig. 4.5(b) indicates, in effect, this fall in marginal utility which has to be matched by corresponding reductions in price, so AB is the consumer demand schedule for widgets. If the same analysis is applied to other goods purchased by the individual then the consumer will attempt to spend his income in such a way as to maximise total overall utility. The consumer will adjust spending on any two (or more goods) until their marginal utilities are proportional to their prices or:-

$$\frac{\text{marginal utility of A}}{\text{marginal utility of B}} = \frac{\text{the price of A}}{\text{the price of B}}$$

In the demand schedule for widgets, if the price falls by 10% the consumer increases the purchase of widgets until the marginal utility of widgets (A) falls by 10%. This means more are bought as the marginal utility falls by 10% as Fig. 4.5(b) shows.

Note: Fig. 4.5(a) and (b) also indicate that the sum of the areas of marginal utilities of 5 widgets in Fig.(a) is the same as the total utility derived from 5 widgets shown in Fig.(b). See Chapter 18 for further analysis.

FIG. 4.5
MARGINAL UTILITY AND DEMAND FOR WIDGETS

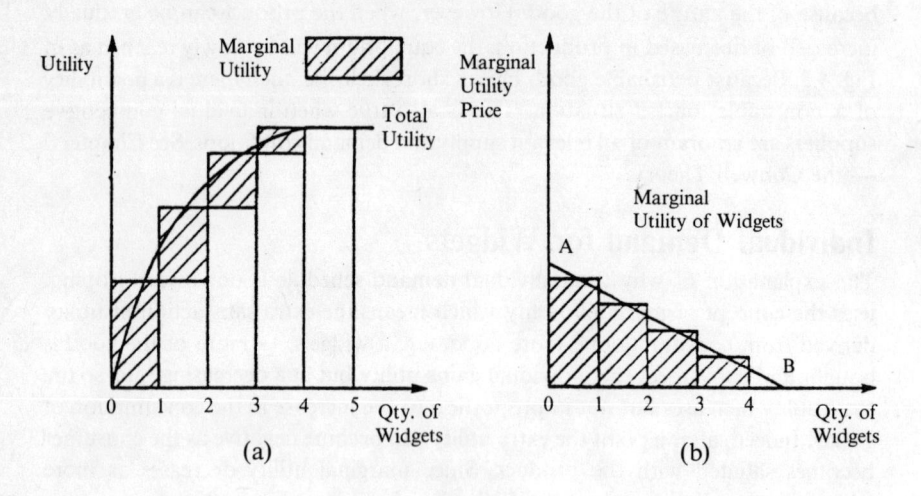

FIG. 4.6
UTILITY AND CONSUMER SURPLUS

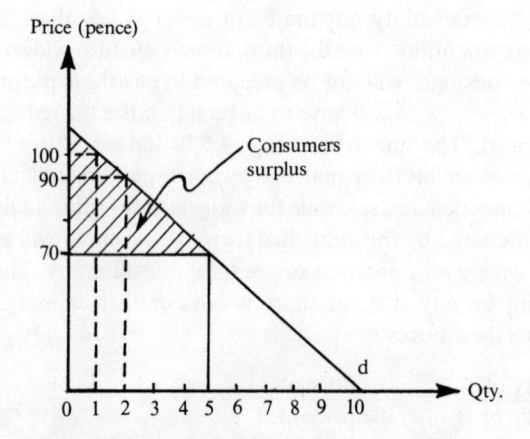

Utility and Consumer Surplus

The demand schedule of an individual relates price to marginal utility as Fig. 4.6 shows. Assume an individual buys 5 widgets at 70p. The demand reflects the fact that the marginal utilities derived from higher prices above 70p., e.g. 100p., 90p., 80., and 75p., will be equivalent to these prices, namely 100 + 90 + 80 + 75 plus the units of extra utility derived from a price of 70p., i.e. in total 415 units of utility.

However, the 5 widgets purchased cost 70p. × 5 = 350p. which is less than the total utility of 415 by 75. This 75 extra utility gained, but not paid for, is called consumer surplus and this is equal to the shaded in area, above price of 70p., as shown in Fig. 4.6. In effect it is the difference between what the individual actually pays and the maximum amount he would be prepared to pay (415p.) if each widget had been purchased individually at the higher prices of 100p., 90p., etc.

Demand for Widgets — Other Demand Factors

A change in demand can occur because factors, other than the price of the product (widgets), change and influence the consumer. At each price an extra 60 units will be demanded. Conversely, a fall in demand means 60 fewer widgets will be demanded at each price, i.e. the price of the good is assumed to remain constant — ceterus paribus. As Fig. 4.7 shows these changes shift the whole demand schedule to the right (or the left) of the original demand. The main factors affecting demand in this way are:-

FIG. 4.7
DEMAND SHIFTS AND IMPACT UPON PRICE

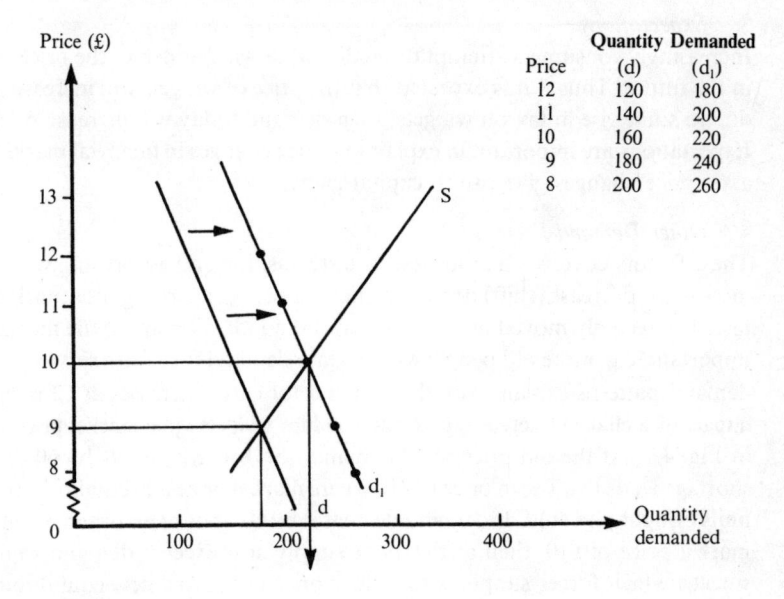

Price	Quantity Demanded (d)	(d_1)
12	120	180
11	140	200
10	160	220
9	180	240
8	200	260

1. *Real Disposable Income (RDI)*
This refers to the value of income, after adjusting for inflation, net of deductions for tax, etc. It is very important in influencing demand for expensive consumer durable goods where income increases also increase the demand for the good, i.e.

they are normal goods. However, in the case of inferior goods less are bought as income rises and in some cases only so much of a good can be consumed (satiation goods) regardless of income. If taxation policies change so high spending incomes are taxed more than before, then this new distribution of tax will lead to a fall in demand, i.e. it will shift demand to the left since disposable incomes have now fallen.

2. *The Price of Related Goods*

The two categories of related goods are substitutes and complementary goods. Substitute goods are alternatives for each other, e.g. coffee or tea, whilst complements are goods which are brought together, e.g. petrol and cars. This means if the price of tea falls we would expect consumers to buy more tea and less coffee, i.e. the demand for coffee would shift to the left. In the case of widgets, if 60 more are demanded, it would have been because the price of the substitute had risen. In the case of complements, a fall in the price of petrol would lead to a rise in demand, so demand shifts to the right. This relationship is also referred to as joint demand. In the case of house purchase and credit, these two products are purchased normally at the same time, so cheaper credit normally increases the demand for houses, i.e. shifts demand to the right.

3. *Expectations*

Increasingly consumers attempt to predict what will happen to the price of a good in the future. Thus if it is expected that the price of widgets will increase, perhaps due to some rise in tax on widgets, then demand today will increase by 60 units. Expectations are important in explaining price changes in financial markets where asset price changes give rise to capital gains.

4. *Other Demand Factors*

These factors cover such influences as taste, fashion and advertising which can all increase or decrease (shift) demand. This is true in consumer goods markets where taste has recently moved in favour of low fat goods. The size of the market is also important, e.g. more old people will increase demand for health services. Seasonal demand patterns explain why the demand for cards increases at Christmas. **The impact of a change (increase) in the demand for widgets upon market price** is shown in Fig. 4.7. At the old price of £9 demand now exceeds supply by 60 units. This shortage leads to a rise in price to £10 where market price is in equilibrium with 220 units bought and sold. If demand decreases by 60 units at an original equilibrium market price of £10, then at this price supply now exceeds demand so there is a surplus which forces suppliers to reduce price down to a new equilibrium of £9.

FIG. 4.8
SUPPLY CHANGES (SHIFTS) AND PRICE

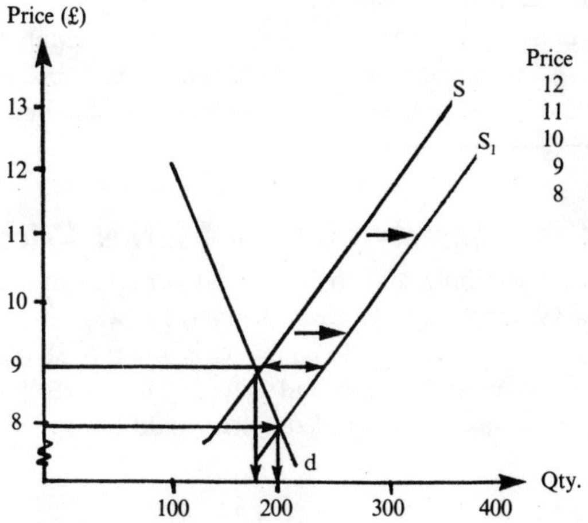

Price	S	S_1	d
12	300	360	120
11	260	320	140
10	220	280	160
9	180	240	180
8	140	200	200

Supply of Widgets — Other Supply Factors

Changes in supply occur when more or less is supplied at each price by suppliers. Alternatively for some output level, e.g. 200, the shift to S1 means in Fig. 4.8 suppliers are willing to accept a lower price, i.e. £8, than before. Factors which shift the supply curve are:- (ceterus paribus)

1. *Productivity Gains*
If unit input costs fall or unit output, per factor input rises, then overall average unit costs will decrease across the whole industry and so suppliers will be willing to offer the same quantity at a lower price. These gains in productivity will be due to improvement in management, better machinery, improved labour productivity or better cost saving technology resulting from innovation or improved techniques. This shifts S to S1.

2. *Factor Cost Changes*
If the unit cost of factor inputs, e.g. wages, rent, interest rates or materials falls, then even if productivity remains constant unit output costs, i.e. selling prices will decline. However, if factor costs fall by the same amount as productivity declines, then supply remains constant. Factor costs can also reduce if cheaper substitute materials can be used, e.g. plastic rather than cast iron gutterings are used in the building industry.

3. *Weather and Agricultural Yields*
In many agricultural sectors the weather can have a considerable impact. A rainy

70 Market Analysis: How Price is Determined

spell can reduce the yield of the agricultural sector and even with the same factor inputs of fertiliser and manpower the supply will shift to the left, i.e. S1 to S.

4. *Government Taxation and Subsidies*

The imposition of an indirect tax, e.g. VAT, will shift the supply from S1 to S and this will have the same impact as a rise in costs or a fall in productivity. A reduction in VAT or a subsidy given to the producer, will shift supply from S to S1 and so act in the same way as a fall in cost.

The Impact of a Supply Shift on Market Price

As shown in Fig. 4.8 supply shifts from S to S1 with demand (d) shown. At the original price of £9 supply now exceeds demand for widgets by 60 units and so market forces push down the price to a new equilibrium of £8 where demand and supply quantity is 200 units. If supply had shifted from S1 to S, due to the fall in the productivity of the industry, the market price would have risen from £8 to £9.

FIG. 4.9
JOINT DEMAND

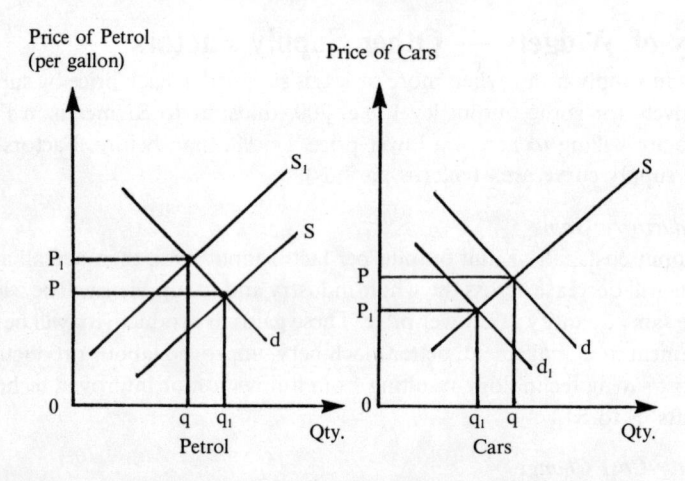

Special Demand and Supply Relationships

The following indicate some applications for the above analysis regarding changes in the demand and supply conditions with respect to particular relationships.

a. *Joint Demand/Complementary Goods, e.g. petrol/cars (see Fig. 4.9)*

In the case of complementary goods, the change in the price of one will affect the demand for the other because they are jointly demanded. If petrol costs rise and price goes from OP to OP_1, this reduces the overall demand for cars from d to d_1 and the price of cars falls from OP to OP_1.

FIG. 4.10
COMPETITIVE DEMAND

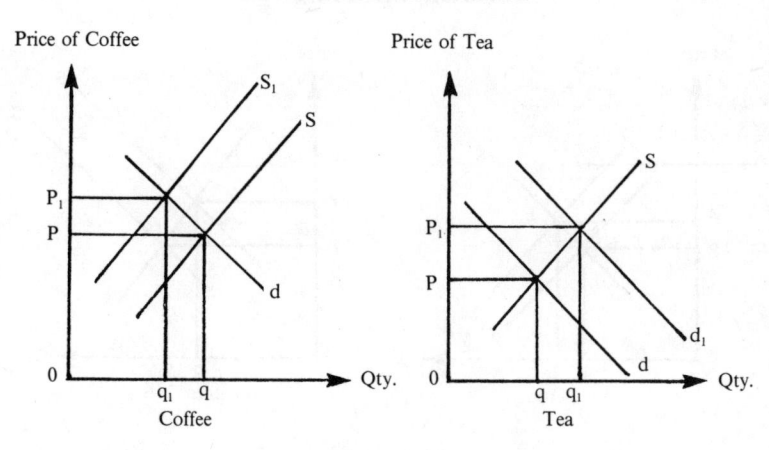

FIG. 4.11
COMPOSITE DEMAND

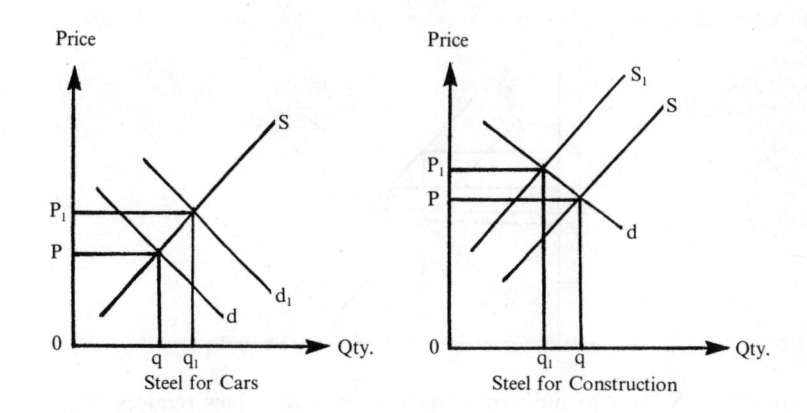

b. *Competitive Demand/Substitutes, e.g. coffee/tea (see Fig. 4.10)*
These two products could be viewed as substitutes and so the demand for one will vary directly with the price of its substitute. If a bad harvest reduces the supply of coffee from S to S1 and pushes up prices from OP to OP1, then demand for tea will increase from d to d_1 as people substitute in favour of cheaper tea. This eventually pushes up tea prices from OP to OP_1.

c. *Composite Demand/Several Uses for the Same Good (see Fig. 4.11)*
Often there are several uses for the same good. Steel can be used to build cars or for construction purposes. If the demand for steel to build cars increases from d to d_1 and pushes up steel prices, this will shift the supply schedule for construction steel

72 Market Analysis: How Price is Determined

FIG. 4.12
JOINT SUPPLY

Beef Cattle

Leather Goods

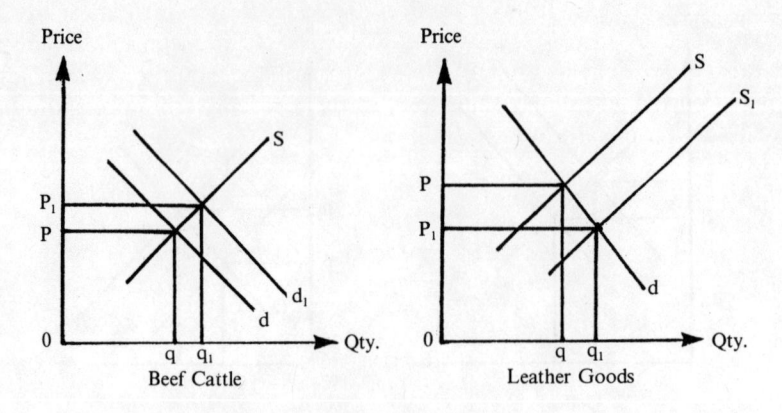

FIG. 4.13
MARKET CHANGES OVER TIME

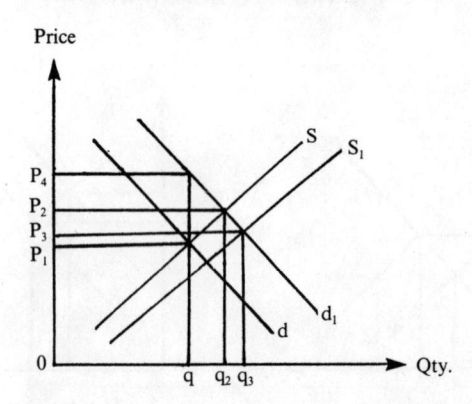

from S to S_1 and so push up construction prices. This reduces demand and quantity falls from oq to oq_1.

d. *Joint Supply (see Fig. 4.12)*
This is where the production of one product, e.g. cows, automatically increases the supply of another, e.g. leather derived from cows. Similarly in air transport an outward journey gives rise to an inward one. When demand for beef cattle rises from d to d_1, cow production increases output from oq to oq_1. This shifts the supply of leather goods from S to S_1 and reduces price from OP to OP_1.

e. *Market Changes Over Time (see Fig. 4.13)*
Although changes in demand shift demand in the short term very quickly, changes in supply, due to cost, etc., normally occur over a longer period. This means for a

given change in demand from d to d_1 price adjustments occur from the immediate to the medium and thence the long-term. In the immediate term supply is often fixed at oq so price rises from op to op_4 as demand increases. In the medium term, output gradually increases, oq to oq_2 as factors of production move into the industry, so price changes to OP_2. In the long-term the industry is able to adjust fully to demand and supply shifts to S_1 so the new long-term price and output equilibrium is op_3/oq_3.

FIG. 4.14
GOVERNMENTS & PRICE CONTROLS

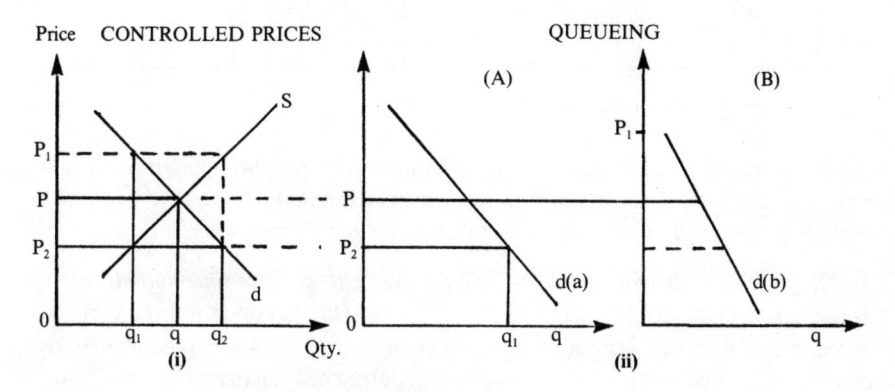

Applications of Market Analysis

1. *Governments and Price Controls*

Governments often wish to fix price above, or as in the case shown in Fig. 4.14(i) below equilibrium price of op at op_2. This may be in order to achieve some social objective such as ensuring all can afford to purchase the good. However, the consequences may be other than was anticipated. In the first place demand now exceeds supply at op_2 by an amount oq_2 less oq_1. This excess demand may now become a problem in other markets. Supply reduces in this market and those lucky enough to obtain the goods do so at a price of op_2. Left to the free market the limited supply of oq_1 may be forced up in price by a 'black market' to a price of op_1 which is above the equilibrium which would have arisen in an unregulated market. If the government wish to allocate oq_1 it could do so by a variety of methods, such as rationing by using coupons, queuing or even by a system of bribery to those bureaucrats allocating oq_1. In the event of a queuing system, person A, see Fig. 4.14(ii), obtains all they need of the scarce good by being first in the queue, i.e. oq_1, whilst person B is unable to purchase anything at all. However, person B values the first unit of the scarce good at a price of op_1, whilst person A values the good at only op_2. Thus trade between them would improve the situation until an overall level of op obtains for A and B. This result would have occurred if left to the free

74 Market Analysis: How Price is Determined

FIG. 4.15
BUFFER STOCKS ARRANGEMENTS etc.

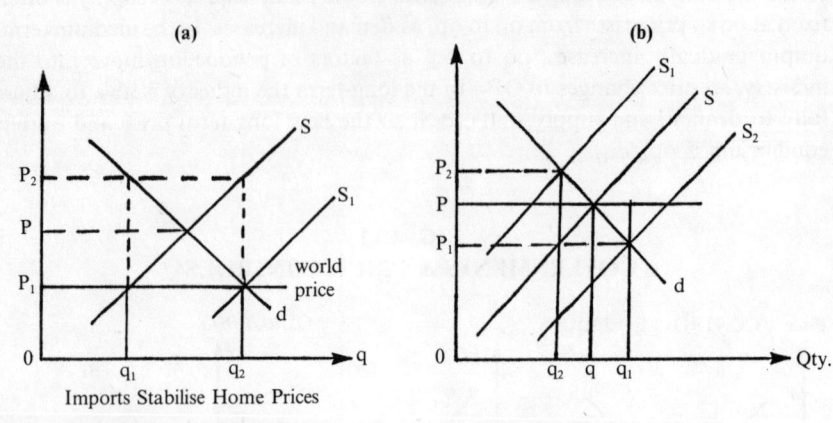

(a) Imports Stabilise Home Prices

(b)

market. Similarly a control price of op_1 in Fig. 4.14(i) above the equilibrium, would have led to an excess supply of oq_2 less oq_1 which could also lead to expensive storage problems as well as a waste of these unwanted resources.

2. *Buffer Stock Arrangements to Stabilise Agricultural Price Fluctuations*

If the government wish the price of eggs to be stabilised at op as in Fig. 4.15(b) it would attempt to plan output of oq so the revenue in the industry is equivalent to op × oq. It may also realise that unplanned output can fluctuate between S_1 and S_2 which would lead to price fluctuations between op_1 and op_2. In order to stabilise price at op the government could operate a buffer stock system. This means it would buy up excess stock of oq_1 – oq in order to push price from P_1 to p and it would sell off this stock in the event of a shortage, i.e. oq – oq_2 to stop the price rising to op_2. However, if producers saw op as a guaranteed price they might be encouraged to permanently produce beyond oq and so taxpayers' money is used to build up increasingly wasteful stocks.

3. *Quotas, Imports and Subsidies etc.*

In order to overcome the overproduction problem a quota system could be used so that each producer is allocated a quota proportional to oq in Fig. 4.15(b). However, this is criticised because it does not encourage the lowest cost producers to produce most because each is given the same output amount to produce. In some agricultural markets, see Fig. 4.15(a) world imports at a price of op_1 may be allowed in the home market. This will lead to a home production level of oq_1 and an import level of oq_2 less oq_1. Home producers may also be paid a subsidy of op_2 less op_1 in order to support the home industry. This may lead in the long-term to a supply shift from S to S_1 which provides self-sufficiency at the world price. A tariff of op_2 less op_1 could also achieve this level of self-sufficiency but a high home price may not encourage long-term self-sufficiency levels. Again, if the government wish to stabilise price at op_1 then when demand increases and threatens op_1 the government could allow imports in: imports are used as a buffer stock to stop home prices rising above op_1.

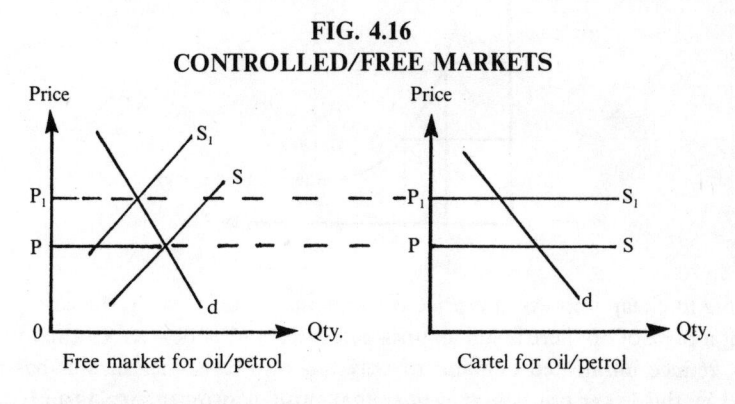

**FIG. 4.16
CONTROLLED/FREE MARKETS**

Free market for oil/petrol

Cartel for oil/petrol

4. *Free and Controlled Prices*

The petrol market exists under both a free market, e.g. the Rotterdam spot market, and a controlled petrol market price, e.g. OPEC. It could be argued that the free market price influences the cartel or control price, see Fig. 4.16. In this case lower non-OPEC oil prices push down world petrol prices from op_1 to op and this forces OPEC to reduce its price from op_1 to op.

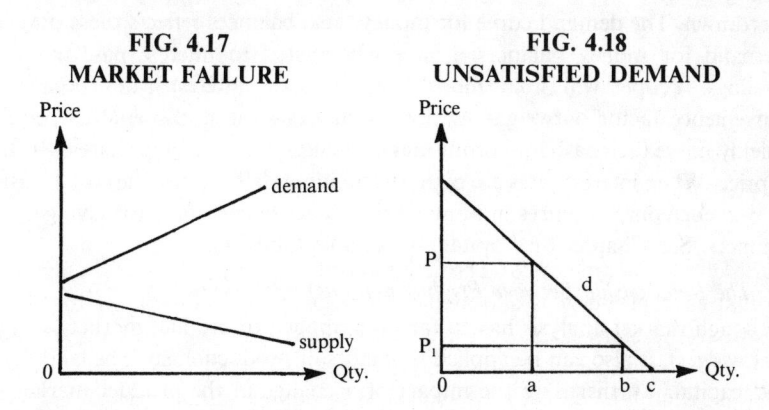

**FIG. 4.17
MARKET FAILURE**

**FIG. 4.18
UNSATISFIED DEMAND**

5. *Market Failure : Unsatisfied Demand*

In the case of unsatisfied demand there will be no price where consumers would be able to purchase because minimum supply price is always higher than the price consumers are prepared to buy, see Fig. 4.17. This problem can be corrected by governments subsidising production, as in the case of cars for the disabled, or by

76 Market Analysis: How Price is Determined

**FIG. 4.19
DEMAND FOR MONEY**

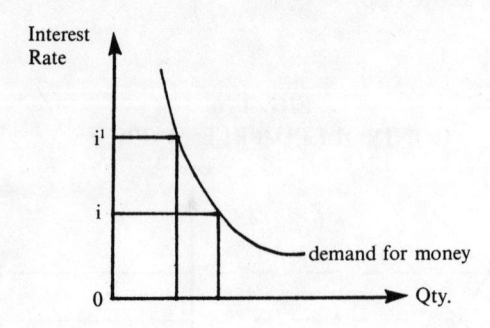

allowing in cheap imports at a price where demand can exist. In the case of Fig. 4.18 at a price of op there is still an unsatisfied demand of oc – oa. Cheap imports at op_1 reduce unsatisfied demand to only b – c so consumer surplus has been gained by this lower price. A zero price maximises consumer surplus and means unsatisfied demand no longer exists.

6. *Demand for Money or Cash Balances, see Fig. 4.19*

The demand for money arises so that people can pay their bills, have cash for emergency purposes or use money in order to speculate and make a profit. If they hold too little in their current account (cash balances) they may run the risk of having to borrow at even higher cost or pay excessive bank charges for being overdrawn. The demand curve for money/cash balances reflects these pressures. Demand for money balances is inversely related to interest paid on money holdings. People will hold more cash at lower interest rates because the convenience factor outweighs the loss of interest, and it also enables people to quickly move their cash into profit making ventures, e.g. buying shares which rise in price. When interest rates are high cash holdings fall because the cost of cash for convenience purposes rises in terms of the higher interest paid for giving up cash balances. See Chapter on Capital — loanable funds theory.

7. *The Relationship Between Product and Factor Markets*

Although market analysis has so far been applied to product markets, e.g. eggs and widgets, it also can be applied to factors of production such as land, labour and capital. Furthermore the impact of a change in the product market with respect to substitute products such as tea and coffee can be traced through factor markets; the supply and demand for labour in the tea and coffee plantations. Fig. 4.20 illustrates these concepts. In the example, demand for tea increases whilst demand for coffee decreases. This pushes up tea prices and reduces coffee prices. Resources (labour) are moved into tea production as the demand for labour pushes up tea workers' wages and at the same time demand for coffee workers pushes down the wages of coffee labourers. The market mechanism operates in order to produce more of what is wanted by using more labour resources. As the wages of tea workers rise they have a greater claim on what is produced, i.e. the what, how and for whom questions of economics are illustrated in this example.

FIG. 4.20
THE RELATIONSHIP BETWEEN PRODUCT AND FACTOR MARKETS

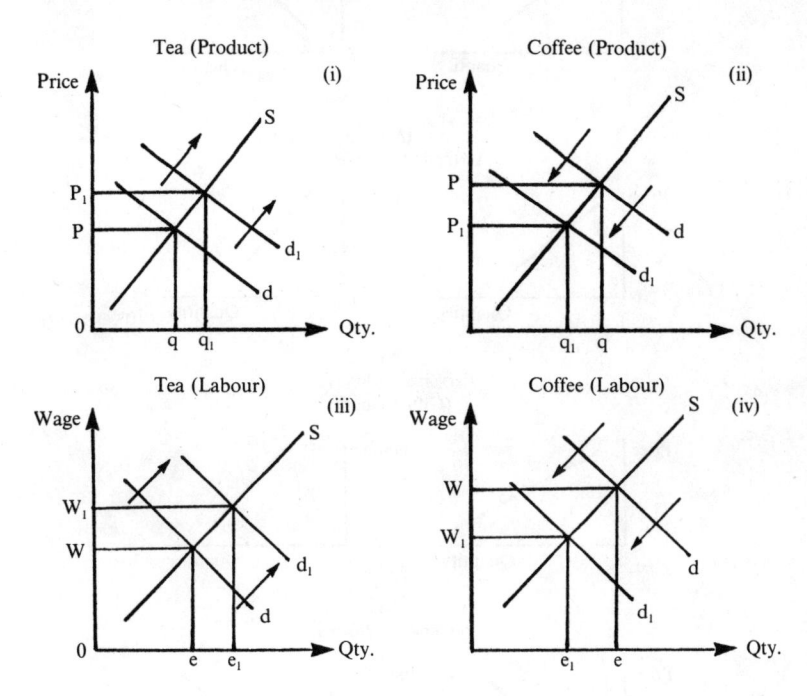

The Perverse Demand Curve/Income and Substitution Effects

The law of demand says that the price of the good and the quantity demanded are usually inversely related. However, there are circumstances when demand curves slope upwards. In order to understand clearly why and how these examples occur, it is important to be clear about price (substitution) and income effects and how they combine to affect the demand curve. Fig. 4.21 column I shows four demand schedules. L and M are normal demand schedules where more is bought as price falls whilst N and O are perverse demand schedules which slope upwards with respect to price. Column II shows how demand changes relate to income changes. A normal response is where more is bought when income rises whilst an abnormal or inferior response is the opposite with respect to income. There are four

FIG. 4.21
NORMAL AND PERVERSE DEMAND

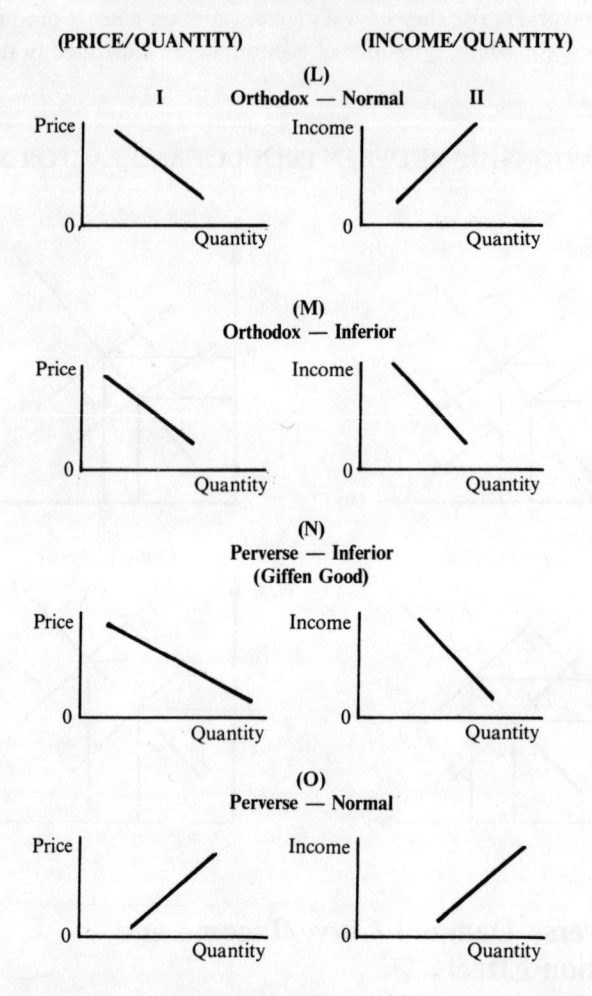

(PRICE/QUANTITY)   (INCOME/QUANTITY)

(L) Orthodox — Normal

(M) Orthodox — Inferior

(N) Perverse — Inferior (Giffen Good)

(O) Perverse — Normal

possibilities when price and income effects are combined with respect to quantity demanded. Situation L is the orthodox or normal case, i.e. income and substitution effects work in the same direction to increase demand when price falls. Situation M shows a case where there is a positive substitution effect which outweighs a negative (inferior) income effect. So overall demand still slopes downwards, e.g. an inferior good such as bread still exhibits overall a downward sloping demand schedule with respect to price. Situation N shows where a negative income effect outweighs a positive substitution effect so overall demand slopes upwards, e.g. the Giffen Good case. Finally, situation O shows where the positive income effect is outweighed by a negative substitution effect so more utility is gained as the price rises, i.e. people want goods of ostentation because of their social appeal. This last case also explains why speculators, who expect prices to rise even more, buy shares even when their prices are increasing. Furthermore, when quality is perceived to be indicative of the price, consumers will often buy more as the price rises because they may feel they are getting a better product. Demand is thus upward sloping with respect to price.

CHAPTER 4 Research

1. *Monitor the price of a good/s you consider to be produced competitively and monopolistically and identify the market forces affecting the price changes.*

2. *Obtain a copy of "Exchange and Mart" and identify as many markets as possible.*

DATA RESPONSE QUESTIONS

Question 1
Taxi-Cab Licences: The Cartel Case Illustrated

Taxicabs in Civis

In Civis, as elsewhere in the UK, taxicabs are licensed (for a nominal amount), by the local authority. The price per mile charged by the taxis is set by the local authority and is the same for all taxi operators. With the decline in public facilities and the development of a new shopping centre, demand for taxi services has doubled in Civis. This has resulted in the price of taxicab licences rising in the free market, representing a form of monopoly profit (i.e. an economic rent of scarcity). In effect it represents the discounted income stream an owner of taxis could earn over time. The authority proposes to increase the number of new licences issued. This move has been met with protest by existing taxicab licence holders.

80 Market Analysis: How Price is Determined

Fig. 1
Supply and demand for travel in taxicabs

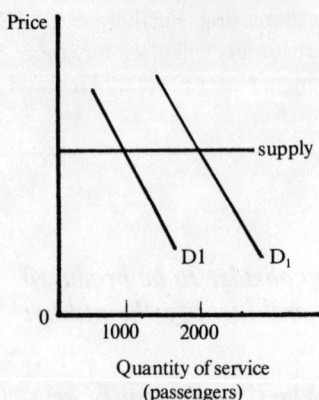

[Graph: Price vs Quantity of service (passengers); supply curve, D1 and D₁ demand curves at 1000 and 2000]

Fig. 2
Supply and demand for licences

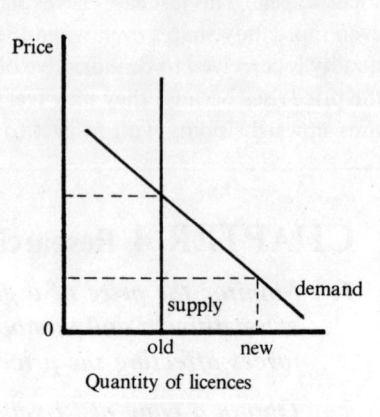

[Graph: Price vs Quantity of licences; vertical supply at "old", shifted to "new", with demand curve]

1. Use Fig. 1 and show the extra income generated by the increase in demand. If the number of licences increased, what would happen to this revenue?
2. Use Fig. 2 to show the economic profit earned by existing taxi-cab owners. If the number of licences increases, show the new price for licences and the position of the existing taxi-cab owners with regard to economic profit earned from owning a licence.
3. Outline the main arguments in favour of limiting/increasing the number of taxi licences.

Question 2 — Using Market Analysis
Keeping Control of the GIs in Yokohama

Late in 1945 I was sent to Japan as part of a military government team stationed in Yokohama. I was put in charge of rationing, price control, forestry, fishing, and mining for Kanagawa Prefecture. That meant I had nothing to do. The occupation was being run exclusively by General MacArthur's headquarters in Tokyo. But we in the military government at lower levels didn't know we weren't supposed to do anything. Neither did the local Japanese officials. We — and they — took ourselves quite seriously.

One day the medical officer of our company came to see me. He was worried about the health of the American troops. They were picking up girls on the street instead of patronizing the brothels' where the girls were given a medical inspection once a week. The medical officer thought the soldiers were picking up girls on the street because the brothels' prices were too high. Since I was in charge of price control, he wanted me to take action.

I sent for the chief of the Yokohama police, asked for a report on prices charged by every brothel in Yokohama, and naively told him why. The conversation was conducted through an interpreter. The chief spoke no English, and the Japanese language instruction provided by the Army program at Northwestern had not taught me the vocabulary needed for the conversation. At the end of the interview, the interpreter informed me that the chief, who was not naive, would like to give me a party, and he wanted my friend the medical officer to come too.

I got to quite a few good parties before the Japanese learned I had no power, but the police chief's party was by far the best. By the time it took place, I had had second thoughts. What if American newspapers got hold of the story that a United States Army Officer was reducing prices in brothels for the benefit of American troops? I quietly abandoned the project. A bulky report on Yokohama brothels went unused. The chief must have thought his party had been a great success.

Years later, when I finally saw the light, I became shocked at the deficiency of my economic training. To be sure, I had been away from economics for three and a half years before this incident, but that was hardly an excuse. I had majored in economics as an undergraduate at Harvard, received an MA in economics from Columbia, taught economics for two years at Harvard, passed the qualifying examination for the PhD, and worked briefly for the Office of Price Administration. Yet it had not occurred to me to apply elementary economic analysis to the problem. The medical officer's proposal would have had exactly the opposite effect from what he intended. But if I had figured that out, I would have missed a hell of a good party.

Source: R. Feis, 'The Price of Sin', in Rendigs Feis, Stephen Buckles, and Walter Johnson, *Casebook of Economic Problems and Policies,* 4th edn, West Publishing Co., St. Paul, United States, pp.26–7.

Copyright: Vanderbilt University.

1. Use a supply and demand schedule to show the market for brothel services. Show the equilibrium price.
2. Using the diagram, indicate the price resulting from carrying out the initial proposal.
3. Use the diagram/s to show why their proposal would have worsened the situation.
4. Use the diagram to show an improved solution to the problem.

Question 4(a) — Comparative Demand Patterns

Consumers' expenditure on fuel and light, 1978–81

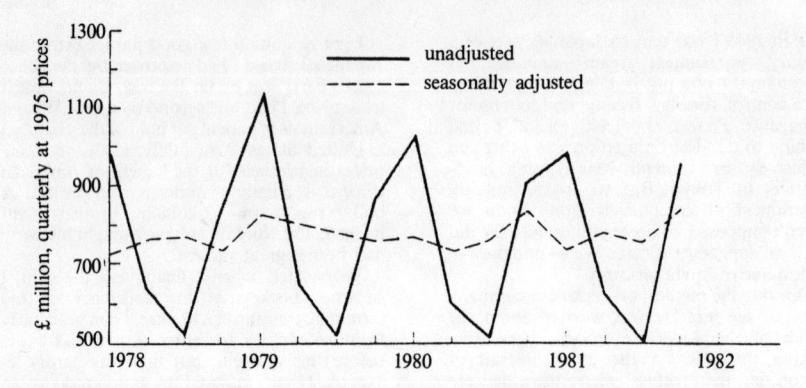

[Graph: £ million, quarterly at 1975 prices, showing unadjusted (solid line) and seasonally adjusted (dashed line) series from 1978 to 1982. Unadjusted fluctuates between approximately 500 and 1150; seasonally adjusted remains around 700–850.]

Source: Economic Progress Report, The Treasury, March 1983.

Orders for new houses, 1978–81

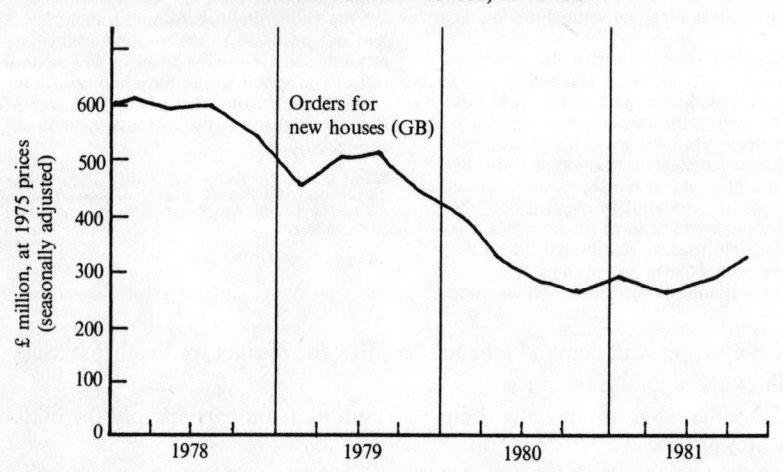

[Graph: £ million, at 1975 prices (seasonally adjusted), Orders for new houses (GB), declining from about 600 in 1978 to around 270–330 by 1981.]

Source: Economic Trends, CSO, March 1982.

1. Explain the terms (i) unadjusted (ii) seasonally adjusted (iii) at 1975 prices. What do (ii) and (iii) attempt to do?
2. Outline the main factors affecting the demand for fuel and light and new houses.
3. Compare the behaviour in each diagram and explain the overall difference using economic analysis.

Question 3
The Crisis in the EC's Common Agricultural Policy

Farming in most rich countries is in a classic mess. As food prices have tumbled on world markets, subsidies to farmers (paid through taxes or propped-up food prices) have spiralled to more than $100 billion a year. Such protectionism only sharpens the appetite for more; it never achieves its proclaimed goals. Farmers' incomes and land prices are falling, bankruptcies are rising. Now the Americans have urged the EEC to agree to abolish all subsidies and barriers to agricultural trade within ten years. The Americans have good reasons for wanting a change: their own spending on farm support has trebled in the past three years.

The main way in which the EEC's common agricultural policy supports farmers is by Eurocrats setting guaranteed prices for dairy products, beef, cereals, sugar. If market prices fall below the floor, intervention agencies buy the surpluses. This rigged system is buttressed by import levies and export subsidies, and its benefits go mainly to the wrong people. Three-quarters of EEC farm support reaches the biggest and richest 25% of farmers, concentrated in the wealthier northern countries. They get nearly $10 000 a year each from Europe's taxpayers. The other quarter goes to the poorer, southern 75% of farmers. They get about $1 000 a year each. Most distortingly, because German and French politicians want their farmers to have average German and French incomes, the EEC pays Karl and Jacques to produce butter at five times the price at which New Zealanders can do it; some of this butter is dumped on world markets at under one-fifth of its true cost, making economic New Zealand butter unsellable.

Europe's farm ministers recognise some of these absurdities, but prefer to tackle the symptoms (eg. through curbing surpluses of milk and sugar by imposing production quotas) rather than the cause (which is the gap between Community prices and world prices). Quotas have sometimes made the gap worse, because farmers have received higher prices to compensate them for not being allowed to produce so much of what is not wanted. Quotas also freeze market shares. Trading in quotas mitigates this, but creates nonsenses of its own. In parts of Britain a farmer's milk quotas are now worth more than his land. Curbs on milk output can just mean more beef or cereals. When everything is in surplus, quotas are a nightmare of red tape, with each farmer having to account for his production down to the last bunch of radishes.

Every statesman knows that a better solution would be sharp cuts in support prices, but these are called politically impossible.

Source: *The Economist, 3 October 1987.*

*A quota system aims to reduce output.

1. Why would the Americans have good reason for wanting a change in the EEC's agricultural policy?
2. Draw a diagram to show the impact of the EEC support policy.
3. How does the trading in quotas reduce the possibility of market shares being frozen? Use the diagram to illustrate.
4. Why does a quota system lead to systematic bureaucracy and accounting?

(b)

Problems in Smallhamlet

A group of market gardeners had for many years sent their tomatoes to be sold at the weekly market in Smallhamlet. However, the Smallhamlet Council decided to ban car parking in the streets near the markets with the result that the number of people shopping in the market decreased substantially. At first the farmers continued to send their tomatoes to the market in the hope that trade might pick up again. However, those farmers living furthest away eventually switched their supplies to Bigtown, where conditions for shopping were more favourable.

Show, by means of a diagram, the demand and supply conditions at Smallhamlet (a) before the parking ban was introduced (b) immediately after the parking ban was introduced and (c) after some supplies had been switched to Bigtown. Explain your diagram with a few sentences.

5 ELASTICITY

AIMS: *To define, explain and discuss*
- *Price, Income and Cross Elasticity of Demand*
- *Factors Influencing Elasticity*
- *Supply Elasticity : Factors Influencing*
- *Price Variations and Elasticity*
- *Governments, Taxation, Market Controls*

KEY CONCEPTS
Price, Income, Cross Elasticity of Demand, Supply Elasticity, Revenue and Elasticity, Buffer Stocks, Incidence of Taxation, Cobweb Theory

Demand elasticity measures the responsiveness of quantity demanded of a good (x) for some given small change in (1) the price of x (2) real disposable income (3) the price of a complementary of substitute good (y) or some other variable, e.g. advertising. Supply elasticity measures the responsiveness of quantity supplied for some small change in the price of the good (x).

(1) Price Elasticity of Demand (P.E.D.)

This measures the responsiveness of quantity demanded for some small change in the price or by formula:-

$$\text{PED (at a point)} = \frac{\%\text{ change in quantity demanded of x}}{\%\text{ change in price of x}} = \text{coefficient of elasticity}$$

The coefficient of elasticity will usually be negative (−) in value since demand falls as price rises and will vary from less than 1 (<1), unity (=1) and then to values greater than one (>1). Giffen goods will be indicated by positive values (+). Fig. 5.1 shows how demand responds with respect to a small change in price and (i) to (v) indicate the different types of elasticity applying the above formula.

If revenue is equal to price (p) x quantity demanded (qd) and price changes as Fig. 5.1 shows then revenue will also change. The extent of this revenue change is measured by comparing areas a and b, the shaded area is common. The results of

86 Elasticity

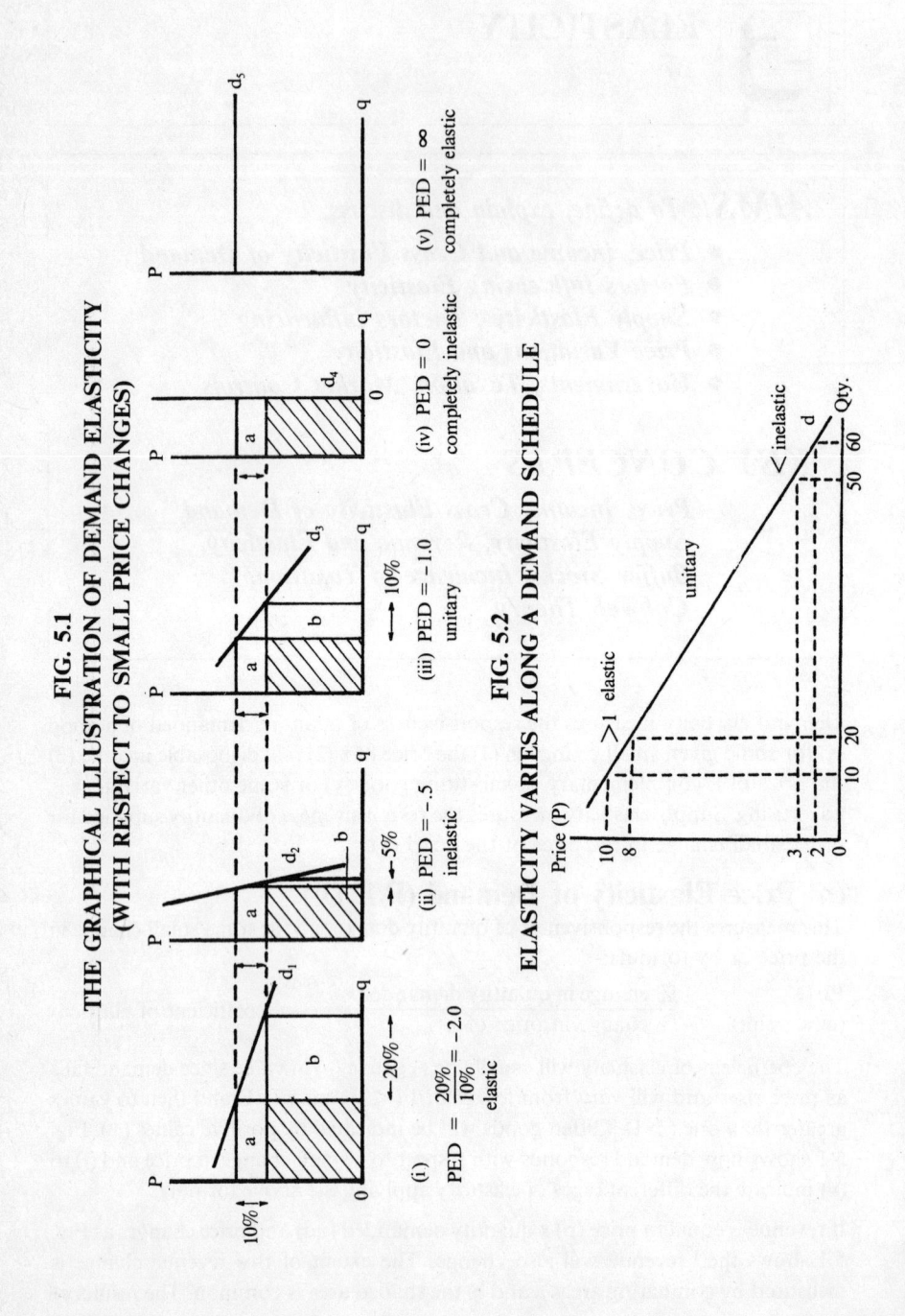

FIG. 5.1
THE GRAPHICAL ILLUSTRATION OF DEMAND ELASTICITY
(WITH RESPECT TO SMALL PRICE CHANGES)

(i) PED = $\frac{20\%}{10\%}$ = -2.0
elastic

(ii) PED = -.5
inelastic

(iii) PED = -1.0
unitary

(iv) PED = 0
completely inelastic

(v) PED = ∞
completely elastic

FIG. 5.2
ELASTICITY VARIES ALONG A DEMAND SCHEDULE

changing revenues with respect to price changes are summarised for (i) to (v).

(i) If demand is elastic (d_1) and the price rises by 10%, then overall revenue falls. If demand is elastic (d_1) and the price falls by 10%, then overall revenue rises.

(ii) If demand is inelastic (d_2) and price rises by 10%, then overall revenue rises. If demand is inelastic (d_2) and prices fall by 10%, then overall revenue falls.

(iii) If demand is unity (d_3) and the price rises or falls by 10%, then overall revenue remains constant.

(iv) If demand is completely inelastic (d_4) and price rises by 10%, then overall revenue rises.
If demand is completely inelastic and price falls by 10%, then overall revenue falls.

(v) If demand is completely elastic (d_5) and price rises or falls by 10%, then revenue increases or reduces by an infinite amount.

Demand Elasticity and the Gradient of a Curve

The simple graphical concept of elasticity stresses how demand responsiveness varies but each price change has to be seen as a very small change over the total demand schedule. This is because, on a demand schedule, elasticity will be different between different prices so it is not the same as the gradient of the line. Use Fig. 5.2 and consider a change from 8p. to 10p. which reduces demand from 20 to 10. These are changes of 25% and 100% respectively, i.e. elasticity equals minus –4 (elastic). However, the price change from 2p. to 3p. leads to a quantity change of 50 to 60, percentage changes of 50% and 20%, i.e. elasticity equals –.4 (inelastic). Thus the line in Fig. 5.2 appears to have the same gradient but elasticity varies along it. In the same way whilst PED from 2p to 3p is –.4 from 3p to 2p PED is equal to a price change of $33\frac{1}{3}$%, a quantity change of 20% so elasticity equals
$$\frac{20\%}{33\frac{1}{3}\%} = -.6.$$
Thus elasticity depends upon whether the change is from 2p. to 3p. or 3p. to 2p. The correct procedure is to take both values and divide by 2, i.e. $.4 + .6 = 1.0 \div 2 = -.5$. However, for practical purposes, elasticity is normally worked on the original price change, i.e. from 2p. to 3p. PED which is equal to –.6.

Determinants of Demand Elasticity: with respect to price

(a) *Degree of Substitutability*
The easier it is to substitute the good for another the more elastic demand will be with respect to price. Thus whilst demand for food may be inelastic overall the demand for butter or margarine may be very elastic as they can be substituted for each other and for other brands of margarine or butter.

(b) *The Time Factor*
In the short-term it is often difficult to quickly obtain a substitute good, but in the

long-term consumers will adapt their behaviour, and alternatives will be available so demand becomes more elastic as consumers are able to buy more alternatives.

(c) *Luxury Versus Necessity*
It is sometimes argued that the more a good is a basic necessity the more inelastic demand becomes, whilst for a luxury demand will be more elastic. However, in affluent economies a luxury, e.g. a motor car, is perceived by many as a necessity.

(d) *The Amount of Consumers' Income Spent on the Good*
If only a small amount of consumers' income is spent on a good then demand will be inelastic. A once yearly purchase of shoe laces which increase in price from 20p. to 30p. is hardly likely to reduce demand. A rise in the cost of house mortgage, which takes up a large amount of the household budget, will reduce demand for housing.

(e) *The Structure of the Market*
Whilst a competitive supplier will face a completely elastic demand, a monopolist faces a more elastic demand for his product. In fact, intensive advertising can mean the demand for the monopolist's product becomes more and more inelastic.

Elasticity of Supply (ES)

This measures the responsiveness of quantity supplied to a change in price. It is the relationship between the proportionate change in price and the proportionate change in quantity supplied. The formula is:-

$$ES = \frac{\% \text{ change in Quantity Supplied}}{\% \text{ change in the Price of the Good}} = \begin{array}{ll} + >1 & \text{elastic} \\ + <1 & \text{inelastic} \\ + =1 & \text{unit elasticity} \end{array}$$

Since supply increases with price, the relationship is positive (+) and varies from inelastic to elastic with other types of elasticity illustrated in Fig. 5.3 (i) to (v).

Factors Influencing Elasticity of Supply

(1) *Time*
In the very short-term the industry (firm) cannot increase the fixed or variable factor very easily so supply will be inelastic. In the short-run the variable factor can be increased and in the long-run all factor proportions can change. The above refers to the flow of goods and services. The stock of land or valuable paintings is often fixed in all but the very long-term.

(2) *Factor or Product Capacity*
If there are unemployed variable factors, e.g. labour, then firms will be able to expand production easily so supply is elastic. If it is possible to import labour or even products, then supply becomes more elastic, i.e. imports are perfectly elastic at the world price.

Elasticity 89

FIG. 5.3
THE GRAPHICAL ILLUSTRATION OF SUPPLY ELASTICITY

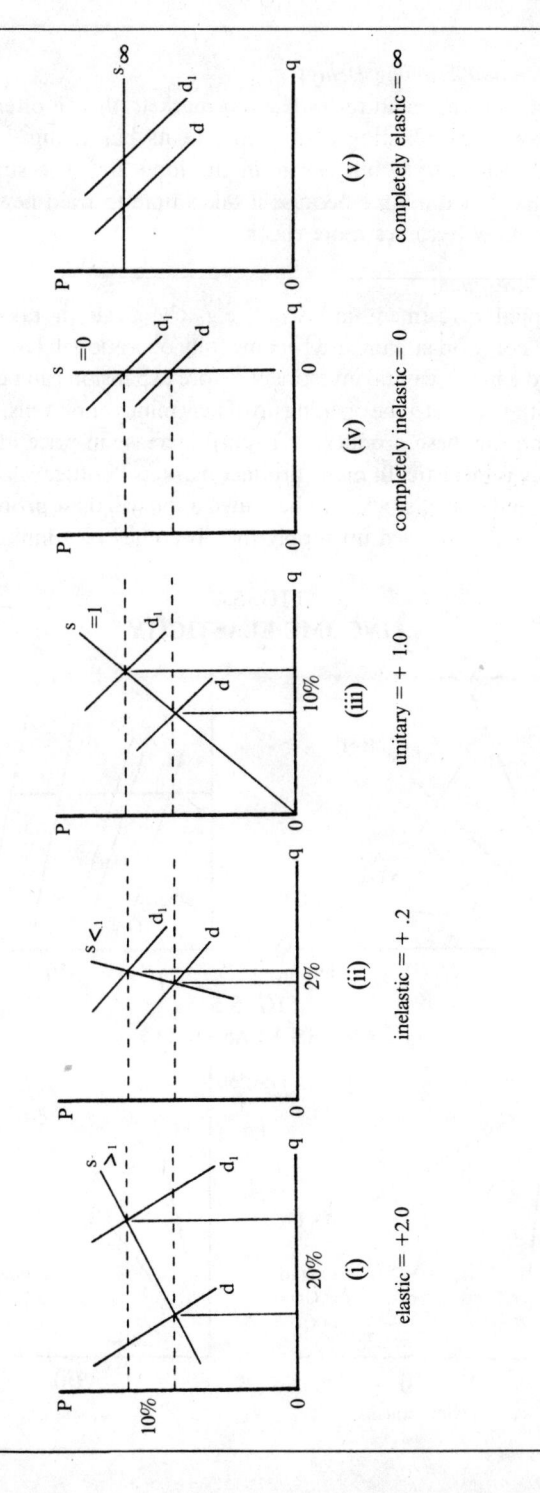

(i) elastic = +2.0

(ii) inelastic = +.2

(iii) unitary = +1.0

(iv) completely inelastic = 0

(v) completely elastic = ∞

90 Elasticity

(3) Production and Training Delays

In the case of certain agricultural and labour markets, there is often a considerable time lag between the planting of a crop and its harvesting, i.e. its supply is inelastic in the short-term but elastic in the long-run. The supply of trained personnel is fixed at one time because it takes time to train new recruits. Once trained supply now becomes more elastic.

(4) Capital Investment

In heavy capital investment industries, e.g. chemicals, it takes time for the investment to come on-stream and become fully operational. Once on-line it then takes time and a heavy capital investment before expansion can be increased. This is also true with respect to the opening up of new mines or oilwells. The impact of a rise in demand for these products is a sharp increase in price in the short-term because supply is inelastic. In many product markets "bottlenecks" appear which push up price and only if stocks can be drawn upon will these problems disappear. Once stocks have been used up supply then becomes very limited (inelastic).

FIG. 5.4
INCOME ELASTICITY

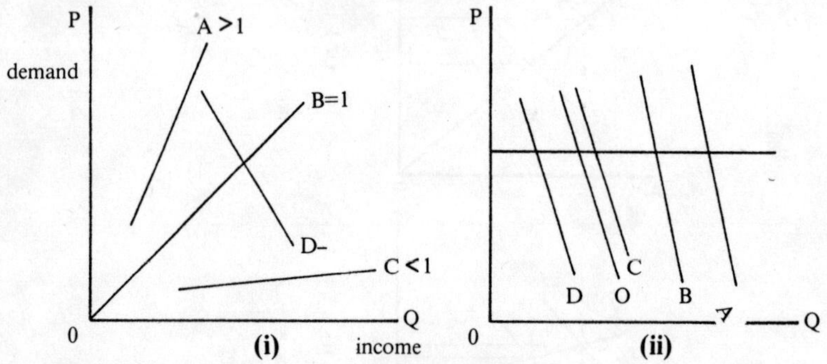

FIG. 5.5
CROSS ELASTICITY

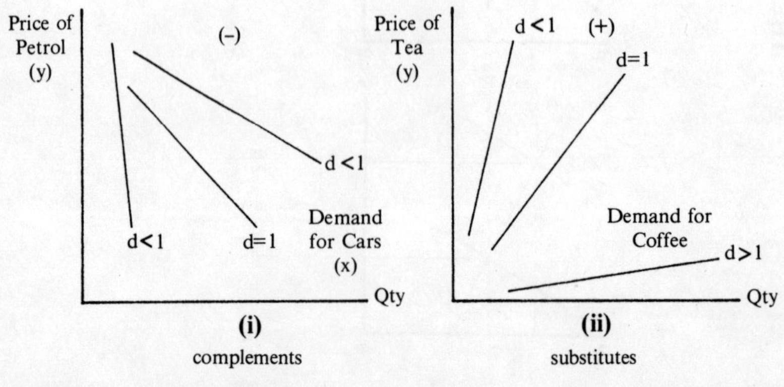

(2) Income Elasticity of Demand (YED)

This measures the response of demand for a good to a change in real disposable income by formula:-

$$YED = \frac{\% \text{ Change in Quantity Demanded}}{\% \text{ Change in Real Income}} \begin{array}{l} = +1 \text{ B unit} \\ = <1 \text{ C inelastic} \\ = >1 \text{ A elastic} \\ = -\text{D inferior} \end{array}$$

These are illustrated in Fig. 5.4(i) where schedules A, B and C illustrate normal goods and where D illustrates an inferior good. In the West, goods such as TV's, videos, cars and capital goods, are likely to be elastic with respect to income so in times of booms and slumps demand for the goods is likely to behave in an erratic fashion. However, for heating and food stuffs generally, demand is more stable and inelastic. Inferior goods, such as cigarettes, are those where, for example, high income groups spend less proportionately than lower income groups. Fig. 5.4(ii) shows how, for some given price, real income increases lead to changes or shifts in demand depending upon the type of income elasticity, i.e. A to D. Original demand is at 0.

(3) Cross Elasticity of Demand (C.E.D.)

This measures the responsiveness of the demand for one good with respect to the price of another, which may be a substitute of a complement. For substitutes the formula give a (+) or direct relationship and for complements a (–) or negative relationship. The degree of substitutability or complementarity is indicated by the value of the coefficient. The larger the value, the closer the relationship. The formula for CED is the same for both complements and substitutes and is:-

$$CED = \frac{\% \text{ Change in Demand for Good x}}{\% \text{ Change in Price of Good y}} \begin{array}{l} = + \text{ or } - \\ \text{and} \\ <1, =1, \\ >1 \text{ etc.} \end{array}$$

Fig. 5.5(i) shows petrol and cars as complements and how elasticity behaves whilst (ii) illustrates tea and coffee as substitutes. Price and income elasticities are given in Tables 5.1 for the U.K. for 1981–86 and 1960–85 in order to illustrate how food elasticities vary.

TABLES 5.1
ESTIMATED PRICE ELASTICITIES OF DEMAND FOR SELECTED FOODS IN THE UK 1981–86

Beef and Veal	−1.46
Mutton and Lamb	−1.67
Pork	−2.01
Frozen peas	−0.88
Bread	−0.26
Tea	−0.19
Potatoes	−0.13

Source: Annual Report of the National Food Survey Committee, Ministry of Agriculture, Fisheries and Food, Household Food Consumption and Expenditure 1986 (HMSO, 1987).

ESTIMATED INCOME ELASTICITIES OF DEMAND FOR SELECTED GOODS IN THE UK 1960–85

	1960	1975	1985
Beef and Veal	0.16	0.25	0.26
Mutton and Lamb	0.38	0.21	0.19
Pork	0.46	0.39	0.14
Frozen peas	1.53	0.43	0.33
Bread	−0.09	0.01	−0.06
Tea	0.03	−0.10	−0.32
Potatoes	0.07	0.01	−0.23

Source: Annual Reports of the National Food Survey Committee, Ministry of Agriculture, Fisheries and Food, Household Food Consumption and Expenditure (HMSO, various years).

Applications of Elasticity

1. *The Incidence of a Tax or Cost of Production Increase*

The "incidence" of a tax on a good, or an increase in the cost of production, refers to who actually pays. Fig. 5.6 illustrates a tax/cost increase which shifts supply to s_1 and so price rises to op_1. At the new price the tax to be paid is a – b. Since price has risen from op to op_1, the consumer pays x amount but this still leaves the producer having to pay the difference, i.e. y. A rise in costs can also be analysed in this way. A fall in tax, a subsidy or a cost reduction will benefit both consumer and producer by the same amounts, i.e. x and y. The incidence of tax or cost increase depends upon the relative elasticity of demand and supply as shown in Fig. 5.7(i) to (iv).

(i) When demand is completely inelastic the tax is equivalent to the extra price consumers pay, so the consumers pay all the tax and output is unaffected, i.e. the tax is neutral.

Elasticity 93

**FIG. 5.6
THE INCIDENCE OF TAX etc.**

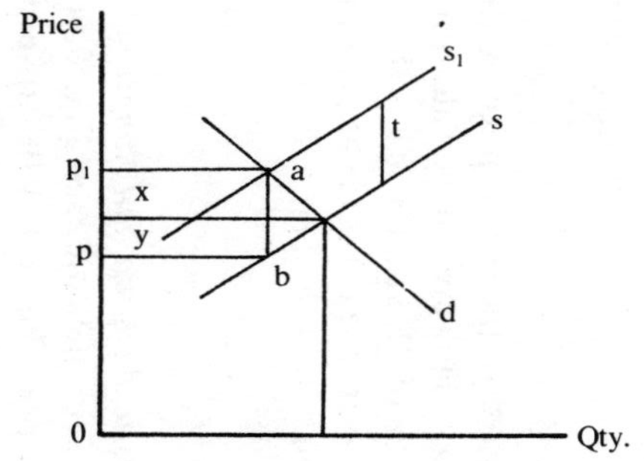

**FIG. 5.8
TAXATION**

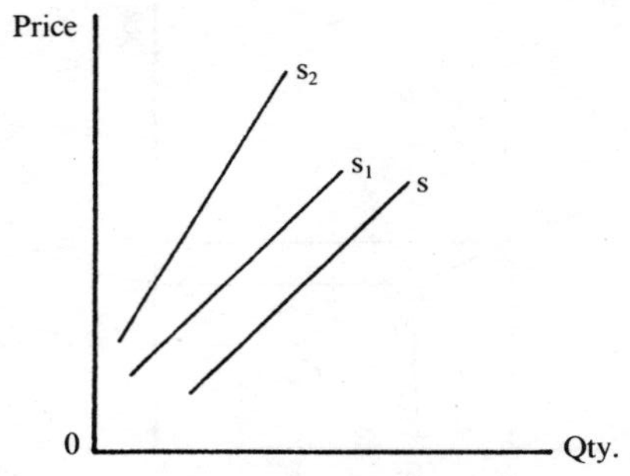

FIG. 5.7

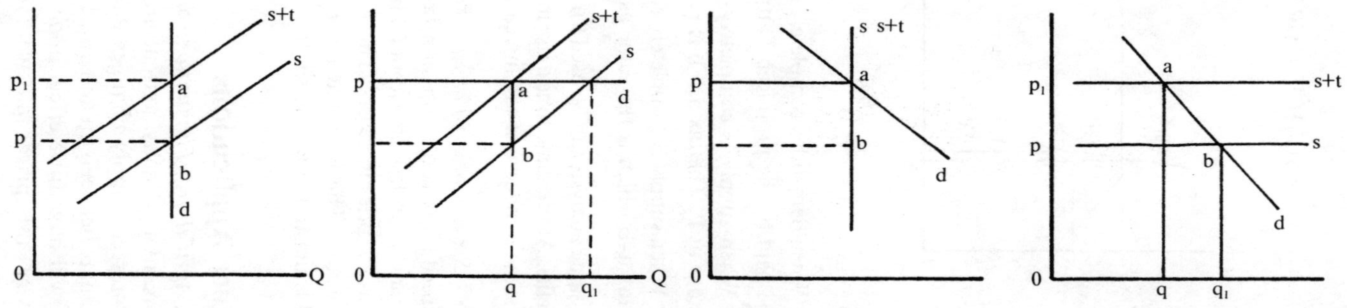

94 Elasticity

FIG. 5.9
AGRICULTURAL PRICE FLUCTUATIONS

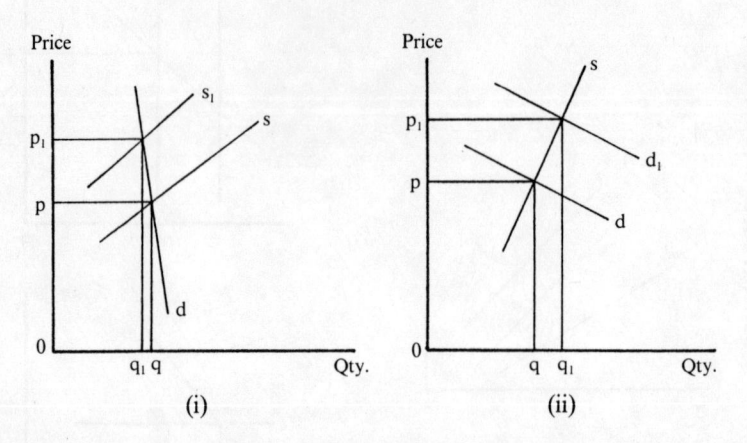

(ii) When demand is completely elastic, the price stays at op but the tax of a–b has to be paid by the producer. Output and employment will also fall (oq_1–oq)

(iii) When supply is completely inelastic supply does not change and the price remains at P. The tax a – b is paid by the producer.

(iv) When supply is completely elastic, then s goes to s + t and the consumer pays the tax a–b which is the same as the price rise op–op_1. Output falls, oq_1–oq.

The same analysis can be used for a subsidy, which shifts s+t to s_1 in terms of who benefits. At the same time a rise in the cost of production can be analysed as having the same impact as a tax increase.

Note Specific or Ad Valorum Tax (see Fig. 5.8)
A specific tax is a lump sum tax which increases the selling price by the same amount regardless of output (value), i.e. s to s_1. However, an ad valorum tax will rise as the price increases. This is because 10% of £1, i.e. 10p. is less than 10% of £10, i.e. £1. This is reflected in a disproportionate rise in the tax as price increases and is illustrated by the shift of supply from s_1 to s_2 in Fig. 5.8

Other Applications
2. *Agricultural Fluctuations due to Inelastic Demand and Supply*
Demand for many agricultural products is inelastic, see Fig. 5.9(i), and unforeseen supply changes due to e.g. a poor harvest, will cause price to fluctuate between op and op_1. This will also increase revenue into the industry but will have little effect upon output, i.e. oq_1 to oq. In the event of a good harvest the price fall will substantially reduce producers' income, so

Elasticity 95

FIG. 5.10
ERRATIC PRICE FLUCTUATIONS: THE COBWEB THEORY

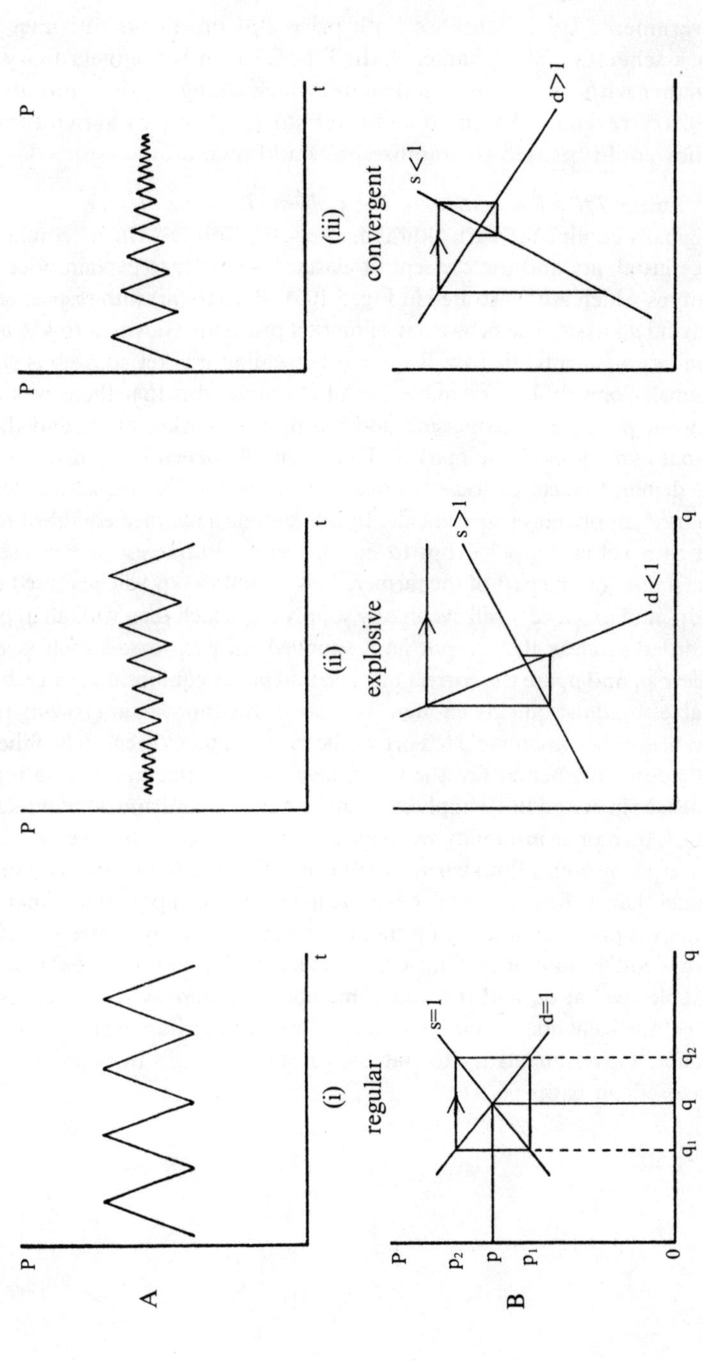

A

(i) regular

(ii) explosive

(iii) convergent

B

(i) $s=1$, $d=1$

(ii) $s>1$, $d<1$ explosive

(iii) $s<1$, $d>1$ convergent

governments try to stabilise both price and producers' incomes by buffer stock schemes. See Chapter 4. In Fig. 5.9(ii) it is the inelasticity of supply together with fluctuations in demand which changes price, output and hence industry revenue. Again some buffer stock scheme or agricultural support policy could be used to stabilise price and income.

3. *Erratic Price Fluctuations – The Cobweb Theory*

Originally confined to agricultural markets, the Cobweb Theory combines market price instability and the concept of elasticity in order to explain price behaviour patterns which are illustrated in Fig. 5.10 A, B, (i) to (iii) with respect to price and demand analysis. The behaviour of market prices are shown in row A and display a variety of forms. In row B the corresponding market cobweb is shown. The original Cobweb Theory made use of a simple idea that there was a time lag between producers recognising and reacting to market price, and the eventual output coming onto the market. Thus if supply depends upon yesterday's price but demand reacts to today's price, it is quite possible for actual demand and planned supply never to coincide. In B(i) assume a planned equilibrium of op/oq but then actual output drops to oq_1 due to a bad harvest or because of earlier uncertainty on the part of the farmer. This output of oq_1 will be forced up in price to op_2 and producers will eventually supply oq_2 which then will fall in price to op_1 in order to clear this output level supplied. In each case suppliers mistakenly believe p_1 and p_2 are the correct market, and hence equilibrium, price, but they are unable to adjust quickly enough (because of the time lag in growing the output) and hence they are unable to correct the problem quickly enough. When demand and supply elasticities are the same, i.e. = 1, the price moves in a regular way. When, as in A and B(ii) supply elasticity is greater than 1 and demand elasticity less than 1, then price instability worsens, i.e. price explodes. However, price gradually converges in A and B(iii) when supply elasticity is less than 1 and demand elasticity greater than 1. Any market can behave in this way if suppliers are unable to adapt to market price conditions or if they believe incorrectly that current market price is always equilibrium price. Only correct market information can help them settle on a stable level at oq and this can come about by improved market research or a more intelligent adaptation to market information, assuming this is up to date and reliable. Governments try to stabilise price fluctuations by support programmes discussed on pages 66 to 67.

CHAPTER 5 Research

1. Survey members of your class, family or friends and collect information regarding how much petrol, bread, sweets or foreign travel would be purchased if the price of each rose/fell. Present your findings in tabular and graphical form.

2. Obtain heating, electricity or goods bills for the year/s and calculate how demand has changed for each product over the year and between years, if records are available. Compare to changes in income and price. Comment.

DATA RESPONSE QUESTIONS

Question 1

Average coefficients of price elasticity for several brands of detergents and pharmaceuticals

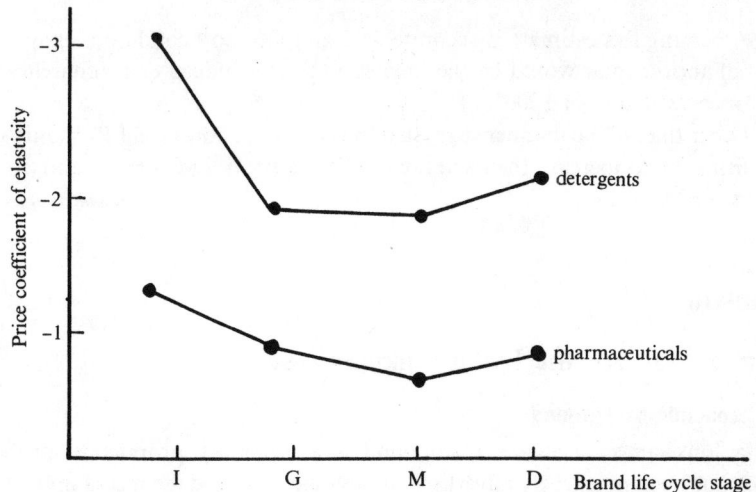

Key:- I = Introduction; G = Growth; M = Marketing; D = Decline

1. Compare the relative price elasticities of detergents and pharmaceuticals over their respective life cycles.
2. How could businessmen use this information?
3. Explain the meaning of the 'Brand life cycle stage'.

Question 2

Price Elasticity of Demand in Ruritania

In Ruritania, a hypothetical country whose currency is the pound sterling (£), the three firms in the car industry together sold in 1985 12 million cars at an average price of £5,000. However, because the economy is in a depressed state the car industry is not working at full capacity and many car workers are not employed for a full working week.

The car workers' union, Vehicle and General Workers, suggest that each producer reduces his price by £200. This action, the Union argues, would result in another 2 million cars being sold while aggregate profits would be maintained at £4,000 million.

a) Calculate the value of the elasticity of demand (correct to one decimal place) assumed by the Vehicle and General Workers Union. Comment on this value.
b) Calculate the average cost with an output of (i) 12 million cars and (ii) 14 million cars. Comment on your findings.

A spokesperson for the Ruritanian car industry points out that government economists have estimated that the elasticity of demand for cars is, in fact, –0.5.

c) Assuming this estimate is accurate, and given the cost conditions assumed in (b) above, what would be the impact on the car industry's profitability of a price reduction of £200?
d) Other than in the manner suggested by the Union, how might Ruritania's car firms try to increase their sales of cars by acting (i) individually and (ii) as a group?

(London, June 1986)

Question 3

Demand factors: the Lydia Pinkham case

The economic background

Lydia Pinkham's Vegetable Compound is a legendary proprietary medicine which has been intensively advertised in both the press and the media in the USA for many years. It is one of the few marketed products for which sales, advertising and price information have been widely and reliably recorded, while the packaging, ingredients and appeal have changed very little. Thus it provides a unique insight into demand influences over time.

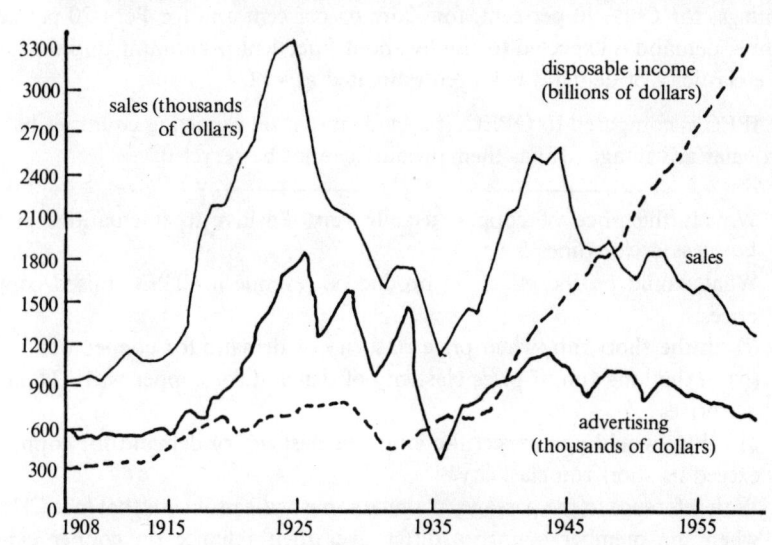

Sales of Lydia Pinkham Company and disposable income, 1908–60

1. Identify the main influence on sales over the period 1908–60.
2. Comment on the apparent overall advertising elasticity of demand for the product between 1915–25 and 1945–55.
3. What market explanations can you offer for the relative decline in sales since 1945?

Question 4

'There has much much speculation about whether oil represents a special case or whether OPEC might be copied by other commodity groups. In particular, likely candidates for cartelisation have been suggested in metallic industries, and one commodity frequently referred to is copper.

Copper is a metal the price of which is usually very sensitive to fluctuations in the business cycle, because of its importance to industries such as electronics, construction and transport. The U.S.A. is largely self-sufficient in copper and is one of the world's largest producers. It is not a major exporter of copper and the same is true of socialist countries. About 70 per cent of copper exports are controlled by a group of producers who, in 1967, formed Conseil Intergouvernmental des Pays Exportateurs de Cuivre (CIPEC). This includes Chile, Peru, Zambia and Zaire. CIPEC aims to co-ordinate the behaviour of members in order to ensure "continuous increase in growth of real earnings from copper exports". Despite some favourable characteristics, CIPEC faces some formidable difficulties. Price stability would require co-operation among a variety of countries. Copper exports represent about 90 per cent of Zambia's total export earnings, for Chile 70 per cent, for Zaire 65 per cent and for Peru 20 per cent. Copper demand is expected to rise by about 4 per cent per annum, and short run price elasticity of demand has been estimated at −1.0.

If CIPEC is compared to OPEC, it is evident that oil exporting countries have a particular advantage in that their product cannot be recycled.'

a) Why is the price of copper 'usually very sensitive to fluctuations in the business cycle'. (lines 5–6)
b) What would be the effect on producers' revenue if CIPEC raised copper prices:
   (i) in the short run, when price elasticity of demand for copper was −1.0;
   (ii) in the long run, if price elasticity of demand for copper was −2.0 at all prices.
c) Why would you expect the long run elasticity of demand for copper to exceed its short run elasticity?
d) With reference to the passage, examine some of the problems that face CIPEC when the member countries differ over their reliance on copper export earnings.
e) What might a group such as CIPEC achieve, other than the enhancement of revenue through supply restrictions?

(London 'A', June 1989')

Question 5

Protectionist Policies: Improving the Terms of Trade

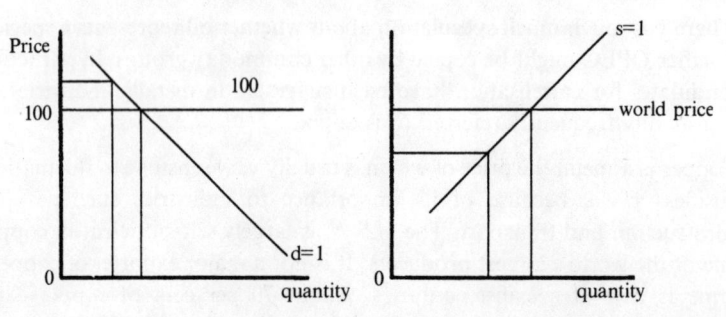

The diagrams above illustrate the import and export demands facing country X. Initially the country is a price taker in world markets for both imports and exports but then becomes a major importer and exporter and is therefore able to influence world import and export prices and reduce import prices in order to gain favourable terms of trade. Note: Demand and supply elasticities with respect to price are −1 and 1 respectively.

1. What will be the terms of trade for country X as a price taker — assume there are no other imports or exports to consider.
2. Identify import and export markets from the diagrams and deduce import and export prices if there is a 10% reduction of exports into the world markets and a 10% reduction in the demand for world imports by country X as a price maker.
3. Calculate the new terms of trade for country X.

5 COSTS, REVENUE AND THE OUTPUT OF THE FIRM

AIMS: To define, explain and discuss
- The Nature and Behaviour of Costs
- Costs and Output Decisions for the Firm
- Short Run and Long Run Decisions
- Scale Economies
- Market Structures and Costs

KEY CONCEPTS
Fixed, Variable, Average and Marginal Costs
Capacity and Optimum Output, Normal and
Abnormal Profit, Long Run Envelope Curve,
Economies and Diseconomies of Scale,
Minimum Scale of Efficiency

General Assumptions

In the long run the business unit exists in order to maximise profits, so Total Revenue (TR) less Total Cost (TC) equals maximum profit, for some level of output. This profit is defined as abnormal profits or economic rent and is different to normal profit. Normal profit includes an imputed cost element in terms of what factor inputs could have earned in the next best use, e.g. if capital could earn at least 10% interest in the bank, then total capital costs include this interest element. The theory of the economic business unit (the firm) also assumes initially that those who manage the firm also own it so there is wholehearted support for the profit maximising objective. There is no conflict of interest between managers and owners, i.e. no divorce of ownership and control, though in the short-term non-profit maximising objectives, e.g. corporate growth, can be pursued in order to ensure maximum long-term profit — see Chapter 10. The last assumption is that in the short-run cost behaviour reflects diminishing return, i.e. costs are U shaped though in the long-run costs can rise, decrease or remain constant depending upon market conditions. This cost assumption is amended in certain examples.

Types and Behaviour of Costs

Types of Costs

Total Costs (TC) are split into total variable (TVC) and total fixed costs (TFC). Variable costs depend upon output, e.g. these are direct or prime costs such as labour, materials or energy, etc. Fixed costs have to be paid regardless of output, e.g. rent, rates, interest charges, etc. In the short-term since these costs have often been paid the firm can, under some circumstances, regard them as having no alternative use, i.e. zero opportunity cost, and so they may not have to be covered. This has led to the notion of "let bygones be bygones" for short-run fixed costs. In the long-run all costs have to be covered because fixed costs become variable.

Costs can also be defined as:-

(i) Average fixed cost (AFC) = $\dfrac{\text{Total Fixed Costs (TFC)}}{\text{output (n)}}$

(ii) Average variable costs (AVC) = $\dfrac{\text{Total Variable Costs (TVC)}}{\text{output (n)}}$

(iii) Average total costs (ATC) = $\dfrac{\text{Total Costs}}{\text{output (n)}}$ = unit costs.

Note (i) + (ii) = (iii), output (n) can be for the number of widgets produced, air miles covered, haircuts, theatre seats, insurance premiums sold, patients treated etc.

The Behaviour of Costs

Fig. 6.1(a–d) illustrates the behaviour of costs. The behaviour of total costs (a) indicates that TFC is constant over some output range and TVC rises reflecting diminishing returns. The behaviour of TC reflects how marginal cost changes (MC), see below.

Fig. 6.1(b) shows average fixed costs fall rapidly as overheads are initially spread over more and more units of output, e.g. 100 ÷ 1 = 100, 100 ÷ 2 = 50, etc. but unit fixed costs (afc) gradually level off as output increases.

Fig. 6.1(c) shows average variable costs (avc) fall initially due to increasing returns but rise as diminishing returns begin to operate. As more of the variable input, e.g. labour, is employed at a constant input price, disproportionately small increases in output lead to unit variable costs increasing.

Fig. 6.1(d) shows average total costs (atc) and reflects the impact of diminishing returns of the variable factor. The lowest point on the atc curve is defined as the optimum or best output level, i.e. lowest unit cost.

FIG. 6.1
COSTS–BEHAVIOUR

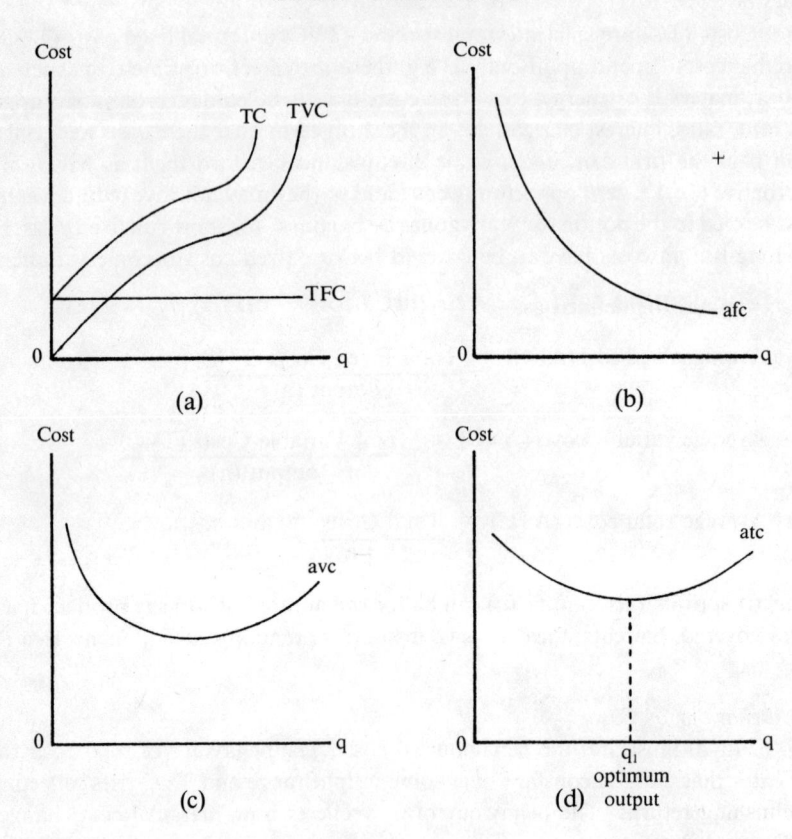

(a) TC, TVC, TFC curves

(b) afc curve

(c) avc curve

(d) atc curve with q_1 optimum output

Marginal Cost, Marginal Revenue (MC, MR)

Marginal Cost (MC) is the extra or additional cost of producing one more unit of output. It is the difference between successive total costs, i.e. $MC_{11} = TC_{11} - TC_{10}$. So the MC of the 11th unit is equal to the total cost of 11, e.g. £100, less the total cost of 10, £93, or the marginal cost = £7. The marginal revenue is the extra revenue from selling one more unit of output. The MR of the 11th unit sold, is the total revenue of 11, e.g. £107, less the total revenue of 10, i.e. £100, so MR = £7. When MC = MR then it defines the most profitable or least loss output of the business so that TR - TC = maximum profit levels.

Costs/Revenue and the Output of the Firm (see Table 6.1)

TABLE 6.1
COSTS, REVENUE AND THE FIRM'S OUTPUT (£'s)

Quantity	Price	Total Revenue	(1) Total Cost	Total Profit (±)	Marginal Revenue	Marginal Cost	
0	20	0	14.5	-14.5	+18	+ 3	
1	18	18	17.5	+.5	+14	+2.5	
2	16	32	20	+12	+10	+ 2	
3	14	42	22	+20	+ 6	+ 3	
(2) 4	12	48	25	+23	+ 4	+ 4	MR=MC
5	10	50	30	+20	+ 2	+ 5	
6	8	48	37	+11	+ 2	+ 7	
7	6	42	46	- 4	+ 6	+ 9	
8	4	32	57	- 5	+10	+110	

Table 6.1 illustrates: total revenue (price x quantity sold), and total cost (fixed plus variable) and hence total profit, also MR, MC for a firm.

Notes

1. Total Cost. At zero output total cost is £14.5 so fixed costs must be £14.50 for all levels of output. Total variable cost is the difference between TC and TFC, i.e. £3.0, £5.5, £7.5, £10.5, £15.5, £22.5, £31.5, £42.5. If the cost of the variable labour input is £.5 each, then variable labour input increases (from zero to eight units of output) as follows:- 6, 11, 15, 21, 31, 45, 63, 85, i.e. proportionately less than more labour input to overall output, so diminishing returns applies.

2. The profit maximising output is where MC = MR at 4 units of output. Here total cost is £25.0, total revenue is £48.0 and total profit is £23.0. From 0 to 4 output units, the extra output increase provides extra slices of profit which

106 Cost, Revenue and the Output of the Firm

FIG. 6.2 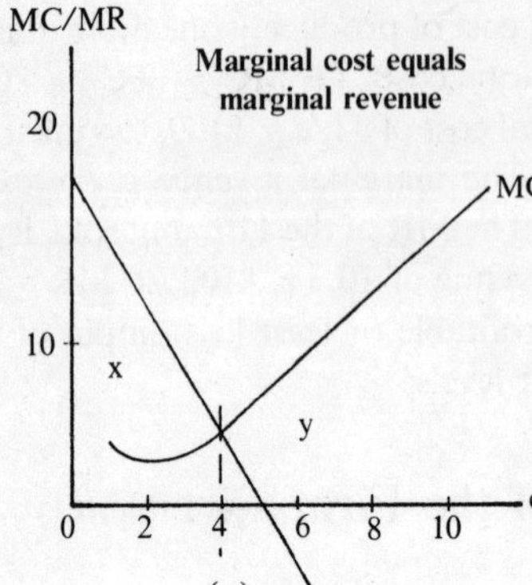
Marginal cost equals marginal revenue
(a)

FIG. 6.4 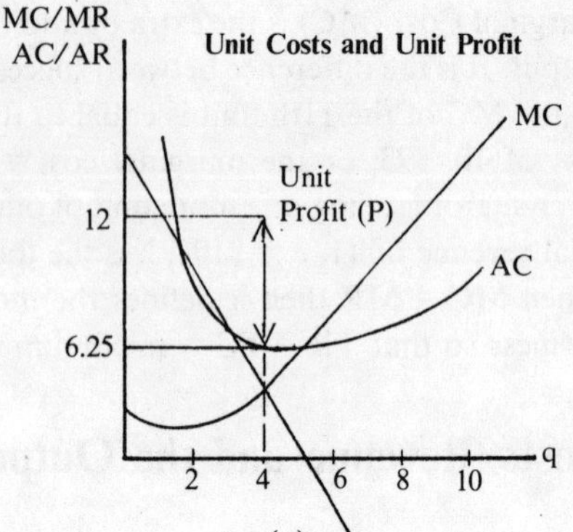
Unit Costs and Unit Profit
(c)

FIG. 6.3 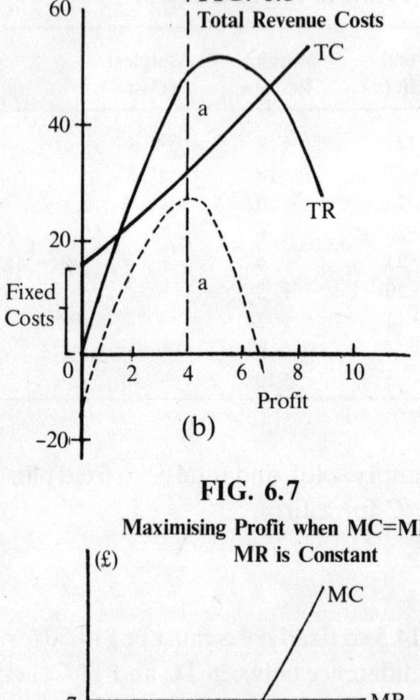
Total Revenue Costs
(b)

FIG. 6.5 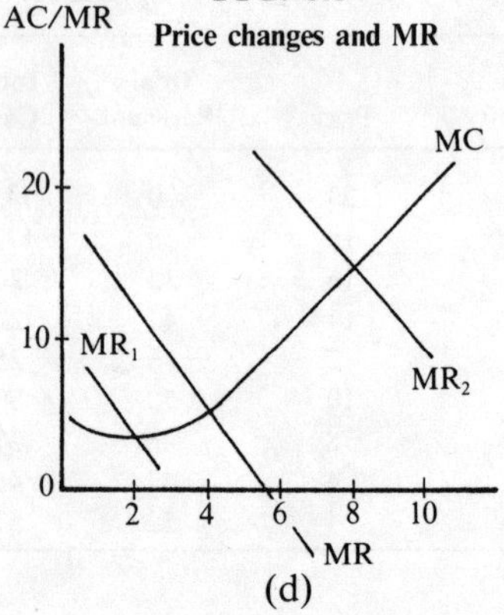
Price changes and MR
(d)

FIG. 6.7
Maximising Profit when MC=MR, when MR is Constant

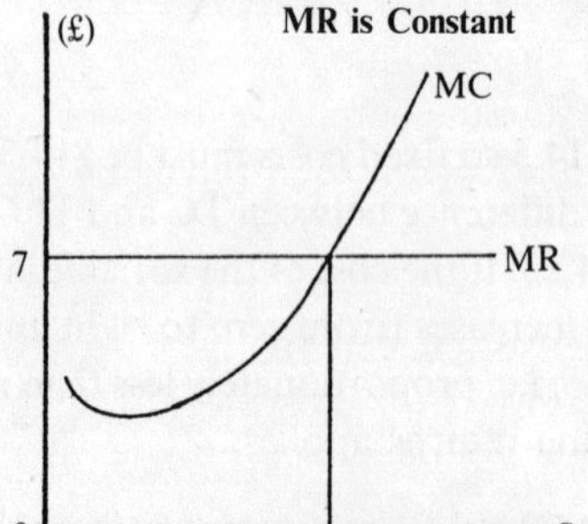

FIG. 6.6
Cost Changes and MC/AC
(e)

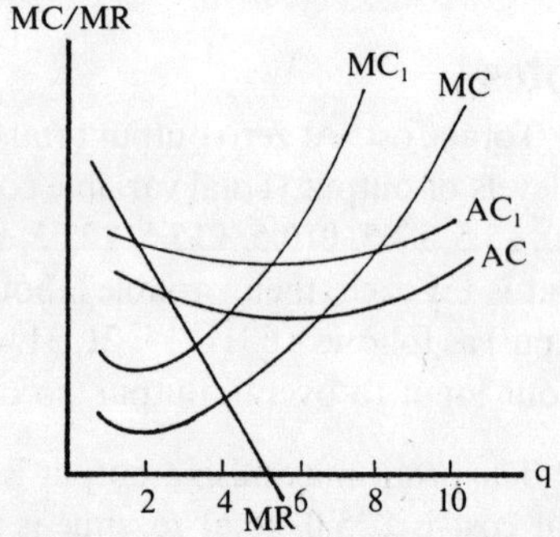

increase overall profits, but beyond 4 units there are negative profit slices which decrease overall total profits.

3. Fig. 6.2 based upon Table 6.1 shows the behaviour of MC and MR intersecting at 4 units of output. Between zero and four contributions to profit are positive, see area x, but after 4 units marginal cost exceeds marginal revenue so contributions are negative, see area y. Fig. 6.3 directly beneath shows total costs, revenue and profit behaviour as output changes and corresponds to the behaviour in Fig. 6.2 above.

4. Fig. 6.4 shows the behaviour of average unit cost (AC) as well as marginal cost (MC). Initially marginal cost falls and then rises rapidly cutting AC at its lowest point. When MC is below AC, AC is falling, and when MC is above AC, AC is rising so MC cuts AC at its lowest point. An example from cricket illustrates. If a batsman has an average of 50 in 10 games, i.e. a total of 500 runs, and the marginal score is 40 then his average falls below 50 and vice versa if his marginal score is 60. In Fig. 6.4 with an output of 4 units average cost is £6.25, price is £12 so unit profit is £5.75 as shown by the arrow.

5. *Applications of Price and Cost Changes, see Figs. 6.5, 6.6.*

If demand increases and price rises at all levels then MR shifts to the right, or left if price falls, and a new profit maximising output is determined as shown in Fig. 6.5. A price fall shifts MR to MR1 and optimum output reduces to 2 units whilst a price rise shifts MR to MR_2 and output increases to 8 units. The impact of cost changes on output depend upon whether the cost change affects MC or AC, see Fig. 6.6. If variable costs rise, due to rising labour costs or VAT, then MC shifts upwards from MC to MC_1 and optimum output reduces below 4 units. If fixed costs rise overall, perhaps due to a rise in a lump sum tax or if fixed costs rise, then MC is unchanged but AC increased, i.e. from AC to AC_1. This means output remains at 4 units but unit and overall profit levels fall.

6. *Constant Marginal Revenue* See Fig. 6.7

Under certain market conditions, e.g. perfect competition or cartel pricing, marginal revenue is the same as the price charged, namely £7, £7, £7, etc. If MC reflects diminishing returns the profit maximising output will be 6 units. Shifts in MR due to price changes, or MC increases due to variable cost changes, will both affect the optimum output as shown in Fig. 6.6.

Costs in the Long Run : Economies of Scale

In the long run the firm can vary both fixed and variable costs and as its scale increases its cost structure also changes so both internal and external economies of scale can be exploited. The long/short run concept does not apply to a calendar year but should be seen in terms of the time period required to change the overall scale of production. A messenger or courier service can double the scale of production overnight by buying a bigger van but a chemical company may require

108 Cost, Revenue and the Output of the Firm

FIG. 6.8

Long Run Cost Behaviour = Envelope Curve of Short Run Costs in an Industry

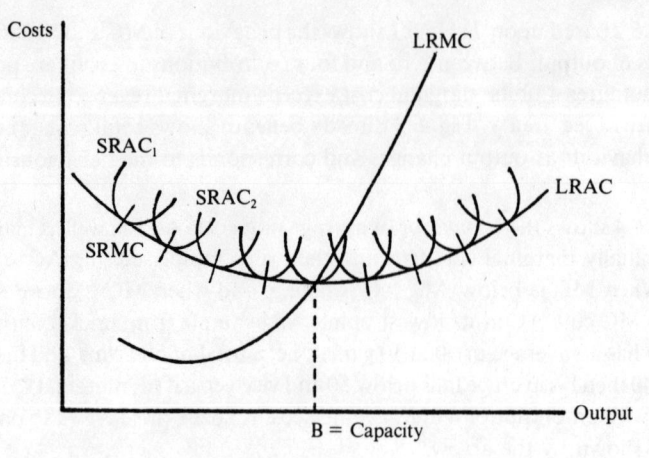

FIG. 6.9

Long Run Manufacturing Cost Behaviour

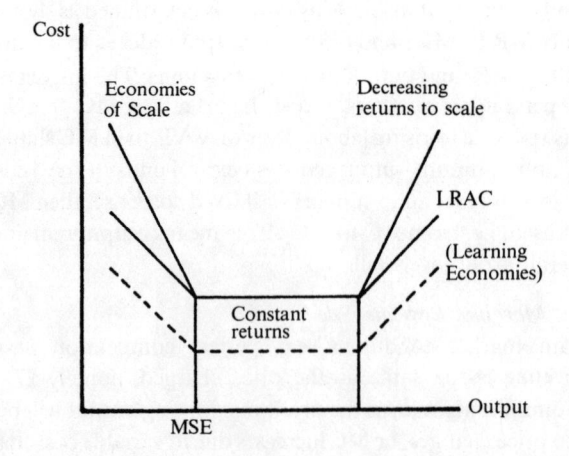

a year or two to double its operational scale of production. The fixed and variable cost proportion also depends upon different firms behaviour so that even in the short-term diminishing returns in a chemical plant take time to operate whilst a business unit employing mainly variable costs incurs diminishing returns very early in their output runs.

Long Run Costs and the Envelope Curve

As new plant and equipment is added the scale of production increases and the firm moves, see Fig. 6.8, from short run average cost ($SRAC_1$) to SRAC 2, etc. with the short run marginal cost (SRMC) cutting SRAC at its lowest point. In the long run plant size is variable and so eventually long run costs increase as short run costs increase exhibiting diminishing returns. By joining up the lowest cost points on the SRAC curves as shown in Fig. 6.8 we can obtain an envelope curve of these points which describe the minimum attainable long run average costs (LRAC). The long run marginal cost (LRMC) is constructed on the same basis and it will cut the LRAC curve at its lowest point. Point B is where LRAC is minimised and shows the long run optimum or capacity in the industry. The downward part of the LRAC is explained by economies of scale and represents decreasing costs whilst the upward part of the LRAC is due to diseconomies of scale representing increasing costs. In the real world manufacturing businesses often experience constant returns and costs as Fig. 6.9 shows. The output level where costs are minimised is defined as the minimum scale of efficiency (the MSE) and this depends upon each individual industry.

Also the slope of the LRAC can be gradual or steep, as Fig. 6.9 shows.

Economies of Scale (Internal)

These operate to reduce long-run unit costs and are under the control of the firm. They are experienced by manufacturing industries and are as follows:- (in note form).

a) *Production or Technical Economies*

Large firms are able to increase the scope for division of labour and specialisation which enables them to use more capital intensive machinery and specialised equipment. By building larger capital units the economies of increased dimensions can be further exploited. In the manufacturing industry robotic techniques of production and automated and computerised technologies are examples of these technical economies.

b) *Financial Economies*

The large firm is able to tap larger sources of finance which enables it to borrow at lower interest rates and experience better credit facilities. Furthermore, it is able to sell shares and obtain capital at relatively cheap rates.

c) *Risk Bearing Economies*
This is for a large conglomerate — the ability to spread risk across a variety of product markets.

d) *Marketing Economies*
These are experienced by the large firms on both the buying and selling side of the business. They are such things as discounts due to buying in bulk, national advertising and brand names, the ability to control input quality, specialised buying staff and preferential transport/sales rates.

e) *Managerial and Administrative Economies*
These cover such items as specialised boards of directors, one unified accounting department using centralised computerised systems and also specialised professional managers.

f) *Learning Economies*
If a management team can improve its efficiency by learning as more of the same operations are undertaken, then over a period of time, and as technology improves, learning efficiencies will influence the whole business and hence overall costs will fall as is shown in Fig. 6.9.

g) *Economies of Scope*
This is when there is a specialised knowledge of e.g. machinery or technology which can be shared across different products, e.g. British Aerospace produce aircraft and cars.

Diseconomies of Scale (Internal)

The increase in scale often brings problems and therefore costs can rise as firms grow beyond their optimum size. These diseconomies derive from labour usage and associated problems of man-management. Therefore communications, co-ordination and control become difficult as departments increase in scale and size. This leads to workers becoming less involved in the business decision making process and labour disputes, e.g. strikes, can increase and lead to cost rises.

Economies of Scale (External)

External economies of scale result from the growth of an industry in a particular region or area. These economies increase the efficiency of the business and hence lower unit costs. They are locational and can take a variety of forms, such as:- (1) a skilled labour force with training facilities, (2) the nearness of component suppliers and sub-contract workers, (3) a good communications and information systems close at hand, (4) a developed infrastructure with road and rail links, (5) associated and complementary product markets in the vicinity. These external economies explain why financial institutions locate in the City of London.

The Business Decision :
Output Levels in the Short and Long Run

In both long and short run the best output level for the firm will be where marginal cost equals marginal revenue. At this output level the decision is then whether to produce or not. In the short run the firm will produce so long as price or average revenue equals or exceeds average variable costs because in the short run fixed costs have to be paid and so can be disregarded, i.e. bygones are bygones. However, in the long run the firm will only produce so long as price covers average total costs, i.e. makes at least normal profits. If average costs are not covered, the firm will go out of business in the long run as Fig. 6.10 illustrates. In the short run, so long as price is op or more production at oq will be viable because op covers average variable costs. A price above op, i.e. in the price region a, will provide a positive contribution to fixed costs and above a price of p_1 abnormal profits are earned. In the long run at output oq price must be at least op_1 or the firm will go out of business. This means that at any price above op_1, in price region b, abnormal profit will be made by the firm.

Demand, Costs and Market Structures

An explanation of how different market structures, e.g. competitive, monopolistic or oligopolistic, develop uses the concept of the minimum scale of efficiency (MSE). The MSE is the output level where long run average cost stops falling and this will be influenced by economies of scale. This idea is used in Fig. 6.11 which shows market demand (d) together with different cost structures, LRAC 1, 2 and 3. Those firms with long run average cost ($LRAC_2$) will have a small part of the total market because MSE occurs at low output levels for the firm and so competitive forces will lead to many competing firms together with a market price of p1. Thus the industry is able to support a large number of producers because of its cost structure. If the industry exhibits long run costs as shown in the Fig. with LRAC1, then the industry will be a natural monopoly so only one firm will be able to exist and exploit potential economies of scale, i.e. MSE occurs at high output levels. A potential new entrant with costs around the level of op4 could not compete with an established monopolist pricing at p3 and making a profit as indicated. There will be a range of market structures and business units between competitive and monopolistic firms. LRAC3 illustrates a cost structure which can support an oligopolistic industry with each producer able to supply around a quarter to say a fifth of the market. This type of industry with four or five firms producing the output gives an MSE of oq3 and price of op_2. Apart from costs explaining market structures, it is also important to recognise that there are other non cost barriers which prevent new firms entering markets. In the case of monopolistic competition it is new product innovation, creating its own market niche, which provides a more likely explanation of this particular market structure. A brief outline of market types, with the main characteristic of each, is given in Table 6.2.

112 Cost, Revenue and the Output of the Firm

FIG. 6.10
PRODUCTION IN THE SHORT AND LONG RUN

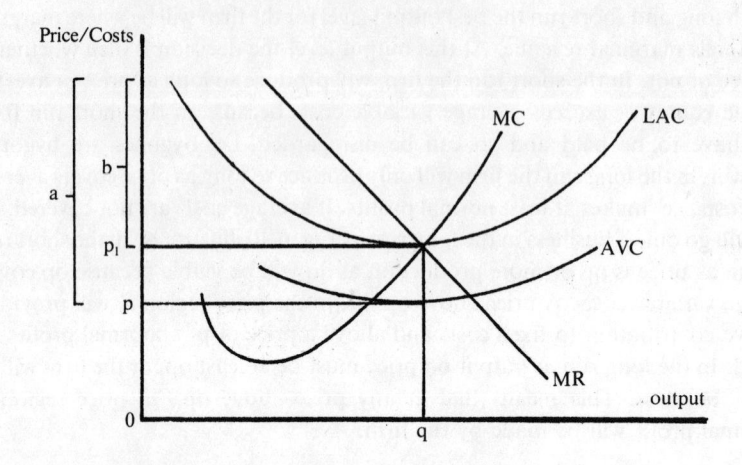

Price/Costs

- MC
- LAC
- AVC
- MR

a, b, p_1, p, 0, q, output

FIG. 6.11
MARKET DEMAND, COSTS AND COMPETITIVE STRUCTURES

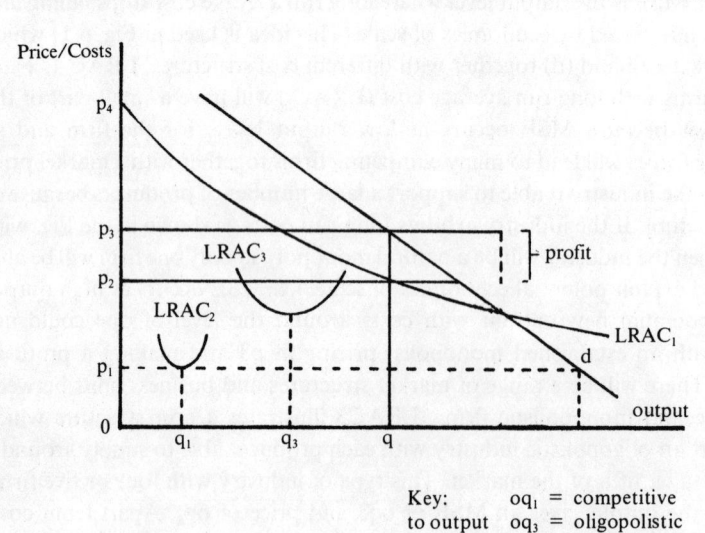

Price/Costs

p_4, p_3, p_2, p_1

LRAC$_3$, LRAC$_2$, LRAC$_1$

profit

0, q_1, q_3, q, d, output

Key: oq_1 = competitive
to output oq_3 = oligopolistic
   oq = monopolist

TABLE 6.2
CLASSIFICATION OF MARKET STRUCTURES

	Characteristics	(i) Competitive	(ii) Monopolistic Competition	(iii) Oligopolistic	(iv) Monopolistic
1.	MSE (output)	Small	Variable	Intermediate	Large
2.	Business Units in Industry	Many	Many	Few	One
3.	Price determination	Supply & Demand	Monopolist Potential Entrants	Oligopolist or Cartel	Monopolist or Overseas pressure
4.	Entry Barriers	None	None	Agreements brand proliferation	Low Cost or barriers
5.	Example (industry) (U.K.)	Chicago grain market	Corner Shop Computer Software	Petrol retailing Brewers High Street Grocers Taxi-Rank	B. Telecom N.H.S./N.C.B. Water Boards

CHAPTER 6 Research

1. *If you have a member of the family who drives a car, obtain the monthly running costs and annual fixed costs and calculate average variable costs – per mile, total fixed costs, average unit costs per mile.*

2. *Using your school or college or club, identify internal economies/diseconomies of scale and try to see what limits the size of the school, college, etc.*

114 Cost, Revenue and the Output of the Firm

DATA RESPONSE QUESTIONS

Question 1 — Transport Costs Compared

The diagram shows the hypothetical relationship between transportation and the volume of goods carried.

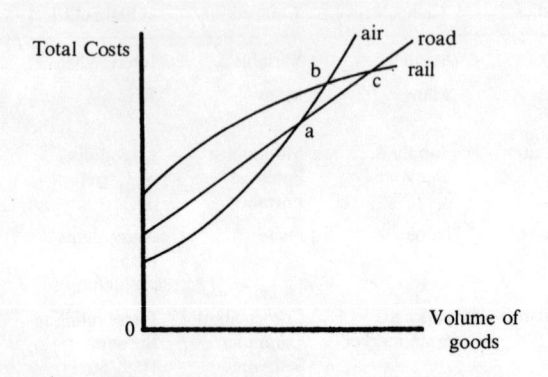

1. Comment upon the fixed and variable cost components for the three modes of transport.
2. Compare the behaviour of marginal costs in each case.
3. What do the points a, b and c indicate?
4. Identify which transport mode you would use in the case of diamonds, tomatoes and coal and give a brief economic explanation.

Question 2 — Full Cost or Marginal Cost Pricing

		Products	
Cost Per Unit £	A	B	C
Materials	2.8	5.2	3.4
Labour	3.6	4.0	5.1
Overheads (200% of labour)	7.2	8.0	10.2
Total Cost	13.6	17.2	18.7
Selling Price	15.7	16.1	20.2
Annual Sales	15,000	20,000	18,000

The accountant provides the above information and advises that Product B should be discontinued as it makes a loss of £1.1/unit × 20,000, i.e. £22,000 p.a.

Further inspection shows that 40% of overheads are fixed. Should Product B be maintained or discontinued? Give reasons for your answer.

Question 3 — Cost Behaviour

The diagram below shows the short-run average total cost functions of three hypothetical companies, A, B and C.

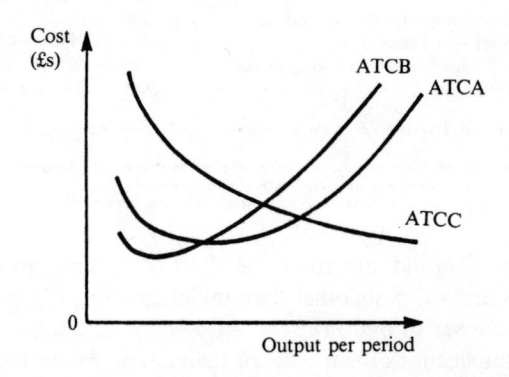

a) What would you expect to be the characteristics of firms A and C?
b) Which, of firms A and B, is the more efficient, and why?

(January 1983, London)

Question 4

Successive units of output	Total cost (£)	Average cost (£)	Marginal cost (£)
1	20	20	20
2	32		
3		14	
4			6
5	50		

Use the data in the above table to calculate:
(i) Total cost at an output of 4 units.
(ii) Average cost when marginal cost is £12.
(iii) Marginal cost when average cost is £10.

Question 5

Study the following data which gives details of development and production costs in the United Kingdom motor car manufacturing industry.

Output of cars (thousand cars p.a. – for 4 years)	100	250	500	1000	2000
Initial costs for model (£ million)	40	50	60	80	110
Costs per car produced over 4 year run:					
Initial costs, £	100	50	30	20	14
Materials and bought-in components, £	290	270	255	247	240
Labour (direct and indirect), £	120	100	92	87	84
Capital charges for fixed and working capital, £	75	65	58	53	48
Total ex-works cost, £	585	485	435	407	386

(Source: C.F. Pratten, Economies of Scale in Manufacturing Industry, Cambridge University Press, 1971.)

Notes: (1) The initial costs include the cost of designing a new model, building prototypes, and 'tooling up', i.e. investing in extra fixed capital equipment.
(2) The output assumes a new model is produced for a period of four years.

a) What does the data indicate about the effect of increases in car output on (i) initial costs and (ii) costs other than initial costs?
b) Explain your answer to part (a).
c) What policy implications for motor car manufacturers are suggested by the data?

(London 'A' Paper, 3 January 1986)

7 COMPETITIVE MARKETS AND BUSINESS BEHAVIOUR

AIMS: *To define, explain and discuss*
- *Business behaviour under competitive conditions*
- *The influence of the short and long run in competitive markets*
- *The firm and industry equilibrium*

KEY CONCEPTS
Competitive conditions, price taker, short and long run supply, price = average variable cost, price = average total cost.

The optimum output of the firm will be determined by equating marginal cost to marginal revenue. Abnormal profit is calculated as the difference between price (average revenue) and average unit cost. Since markets differ the behaviour of the firm will change depending upon market structures. It is important to note that business behaviour will vary because firms operate in different market types at different times, e.g. a competitive firm may become a monopolist and vice versa. The behaviour of the firms under each market structure is outlined over Chapters 7 – 10.

I. Perfectly Competitive Market Conditions, e.g. The Chicago Grain Market

Perfectly competitive markets are a highly idealised type and rarely exist in the real world. The conditions which create such a market are:-

a) Freedom of entry and exit to the market for the buyer and seller. This means there is costless entry and exit (see Contestable Markets) and this implies perfect mobility of goods and factors of production.

b) Similarity or homogeneity of products, i.e. all goods, services and factors of production bought and sold are identical.

c) Perfect knowledge, i.e. everyone has full information regarding market price.

d) It is possible to buy and sell any amount of the product or factor at the going market price.

e) There is no government interference which distorts market conditions, such as taxation.

f) There are a large number of competitive buyers and sellers acting independently so no one firm or group of firms is able to influence market price.

If these conditions, a) to f) are relaxed, it is possible for imperfectly competitive market structures, e.g. monopolies, to develop in both product and factor markets.

Competitive Markets and the Firms Revenue

In view of the above conditions, overall market forces of supply and demand set the price in the competitive product market. As the product is identical, e.g. cucumbers, the consumer will only pay the market price and so the producer becomes a price taker in the sense that the demand for his cucumbers can be viewed as perfectly elastic at the going market price. This means the producer cannot influence the market price. If any attempt is made by the producer to sell cucumbers above the going price, consumers will not buy but will seek out cheaper market prices for cucumbers. Fig. 7.1 illustrates. The market price for cucumbers is 10p. each, see (i) and this means the producer can sell as many as he likes at 10p. Thus total revenue increases as follows, 10p., 20p., 30p., 40p., etc. for each additional cucumber sold. The extra revenue or marginal revenue is always 10p. and so the average revenue is also 10p., i.e. the same as the price. This is shown as a horizontal line for the producer at 10p. or 15p. in the event that demand pushes up market price in 7.1(ii). The total revenue (TR) for the producer at 10p. and 15p. is shown in (iii) and here TR increases at a constant rate for both 10p. and 15p. market prices.

FIG. 7.1
CHANGING MARKET PRICE AND ITS IMPACT UPON THE REVENUE OF THE FIRM

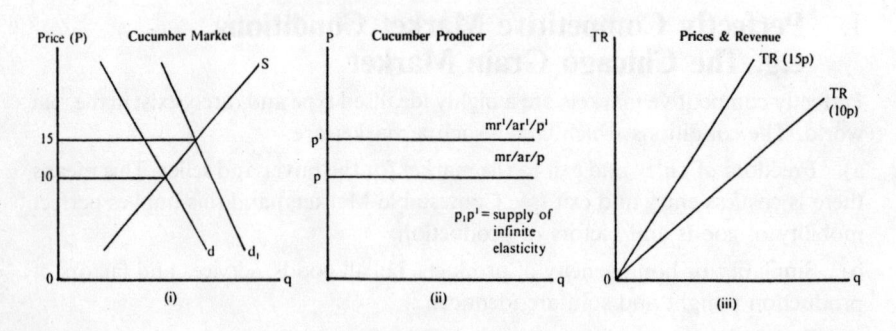

The Equilibrium of the Firm and the Industry in the Short Run (see Fig. 7.2)

In the short run the firm will experience diminishing returns so both marginal and average cost will increase and be U shaped. The firm will continue in business in the short run so long as it covers its average variable costs; though it will hope to cover all its costs and even make above normal profits. Fig. 7.2 (a) and (b) illustrate short run equilibrium for the industry and the firm. Initially, industry cucumber prices are 10p. and at this level mc = mr at oq output for the firm. At this price, average variable costs are just covered so any price below 10p. will lead to the firm immediately going out of business because ongoing variable expenses such as wages cannot be paid. In other words, at 10p. a cucumber the producer is a loss maker. If demand pushes up prices to 12p. per cucumber, the producer is now able to cover all costs, i.e. p = atc so normal profits are earned in this case by the marginal firm and as price increases again to 15p. supernormal profits are earned at op2, where mc = mr^2, since price is now above average total cost. The extra output produced by the producer/s, i.e. oq1, oq2, is identified by the arrow in Fig. 7.2(a) and for the industry is shown by the slope of the combined individual producers supply when this is above average variable costs. In the short run with one fixed factor, supply will be relatively inelastic and this is shown in Fig. 7.4(a) and (b) with respect to the SRMC and SRS for the firm and the industry respectively.

FIG. 7.2

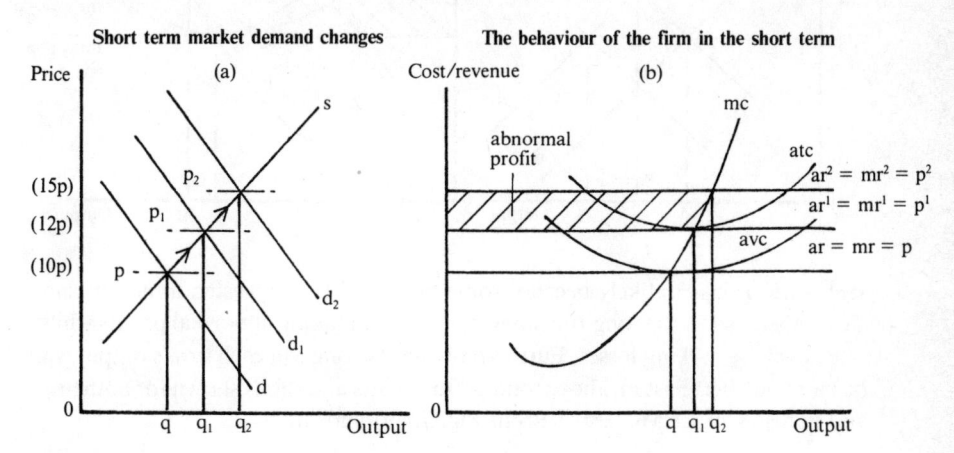

Short term market demand changes (a)

The behaviour of the firm in the short term (b)

The Equilibrium of the Firm in the Long Run

In the long run the firm is able to view all factors of production as variable and will seek the lowest cost limits of factor input. Furthermore, free entry into the industry means firms will be able to come and go without incurring costs. The firm will now be on its long run average and marginal cost schedules. The behaviour of the industry and firm in adjusting to long run equilibrium is shown in Fig. 7.3(a) and (b). Initially the market price is 10p. a cucumber which is the long run equilibrium in the market and for the industry so oq is the capacity or optimum output. In this case, assume all firms have similar costs, so the LRATC for each firm is identical. By definition, for any given LRATC there will also be a short run average total cost (SRATC) and marginal cost which in this case will be the same as the long run equivalent, (LRMC=SRMC). If demand now increases to d2 at a price of 15p., short run output increases to oq1 where firms now make abnormal profits because price exceeds short run and long run average costs. In the long run, the output of the existing suppliers increases and new entrants are attracted into the industry which shifts supply to s1. There are now more producers in the industry and this pushes price down to 10p., s to s1, and wipes out abnormal profits for the industry. Also, industry output at oq2 is stable in the long run and oq is the long run optimum output for each firm — assuming each firm's costs are identical. In the

FIG. 7.3

Long run equilibrium for Industry & Competitive Firm

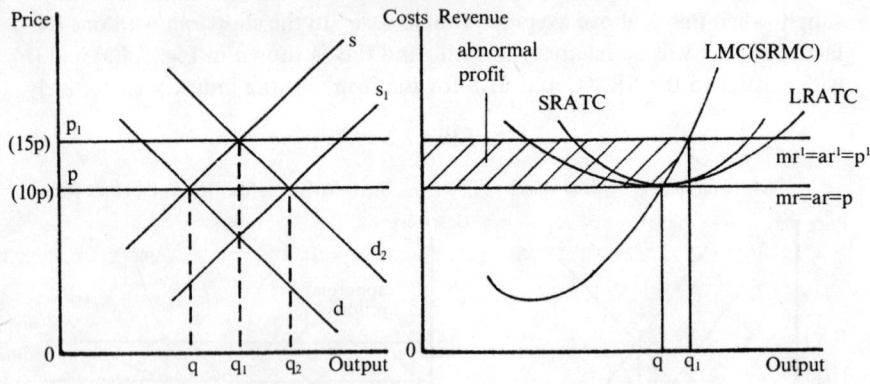

real world this is unlikely because some firms will have invested in newer plant than others, so in the long run some may still be making abnormal profits whilst others will be making losses. Furthermore, in the long run each firm's output will be more flexible (elastic), above total average costs and this is shown for both firm and industry in LRMC and LRS in Fig. 7.4(a) and (b).

FIG. 7.4
THE FIRM

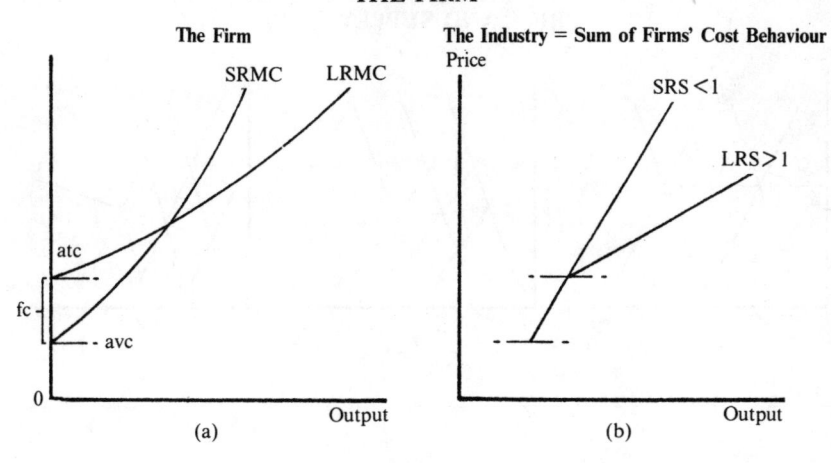

The Firm — SRMC, LRMC, atc, fc, avc, Output (a)

The Industry = Sum of Firms' Cost Behaviour — Price, SRS <1, LRS >1, Output (b)

Supply Price in the Long Run (LRS1, 2, 3) (see Fig. 7.5)

In the very long run demand changes, shown in Fig. 7.5 by d to d2 will, after firms enter and leave the industry, influence long run price depending upon cost and supply conditions. Fig. 7.5 a, b, c, show industry cost behaviour varying from constant, decreasing or increasing factor input costs. Note, in the short run input costs are constant but in the long run diminishing or increasing returns can lead to factor costs changing. The stable price of op1 (LRS1 in Fig. 7.5(a)) reflects constant supply costs as new firms enter or leave the industry. This is because they use such small amounts of total factor inputs that they have no effect on overall input costs. In Fig. 7.5(b) LRS2, costs decrease because the extra output allows suppliers of factor inputs to increase specialisation and reduce factor input costs over the whole industry, i.e. the industry experiences external economies of scale. Finally, in Fig. 7.5(c) LRS3, expansion by new and existing firms bids up the long run price of factor inputs so marginal costs rise and long run supply shifts upwards. Thus overall demand changes can affect market price in the long run. With a decreasing cost industry (LRS2) a fall in demand will lead to a rise in factor costs and product costs, but when demand increases factor costs and long run prices fall.

FIG. 7.5
THE BEHAVIOUR OF LONG RUN INDUSTRY PRICE AND SUPPLY (LRS)

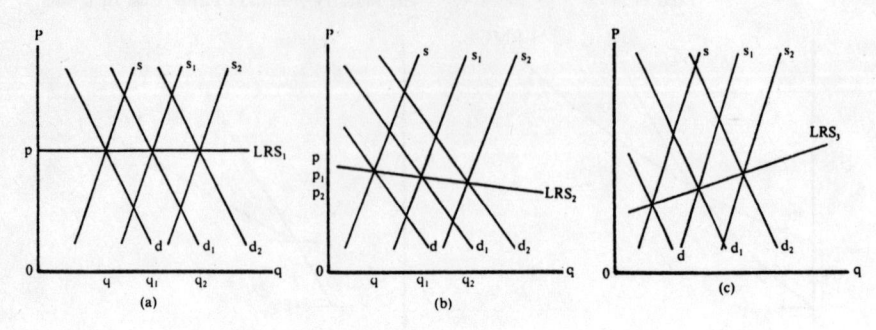

CHAPTER 7 Research

1. *Visit your local produce street market and supermarket and compare prices for food stuffs and flowers and explain why these prices are stable/fluctuate.*

2. *Identify those markets you consider competitive and monitor how the businesses in these sectors change, grow, decline, etc., e.g. use Estate Agents, Free Newspapers, local plumbers, schools and colleges, etc.*

8. THE ECONOMIC BEHAVIOUR OF THE MONOPOLIST (MONOPOLISTIC COMPETITION)

AIMS: To define, explain and discuss
- The behaviour of the monopolist in the short and long run
- Monopolistic competition
- Short and long run equilibrium and barriers to entry
- Monopolists and price discrimination

KEY CONCEPTS
Barriers to entry, price greater than mc, abnormal profits, competition, price discrimination.

Definition

Monopoly in the product or factor market indicates the existence of a sole supplier or buyer (monopsonist). The monopoly can take the form of a dominant firm or as a group of producers who act as if they were a monopoly, i.e. a cartel. Monopolies arise for a variety of reasons, e.g. cost barriers to entry, etc. Instead of being a price taker they face their own demand schedule and are able to set a price or an output level but not both, unless demand is completely inelastic. The demand conditions given in the Table in Fig. 8.1 show the marginal and average revenue of the monopolist which is plotted in Fig. 8.1. The price, quantity demanded schedule, is the same as the average revenue for the monopolist and the marginal revenue curve slopes downwards at twice the rate of average revenue — see Chapter 18 for a mathematical proof.

The Equilibrium of the Monopolist in the Short/Long Run

Fig. 8.2 shows average and marginal revenue behaviour together with marginal and average costs which reflect diminishing returns for the monopolist. This can now be used to analyse the short and long run behaviour of the monopolist. In the short and long run the profit maximising monopolist will set output where marginal cost equates with marginal revenue, and at this output (3) price will set to demand or average revenue, i.e. £8. In the **short run**, with barriers to entry, the monopolist has no competition and makes abnormal profits as shown in Fig. 8.2(i)

FIG. 8.1
MONOPOLIST BEHAVIOUR OF mr, ar

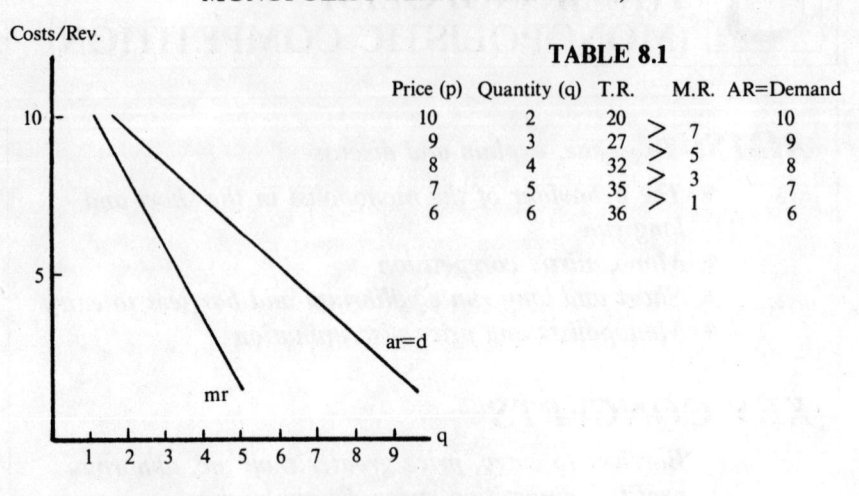

TABLE 8.1

Price (p)	Quantity (q)	T.R.	M.R.	AR=Demand
10	2	20	7	10
9	3	27	5	9
8	4	32	3	8
7	5	35	1	7
6	6	36		6

FIG. 8.2
SHORT AND LONG RUN WITH BARRIERS TO ENTRY

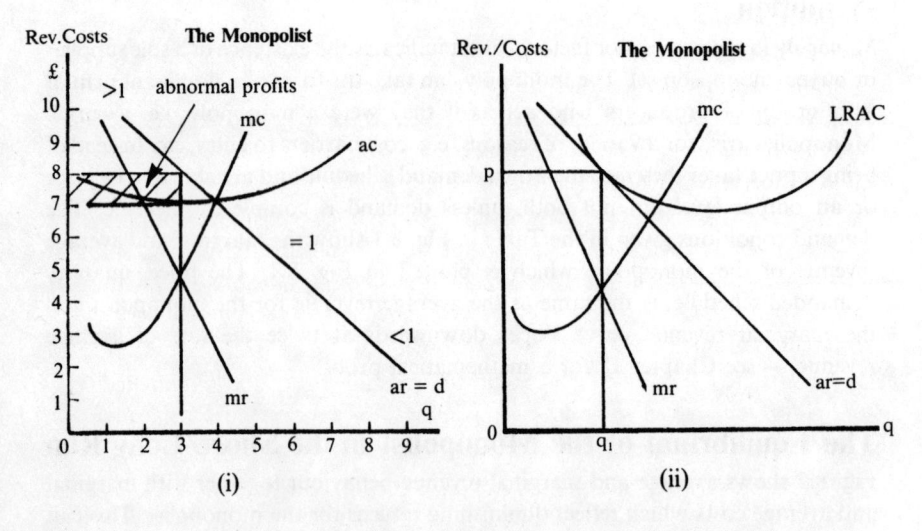

(i)   (ii)

If barriers exist in the long run, these profits will continue to be made. However, in the long run it is likely that new firms will enter the market and reduce these barriers and/or governments will reduce these market constraints, e.g. by outlawing restrictive practices, which both reduce demand and marginal revenue so that only normal profits are earned, as shown in Fig. 8.2(ii).

Demand Elasticity and the Monopolist

As discussed in Chapter 5, a demand schedule, similar to the one facing the monopolist, varies from an elasticity of more than 1 (>1) at the top of the curve, to an elasticity of less than 1 (<1) for lower prices at the bottom of the demand curve. This means the monopolist will price somewhere between the elastic range at the top (high prices) to the mid-point where price elasticity is equal to 1, i.e. unity. If the monopolist reduced price into the inelastic region at the bottom of the demand schedule, total revenue and profits will fall. Only monopolies with other than profit maximising objectives will be able to reduce price into this region in order to maximise market share or other sales objectives.

Barriers to Entry

Monopolies in the form of a dominant firm or cartel are able to exclude potential competitors by a variety of barriers. These are:-

a) *Cost advantages.* Economies of scale and other efficiencies, enable costs to reduce to such low level, especially for natural monopolies, that competition is excluded. These natural cost barriers exist in the distribution of gas, electricity, and telecommunications services, etc. See Sections on Limit Entry Pricing and Natural Monopolies below.

b) *Patents, Licences and Copyright.* A patent protects a firm from competition and is important in high-tech industries, e.g. Rank Xerox, by virtue of patent rights had the whole U.K. market for dry copying in the 1960's and made large profits. Copyright given to authors is a protection of intellectual property and stops copying in the book publishing market. A licence to provide a service is often required before a business is able to supply, e.g. taxi cabs and independent regional television companies. Cable and satellite T.V. is now providing competition for regional independent television monopolists.

c) *Capital Needs.* Certain industries, such as manufacturing, require huge capital investment before production can take place, e.g. chemicals. Not only will the amount of the investment deter potential entrants but the likelihood of failure and the associated costly exit from the industry means business units will hesitate before entering this type of industry.

d) *Product Advertising.* Consumer goods industries are dominated by monopolists who have, over the years, spent heavily on brand advertising in order to differentiate their product in the eyes of the consumer and so earn consumer loyalty, e.g. Coca-Cola and Kelloggs Cornflakes. A would be competitor needs to overcome this advantage which may require substantial advertising investment. At the same time, national advertising leads to economies of scale in marketing, so when demand increases the firm is able to increase its minimum scale of efficiency and hence entry cost barriers become larger.

e) *Channels of Distribution/Locational Advantages.* Existing firms in the market may have a high degree of control over the channels of distribution which means new entrants are unable to sell their products on a large scale. One alleged restrictive practice is retail price maintenance on books and records. Sales product prices are fixed and producers can exclude new entrants wishing to reduce price by blacklisting retail outlets if they do not maintain these controlled prices. A similar barrier in the retail sector is when a retail outlet has a locational monopoly position which gives it a special advantage over its competitors.

f) *Strategic Entry Barriers.* These barriers are deliberately set up by incumbent firms in order to deter would be new entrants. They take a variety of forms ranging from:- i) heavy advertising expenditure on the existing range of products, (ii) developing a product mix so that there are no market niches or openings for a new brand, iii) the development of capacity which enables the encumbent to cut costs and prices. These strategies are designed to put off competitors and work so long as the threats of the incumbent firm are credible and believable.

g) *Government Created Barriers.* Acts of Parliament create privileged state monopolies. These range from the granting of licences to supply a television service, e.g. the BBC, the creation of nationalised industries to supply a service, e.g. British Rail, or the provision of education of health care, e.g. the NHS.

Barriers to Market Entry ensure that supernormal profits are earned and the greater these profits, the greater the incentive for competitors to enter a market. Schumpeter argued that monopoly powers cannot last for ever as profits act as a spur to new entrants and existing monopolies try to reduce the threat of competition by continually inventing new products in order to maintain their profit levels. Schumpeter defined this as a process of 'creative destruction' whereby existing firms try to create new products whilst new firms try to destroy the control of existing firms by inventing better and more suitable products.

Limit Pricing Barriers (See Fig. 8.2)

If the monopolist maximises short run profit where mc = mr, i.e. at 3 units, there is room for a new entrant because average costs (AC) are similar to the price of £8. If costs initially are below entry price, then new entrants could come into the market unless the existing supplier artificially keeps price below costs and increases output to prevent entry in the long run. Then the new entrant will find the price always below start up average costs and so limit pricing excludes new competition. This practice is sometimes referred to as predatory pricing. In this case, see Fig. 8.2, the firm will attempt to prevent new entrants by pricing at £7 and producing up to 5 units, i.e. the competitive equilibrium. This means average costs at £8, for new entrants, will be higher than a price at £7 in the short run so losses will be incurred. The monopolist will, in the long run, without any competition, increase price to £8 and make abnormal profits because would be entrants have now been forced out of the market.

Monopolistic Competition

Monopolistic competition is where there are many different, often small, firms producing goods and services which are differentiated from each other in at least one respect. They are close but not perfect substitutes. Since the products are sufficiently alike, new entrants may come into the market and produce a slightly different product which will reduce demand for the output of the existing firms. The ease of entry into the market is the essential condition, so in the case of school and college book publishing copyright on the author and title provides a monopoly right to the publisher. However, new firms can easily enter the market and produce a similar book which reduces sales of the existing title.

Diagrammatically the short and long term situation of the profit maximising monopolistically competitive firm can be seen in Fig. 8.3. The firm faces the downward sloping demand curve of the monopolist AR1 and marginal revenue MR1, with its average and marginal cost AC, MC. At output OX1 the firm will be maximising profit and pricing at OP1 and making supernormal profits. In the long run as new firms enter the market, the demand of the existing firm will reduce and will move inwards on the diagram until supernormal profits are reduced to zero. Here the demand curve AR2 is at a tangent to AC and normal profits only are earned at output OX2. Furthermore, as output reduces from OX1 to OX2 there will be surplus capacity within the firm and an increase in output (from OX2) would lower unit costs and thus increase cost efficiency.

**FIG. 8.3
MONOPOLISTIC COMPETITION**

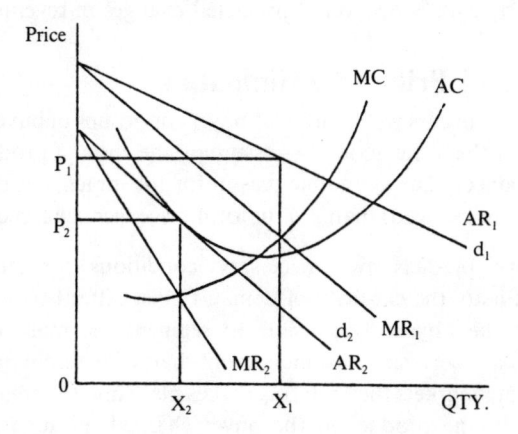

In the above analysis it was assumed that the firm tried to maximise profits where marginal cost equals marginal revenue. In the real world this may not be the case. Businessmen do not always understand that profit maximising implies mc = mr and even if they did they may not be able to provide sufficiently accurate cost and revenue information showing how each changed with respect to the extra unit produced or sold. Assuming they could provide this amount of detail the administration necessary may prove too costly in terms of extra accounting, staff, etc. Furthermore, they may be deterred from pricing where profits are maximised since they may fear competition from new entrants which could ultimately reduce their profits. If the firm announced that a particular range of school and college titles sold were very profitable, new entrants could come into the market and eventually only normal profit would be earned. Indeed, union wage negotiators who saw high profits would immediately increase their demands and bid up wage costs in the industry which the firm may not be able to match, especially if it had a poor cash flow. Excessive profits could antagonise customers and lead to government action in the form of a monopolies commission investigation, etc.

Furthermore, both businessmen's behaviour and newer economic theories suggest that profit maximising is not the sole nor the most important objective of the firm. The firm could set price to maximise its market share or its sales revenue. Most firms in these markets offer a range of products so their long-term relationship with both retailers, wholesalers and customers have to be considered. These may be best suited to a less than profit maximising price. "Satisficing" theories, associated with Simon, Cyert and March, suggest firms set prices which provide a satisfactory level of profits, wages, taxation, etc. Indeed where the firm is a government run nationalised industry, it may be attempting to offer a national level of service which may lead to a breakeven only price level. Indeed, Professors Machlup and Stigler argue that even if businessmen do not know about marginal costs and marginal revenue they still act "as if" their long-term objective is to maximise profit by equalising overall predicted changes in revenue and cost.

Monopolies and Price Discrimination

Price discrimination occurs when different buyers or groups of buyers are charged different prices for the same good/s — assuming the costs of production are the same for the producer. The economic reason for this practice is that profits are higher (or losses are reduced) than if a uniform price were charged to all buyers.

Economic theory predicts two necessary conditions for successful price discrimination. Firstly the elasticity of demand must differ between buyers and secondly it must be physically possible to segment the market and prevent leakages taking place between consumers being charged different prices. If it is not possible to separate markets then arbitrage takes place and the consumer charged the low price sells the product to the buyer charged the high price until an equilibrium prevails with a uniform rate throughout both markets, i.e. discrimination is only economic if the cost of separating markets is less than the extra revenue generated.

These two conditions can only apply when a single seller, the monopolist, exists in the market and the economic case for price discrimination can be shown graphically in Fig. 8.4.

FIG. 8.4
MONOPOLIES AND PRICE DISCRIMINATION

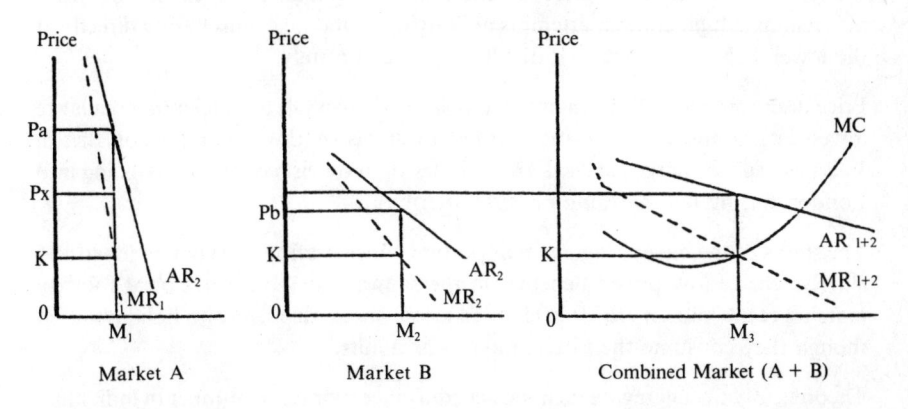

Market A — Market B — Combined Market (A + B)

Fig. 8.4 shows the monopolist selling into two distinct markets A and B. In the absence of price discrimination marginal cost and revenue conditions would indicate a uniform price of Px in both markets. This price would be too low in market A and too high in market B. If the markets could be separated the intersection of the combined MR/MC would now indicate separate output/prices in both markets of Pa and Pb (i.e. where individual MR/MC intersections occur) at K. This exploits the consumers inelastic demand in market A, giving more profit and revenue, and in market B the gain in demand increases revenue as the price falls because of the elastic nature of demand. See prices Pa, Pb.

Price discrimination occurs in a host of markets though its economic basis varies. Geographical price discrimination occurs when regions or countries pay different prices for the same product. Thus U.K. car buyers pay more for a Mini Metro than purchasers of the same car in Belgium, France, Germany etc. This helps Rover make more profit on the U.K. market though cost conditions are roughly similar in both market areas. This geographical variation in price occurs in other sectors. The American air traveller pays far less per mile for internal USA flights, because of cut price competition, than for transatlantic air travel where scheduled flights are high priced to exploit the U.K. businessman's inelastic demand.

In book publishing it is common practice for U.K. publishers to sell the exclusive geographical distribution rights to another distributor or publisher. The same book can bear two prices on its back cover, a U.K. price and, say, an Australian price, and the U.K. publisher is unable to sell into the Australian market. Even

130 The Economic Behaviour of the Monopolist

after handling charges have been deducted the Australian price represents a very high sterling price equivalent and very often Australian purchasers try to buy direct from the U.K. publisher at the lower U.K. price. Whilst the U.K. publisher may refuse to sell to Australia, in view of the exclusive sales agreement, leakage may still occur if other U.K. booksellers sell directly into the Australian market. Therefore even though price discrimination agreements exist if the price differential is high enough attempts at "buying round", i.e. purchasing directly at the lower U.K. price will be difficult to stop completely.

Price discrimination often occurs on the basis of time. Off peak telephone calls are lowest late at night, early in the morning or at weekends. Commuters on British Rail pay higher charges at peak travel times than tourists or shoppers going into London during late morning or early afternoon.

The status of the buyer is again an important consideration. The unemployed and elderly receive low priced benefits on the railway, at the cinema or at football matches etc. Children are often charged lower prices for travel and holidays, even though they consume the same amounts as adults.

Theoretically the aggregate demand schedule incorporates a number of individual demand preferences and therefore reflects different elasticities of demand. If this is the case the logical outcome of a price discrimination policy is to charge an almost infinite number of prices to different individuals along the demand schedule which would help the firm maximise its profits or, in the case of British Rail, reduce its loss. However, separating the market into this number of segments proves almost impossible in practice and explains why it is only done in most markets in a piecemeal manner.

Perfect Price Discrimination — The Airline Case

When a monopolist is able to discriminate between consumers so that each group of consumers is prepared to pay a different price for the same product, then the extra profits earned will be equal to the area of triangle CDE in Fig. 8.5. In the case of airlines who are able to discriminate in this way, then the carrier which faces a constant marginal and average cost as shown in Fig. 8.5 will produce up to an output capacity of oq4. The profit maximising output/price level will be oq/op where marginal costs and marginal revenue are equal at D. This produces a profit of area pCD p4. If the airline can also separate out the customers willing to pay different prices, by varying ticket purchase agreements, then the extra revenue exceeds the extra costs by the area shown as triangle CDE. These discriminatory purchasing price arrangements could be for example:- p^3 may represent low priced stand by tickets, p^2 one week in advance booking prices, p^1 one month in advance booking prices (a club arrangement) and so on. In theory it may also be possible to charge even higher prices to customers purchasing tickets from 0–oq

FIG. 8.5
PERFECT PRICE DISCRIMINATION: THE AIRLINE CASE

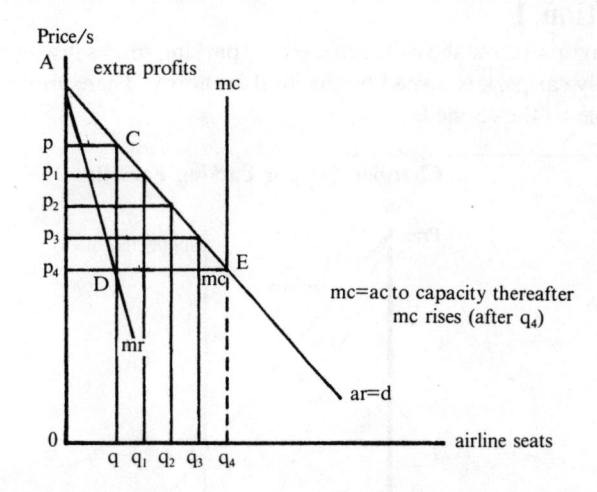

and so cream off the extra profits shown by the triangle ApC. In effect perfect price discrimination has provided extra profits to the airline at the expense of the consumer who loses consumer surplus equivalent to CDE.

CHAPTER 8 Research

1. *Identify a local/national monopolist and outline the main entry barriers you consider important.*
2. *With regard to Rail, Electricity, Post, Airlines, etc. obtain information which illustrates price discrimination at work.*

132 The Economic Behaviour of the Monopolist

DATA RESPONSE QUESTIONS

Question 1
The diagram below shows the market for parking spaces in a small country town. The only car park is owned by the local authority. There are a variety of options available to the council.

Charging for Car Parking Facilities

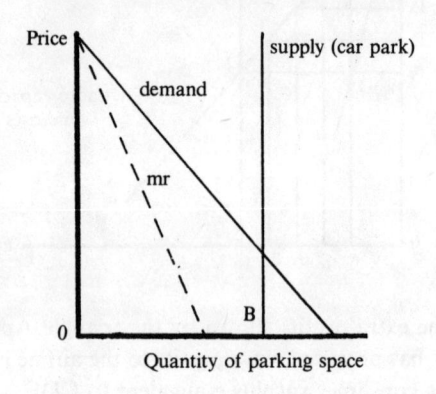

1. The council decides to provide free car parking. Show what happens in this case. (Assume there is no uncertainty on the part of potential car park users about getting a space).
2. The council wishes to ensure a free market equilibrium in order to reduce the number of motorists searching for a space.
   (a) Why would they wish to do this?
   (b) Show the impact of this decision on the diagram.
3. If the council decides to use ratepayers' money rather than charge users for parking, what will they do? Show it on the diagram.
4. Show the impact of a council policy designed to maximise profit with the existing car park. Outline the social costs of such a policy.

Question 2 — The Monopolist and Competition

A monopolist, at present producing an unbranded product for the home market only, is faced by the following revenue and cost schedules.

Price	Demand	Fixed Costs	Variable Cost
20	20	200	260
18	30	200	370
16	40	200	400
14	50	200	425
12	60	200	460
10	70	200	500
8	80	200	680

1. Calculate the monopolist's equilibrium price and output.
2. Assuming the same cost conditions, what was the long run equilibrium price and output levels be if the industry were perfectly competitive? (Assume costs include normal profit.)
3. Why might the cost conditions be different under perfect competition?

Question 3 — The Monopolist: Three Market Situations

(I) A profit maximising monopolist sells in market 1 and is considering going into market 2 with the same product. The cost and revenue conditions are shown.

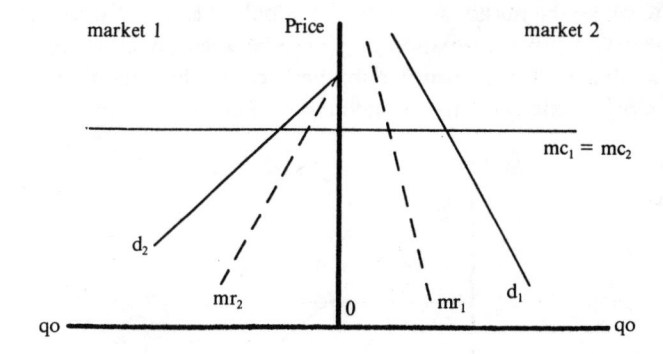

1. What would happen if the monopolist went into market 2 with the price he sets in market 1.
2. Under what conditions could the monopolist set a different price in market 2?
3. Show the price and profit in both markets when price discrimination is practised. Give real examples of price discrimination.

134 The Economic Behaviour of the Monopolist

(II) A monopolist operates under market conditions shown in the diagram.

1. How would you describe the monopolist? Give real examples.
2. Why would costs decrease?
3. Mark and show the price, output and profit in each case if the monopolist decided to maximise profit (p¹q¹), break even (p2q2) and maximise the communities economic efficiency (p3q3).
4. Outline the economic problem of outcome p3q3.

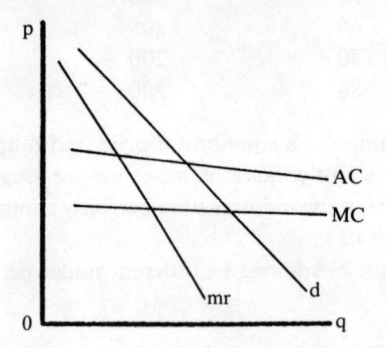

(III) A publisher has the cost and revenue conditions shown.

1. Show the price, output and profit for the profit maximising publisher.
2. The author receives a royalty, calculated as a constant percentage of sales. Show where the author would wish the publisher to set price and output.
3. Show why a conflict situation may arise between publisher and author.
4. Show what would happen if publisher's copyright were abolished and the industry became perfectly competitive. Comment upon the outcome.

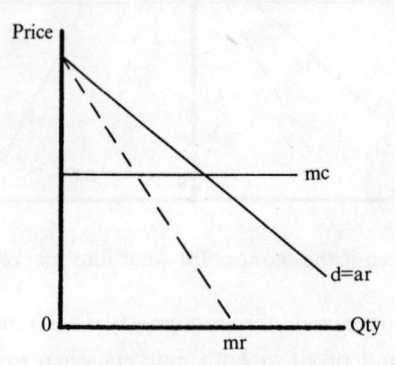

Question 4 — Average Pre-Tax Prices in Europe — Motor Cars

Average pre-tax car prices		
cheapest = 100	1987	1989
Denmark	100	100
Greece	n.a.	107
Belgium	121	123
Luxembourg	122	127
Holland	122	130
France	128	132
West Germany	128	137
Portugal	127	140
Ireland	130	145
Italy	129	148
Spain	142	149
Britain	144	161
Source: BEUC		

Source: Economist, 13 January 1990.

1. Explain the meaning of the index "cheapest = 100" and hence the position of Denmark.
2. How have average car differentials changed from 1987–89 with respect to Spain and Britain.
3. What economic principle does this data illustrate?
4. What conditions does the principle in Q3. require in order to be maintained. Relate these conditions to the fact that the above countries are members of the EEC.

Question 5 — Price Discrimination and the Monopolist

A monopolist faces the following cost and demand schedules:

	COST		DEMAND	
Q	Fixed (£'s)	Variable (£'s)	Price (£'s)	Demand
1	100	50	70	1
2	100	95	65	2
3	100	130	60	3
4	100	150	55	4
5	100	155	50	5
6	100	160	45	6
7	100	185	40	7
8	100	270	35	8

1. What level of output will this firm choose to produce at?
2. As a result of a fall in consumers' income the firm's demand schedule is

Price	Demand
60	1
55	2
50	3
45	4
40	5
35	6
30	7
25	8

    How will the firm to respond to this changed situation?
3. What would the firm do if, after the fall in demand, it engages in perfect price discrimination?

9 OLIGOPOLISTIC MARKETS — AND THE BEHAVIOUR OF THE OLIGOPOLIST

AIMS: To define, explain and discuss
- The nature of oligopolistic markets
- Collusive and competitive models of behaviour
- Strategic entry deterrence and game theory
- The competitive fringe and the dominant firm.

KEY CONCEPTS

Interdependence v independence, cost plus, price stability, kinked demand curve, game theory, strategic entry barriers, competitive fringe.

Oligopolistic markets are those dominated by a few firms, usually similar in size, who behave in either a competitive or non-competitive (collusive) manner. There are so few sellers that each firm is affected by the action of its rivals; unlike monopolies whose barriers to entry protect the market from competition. Thus the behaviour of the oligopolist is interdependant, i.e. depends upon the action of its rivals whilst monopolies behave independently of each other. Oligopolistic structures are commonplace in markets such as steel production, petrol retailing and high street banking where products and services are very similar. Oligopolists also operate where brand differentiation is high, e.g. the market for cars, beer and bread.

Characteristics of Oligopolistic Markets

Oligopolistic markets are, by definition, heavily concentrated so much of an industry's output is in the hands of a few producers, e.g. the $CR_5 = 70\%$, etc. which means the five largest producers are likely to have over 70% of the market output. Research has shown also that in the U.K. and the U.S.A.:-

1. Oligopolistic industrial concentration ratios are increasing in manufacturing sectors.
2. Profit rates are usually higher in the more concentrated market sectors.
3. Product advertising and non-price competition is commonplace.

138 Oligopolistic Markets

4. Average variable and marginal costs are saucer-shaped under oligopoly, i.e. they often appear 'L' shaped.

5. Unlike perfectly competitive and monopolistic market models which predict a unique price/output combination, oligopoly behaviour suggests there is more than one output level where profit is maximised.

6. Oligopolists often use a full variable cost plus profit mark-up formula in order to set price which then tends to be rather sticky compared to the volatile price movements in many competitive markets. This price stability is illustrated in Fig. 9.1. which shows the oligopolistic price charged at the pump by Shell compared to the free and volatile market price for petrol determined on the Rotterdam spot market during August/September 1990.

7. Oligopolists compete or collude in markets. Table 9.1 outlines the circumstances under which each is likely to occur.

FIG. 9.1
INCREASES IN SHELL UK PUMP PRICES VERSUS INCREASES IN ROTTERDAM SPOT PRICE (AUGUST–SEPTEMBER 1990)

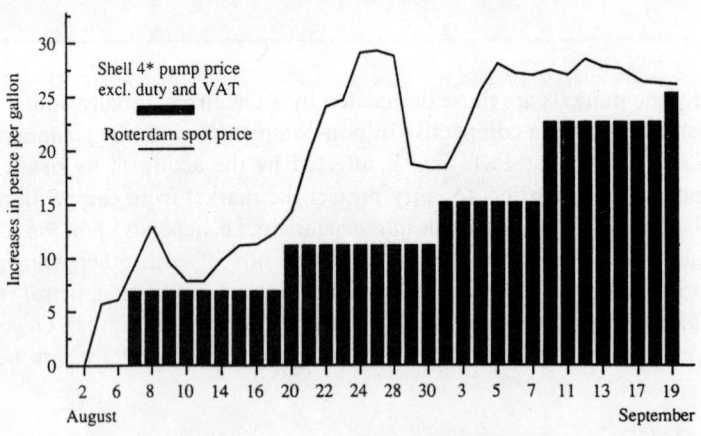

Source: Shell Shareholders Bulletin, Sept. 1990.

TABLE 9.1
OLIGOPOLIES: COLLUSION OR COMPETITION

Factor	Encourages collusion:	competition if:
Barriers to entry	✓	
Product is non-standard		✓
Demand and costs are stable	✓	
Collusion is legal	✓	
Secrecy about price and output		✓
Collusion is illegal		✓
Easy communication of price and output	✓	
Standard product	✓	

Models of Oligopolistic Behaviour — (Competitive)

A. *The Monopolistic Model*

Applying the above characteristics of oligopolistic markets above, one explanatory model is illustrated in Fig. 9.2 which incorporates saucer-shaped costs together with a monopolistic theory of behaviour with respect to the change in demand from d2 to d1. This shows that even with this change because of relatively flat average variable costs, the equating of marginal cost and marginal revenue means that the price is relatively stable at op_1 between the output range oq and oq1. This also can be interpreted as a full variable cost plus fixed cost mark up as the figure illustrates. At the same time if similar sized oligopolies in an industry have similar costs and products, then it is not surprising to find similar and stable prices in these markets, e.g. in petrol retailing.

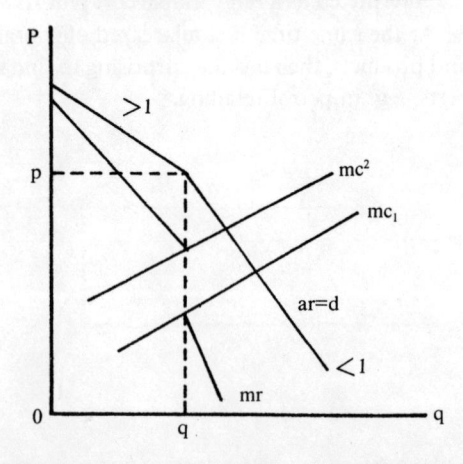

FIG. 9.2
A: COMPETITIVE OLIGOPOLISTIC BEHAVIOUR

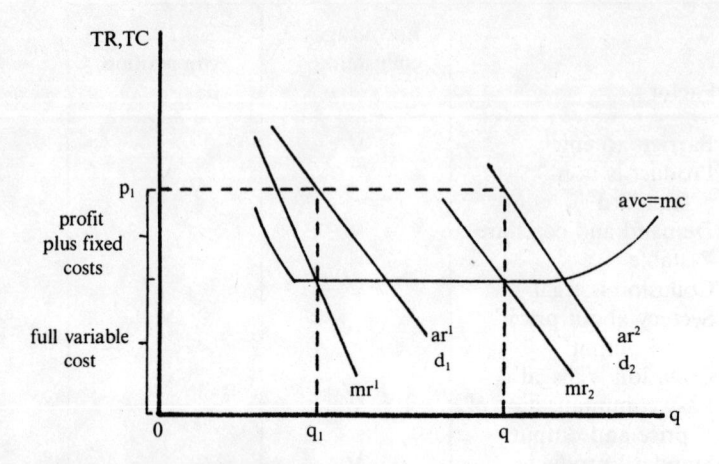

B. *The Kinked Demand Theory*

This theory assumes the demand facing the individual oligopolist is kinked at the current price level. The price stability at op, the kink, is determined because the firm believes that if it cuts this price its rivals will follow so no extra revenue is generated, i.e. demand is inelastic. Furthermore, if it raises its price its rivals will not follow suit so its revenue will suffer, i.e. demand is elastic. This is illustrated in Fig. 9.3 which shows the demand schedule and a discontinuous marginal revenue schedule. Thus even with a change in marginal cost from mc1 to mc2 the price stays at op. However, this theory does not explain why the price is originally at op.

FIG. 9.3
B: THE KINKED DEMAND CURVE

FIG. 9.4
C: COLLUSIVE OLIGOPOLIES

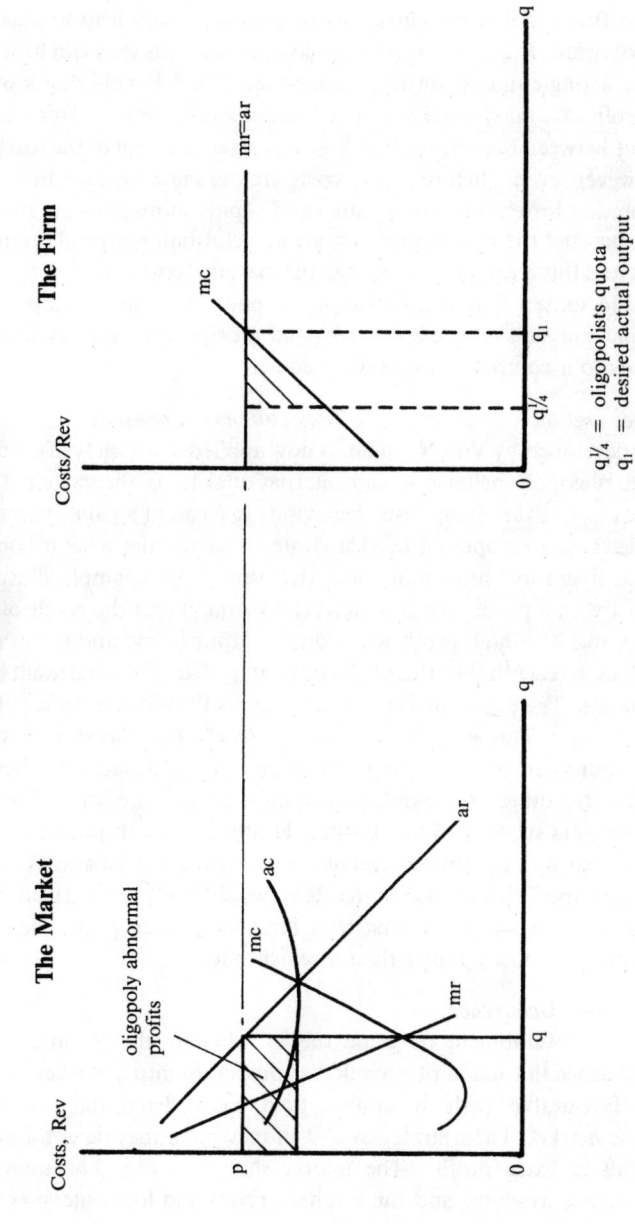

The Market

The Firm

$q\frac{1}{4}$ = oligopolists quota
q_1 = desired actual output

C. Collusive Oligopoly Models

The collusive cartel model is useful when there are a small number of firms selling a similar product and when a fierce price war would be harmful. In this case the firms recognise that a policy of mutual interdependence may help to maximise overall industry profit. If it is assumed they have similar costs they can be treated as if they were a single multiplant monopolist, see Fig. 9.4. This shows overall oligopolistic profits are maximised at a price/output level of op/oq. This output is then shared out between the oligopolists, e.g. a quarter or a fifth of the market to each one. However, even when marginal costs are the same for each firm, there will be a temptation for each to break ranks and supply more than the allocated share, i.e. oq_1, because the ruling price appears as a constant marginal revenue to the oligopolist and this is always greater than the marginal cost as the figure shows. This may lead to some selling at a slightly lower price than the agreed price, op, and this will put pressure on the agreement and a price war may develop. This eventually leads to a competitive supply schedule.

D. Oligopolies and the Game Theory – Competition or Collusion

Game theory, developed by Von Neuman, is now applied to a variety of economic topics, such as oligopoly behaviour and international trade theory, etc. Game theory attempts to analyse oligopolists' behaviour in terms of a game where each firm tries to determine its optimal market strategy, aware that what it does will influence its competitors' behaviour, and vice versa. An example illustrates. Assume there are two producers in a market (duopoly) and the result of each pricing strategy means a high profit when one's output is low and the others is high. How will each react to the others behaviour and what will be the result if they compete or collude? The matrix in Fig. 9.5 summarises the profit outcome of each firm's output decision. This is for firms A and B. As the Fig. shows, if they both have a high output strategy, then competitive profits are £1m each. If either goes for a low output, the other firm stands to gain more profit, i.e. £3m or £2m more than a corresponding strategy of low output. However, if both pursue a selfish policy, they will return to £1m profit level outcomes each as can be seen. As shown by the solution of the Prisoners Dilemma, they would both be better off by co-operating and reducing output so that they both make £2m profit each. This implies a co-operative policy rather than a selfish one.

E. Strategic Entry Deterrence

This theory is a development of game theory whereby the incumbent firm attempts to influence the action of a would be competitor into a market in such a way that it is favourable to the incumbent firm, e.g. it deters the new entrant coming into the market. These strategies cost money but if they deter the entrant they may result in extra profits. The matrix shown in Fig. 9.6 outlines the alternative strategies available and the resulting profit and loss outcomes to the incumbent and would be entrant when different decisions are taken, i.e. to come into the market or stay out, or to fight or not to fight, etc. The best strategy for the

Oligopolistic Markets 143

FIG. 9.5
THE DOMINANT FIRM AND THE COMPETITIVE FRINGE

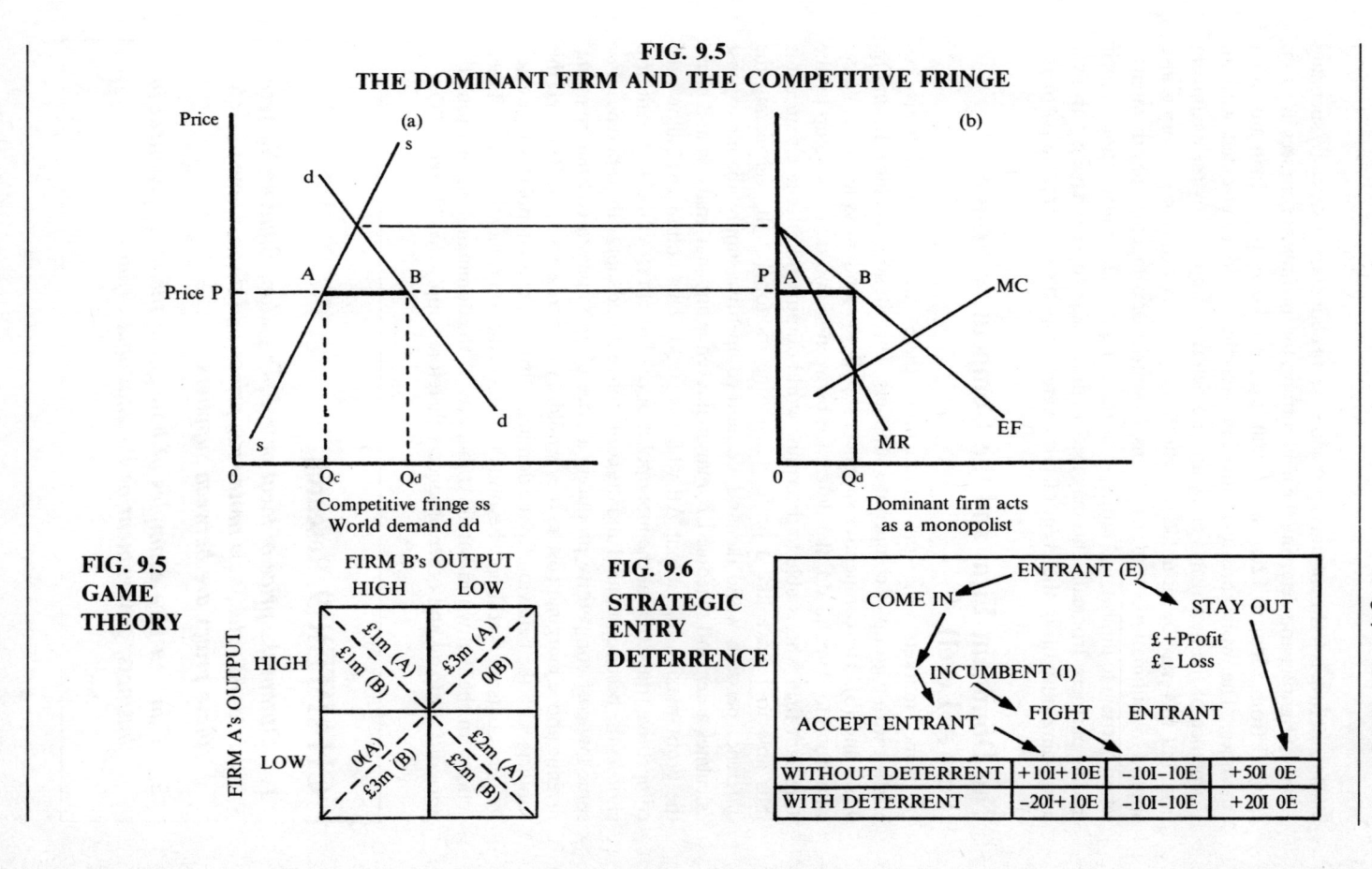

(a) Competitive fringe ss
World demand dd

(b) Dominant firm acts as a monopolist

FIG. 9.6 STRATEGIC ENTRY DETERRENCE

ENTRANT (E)
COME IN / STAY OUT
INCUMBENT (I)
FIGHT / ACCEPT ENTRANT
£ +Profit
£ −Loss

	ACCEPT ENTRANT	FIGHT ENTRANT	STAY OUT
WITHOUT DETERRENT	+10I+10E	−10I−10E	+50I 0E
WITH DETERRENT	−20I+10E	−10I−10E	+20I 0E

FIG. 9.5 GAME THEORY

FIRM B's OUTPUT

	HIGH	LOW
FIRM A's OUTPUT HIGH	£1m (A) / £1m (B)	£3m (A) / 0 (B)
FIRM A's OUTPUT LOW	0 (A) / £3m (B)	£2m (A) / £2m (B)

incumbent firm is if the entrant is persuaded to stay out of the market. By spending £30m on fighting and deterring the new entrant, the incumbent firm sees its profit reduced from £50m to £20m which still gives it a larger profit than any other outcomes. The worst possible situation, a fight, could be avoided with an acceptance of the new firm's entry and no deterrent imposed by the incumbent firm, but this may be an unlikely event. Strategic entry deterrence theory is also applied to multinational trade situations. Countries or companies may threaten to set up barriers to import, e.g. tariffs, in order to frighten off similar action by their trading partners. Ironically this may lead, in due course, to them having a stronger bargaining position in the event of tariff agreements between trading partners.

The Dominant Firm and the Competitive Fringe (Post A Level)

In some markets, e.g. oil production, there are dominant firms co-existing with a group of competitive suppliers. This situation is illustrated in Fig. 9.5(a) and (b). The competitive suppliers supply the amount ss in Fig. 9.5(a) so with a world demand dd, the difference between ss and dd is made up by the dominant firm who is able to determine world output and price levels since it is thus able to behave like a profit maximising monopolist. By calculating the difference between world demand, dd, and competitive supply, the monopolist calculates a demand schedule EF, marginal revenue and marginal cost and hence the profit maximising output AB which is 0Qd. This output level allows the competitive fringe 0Qc at the monopolist price of op. In effect the dominant firm chooses the best output level and the competitive fringe supply the difference. For some low cost competitive producers a price of op implies a constant marginal revenue above marginal cost so they would try to increase output. However, this conflicts with the behaviour of the dominant firm so the monopolist will threaten to increase its market supply beyond 0Qd unless the fringe members control their actions. In the real world Saudi Arabia acts as the dominant firm in setting the price of OPEC oil and other producers therefore supply the difference 0Qc.

CHAPTER 9 Research

1. *Obtain the price of local petrol per gallon, Building Society interest rates, new motor car prices and discuss how flexible these prices are between suppliers.*

2. *Can you give examples of how game theory is practical in business, government or international affairs?*

DATA RESPONSE QUESTIONS

Question 1 — Cartels: Theory and Practice

The oil market is unlike most other commodity markets such as tea, coffee or copper. It is riddled with market imperfections. These imperfections stem from OPEC, a cartel of thirteen countries which seeks to maximise the collective benefit of member states. Since 1973 OPEC has deemed it in the interest of its members to raise price considerably on two occasions (1973 and 1979), with only a marginal effect on demand.

However, with the onset of the world recession in 1980 the demand for oil was dramatically curtailed. Throughout 1984 the oil market was working strongly against OPEC and several member countries such as Nigeria and Ecuador broke ranks and produced up to 40% more oil than the agreed quota. Several crisis meetings have taken place to retain the credibility and effectiveness of OPEC.

If the OPEC cartel does finally collapse this would have a severe impact on oil prices with some experts suggesting a fall in price of up to one-third. Such a price fall could have dramatic repercussions, not only for OPEC members but also for the United Kingdom and other non-OPEC oil producers.

1. Define a "cartel" (line 3).
2. How has OPEC sought to maximise the collective benefit of member states (line 4)?
3. With reference to the text, discuss the circumstances in which a cartel might collapse.
4. Why might the price elasticity of demand for oil be different in the long run from that in the short run?
5. Explain the likely impact on the United Kingdom economy of a substantial fall in oil prices.

(London 'A' Paper, 1988.)

Question 2   "The Rewards to an Individual Producer from Cheating on the Cartel"

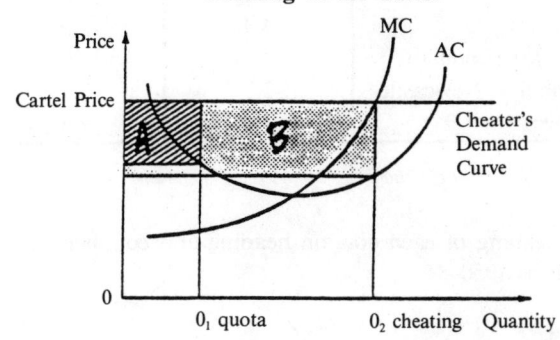

146 Oligopolistic Markets

Use the figure to answer the following:-
1. Why is the cartel price the same as the "Cheaters" demand curve?
2. Why will the producer be tempted to increase production beyond OQ_1?
3. Why will the "Cheat" stop at OQ_2?
4. Identify and explain the shaded areas A and B.

Question 3

Table 1
The U.K. Brewing Industry 1950–85

Year	Total Production (million bulk barrels)	Brewery Companies No. of firms	No. of plants	Average Output per plant (thousand bulk barrels)
1950	24.9	360	560	44
1955	24.5	320	460	53
1960	26.1	247	358	73
1965	29.9	180	274	109
1970	34.4	96	177	194
1975	39.2	82	147	267
1980	38.9	80	145	268
1985	36.5	68	117	312

Table 2
The Principal Brewery Companies in 1985

Firm	Production (million bulk barrels)	% U.K. Production
Bass	7.7	21.0
Allied-Lyons	4.9	13.5
Whitbread	4.4	12.0
Grand Metropolitan	4.0	11.0
Scottish and Newcastle	3.7	10.0
Courage	3.3	9.0

Source: C.S.O. Dept of Trade.

1. Define the meaning of each column heading and comment on the fall in number of firms 1950–85.

2. Discuss with suitable examples the economic principle at work with respect to average output per plant 1950–85.
3. What has been the pattern of production between 1950–85 and give reasons to explain this behaviour.
4. Use Table 2 to explain the market structure of brewing and discuss how you would expect the companies to behave within this structure.

ALTERNATIVE THEORIES OF THE FIRM

AIMS: *To define, explain and discuss*
- *Alternative theories of the firm*
- *Managerial and behavioural objectives of business*
- *Contestable markets and business behaviour*

KEY CONCEPTS

Divorce of ownership from control, managerial objectives, satisficing theory, acceptable profit levels, organisational slack, marginalist/neoclassical, consumer sovereignty, contestable markets, strategic entry deterrence.

The assumption of profit maximising in the business unit is possible only if managers and owners work together and there is no division between those who own and those who manage the firm. However, in the real world, in large companies, there is a difference between those who own, shareholders, and those who manage, directors, and this means it is possible for other than profit maximising objectives to be pursued. This divorce of ownership from control has led to other theories of the firm being developed and these stress managerial behaviour designed to:-

1. *Maximise Sales Revenue and Market Share*

The performance of management is often rewarded financially if there is an increase in the firm's market share or sales so long as this is achieved alongside an acceptable level of profit. This allows management to buy sales by advertising which reduces profit levels and promotional costs rise. This theory of sales maximisation is associated with W. Baumol. Fig. 10.1 illustrates this concept and uses the model of a profit maximising monopolist. Profit maximising is achieved at output oq given costs and revenue. If there is some normal market level of acceptable profits, op_r, then output and sales can be increased by advertising up to outputs of oq1. This level of output boosts revenue at the expense of profits. Critics of the sales maximisation theory allege that long term profit maximising is still the objective of the firm even with short term sales maximising and this short

FIG. 10.1
MAXIMISING SALES REVENUE

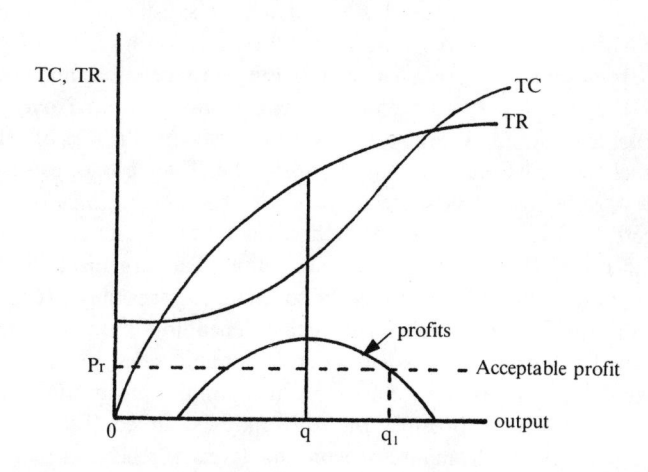

[Figure: Graph with axes TC, TR (vertical) and output (horizontal). Curves shown: TC, TR, profits, with horizontal line at Pr marked "Acceptable profit", and points q and q₁ on output axis.]

term objective allows the firm to gain monopoly power in the long run in order to maximise its profit.

2. *Managerial Theories of Behaviour*

If shareholders are not able to control management and if the business unit operates under monopolistic conditions, then it is alleged that managers may pursue their own goals within the business. This can be such things as increasing their salaries, building up non-taxed expenses and generally increasing the size of their departments or offices or their own tax free perks, etc. This view does not refute the view that profit is the firm's objective since the more profit the manager earns for the company the more his salary increases. Nevertheless, the idea is that managers associate the growth of the company with their own self advancement and salary performance and this management behaviour may not always be consistent with profit maximising. Thus it could be that management will seek to increase the size of the firm but at the same time they will fight off a takeover bid by another company since this could threaten their own job, salary and status. This could lead to a potential conflict situation between dividend policy and future management security because if dividend and share prices are high, as shareholders would wish, this will reduce the retained profits available for internal growth which ultimately benefits management. This factor may lead to management fighting off a takeover bid which could provide not only a capital gain for shareholders, but also a guaranteed future dividend growth.

3. Behavioural Theories of the Firm

Management face a complexity of data and instead of maximising one particular objective, e.g. profit, they seek instead to achieve satisfactory performance levels over a whole range of goals. These could be satisfactory levels of profits, sales growth, labour relations, publicity or relations with the public and government. If each of these goals are achieved then it can aspire to improve overall standards including profit levels. These are known as 'satisficing' theories of behaviour and are associated with Simon and Cyert and March. These economists took the view that the organisation could be seen as a group of conflicting interest groups such as managers, workers, creditors, shareholders and government who each have different objectives within the business unit. The organisation survives and resolves these conflicts by a process of continuous bargaining. At the micro level within the firm there also are other goals depending upon the function of the manager. These can be classified as stockholding, sales, production, credit or promotional goals. At any one time, for example, the production goal is to produce as much as possible but this may be in conflict with the stockholding goal which is to maintain economic levels of stock. As the goals conflict compromise is needed and often a goal may be more than satisfactorily achieved, in which case there will be organisational slack or 'excess fat' within the department. There are more resources available than are necessary to meet the current goal. This slack allows for change in the organisation without too much conflict arising because side payments can be made which allows for compromise within the organisation. These theories were developed because it was alleged that the marginalist, i.e. neoclassical, theory of the firm's behaviour, did not seem to coincide with the actual behaviour of businessmen. For one thing businessmen may not know their marginal cost or marginal revenue and furthermore it was alleged that businessmen priced on the basis of full cost plus a profit margin so that the marginalist theories used unreal assumptions and should therefore be changed to accommodate the real world. However, Machlup and Friedman still maintain the marginalist theories of the firm are still valid regardless of the reality of their assumptions. More important, they allege, is how far the neoclassical theories are able to predict testable implications about business behaviour with respect to price, output and profit, i.e. do businessmen behave as if they were seeking to maximise profits.

4. Galbraith Theory of the Firm's Behaviour

Advanced by J.K. Galbraith, this theory questions the idea of consumer sovereignty in the market place. It alleges that business units invest huge amounts of capital in new product lines and then use manipulative advertising to ensure that consumers buy their products. He supports this notion by pointing to the fact that monopolistic market structures are typical in many consumer goods industries and that little competition is really experienced. However, critics of this theory point to the failure of the Ford 'Edsel' motor car in the U.S.A. and the

Strand cigarette brand in the U.K. where both products were heavily advertised yet proved to be failures because the consumer ultimately decided they did not want to purchase them.

5. *Game Theory and Strategic Entry Deterrence* (see under Oligopoly Theory)

6. *Contestable Markets*

This is a new theory of market behaviour developed by Baumol which uses many of the traditional neoclassical ideas of the firm. The theory explains why the results associated with perfectly competitive markets can be experienced in circumstances of scale economies, usually experienced by monopolies. Contestable market theory explains therefore why the behaviour of monopolies can appear as if competition was present. Contestable markets are those with the following characteristics, namely:- (a) free entry and costless exit so that any capital investment can be fully realised in the event of bankruptcy (b) there are no perceived differences in terms of the product sold in the market and (c) price taking behaviour is not necessary and this is a critical difference between competitive and non-competitive market behaviour. In essence contestable markets provide the basis for hit and run entry, i.e. competition conditions, and this means incumbent firms, even monopolists, have to move towards least cost production methods. Also price has to equal marginal cost where these prices are set by competitive conditions, and make no more than normal profits in the long run. Otherwise the fear of hit and run entrants reduces profits to zero and could even lead to the incumbent firm going out of business. Contestable market theory is useful in explaining the similarity in behaviour in both competitive and monopolistically competitive markets in the long run. However, many oligopolistic markets still have costly entry and exit conditions so this theory is less applicable in oligopolistic and pure monopolistic market conditions.

CHAPTER 10 Research

1. *Ask your friends, relatives, businessmen, teachers or lecturers what they perceive to be the objectives of the institution they work for.*

2. *Can you identify in any institution you are familiar with the following: organisational slack, side payments, empire building, consumer sovereignty, consumer ignorance and manipulation?*

FACTOR INCOMES — WAGE DETERMINATION

AIMS: To define, explain and discuss
- Market theory of income determination
- Marginal revenue product and incomes
- Supply influences on factor incomes
- Monopolistic market behaviour

KEY CONCEPTS

Marginal revenue (physical) product, demand/supply elasticity, derived demand, monopolists, wage discrimination, economic rent, transfer earnings.

Wages are the payment for labour services, rent for land, interest and profit for capital services and profit the reward for enterprise. The distribution of factor incomes applies supply and demand analysis in order to answer the question of "for whom are the goods and services produced?" Market analysis treats the rewards of factor inputs as a price determined under competitive market conditions. These are relaxed and monopolistic market conditions are treated later in the chapter. These competitive factor markets are characterised by the following:-

a) buyers and sellers of factor inputs are price takers, i.e. there are no monopoly buyers or sellers.

b) labour and other factors are homogeneous or identical.

c) there is full information about the price and quality of factor inputs.

d) factor prices are freely allowed to fluctuate in order to equate demand and supply.

e) there is free mobility of factors, e.g. labour can and will move freely between regions, occupations or industries.

f) factor inputs move in order to receive their highest income and best employment.

g) entrepreneurs employ factors in order to maximise the profits of the business.

FIG. 11.1 SHORT RUN

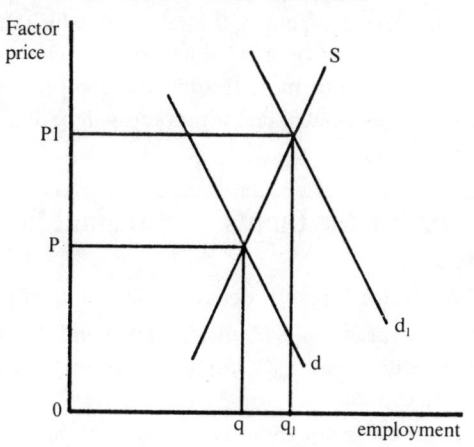

FIG. 11.2 LONG RUN

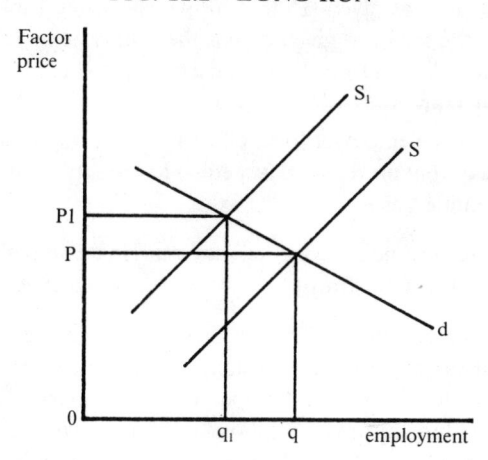

FACTOR PRICE CHANGES IN THE SHORT AND LONG RUN

Factor Price Determination

In its simplest form the market theory explains factor price and employment in terms of movements in demand and supply. In the short term it is normal for demand forces to be the main determinant so, as Fig. 11.1 shows, the rise in factor prices and employment responds to demand in the main. In the short term many factor inputs are assumed to be fixed. In the long run the main influence in factor markets is due to changing supply conditions since in the long run all factor inputs are variable. In Fig. 11.2 this is shown as an overall reduction in factor supply, S to

S1 which causes price to rise and employment to reduce. It is important to note that although factor markets are competitive the ease with which they adjust depends also upon the degree of competition in product markets. Thus, in the long run, it is assumed product markets will be more flexible and competitive as entry barriers reduce and this will mean associated factor markets will be able to react in a more competitive manner.

The Demand for Factor Inputs – Marginal Revenue Product Characteristics

1) The demand for factor inputs is derived from the final product or service.

2) The demand for factor inputs is often a joint demand. Thus when the demand for labour increases, due to cheaper labour or more profit, so also does the demand for land and capital.

3) Market demand for a factor input is the result of total individual employer demand. In competitive product and factor markets the employer, as producer, takes the product price as given (£5 in example shown in Table 11.1), and also takes the price of the factor as given (£20 is the wage rate in Table 11.1). This is because the small individual producer and employer is unable to influence the product or labour market.

4) The demand of the employer for the factor will be up to the point where the value of the extra output produced is just equal to the extra cost of employing the factor. This is identified as:-

marginal revenue product of = marginal cost of factor
factor input (mrp)   input (mc)

5) In terms of the labour market the mrp is equal to the marginal physical product of labour times the given product price, in the competitive market, and the mc is the wage rate given by the competitive labour market. The behaviour of mpp reflects diminishing returns, i.e. labour is the variable input with capital the fixed factor. Table 11.1 and Fig. 11.3 illustrate how mrp is derived with the following implications:-

a) The downward sloping portion of the mrp, shown in Fig. 11.3, is the businessman's demand for labour. If the wage rate (mc) is £20 then demand will be up to eight men and only six will be employed if the wage rate rises £35, etc. The total product of labour, etc. is the area under the mrp curve. Of this the wages bill is 8 x £20 = £160 and so the rest goes as a reward to other factors employed, up to the point where mrp equals mc, i.e. the mrp of land equals the marginal cost of land, etc.

b) If either the price of the product rises, from £5, and/or the marginal physical product of the workforce increases, then the mrp or demand for labour shifts to the right. A leftwards movement occurs for the opposite reasons. The results are

Factor Incomes – Wage Determinations

TABLE 11.1
CALCULATING MARGINAL REVENUE PRODUCT AND THE DEMAND FOR LABOUR

No. of Men Employed	Total Output	Marginal Physical Product (MPP)	×	Product Price £5	=	Marginal Rev. Product (MRP)	
1	5	5				25	
2	12	7	Increasing Returns			35	
3	22	10				50	Wage cost = £20
4	33	11				55	or £35 etc.
5	43	10				50	
6	50	7	Diminished Returns			35	
7	55	5				25	
8	59	4				20	
9	62	3				15	
10	64	2				10	

FIG. 11.3

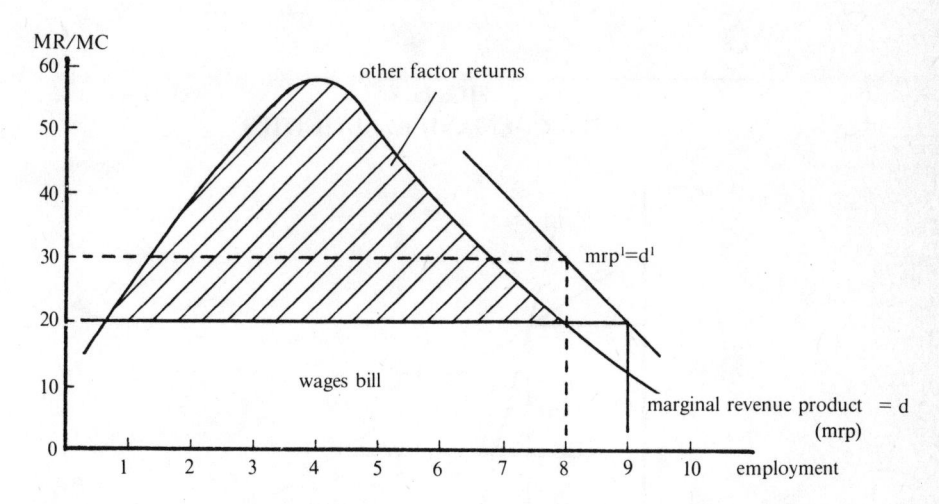

illustrated in Fig. 11.3 and show that either the existing workforce of 8 men receive a higher wage of £30 or more men are employed at £20, i.e. 9. The price of the product may rise because it becomes popular or supply reduces whilst the increase in labour productivity could be the result of better technology, a rise in the demand of all other factor inputs or an improvement in the management of labour relations in the business unit, etc.

FIG. 11.4
INDUSTRY DEMAND FOR LABOUR (XY)

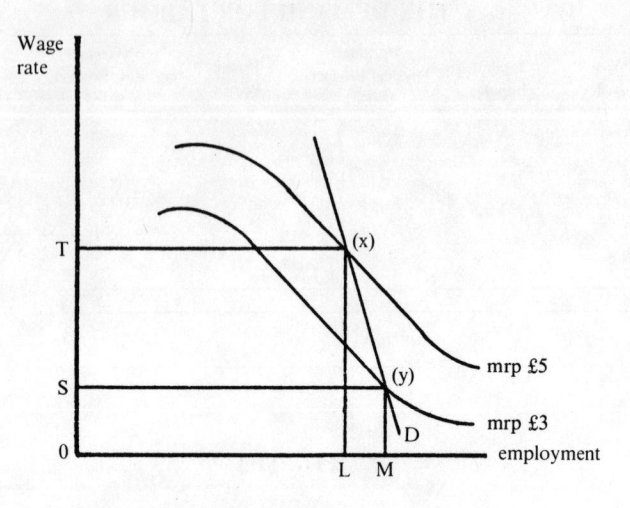

FIG. 11.5
FACTOR DEMAND ELASTICITIES

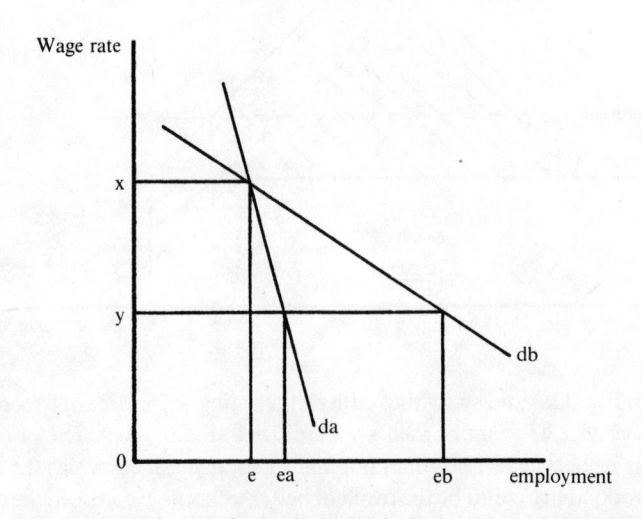

c) The factor demand curve in the industry is derived from individual employers demand schedules and will be more inelastic in nature, see Fig. 11.4. This is explained as follows. If the price of the factor (labour) falls then all firms hire more labour causing a rise in output and a fall in product price, e.g. £5 to £3. This causes a shift of the mrp to the left because the fall in price from £5 to £3 will reduce the value of the marginal revenue product. At the original price, OL are employed at OT wage rate but with the fall in the price of the product the price of the factor also falls from OT to OS. Thus with mrp equal to £3 and the lower factor price of OS, only OM will be employed. If points x and y are joined up, the demand for the industry is shown as the inelastic line XY.

Demand and Factor Elasticity

Consider two industries A and B in Fig. 11.5 employing the same factor, labour, but their respective demand schedules da/db have different demand elasticities. This means that for any given fall in the wage rate, more of the factor is employed by industry B than by industry A, i.e. if the price of labour falls from x to y, industry B's demand for labour increases from e to eb whilst industry A's increase is from e to ea. The reverse would happen if the wage rose from y to x. Factor elasticity of demand is important and will depend upon:-

a) The elasticity of demand for the final product. The more inelastic the demand for the final product, then the more inelastic the demand for labour becomes.

b) The substitutability of one factor for another. The more substitutable the cheaper factor is in terms of other factors, then the more elastic its demand becomes.

c) The amount the factor cost proportion represents in terms of the final cost bill. In industry A the labour factor cost is less important than in industry B in terms of their overall costs.

d) The profitability of the industry. If an industry is making large profits it will have an inelastic demand for the factor because even if factor price increases it will be able to afford these extra costs. Less profitable industries will have a more elastic demand schedule.

e) The time factor. In the short term it is more difficult to substitute other factors for labour when the wage rate increases. However, in the long term a firm will be able to respond by using other factors if the wage rate rises. This means demand will be inelastic in the short term and elastic in the long term.

f) The political climate. If wage increases can be passed on to the customer, then inflationary price increases are expected by customers, so large wage increases can be more easily negotiated by unions when it is believed that governments relax controls on inflation, e.g. at an election time.

The Long Term Demand for Factors

In the long term the profit maximising firm will apply the mrp = mc(p) rule in all factor markets. The least cost combination of factors, at any output level, will depend upon the marginal physical product of each factor, not mrp since sales (price) are now less important. This means the factor employment which minimises costs will be:-

$$\frac{\text{mpp of labour}}{\text{price of labour}} = \frac{\text{mpp of land}}{\text{price of land}} = \frac{\text{mpp of capital}}{\text{price of capital}} \quad \text{and so on.}$$

Non-Competitive Labour and Product Markets

a) *Monopolistic Product Markets.* When one more worker is employed to produce, e.g. four extra units, the monopolist will have to reduce the product price in order to sell the extra product. This is because monopolists face a downward sloping demand schedule. The change in the monopolist's schedule is shown:-

		Total Revenue
If the monopolist sells 100 at £50	=	£5000
If the monopolist sells 104 at £49	=	£5096
Marginal revenue product of extra worker	=	£ 96 (mrp)

However, the value of the marginal product = 4 x £49 = £196 (vmp)

This means the value of the marginal product, to a monopolist, is always higher than the marginal revenue product of the extra worker. Fig. 11.6 shows this with a competitive supply schedule of labour. The competitive supply of labour is also the same as the marginal cost to the monopolist. This means, as Fig. 11.6 shows, that for the nth worker employed, there is a difference between the vmp and the mrp. If the monopolist pays the value of the mrp, i.e. £96, it will be less than the value of the marginal product produced, i.e. £196.

b) *Monopsonistic Labour Markets.* In this situation there is only one buyer of labour which is still offered competitively, i.e. there is no union. The monopolist sells into a competitive product market, i.e. vmp = mrp. In this case, when the monopolist hires more labour, it bids up the price it pays to all its existing workers. For example, if the monopolist hires 10 workers at £20 each, the wages bill is £200. In order to have the 11th worker, the monopolist has to pay £21 to all employees which increases the overall wages bill to 11 times £21 = £231. The average cost per worker given by the supply of labour is £21 but the marginal cost of the extra worker is £31, i.e. £231 - £200. This is shown in Fig. 11.7 where, for any level of employment the marginal cost is higher than the average price. The monopolist will employ up to 11 men if his mrp equals vmp equals mc, at £31, but the workers will only receive a wage of £21. Note: If a union were to enter this industry and set a union rate of £26, which now becomes the labour supply schedule, i.e. mc = ac, the monopolist will have to pay this rate and will increase employment in the industry to 13 workers, i.e. a union raises wages and employment in a monopolistic labour market.

FIG. 11.6
LABOUR MARKETS AND THE MONOPOLIST PRODUCER

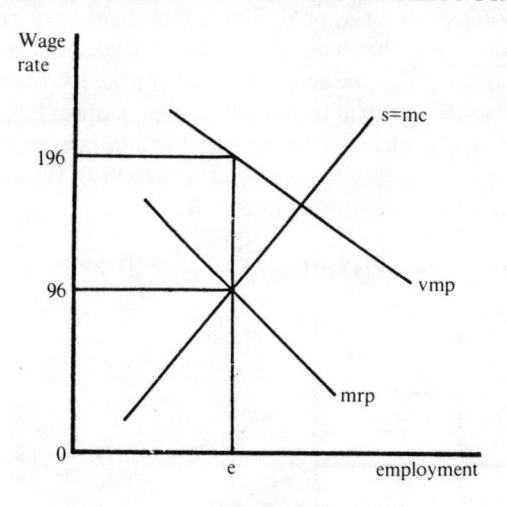

FIG. 11.7
LABOUR MARKETS AND THE MONOPSONIST EMPLOYER

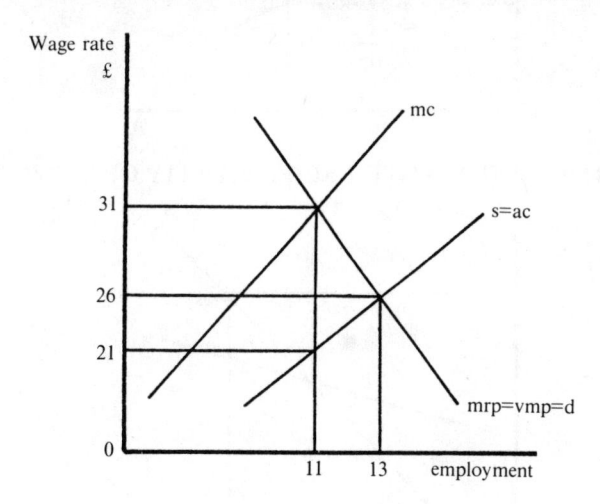

Supply of a Factor of Production, e.g. Labour etc.

Supply can mean any of the following:-

1. *The Total Physical Supply of a Factor*

A physical stock in the short term is likely to be fixed and difficult to change, e.g. the stock of land, skilled labour, capital. This will change over time, see Fig. 11.8 which shows the increase in the stock of land after reclamation, i.e. S to S1. This means as demand increases, in the short term, factor price increases from P to P1 to P2, but as the stock increases in the long term overall prices fall, see arrows. In the case of labour supply, increases in the participation rates by such groups as women, old age pensioners, overseas immigration or school leavers, can increase the stock of labour and hence shift from S to S1.

FIG. 11.8 PHYSICAL FACTOR SUPPLY

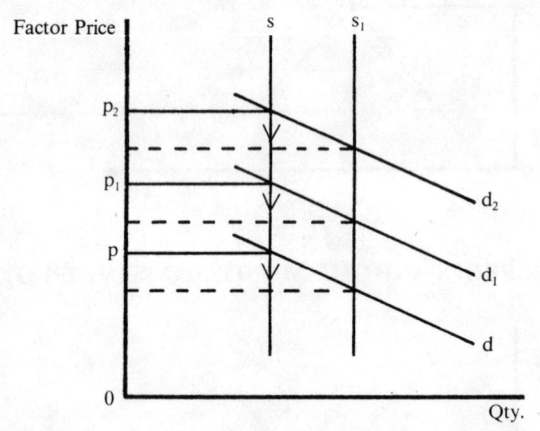

FIG. 11.9 ALTERNATIVE USE/ELASTICITY OF SUPPLY

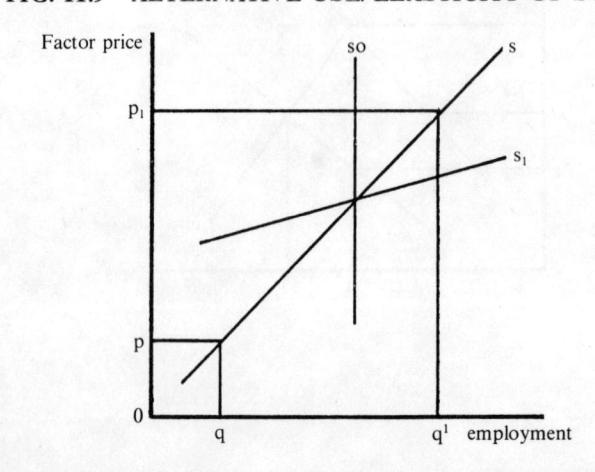

2. The Supply of a Factor in a Particular Use

Labour and other factors can move between alternative uses and in this case the price in the next best use will influence how much labour must be paid in a particular use. This will depend upon the relative wage rates and the alternatives and opportunities available to labour. It will also depend upon the flexibility of a factor of production and how easily, for example, labour is willing and able to move between jobs or regions or industries. The overall mobility of labour between occupations and regions can be influenced by Government retraining schemes and the cost of housing in different parts of the country and land uses can also be influenced in terms of their location and the planning restrictions placed on their development. The supply schedule S in Fig. 11.9 reflects these ideas. In order to attract oq labour at least op must be paid in wages since labour can obtain this elsewhere. In order to attract oq_1 labour up to op1 must be paid in wages. In deciding between jobs, workers take into account not only monetary rewards but they also place a value upon non-monetary factors (non-pecuniary advantages). These are such things as working conditions, pensions, holidays, job satisfaction, etc. These, together with financial reward, add up to the net advantage of an occupation to a worker.

3. Shifts in Supply

There are non price wage changes which will affect the supply of labour in the real world. These influences will move supply from S1 to S2 in Fig. 11.10 and they are as follows:-

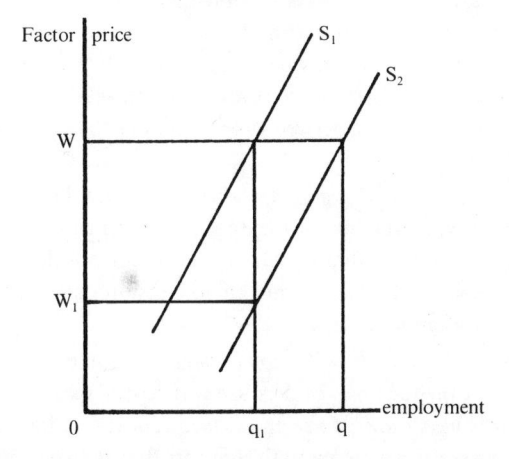

FIG. 11.10
A SHIFT IN SUPPLY

(i) Overall wages or net advantages in one occupation are higher than in other competing occupations, so workers move to this particular industry or occupation, i.e. S_1 to S_2. Unemployment in the economy or in a region could also increase, which overall reduces wage expectations which shifts labour from S1 to S2.

(ii) Labour now freely enters the economy or a region from other lower wage areas (immigration).

(iii) An increase in the labour force can result from a population bulge or from a shift in the age structure so that the working population in general terms increases. This could also result if more women entered the working population or if, say, the school leaving age was reduced.

(iv) As mentioned, women could be attracted to return to work because of a successful advertising campaign or more attractive employment packages, e.g. creches for working mothers, etc.

(v) A weakening of restricted practices, as exercised by closed shop agreements or professional qualifications, could result in more qualified personnel entering a particular industry after a shorter training time period.

The overall impact of the supply shift from S1 to S2, shown in Fig. 11.10, is to increase the amount of labour at each wage rate and also for each amount of labour supply, e.g. oq_1 a lower wage has now to be paid relatively in order to attract this amount of labour into the market, i.e. ow to ow_1.

4. *Elasticity of Factor Supply*

The response of labour supply to a wage change, or any other factor supply, can be measured in terms of elasticity as Fig. 11.9 shows. The normal supply S is compared to two other supply schedules, S0 and S1 which reflect inelastic and elastic supply schedules respectively. Factors which influence the elasticity of supply are:-

(i) *Time*. In the short term factors are not usually able to move quickly to a new use so supply is inelastic. It takes time for labour to obtain information about alternative jobs, time to hand in one's notice and then move to the new job. Workers may also see a wage rise in another occupation as temporary. In the long run factors are more adaptable between uses so that both labour and land can now be used for different purposes.

(ii) *Geographical and Occupational Mobility*. If labour becomes more able or willing to move between regions or occupations, then supply will become more elastic. This factor will be influenced by government policies designed to allow flexibility between occupations, e.g. moveable pension plans or the ability to find cheap housing in different regions.

(iii) *Controls on the Flow of New Factor Entrants*. If trade unions exercise closed shop agreements or professional bodies use restrictive rules on qualifications, the supply of labour is likely to be fixed in both the short and long run. Patents can have the same impact on new capital entering the industry. Planning controls which reduce the use of a piece of land to one specific purpose will also mean land supply is inelastic in both the long and the short term. A weakening of these restrictions, either by more competitive product markets, less bureaucratic interference, or an easing of all factor markets will help to make supply more elastic.

FIG. 11.11
ECONOMIC RENT

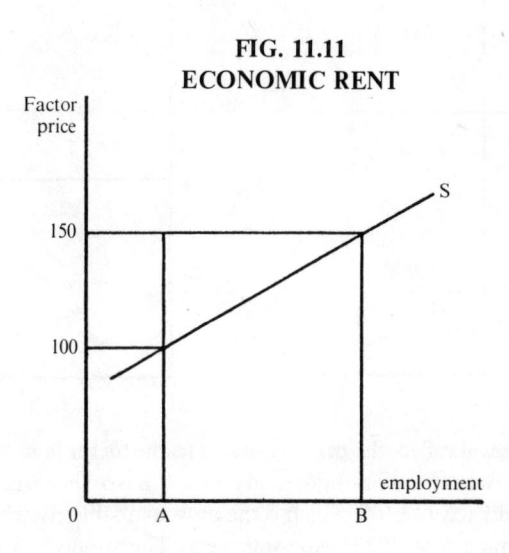

FIG. 11.12
ECONOMIC RENT & TRANSFER EARNINGS

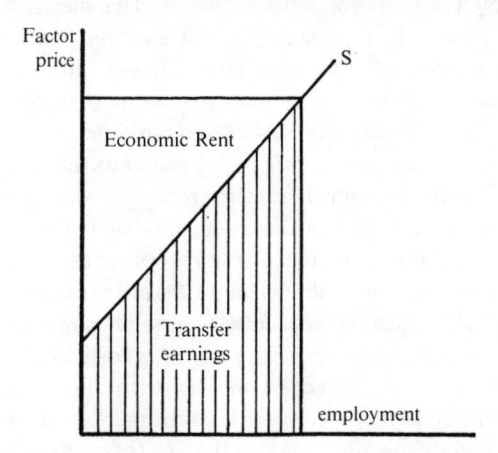

Supply Elasticity and Economic Rent (Producers' Surplus)

The Pareto definition of Economic Rent is "the amount that has to be paid over and above the minimum necessary to keep the factor of production, e.g. labour in a particular use." The minimum payment necessary is called the transfer earning

FIG. 11.13
ALL RENT

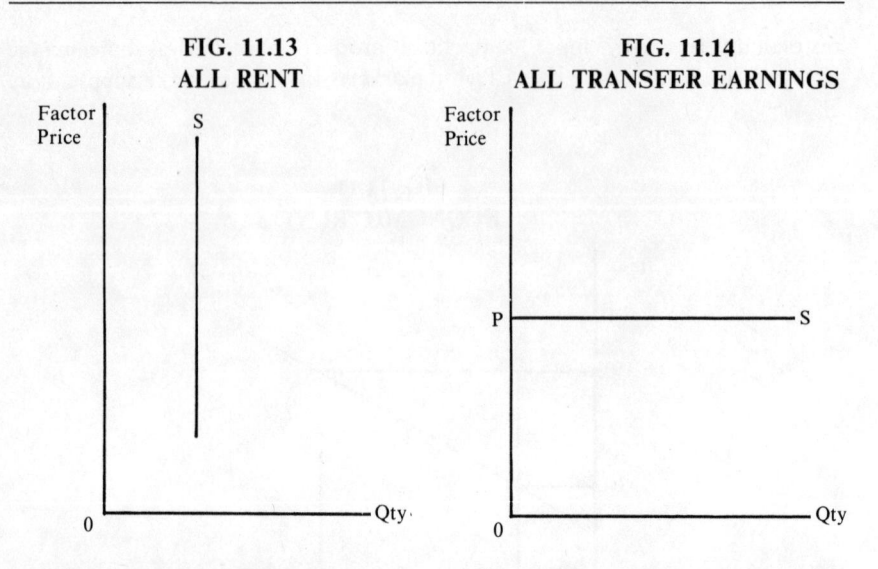

FIG. 11.14
ALL TRANSFER EARNINGS

and this amount will reflect the price available to the factor in its next best use, i.e. it reflects its alternative use or opportunity cost. If a worker earns the market rate of £150 but would accept £100, which is the most available elsewhere, then £100 is the transfer earning and £50 is economic rent. The supply schedule of a factor incorporates many similar workers who could earn different amounts elsewhere. In Fig. 11.11 A would accept £100 but B must be paid £150 so there is no economic rent for B, but £50 worth of economic rent for A. This means the area under the supply curve in Fig. 11.12 represents transfer earnings and the area above is economic rent. If a factor is fixed in use so that it has no alternative uses available, then all the payment made is in the form of an economic rent, see Fig. 11.13, whilst if the supply of a factor is perfectly elastic (zero economic rent), then all payment will be in the form of a transfer earning or will reflect its full opportunity cost, see Fig. 11.14. In this latter case, unless the factor receives a wage of op, no factors will enter the market because they can all receive around op in their next best use. This supply schedule would also reflect the long run supply of an industry with constant costs where no economic rent or abnormal profits are earned. The normal supply of output, see Fig. 11.12, reflects the fact that economic rent is abnormal profits to producers, whilst transfer earnings reflect resource costs in alternative uses. For capital, e.g. cash or money, which is mobile, then all payments are transfer earnings because unless money receives at least the market rate it will immediately move elsewhere. In the short run capital in the form of machinery, etc. in a specific use, receives a payment which is a profit or a quasi rent, after Marshall, because it has no alternative use. A computer, for example, is only able as a piece of capital to do one specific job. However, in the long run the entrepreneur can invest in different forms of machinery. Economic rent is discussed with respect to land later in the chapter.

Applications of Economic Rent

(a) *Taxation of Economic Rent*

Henry George advocated the taxation of factor rewards when they were paid all economic rent. In particular he advocated taxing the landlord earning high rents because of the particular location of a piece of land. Fig. 11.15 shows how demand increasing from d to d1 would increase the economic rent or windfall profits to a landlord who owned a piece of land by the shaded area, as price rose from p to p1. Since the factor (land) would remain in the particular use, even with as low a price as op, Henry George and others advocated the full taxation of this area because it

FIG. 11.15
TAXATION OF ECONOMIC RENT

(a)

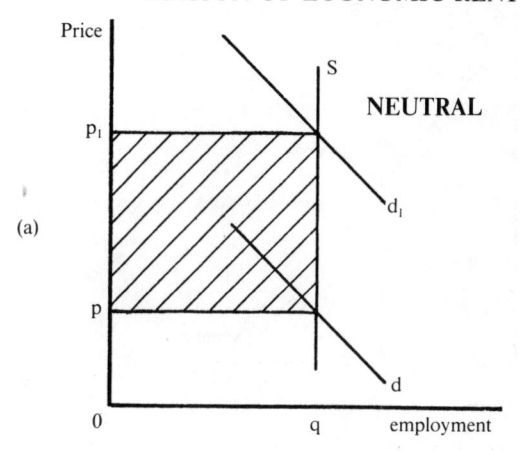

FIG. 11.16

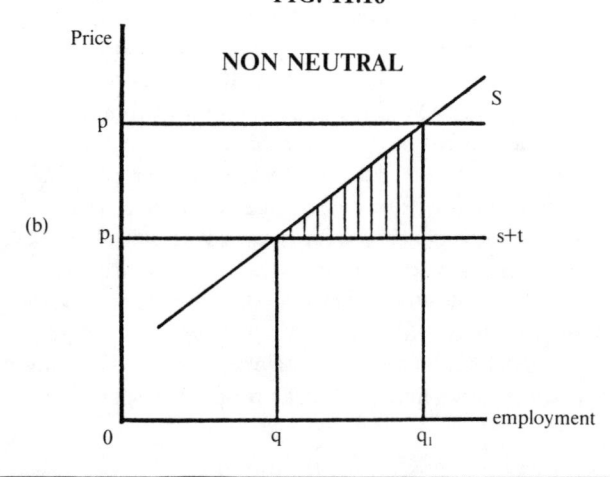

(b)

166 Factor Incomes – Wage Determinations

would not reduce factor supply from oq. Since land would not be affected by the tax in any way, i.e. it would be neutral in its impact, the general principle has developed whereby a tax on an inelastic factor is seen to be an efficient tax because it does not affect a factor's supply. However, as Fig. 11.16 illustrates, a factor supply shown by S which is then taxed has its income reduced as price falls from op to op1 and the tax effectively reduces the factor's transfer payment by the shaded area and also reduces the supply of the factor from oq1 to oq. In this case the tax is non-neutral and can have an impact upon the efficiency of a factor market. This is discussed in Chapter 14.

FIG. 11.17
COMPETITIVE v MONOPSONISTIC LABOUR MARKETS

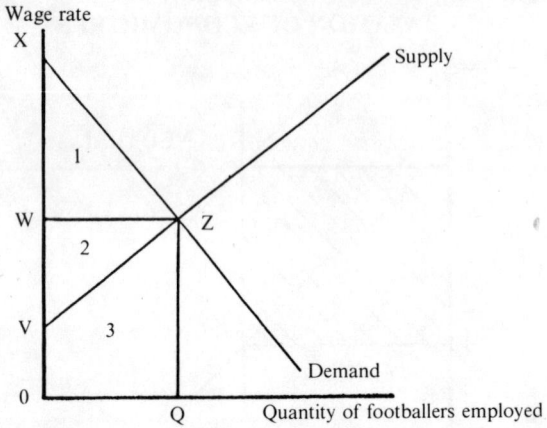

(b) *Competitive and Monopsonistic Factor Markets, e.g. Footballers' Wages*

Footballers receive the market wage of ow, in Fig. 11.17, which represents a competitive market. In this case area 3 reflects the transfer earnings, area 2 economic rent to the footballers and area 1 the residual income received by the football clubs used to pay other factor inputs. If wage discrimination is now introduced by the employers who form themselves into a monopsonistic league willing to pay only the footballers their transfer earnings, i.e. area 3, then the employers will now receive area 1 plus area 2 and thus their profits will rise. The footballers could respond by forming themselves into a union or players association and negotiating a standard wage of ow payable to all footballers in the league. Otherwise competition from overseas for home based players could also reduce the power of the employers so they may be willing to pay a standard wage of ow rather than risk losing all their players to overseas clubs. Individual contracts of employment and different wage payments are used in many industries to exercise wage discrimination and gain extra profits on the part of the employer.

Factor Incomes – Wage Determinations 167

CHAPTER 11 Research

1. *Compile a list, from local and national newspapers or by visiting your local employment agencies, of occupations together with their corresponding salaries. Identify the factors you feel explain such wage differences.*

2. *Use local sources, e.g. newspapers, etc., to determine where most job vacancies occur. Why do you think this is so?*

3. *Do workers in your area commute or travel to work? Why do they do this and not move closer to the work? Identify the main reasons, e.g. house prices, children at school, etc.*

4. *Is there any evidence of workers doing similar jobs in your area being paid different wages?*

DATA RESPONSE QUESTIONS

Question 1

Factor Markets and the Profit Maximising User

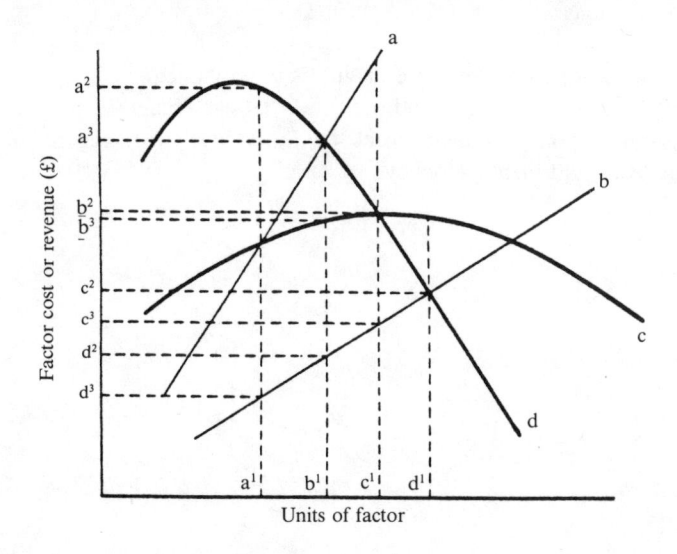

1. Identify using the diagram (i) marginal factor cost (ii) average factor cost (iii) marginal revenue product (iv) average revenue product.
2. Identify factor employment and wage levels the profit maximising employer employs when (i) competitive (ii) monopolist conditions.
3. Show the return to the factor, the entrepreneur, other factors for 2(i) and 2(ii).

Question 2

The Market for Business Studies Teachers

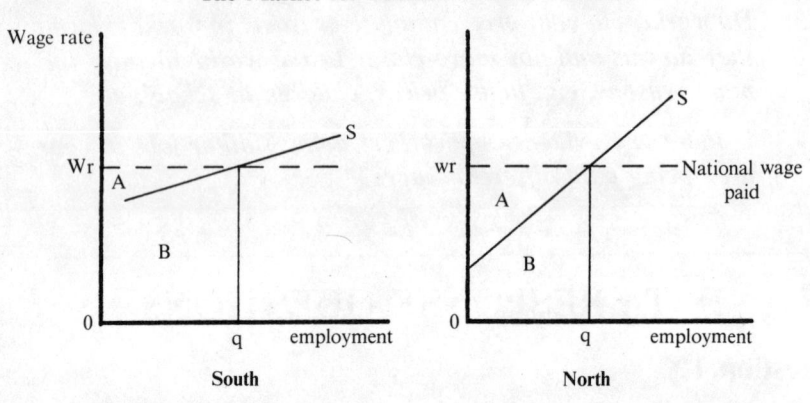

South

North

It is often alleged that market conditions for different teachers vary in the North and South of England.

1. On what basis could the above diagrams be explained?
2. Identify the areas A and B and indicate what each diagram shows.
3. How might policy makers react to the above with regard to wage negotiations and taxation policy?

Question 3

The U.K. Labour Market

The labour market in this country is one of the most studied but probably least understood of all markets. There are a wide range of views about the nature of the labour market. On the one side there are the "equilibrium theorists", who argue that the labour market is not dissimilar to competitive markets, like that for cabbages or foreign exchange. At least they say it has more in common with such markets than is commonly supposed. Thus the price in each market, be it cabbages or labour, is determined by the equality of supply and demand. Equilibrium theorists argue that real wages adjust quickly to changes in supply and demand.

An important part of the equilibrium approach is the explanation it suggests for the pattern of rising real wages and unemployment. The explanation advanced is couched in terms of upward (leftward) shifts in labour supply, these reductions in the supply of labour being the result of increases in the value of social security benefits and of increasing pressure on the labour markets by trade union activity. In an equilibrium model, measured unemployment is then explained by the rational supply decisions by workers, although it is also recognised that there will be frictional unemployment even in a competitive labour market. Such frictional unemployment is, of course, an almost inevitable feature of a flexible, changing economy, and as such is not evidence of problems in the labour market. In the main, the argument put forward by the equilibrium theorists is a supply-side explanation of changes in measured unemployment. Put another way, they argue that the natural or equilibrium rate of unemployment increased substantially during the 1980's, largely due to these supply side effects.

The other or opposite view of the labour market is that it is more or less permanently in disequilibrium, with the supply of labour not being brought into equality with the demand, by smooth quickly adjusting real wages. According to this alternative, real wages are rigid, especially downwards. Hence a fall in the demand for labour, for example, will be reflected in an increase in unemployment, which is largely involuntary, and which will tend to persist. "Disequilibrium theorists" generally advocate demand reflation as a means of reducing unemployment.

Source: Lloyds Bank Review, number 165, July 1987.

a) Explain the similarities between the market for cabbages and the market for labour.
b) Use a diagram to explain the patterns of rising real wages and unemployment to the labour market.
c) Discuss the alternative policies to reduce unemployment likely to be advocated by the two groups of theorists in the passage.

12 LABOUR & LAND MARKETS — INDUSTRIAL APPLICATION

AIMS: To define, explain and discuss
- The role of Trades Unions
- The impact of unions on labour markets
- Non-clearing markets and mrp
- Land markets and their behaviour

KEY CONCEPTS
Productivity deals, wage differences, non-competitive groups, Ricardo and rent, bid rent, urban yields.

A. Trades Unions — Role and History

Trades Unions are workers organisations set up to:-

(i) Improve the pay and working conditions, e.g. safety, of its members.

(ii) Reduce wage discrimination between, for example, male and female workers.

(iii) Bargain collectively at a local or national level on behalf of its members.

(iv) Influence the economic and social policy of governments.

(v) Increase the promotion prospects, opportunities and security of its members.

(vi) Safeguard and protect members against dismissal and ensure that benefits are paid to members who are ill, injured or unemployed.

Trades unions developed in the U.K. in the 19th century especially in such basic industries as steel, coal, shipbuilding and agriculture primarily to improve working conditions and safeguard pay and employment where possible. In the 20th century unions also flourished in the newer consumer goods and service sectors, for example, teachers, civil servants, engineering workers, and overall union membership reached a total of 13 million or around 54% of the workforce by 1979. Subsequently membership has fallen mainly due to anti-union legislation of the Thatcher era, see Table 12.1, unemployment and the increase in non-unionised industries. In the 1970's trades unions with the Labour government played an important role in formulating economic and social policy but since 1979 governments have largely ignored unions in forming policies and have specifically legislated to outlaw such practices as secondary picketing and the closed shop.

TABLE 12.1
TRADE UNION REFORM

Measure	Purpose
Employment Act (1980)	To give employers legal remedies against secondary picketing and secondary action.
Employment Act (1982)	To make closed shop agreements slightly more 'democratic'; to outlaw 'union labour only' requirements; to give employers legal remedies against political strikes; and to make trade unions (rather than officials) liable for damages for unlawful strikes.
Trade Union Act (1984)	To extend democracy in trade through, *inter alia*, the introduction of secret ballots before strike action is taken.

FIG. 12.1
UNIONS AND LABOUR MARKET

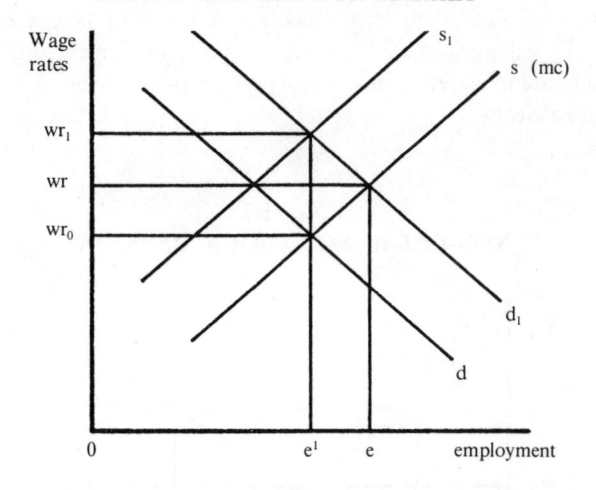

The Impact of Trades Unions upon Labour Markets

Using Fig. 12.1 the influence of trades unions can be analysed as follows:-

(i) *Negotiating Productivity Deals*. If unions agree with management practices designed to improve productivity this will have the impact of shifting the original equilibrium wage/employment levels of owr/oe^1 to owr/oe because productivity deals increase the demand for labour from d to d1 in a competitive industry. Many argue that closed shop agreements are a form of productivity deal because management only has to negotiate with one employee representative which saves time and rationalises practices.

(ii) *Controlling the Supply of Labour.* In the short term the union can, by closed shop agreements, limit labour supply to oe^1 in Fig. 12.1, so that the wage rate rises to owr$_1$ when demand increases to d1. In the long run inflexible practices and determined entry controls exercised by a union could even reduce supply to S1 which will maintain long term wage rates at wr1. Some claim these practices have resulted in unionised labour earning 11.5% more than their non-union counterparts in industries which are non-competitive:

(iii) *Counteracting Monopsonistic Employers.* As discussed in Chapter 11 a single employer setting wages to marginal costs rather than supply will employ oe^1 at a wage rate of wro as shown in Fig. 12.1. A union entering this market can counteract monopsonistic power and set the union rate of owr which, with a monopsonistic demand of d1 will also increase employment to oe.

B. **Non-Clearing Labour Markets**

In the labour market illustrated in Fig. 12.2 wage flexibility ensures that the free market clears and there is an equilibrium wage rate and employment level of wo/Lo. However, in the real world, labour markets do not always clear so it is possible for a wage of w2 to exist which means there is a permanent surplus of labour L2 – L1 willing to work but unable to find employment at this wage level. The following are micro economic factors advanced to explain why some labour markets fail to clear:-

FIG. 12.2
NON-CLEARING LABOUR MARKETS

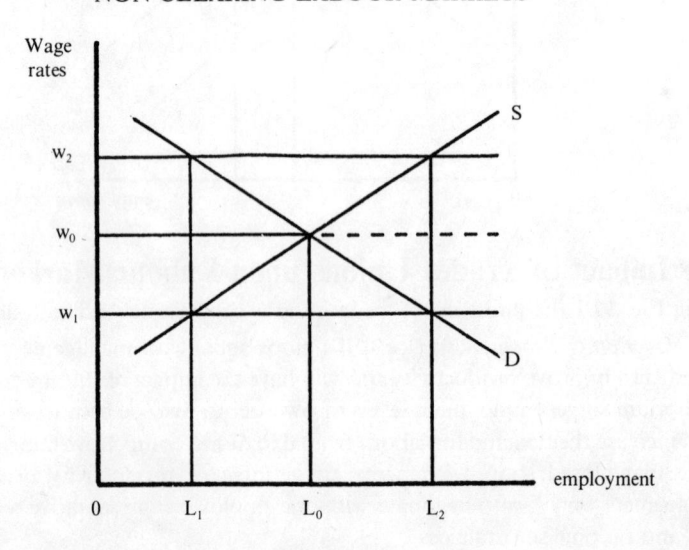

(a) *Minimum Wage Agreements.* If a minimum industrial wage of w2 was established this would not enable the labour market to clear at wo, i.e. L2 - L1 are involuntarily unemployed. In the U.K. "Whitley Councils" were set up originally to maintain minimum wage levels in traditionally low paid industries, often dominated by monopsonistic employers. They were abolished in the 1980's which led many to fear that wages would fall to wo which may well have been near poverty levels. In the absence of legislation a strong trade union could also negotiate minimum wages at w2 and/or limit labour supply to OL1. This would have the same effect as legislation establishing minimum industrial levels.

(b) *Entry Barriers by Firms and Existing Employees.* If there are existing entry barriers in product markets (see Chapter 8, Fig. 8.2), because of imperfect market conditions, labour employment could reduce to OL1 with a wage of ow2. Though theoretically the employment of more labour will reduce wage rates to owo and hence clear the market, which has a monopolistic output at OL_1, it may be difficult or expensive to recruit more labour; or those in a job may threaten industrial action to those employers if new recruits are taken on. This may be an important threat if monopoly profits are high. The cost of recruitment and selecting the correct applicants, i.e. L0 - L1, will be high because often there is a lack of reliable information regarding their past job achievements. This means employers are prepared to pay existing workers, i.e. OL_1, a wage in excess of the wage workers will on the whole accept, i.e. W2 rather than W0. This can lead to those looking for a job at a wage between W2 and W0 leaving the market. In the long run this could aggravate the labour market generally and increase vacancy rates for any given level of employment, i.e. the Beveridge curve. This is the inverse relationship between unemployment and vacancy rates and has shifted outwards from the origin over the long term which tends to support the above analysis.

(c) *Non-Competing Groups.* Because labour is not similar, the excess supply or shortage in one market may not influence the other, i.e. it is possible to have an excess supply of history teachers and at the same time vacancies for mathematicians within the educational sector.

Wage Discrimination

Wage discrimination exists when the same job pays differently depending upon the employee's sex, status, creed or religion, etc. It is alleged that in the U.K. wage discrimination exists with respect to colour or sex or between unionised and non-unionised labour doing the same work. The result of this discrimination is that unfair wage differences occur because free market forces are unable to operate. Fig. 12.3 illustrates wage discrimination between male and female workers. The labour market operates inefficiently in such a way that men are paid owm, and women receive oww because of the lower discriminated demand of dw. If discrimination disappeared, due perhaps to equal opportunity legislation, the combined demand and supply forces operate after discrimination to determine a

174 Labour and Land Markets – Industrial Application

FIG. 12.3
ECONOMICS OF SEX DISCRIMINATION

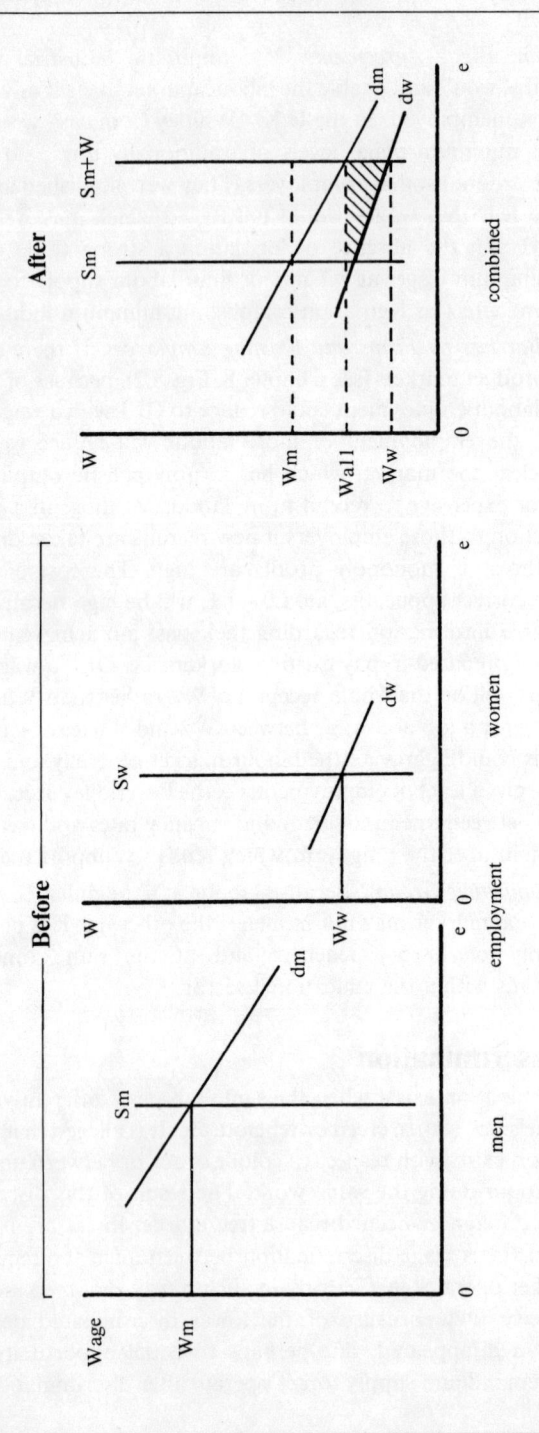

general wage level of OW all. This is lower than the male wage rate before discrimination and the extra income now paid to women in the market is shown by the shaded area, i.e. there is a redistribution of income from men to women.

Marginal Revenue Product Theory and the Labour Market

Although the mrp theory explains the relationship between wage rates and productivity it suffers from some major drawbacks.

(i) MRP theory assumes market operations determine wage and employment levels. However, in the public sector, e.g. health and education, no such global markets exist. This means neither product nor product prices are obvious and furthermore within health there may be many separate sub markets which lead to complications. Lastly, it is very difficult to define the output of the health service and hence quantify it.

(ii) The theory assumes all labour in a market is identical. This is rarely the case and has led some to suggest each person constitute their own unique labour market.

(iii) Immobility of labour between regions and occupations exists which distorts market movements. This can also occur if people are unaware of the opportunities that exist elsewhere.

(iv) Wealth is a major source of income differences. Since much wealth is inherited it is outside market analysis. Inherited wealth allows some groups privileged access to the labour market, e.g. the 'old school tie' in the legal profession or in the city.

TABLE 12.2
U.K. LABOUR STATISTICS 1979, 1984, 1989

Manpower and incomes		1979	1984	1989
Total working population (June)	'000s	26,627	27,265	28,606
as a % of population		47.3	48.3	50.0
Total employees in employment (June)	'000s	23,173	21,238	22,826
of which men	'000s	13,487	11,888	11,996
women	'000s	9,686	9,350	10,830
Wholly unemployed (June)	'000s	1,235	3,030	1,799
as % of working population		4.6	11.1	3.1
Vacancies (annual average)	'000s	243.0	246.2	218.4
Industrial stoppages	m working days lost	29.1	27.1	4.1
Sickness (6)	m working days lost	385.3	324.9	362.4
Weekly hours worked by men (7)		43.2	42.8	43.4
Weekly hours worked by women (7)		37.2	38.1	38.6
Average weekly earnings of men (7)	£	98.28	157.50	229.87
adjusted for inflation to 1989 prices	£	199.68	203.41	229.87
Average weekly earnings of women (7)	£	58.44	96.30	139.93
adjusted for inflation to 1989 prices	£	118.74	124.37	139.93
Income from employment as % of gdp (3)		67.6	64.7	64.6
Gross trading profits as % of gdp (3)		13.0	16.1	16.7

Source: 'Lloyds Bank Profile of Britain 1990'.

(v) Differences between wage rates in occupations are often the result of historical precedent, the social norm, or political expediency, e.g. paying nurses more as an election approaches.

(vi) The theory assumes it is possible for the employer to estimate marginal revenue product. However, in the real world the employer may not know or be able to estimate mrp.

(vii) Alternative wage theories stress the importance of industrial profit levels as well as industrial power and the marginal cost, marginal benefit equilibrium for both unions and businesses in settling wage disputes.

Table 12.2 provides selected statistics regarding U.K. labour markets 1979, 1984 and 1989.

Market Theory and Land Prices

Ricardo and Rent

Ricardo analysed high land and food prices at the time of the Napoleonic Wars in Europe in the 1800s when the U.K. was blockaded and unable to import cheap corn from Europe. He showed that with a fixed supply of agricultural land and a rising demand for food, land rents and hence food prices, were bound to rise, see Fig. 11.8. These high land prices could be viewed as taxable windfall profits, see Henry George, though Ricardo saw this profit as providing the basis for future capital investment in other industrial sectors. Ricardo identified the return as a rent and in terms of previous analysis it can be seen as a form of economic rent which increases as demand shifts to the right in Fig. 11.15. The conclusion of his analysis was that high land prices were the result and not the cause of high food prices.

The Demand for Agricultural and Urban Land

(a) *Agricultural Land Values and Ricardo*

As a land owner, Ricardo analysed the demand for land and hence its value in terms of the value of output it was able to produce, e.g. the corn yield of land. Initially the best land unit would be cultivated and its yield, and hence the rent it could command, would be high as Fig. 12.4 shows. The next piece of land (unit 2) would have a lower yield and hence value, and so on until at a rent of op it is just worth cultivating the marginal piece of land, unit 4. Rising food prices could push up the yield of all four pieces of land and hence at op the marginal piece of land now increases in value. This analysis is similar to diminishing marginal revenue product theory with land as the variable product, though Ricardo never discussed land values in these specific terms.

(b) *Urban Land Values*

In modern urban land value theory agricultural land yield is replaced by the concept that urban yields, or derived profits, depend upon locating close to the city centre (market), and values generally decrease as property locates away from this

FIG. 12.4
PRODUCTIVITY OF LAND

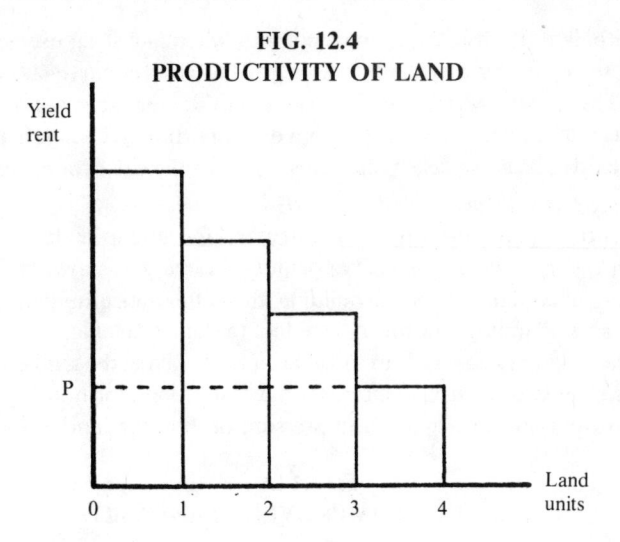

Yield rent vs *Land units*, with bars at 0-1, 1-2, 2-3, 3-4 of decreasing height; P marked by a dashed horizontal line at the level of the 3-4 bar.

FIG. 12.5
LAND VALUES AND USES

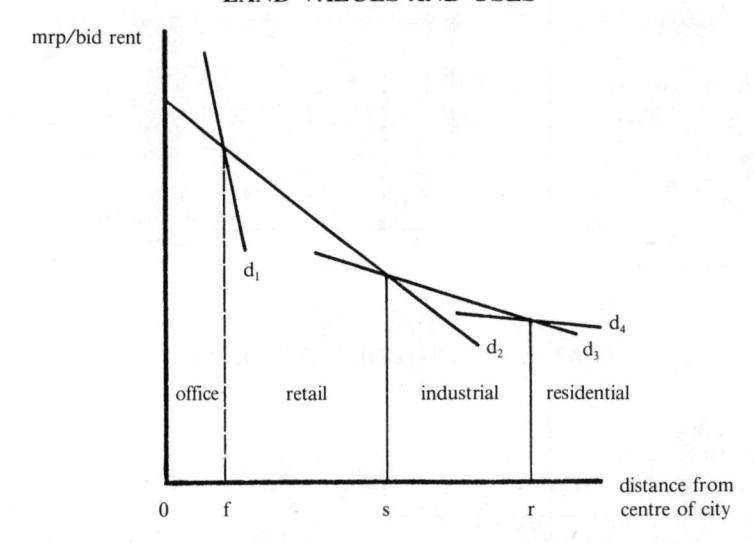

mrp/bid rent vs distance from centre of city; demand schedules d_1 (office, 0 to f), d_2 (retail, f to s), d_3 (industrial, s to r), d_4 (residential, beyond r).

central position. At the same time land has different uses, shown in Fig. 12.5, as office use (d1), retail (d2), industrial (d3) and residential (d4). The revenue produced by each use is reflected in the shape and height of each demand schedule. Office use can afford to bid high rents in order to be at the centre because yields or profits are also high, but they fall dramatically as offices locate further from the centre. Other uses with their own corresponding yields can afford rents as shown by particular demand schedules and as uses move from the centre then retail takes

178 Labour and Land Markets – Industrial Application

over or outbids office use, at of, until point os when industrial use now outbids retail, and so on. Joining up these points gives a bid rent curve shown as dx in Fig. 12.6. The impact of improved transport in the area increases overall yields and rents, e.g. dy, and in this case there is a disproportionate change in land values as suburb land values rise faster than those close to the city centre. See Fig. 12.6.

(c) *Planning Controls and Windfall Profits*

In the absence of planning controls the demand for land to build houses would compete in the land market against agricultural use and as shown in Fig. 12.7 it would use up to oq_1 land for house building, thereafter agricultural land use is the most profitable. Planning controls now reduce the land available for housing to oq and this scarce land is now bid up in value to Lp so giving the landlords windfall profits, see shaded area. It also increases the cost of land for housing and hence prices rise so putting further demand pressure on housing land elsewhere.

FIG. 12.6
IMPACT OF IMPROVED TRANSPORT

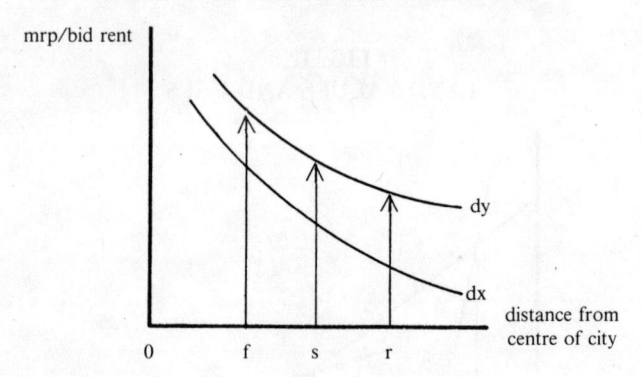

FIG. 12.7
PLANNING CONTROLS AND PROFITS

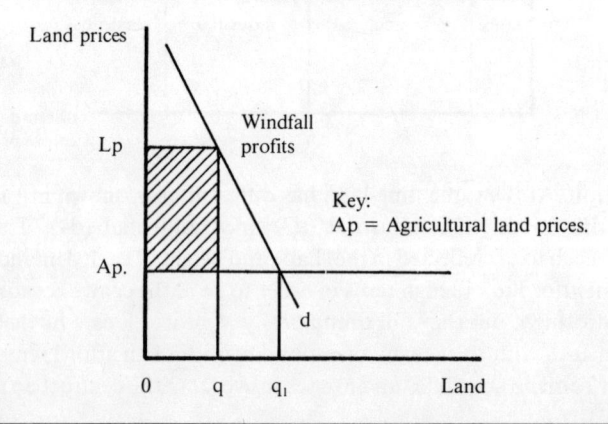

Key:
Ap = Agricultural land prices.

CHAPTER 12 Research

1. *Try to find out how much land costs in your area – use local estate agents, etc.*

2. *Discover how far the cost of land influences the price of houses. Again use estate agents and obtain local house prices, office and industrial rents and compare different locations and their respective prices or leases. Identify locational, transport, market, social and other factors which may play a part in influencing these prices.*

DATA RESPONSE QUESTIONS

Question 1 — Labour Market Equilibrium

The diagram shows marginal cost, marginal product of labour and the wage rate for the firm.

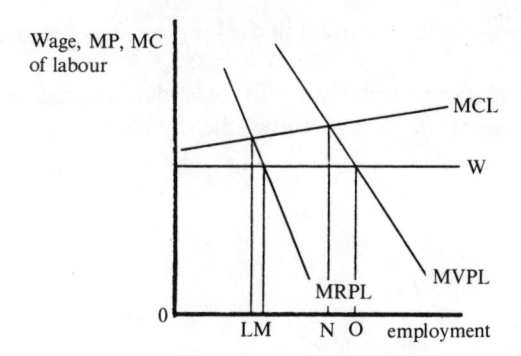

Show the profit maximising output level for each of the following:-
1. A firm facing a downward sloping demand curve for its product with a competitive labour market.
2. A firm facing a downward sloping demand for its product which acts as a monopsonist in the labour market.
3. A competitive firm facing a competitive labour market.
4. A firm unable to influence the price of its output which acts as a monopsonist in the labour market.

Question 2 — The Demand for Land

A region has two sectors: industrial and residential. The diagram shows their demand schedules (D1 and DR), SS shows the fixed supply of land.

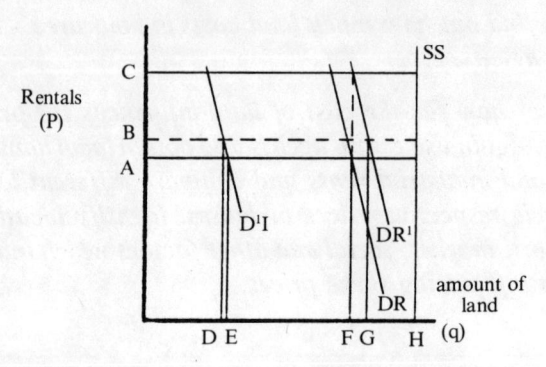

The government decides to subsidise house purchase and this shifts demand for residential land to DR^1.

1. Given the equilibrium rental show initial allocation of land.
2. After the subsidy has been given show the rental rates in the sectors in the short run.
3. What will be the equilibrium position in the long run in terms of (p/q) for both sectors.
4. Show the short term gain in rental values to the landlords of residential land.
5. What will be the impact in the long run of the subsidy?

13 CAPITAL: NATURE AND ANALYSIS

AIMS: To define, explain and discuss
- The nature and role of capital
- Capitalisation and discounted cash flow
- The businessman's investment decision
- Capital, growth and interest theories

KEY CONCEPTS

Net present value, depreciation, yield, discount factor, marginal value product of capital, productivity of capital, loanable funds theory, rate of profit/return on capital.

Capital is represented in an economy by the stock of machinery, plant, offices, hospitals, roads and houses, etc. owned by the public and private sectors. Companies identify capital in the form of fixed or current assets within the balance sheet and these are used to produce a profit. The stock of capital is used to provide the flow of capital services which overall increase company profits and private and public sector benefits. These benefits take the form of improved housing services,

FIG. 13.1 SHARE OF FIXED INVESTMENT (U.K.)

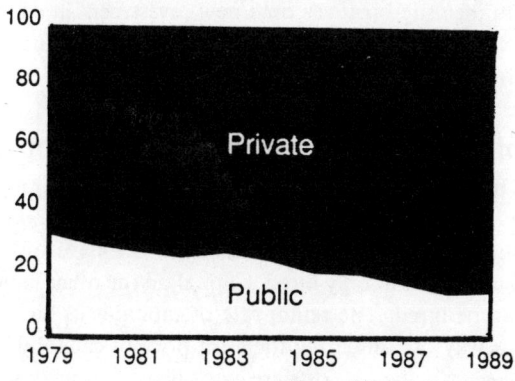

Source: Lloyds Bank Economic Profile of G.B. 1990.

better roads or transport facilities and a steady flow of health and educational services. The share of fixed investment provided by private and public sectors are shown in Fig. 13.1

Capital formation in the U.K.
Manufacturing industry accounted for 13 per cent of gross domestic fixed capital formation in 1989. Transport and communication took up 8 per cent and petroleum and natural gas 8 per cent. Leasing expanded rapidly as a means of finance in the 1980s and now accounts for 14 per cent of manufacturers' capital expenditure. Since 1979, the share of public sector investment as a proportion of total investment has fallen sharply, because of tight control of public expenditure.

Broken down by type of asset, plant and machinery takes up 42 per cent of gross domestic fixed capital formation, vehicles, ships and aircraft 10 per cent, housing 18 per cent and other construction the remaining 30 per cent. Machinery and equipment investment accounted for 8.0 per cent of gdp in 1989. This is comparable with other countries such as the USA (7.5 per cent) and West Germany (also 7.5 per cent).

The net capital stock of the U.K. was valued at £1,147.8bn at the end of 1987 in terms of the current replacement cost of fixed assets. The book value of stocks held at the end of 1988 was £96.5bn.

Definitions
The total annual increase in the capital stock is defined as the Gross Domestic Fixed Capital Formation (GDFCF) plus the net addition to manufacturers stocks. After deductions for capital wear and tear (depreciation) the residue is net investment flow identified over a specific time period. This is represented as the purchase, by the business and public sectors, of additional units of capital to add to the existing capital stock. This means that in the short term the capital stock is usually fixed and inelastic but over time new investment in capital increases the total quantity of stock as long as the extra revenue of additional capital stock exceeds the extra cost of provision.

The Price of Capital, i.e. Asset Price or Rent Charge?
Labour is hired by the businessman so the wage rate is a hire or rental rate which is matched by an equivalent flow of labour services or product according to marginal revenue product theory. Labour does not have an asset price since people cannot be owned but only hired. Capital on the other hand can be bought outright or it can be hired. The rental rate of capital is its hire rate. This means there has to be a way of comparing the asset price of capital with its future hire price, in order to see whether its costs are equivalent to its income. The analysis to

do this is as follows:- Assume an asset (V) receives a fixed income of £1000 (A) for ever and the current interest rate is 10% (i). Then the present capital value (V) equals $V = \frac{A}{i}$, i.e. $\frac{£1000}{.10} = £10,000$. This means that, assuming no other factors are taken into account, and if there is no inflation or tax, a current capital asset priced at £10,000 is exactly equal to a permanent hire cost or rate of £1000 per annum at 10% interest cost. If, however, all prices, including rental prices, are rising by 5% annually (inflation) then the real interest rate is the nominal rate of 10% less 5% inflation, i.e. 5%. In this case the real value of the capital asset is not £10,000 but $\frac{£1000}{.05}$, i.e. £20,000. The rest of the analysis assumes nominal and real interest rates are the same, i.e. inflation is zero.

The Price of Capital — Present Value Analysis

The future capital value (Sm) of a sum of money, either representing a cost or a profit, with a present day value of £100 (P) can be calculated if the time period (n) and the interest rate (i) are known by using the compound formula of $Sm = P \times (1 + i)^n$. In the case of £100 invested for 3 years at 10% interest, this will be £100 × (1.10)³ which equals £133. Discounting is this capitalisation process in reverse. Instead of asking the future value of a present sum, we calculate the present capital value of a known future sum. The present value of £100 to be received in two years' time at a 10% cost of interest means that we are giving up the interest on £100 for 2 years, so the amount representing this foregone interest or opportunity cost should be taken off or discounted from the £100 in order to find its current capital value. The actual value is £82.64 which is obtained from the discount tables, see Table 18.2(2), or by using the formula:-

$$\text{Present capital value (P.V.)} = \frac{R \times 1}{(1+i)^n}$$

with P = £100, i = 10%, and n = 2 years. If the investment produced a stream of rentals or costs of £100 per annum over the next 5 years, the present value sum would be, using the formula = $\frac{£100}{(1+.1)} + \frac{£100}{(1+i)^2} + \frac{£100}{(1+i)^3} \ldots \frac{£100}{(1+i)^5}$ i.e. £379. In the case of a constant amount, e.g. £100, the cumulative discount tables in Table 18.2(4) can be used. So £100 × 3.79 = £379. The value 3.79 is the cumulative addition of the discount factors given by $\frac{1}{(1+i)}$ over 5 years and will be symbolised as Σ df. When costs or rental incomes are constant, then the present value of the capitalised stream is equivalent to PV = R × Σ df where rentals are constant and time and interest rates are given. In the above £100 × 3.79 = £379, n was for 1 to 5 years and the interest rate was 10% (real). Using the formula allows us to calculate, by rearranging the symbols, other useful concepts in investment economics:-

184 Capital: Nature & Analysis

(a) *Equivalent Rental or Costs Over Time.* If the present capital cost is £379 then how much would this represent on an annualised basis if the investment lasts 5 years and the current interest (capital cost) is 10%. Rearranging the formula we obtain rentals as the subject, i.e. $R = \frac{PV}{\Sigma df}$ or $\frac{£379}{3.79}$ = £100 p.a. This is the equivalent annual cost of an investment of £379 over 5 years at 10% interest.

(b) *Pay Back Time or Yield*

The pay back time (n) or yield (i) can also be calculated if the annualised income and capital costs are known simply by rearranging the formula, i.e. $\Sigma df = \frac{PV}{R}$ for some (1) pay back time or (2) interest rate or yield. So for

(1) $= \frac{£379}{£100}$ = 3.79 at 10% which gives 5 years pay back time by using the tables.

(2) Yields can also be calculated using the formula so, $\frac{£379}{£100}$ = 3.79 which over a 5 year pay back time represents a 10% yield, using the tables.

Calculations can be checked by using the tables in the Table 18.2(4) When uncertainty is introduced into the analysis then the simple methods to deal with problems of risk are:-

(i) Increase the capital cost proportionately.

(ii) Reduce the time period, i.e. go for earliest possible pay back.

(iii) Increase the interest rate charge which will then give a lower discounted income value.

(iv) Reduce net income benefits of those investment projects which have the highest risk factors.

More sophisticated techniques such as 'most/least' likely outcomes and also probability analysis lie beyond the scope of this book.

The Businessman's Demand for Capital Assets or Services

The rental rate or cost of capital services is treated analytically in the same manner as the wage rate and according to marginal revenue product theory this rate or cost will be equated to the value of the extra revenue product produced by the unit of capital employed. This is known as the marginal value product capital, or MVPK.* As more capital units are hired or bought marginal product declines, due to diminishing returns to the variable factor, so the MVPK schedule is downward sloping. The product price to the hirer of capital is given since he sells into a competitive market where the product price is determined. Furthermore, since the capital hirer is unable to influence the capital market, the cost or price of hiring the capital is given by overall market forces, he is also a price taker in terms of factor costs. Figs. 13.2 and 13.3 show the equilibrium situation in both the

---

*Also referred to as the marginal efficiency of capital (M.E.C.) or marginal revenue product of capital (mrpc).

Capital: Nature & Analysis 185

FIG. 13.2
THE CAPITAL MARKET
(A)

FIG. 13.3
BUSINESSMAN'S DEMAND FOR CAPITAL
(B)

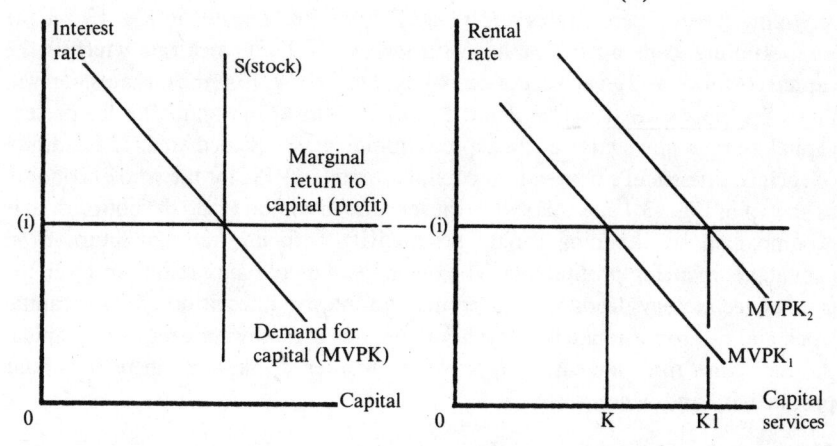

FIG. 13.4
RETURN ON CAPITAL (PROFIT)

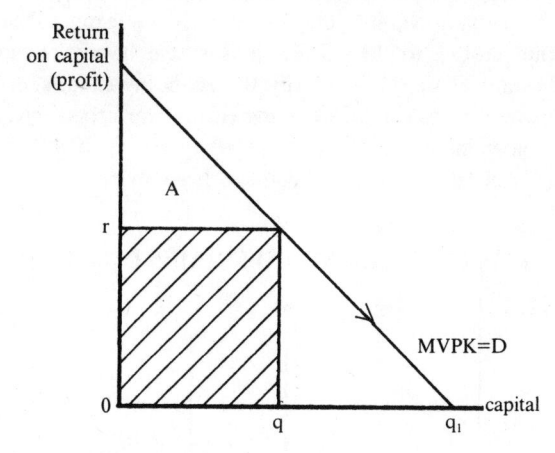

capital market A and for the individual hirer of capital services B. The overall capital market determines the cost of capital, i.e. the interest in real riskless terms, and this, given the MVPK of the businessman, determines how much capital he can afford, i.e. level OK. The businessman can either buy assets up to OK or, by using present value analysis, estimate the equivalent capital cost of hiring these services. In the event of a rise in the product price, or an increase in the productivity of the capital used, then $MVPK_1$ will shift to MVPK2, in Fig. 13.3 and the businessman will increase his demand for capital from OK to OK1. At this point the marginal cost equals marginal revenue product. In the real world, the individual businessman's demand for capital will thus reflect capital costs or higher rentals, the profitability of hiring capital (MVPK) as well as expectations regarding future interest rates and risks. The MVPK schedule in Fig. 13.3 is the businessman's demand for capital with respect to the interest rate which is the capital cost. For any given cost of capital, i.e. Or, see Fig. 13.4, the businessman will invest oq units so that the discounted future profits are just equal to the present capital asset or hire charge of the capital equipment, see shaded area. The addition of each businessman's demand for capital gives an MVPK for the whole economy as shown in Fig. 13.4 and this shows the increase in capital along the bottom axis is accompanied by declining capital productivity or falling rates of return from capital, i.e. reducing profitability. The outcome of increasing capital use, given the state of technology, leads to zero profits and interest rates at oq_1, a large capital stock and disproportionately low output rates due to diminishing returns to capital. At the same time increasing capital per worker is likely to increase labour productivity and hence wage levels.

Economic Growth and Investment (see Fig. 13.5)

In the long term new investment opportunities, made available by new waves of technical innovation, work to shift the MVPK or demand for capital to the right, i.e. d to d1 to d2. These opportunities may occur at the same rate as the increase in the long term capital stock s to s1 to s2 and in this case the cost of capital and its return remain constant at or. Dynamically the economy experiences short run falls in profitability, r to r_1, as capital stock increases from s to s1, given d, until a new wave of technology increases capital productivity, d to d_1. This process pushes up profit rates and capital returns once again increase to or.

FIG. 13.5
LONG RUN CAPITAL AND INVESTMENT GROWTH

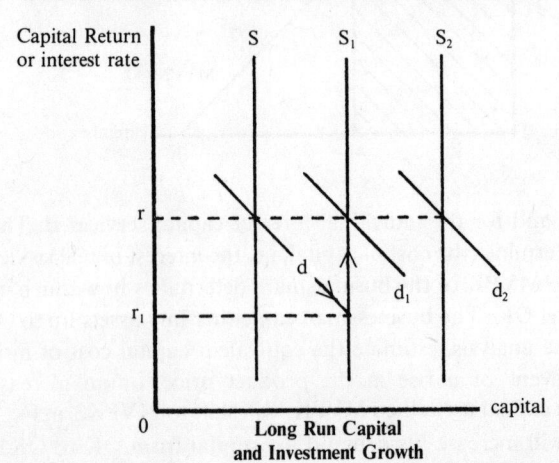

FIG. 13.6
FACTORY UNITS (PLANNING CONTROLS)

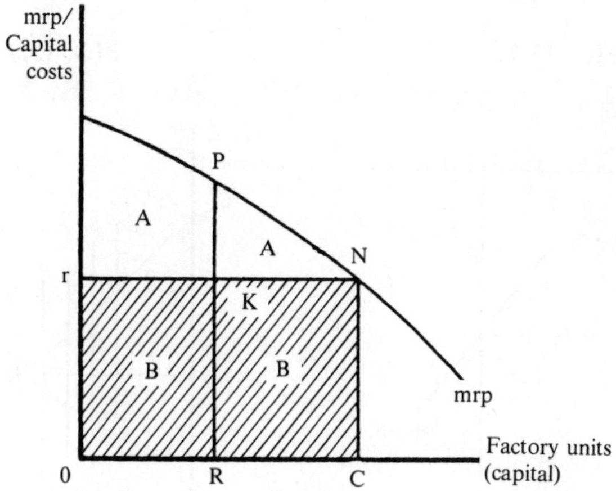

Applications of Capital Analysis

(a) *Factory Units and Planning Controls, Fig. 13.6*

Assume a businessman has a piece of land, a fixed factor, on which he can build a number of factory units. This means capital is now a variable factor. According to the mrp theory, factory units will be built on the land up to the point where the marginal revenue product, in terms of discounted rentals, will be equal to the long term capital cost. In Fig. 13.6 this will be at OC units at or cost. Capital investment is represented by shaded area B with A representing the profit, land rents and other factor returns. If planning controls are introduced forbidding building beyond OR units, then profit maximisation will not occur. Area RKNC represents the cut back in investment and area PKN the fall in land values when only OR units are built.

(b) *The Capital Market in the Short and Long Run, Fig. 13.7*

In the short run the economy has inherited a given stock of capital from previous investment decisions. The intersection of this stock S with the current demand for investment gives the real riskless interest rate at 3%, i.e. lenders receive and borrowers find their interest rate and returns on investment (profit) just equal to 3% in a riskless and inflation free world, see Fig. 13.7. If risk varied between projects then so will the rate of return and capital costs (see below). In the long run as people go on saving loanable funds and thus accumulating capital, they will save more as interest rates rise and less as interest rates fall. The long run supply of capital is shown as S in Fig. 13.8 together with short run supply schedules of S to S4. At 3% the long run supply of capital (saving) exceeds demand. This means in the long run people desire to accumulate more capital so in short run periods the capital stock increases from S to S1. This process moves the short run supply to a long run equilibrium at 2%. The real rate of return and interest costs move

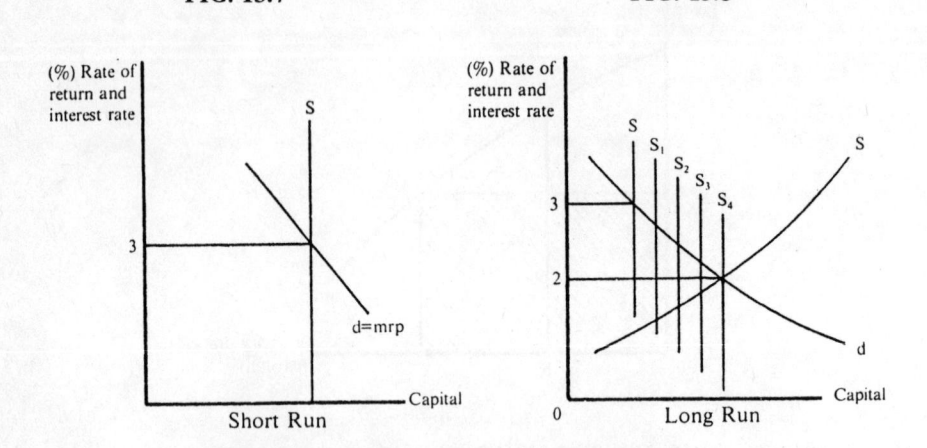

FIG. 13.7 **FIG. 13.8**

CAPITAL MARKET : SHORT & LONG RUN EQUILIBRIUM (RISKLESS/ZERO INFLATION)

downwards in the long run towards 2% because of long run diminishing returns to capital. However, should long run demand (d) shift upwards because of overall improvement in technology, etc., then long run profit returns and interest rates will also increase from 2%. In the real world the return on capital, i.e. profit, will incorporate a variety of factors. The 2 or 3% return discussed above reflects a riskless return and a time preference payment to savers when inflation and business risk are zero. Returns in the real world incorporate a payment to offset the cost of depreciation on capital, a premium to offset risk and a payment to provide a residual profit for efficient management.

(c) *The Determination of Market Interest Rates (Loanable Funds)*
The loanable fund theory of interest rate determination uses the above analysis concerning the marginal efficiency of capital (time preference) and then applies to this a more realistic analysis of what happens in the real world with respect to the supply and demand of loanable funds. The following additional assumptions are made:-

(i) *Risk and Administrative Costs.* The risk and the cost of business investment (demand for capital) varies according to industry and project and therefore the required returns also vary. This will affect the demand for loanable funds.

(ii) *Inflationary Expectations.* If inflation exists then a premium will have to be paid to compensate savers and investors for this. Thus nominal interest rates will differ from real rates by the inflation factor. If uncertainty exists regarding future inflation, then this will increase the compensatory factor and may well outweigh actual inflation rates.

(iii) *Money As a Speculative Medium.* Money is used not only as the medium of exchange for capital but is also used for other speculative or profit making purposes in money markets. This demand can perversely affect the demand for capital and distort interest rates. See Keynesian and other theories of investment in "Essential Concepts in Macro-Economics" by N. Proctor.

(iv) *Governments and the Banking Sector.* Governments, in an effort to achieve macro-economic objectives will attempt to influence and control interest rates and this could distort both capital and money markets.

The Loanable Funds Theory (see Fig. 13.9)

This theory shows the demand for loanable funds as reflecting the marginal efficiency of capital, i.e. demand, and the flow of savings (S) over a time period. The supply of savings on loanable funds are predicted to increase as the interest rate rises whilst demand falls. The supply of loanable funds will be responsive to inflationary expectations and the profit gains from holding capital in cash or other liquid forms, etc. Thus, if overall business risk reduces and profitability increases, the demand for loanable funds will shift to the right whilst higher levels of expected inflation will shift the supply of available funds to the left. This will increase overall levels of interest rates. Governments and banks can keep interest

**FIG. 13.9
LOANABLE FUNDS THEORY OF INTEREST RATES**

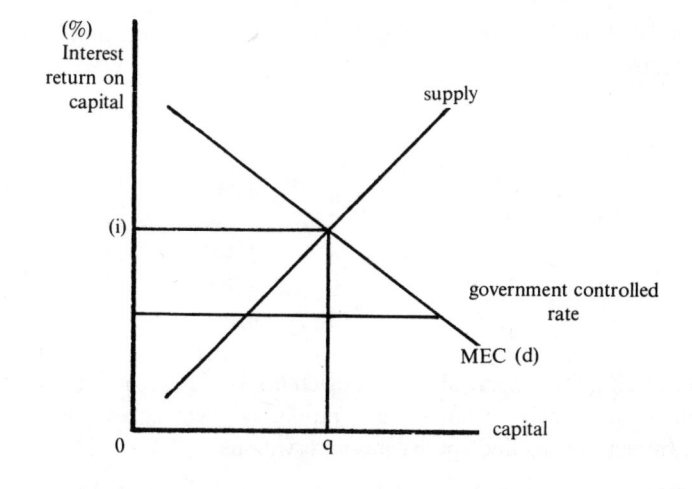

190 Capital: Nature & Analysis

rates below the equilibrium (i) and then ration out the available capital. Interest rates will not always reflect the true demand and supply of loanable funds, but will often be controlled so that certain macro-economic objectives can be met.

CHAPTER 13 Research

1. *Using information obtained from your local bank or building society, identify the different types of interest rates paid and charged and explain why these variations exist.*

2. *Consult national newspapers, magazines or bank reviews in your library and compare capital accumulation (investment) between countries, sectors or industries.*

DATA RESPONSE QUESTIONS

Question 1

a) The Board of Directors of Cando plc, which manufactures prefabricated units, are considering a proposal to invest £61,450 in new production facilities. They are concerned as to whether this outlay would be recouped. The new facilities would have a life of 10 years and the company requires a 10% return on all its investment projects. The product is sold in units which provide a profit of £200 per unit before depreciation.

How many extra units would have to be sold per year to meet the 10% rate of return criterion?

Note: The present value of £1 receivable each year for the number of years is as follows:-

10%

Years					
1	0.909	6	4.355	11	6.495
2	1.736	7	4.868	12	6.814
3	2.487	8	5.335	13	7.103
4	3.170	9	5.759	14	7.367
5	3.791	10	6.145	15	7.606

b) The results of an appraisal of three machines are shown in Table 1. Advise on which machine(s) should be purchased, giving reasons for the recommendations and specify any reservations.

Capital: Nature & Analysis 191

Table 1

	Machine X	Machine Y	Machine Z
Capital Cost £'000	8	10	15
resulting net cash inflow £'000 in Year 1	4	4	5
2	4	4	5
3	1	4	5
4	–	2	5
5	–	–	3
Net Present Value at 0%	1	4	8
Net Present Value at 15% (mid year discounting)	−0.22	+1.02	+1.91
Internal Rate of Return	11%	22%	22%
Payback period in years	2	2½	3

c) You are a property company considering buying a 5-year lease for a capital value of £75,000 on which you will receive a guaranteed yearly rental income of £22,000. The cost of capital is 10% for the first four years and 15% for the fifth year.

Calculate whether you should purchase the lease for £75,000, using the most appropriate method (ignore inflation and taxation, etc.). Name the method you use.

Question 2

Investment in Energy Savings — D.C.F.

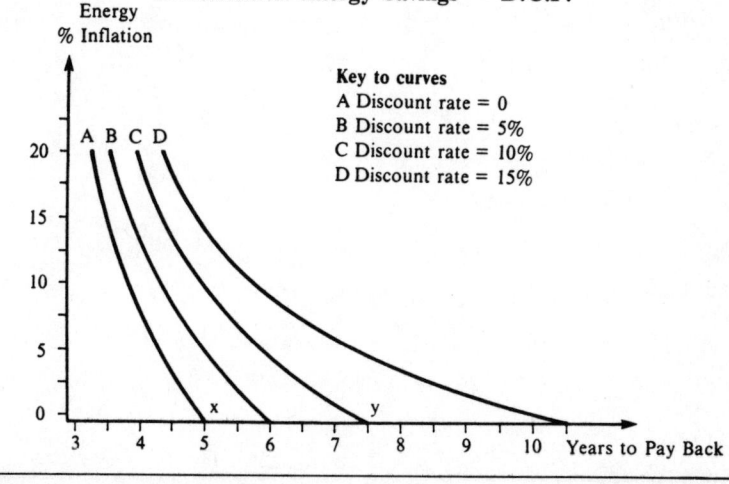

Key to curves
A Discount rate = 0
B Discount rate = 5%
C Discount rate = 10%
D Discount rate = 15%

(Graph: Energy % Inflation vs Years to Pay Back, showing curves A, B, C, D with points x and y marked)

192 Capital: Nature & Analysis

The chart shows the effects of interest or discount rates and inflation on energy saving payback periods. In the example, if regular yearly energy savings are £200 with an initial investment of £1,000 then after 5 years, with no inflation on energy prices and no capital costs, the investment will be recovered as shown as point X on schedule A. Line C assumes the same conditions but there is now a capital cost of 10% interest p.a. This means the payback period becomes about 7½ years, i.e. point Y.

1. Use schedule A and explain what happens to the payback period as energy prices rise.
2. Why does the 10% interest rate shift the original schedule A to C and increase the payback time? Name and describe the economic principle being used.
3. What could the chart illustrate about consumers' buying decisions with regard to energy savings and other home improvements. Relate your answer to actual consumer behaviour.

14 GOVERNMENTS & MARKETS — MICRO ECONOMIC POLICY

> **AIMS:** *To define, explain and discuss*
> - *Pareto optimum and markets*
> - *Market failure and weakness*
> - *Remedies for market failure*
> - *The economics of pollution*
>
> ## KEY CONCEPTS
> *Cost and allocative efficiency, Pareto optimum externalities, public goods, merit goods, marginal costs of pollution and abatement, pollution quotas, equality and efficiency, taxation (regressive/direct), information assymetry.*

Governments and Markets — Micro Economic Policy

In order to understand why Governments intervene in markets it is important to define economic efficiency. **Economic efficiency**, according to the Pareto definition (Pareto optimum), is the idea that, for a given range of demand tastes, resources and technology, it is impossible to move to another allocation which would make some people better off and nobody worse off, i.e. the economy has achieved the best possible distribution of goods. A Pareto optimum is illustrated in Fig. 14.1. Here the present allocation is at z for both individuals A and B. Using the idea of a Pareto optimum, only points in region 3 guarantee an improvement for both A and B. In region 2 both are worse off whilst in regions 1 and 4 one is better off at the expense of the other. In economics a Pareto optimum also requires cost efficiency in order to ensure allocative efficiency, (see Fig. 14.2). This shows that for productive or cost efficiency, marginal cost, for the firm, must be minimised at MC and not MC_1. The shaded difference between the two could be due to monopolistic inefficiency or organisational slack. Furthermore the firm should also operate at the lowest point on its long-run average cost curve, i.e. LAC. Under monopolistic conditions, with excess capacity, the industry could be operating inefficiently at points a or c. Competition ensures an output of oq which minimises costs at b and this, in the long run, will be where market demand equals supply. In a free market, economic efficiency is maximised if price equals both MC

FIG. 14.1
PARETO OPTIMUM

FIG. 14.2
PRODUCTIVE/ALLOCATIVE EFFICIENCY: THE FIRM

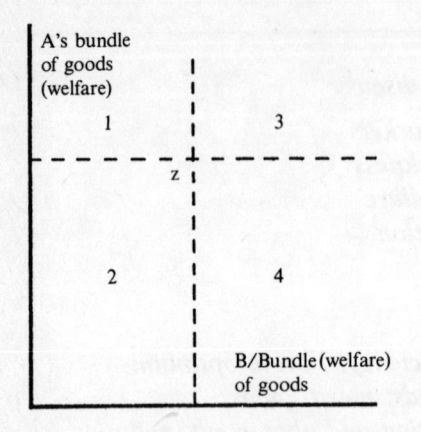

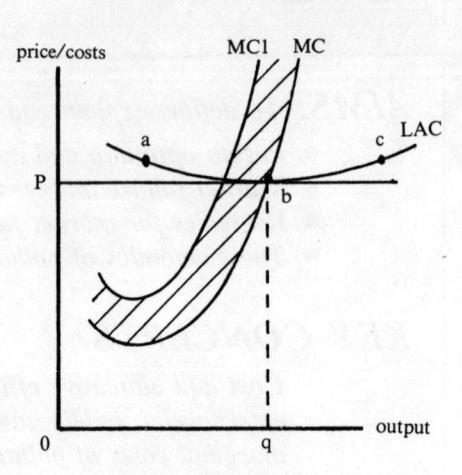

FIG. 14.3
PRODUCTIVE/ALLOCATIVE EFFICIENCY: THE MARKET

FIG. 14.4
CONSUMER & PRODUCER BENEFITS: MAXIMISE NET BENEFITS

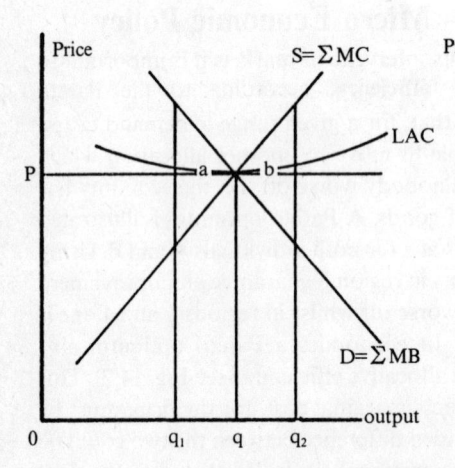

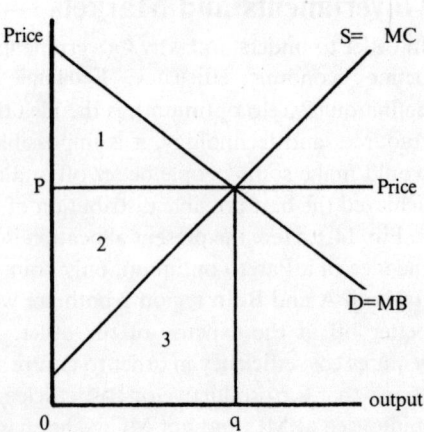

and LAC at b, since it also equals marginal utility, i.e. resources could not be reallocated without making someone worse off. Fig. 14.3 shows the supply schedule as the sum of private marginal costs for firms whilst demand is the sum of private marginal utility or benefits for consumers. The long-run equilibrium for price and output is op/oq which is also at the lowest point on the long-run average cost curve LAC, i.e. it is a Pareto optimum. Suppose the free market equilibrium were disturbed so the market moved to either output oq_1 or oq_2. At oq_1 marginal benefits (D) exceed marginal costs (S) so society would gain triangle a by moving to output oq. At oq_2, MC exceeds MB so society would gain triangle b by moving to output oq. Thus oq is a Pareto optimum.

Consumer & Producer Surplus

Another approach illustrating the Pareto Optimum is one which uses the idea of consumer and producer surpluses, (see Fig. 14.4). The area under the demand curve, at price op, reflects total benefits paid for (areas 2 plus 3) plus consumer benefits not paid for (area 1). The supply curve reflects resource costs at output oq (area 3) plus the producer's profits or surplus (area 2). The free market optimum op/oq maximises the net benefits to the community. These net benefits are areas 1 plus 2, i.e. consumer surpluses (1) and producer surpluses (2). Total net benefits cannot be improved upon at any other output level. This approach has been developed in "area analysis" which is used to analyse comparative market situations. (See Chapter 14: Data Questions).

Advantages of Free Markets

The above analysis illustrates how the free market equilibrium, at op/oq:-

(a) maximises productive and allocative efficiency, i.e. achieves a Pareto optimum;

(b) co-ordinates consumer and producer decisions without the need for conscious and expensive direction of a bureaucracy;

(c) automatically relates price to private costs and benefits and so maximises social benefits;

(d) directs resources to where marginal revenue equals marginal costs;

(e) acts as an information system for both producers and consumers. Hayek argues that the free market is a discovery process whereby consumers signal their preferences to producers by price movements and resources are re-allocated as these preferences are revealed in the market system. Government intervention can, says Hayek, often distort these signals and confuse producers and consumers.

Drawbacks of the Free Market

The free market's use of resources to achieve a Pareto optimum only works under certain conditions which are often unrealistic and which have to be corrected by government intervention. These qualifications are listed below and then discussed in detail:-

(i)   Markets are perfectly competitive
(ii) There are no public goods in the economy

(iii) There are no merit or demerit goods
(iv) There is no price instability in markets
(v) There is no risk or uncertainty
(vi) Correct information is freely available to producers and consumers
(vii) There are no externalities in consumption or production

FIG. 14.5
MONOPOLISTIC & COMPETITIVE EQUILIBRIUM

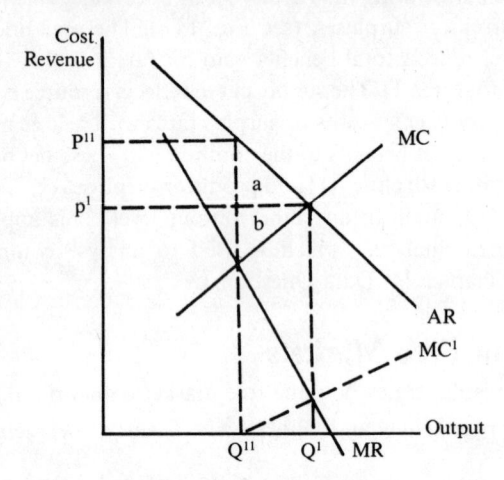

(i) *Markets are Perfectly Competitive*
The existence of monopoly power, other things equal, causes output to fall and price to rise. Under perfect competition, where AR = MR, equilibrium output is Q′ where MC = MR = AR and price is p′ in Fig. 14.5. Suppose that the industry becomes a monopoly. The monopolist can sell a greater output only by reducing the price and therefore faces a downward sloping AR curve with a diverging MR curve beneath it. Profit-maximising equilibrium output falls to Q″ where MC = MR and price rises to p″. The extent to which social welfare fails to be maximised, that is, the extent to which resources are misallocated, is shown by the welfare triangles a and b, a representing the loss of consumers' surplus and b the loss of profit caused by the reduction in output from Q^1 to Q^{11}. There is no such thing as a perfectly competitive market in the real world and so in practice the free market economy fails to make the best use of resources to the extent that its constituent markets embody monopoly power. If, however, a monopoly leads to the attainment of economies of scale, the MC curve will move outwards and the efficiency gains will restore some of the output lost under monopoly. This shifts the MC downwards to MC^1 which cuts MR at an output of oQ^1 or beyond. In this case the monopolist can produce at an output level and at a price which is

compatible with the free market one of op_1 where MC = AR. Monopolists and government are discussed further in Chapter 15.

(ii) *There are no public goods*
A pure public good exhibits, firstly, non-rivalry in consumption, as in the case of nuclear defence, where the supposed benefit to A of being protected from nuclear attack does not mean that there is less benefit left for B. The second characteristic of a pure public good is non-excludability: once the good is provided for A it is impossible to exclude B from its benefits. For example, providing a "nuclear umbrella" for one person automatically affords equal protection to her neighbours. B will not pay towards providing a public good, because no rational agent will pay for benefits she is going to receive for nothing. When A sees that B is a "free rider" she too will refuse to pay. Thus, the free market is incapable of providing public goods, despite the fact that society (both A and B in the example) would be better off with the good than without it. Street lighting and other local services are public goods and were paid for by local rates. It was alleged, however, that this system allowed some to use local services freely because rates were not paid by all who lived locally but only by house owners, i.e. they were "free riders". This was one reason why the community charge or "poll tax" was introduced because this had a broader tax base and so everyone over 18 years (with some exceptions) contributed to the financing of local services. — see Chapter 1.

(iii) *There are no merit/demerit goods*
Merit goods are those goods the consumption of which is believed to be meritorious. Thus, a good might provide greater benefits to an individual than he/she herself realises. For example, it is considered to be in a child's own long-term interests to be compelled to attend primary school even if this is not apparent to the child herself, or perhaps to her parents. From this perspective, a free market, by responding to consumer preferences alone, would supply less than the optimal amount of primary schooling. The benefits of a child's education might accrue to other people as well as to the child herself, a possibility which raises the issue of externalities.

Demerit goods are those goods the consumption of which is considered, by the state, to be bad for the individual and society. Thus excessive smoking or drinking of alcohol is harmful and costly and these are demerit goods, i.e. they are bad for you. The state attempts to increase the consumption of merit goods, e.g. education and/or health, and reduce the consumption of demerit goods by using a mixture of taxation and subsidies as Fig. 14.6 illustrates. A free market solution is shown by price/output of op/oq. The government considers the good to be of merit and wishes to encourage consumption to oq_1, i.e. this is a Pareto Optimum. This level can be achieved by (i) state provision of oq_1 by (ii) an advertising campaign increasing community awareness of the benefits of the good which then increases demand to D_1 or by (iii) a subsidy, S to S_3, which reduces the free market

FIG. 14.6
DEALING WITH MERIT/DEMERIT GOODS

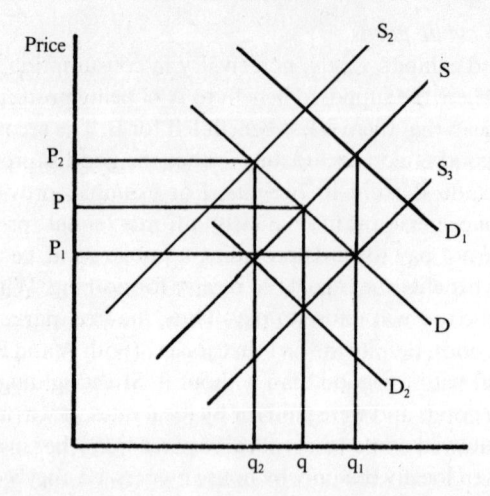

price to op_1. A demerit good can be similarly treated. A government wishes only oq_2 to be consumed. It may achieve this by (i) allowing only oq_2 on to the market, (ii) a tax could be placed on the good so shifting S to S_2 and price rises to op_2. Alternatively an advertising campaign, warning of the dangers of the product, could reduce demand to D_2. In effect by providing more information of the merits or demerits of the good the individual is made aware of the true value of the good through the market system. The role of the government in this is to provide the correct information.

(iv) *There is no price instability in markets*
Many agricultural and raw material markets are characterised by price and income instability. This is due to (i) poor market information by suppliers, (ii) a time lag between recognising a demand change and being able to provide for it and (iii) because forward output planning is difficult due to poor market operation. The result of price volatility is that producers have an uncertain income and forward investment in future output is patchy, uncertain and inadequate. The role of government under these circumstances is to stabilise markets by supporting farmers incomes or market price as discussed in Chapter 4.

(v) *There is no risk or uncertainty*
Many markets are characterised by risk and uncertainty with regard to the future. Whilst insurance and other contingency techniques have reduced this risk many markets still suffer from product uncertainty due to moral hazard or adverse selection. Furthermore, when forward markets are unavailable then consumers cannot make their future preferences known. As many futures markets do not exist and because risk can reduce output below the Pareto optimum then

inefficiency increases. The role of the government in these circumstances is to encourage markets to develop by covering possible losses as in the case of overseas trade risk, e.g. E.C.G.D. Governments can also provide health provision, e.g. care for the elderly, which could not be adequately provided by the private sector due to problems of adverse selection within the insurance markets.

(vi) *Information Problems – Asymmetry*
Because of moral hazard and adverse selection problems (see Chapter 3), consumers and producers may know more than each other (asymmetry) so they may never trust the market price as an indicator of benefits or production costs. In financial markets consumers may not be fully aware of product safety, quality or reliability and in financial markets "insider trader" dealings can increase consumer distrust in capital markets. Providers of insurance may find, because of moral hazard and adverse selection problems, actual provision costs greatly exceed budgeted costs which may lead them to withdraw from markets, i.e. markets will then operate inefficiently. Efficient markets are those where all possible information is equally and readily available to producers and consumers and so the role of the government is to ensure this condition applies. This would lead governments to insist, to both consumers and producers, upon full disclosure of relevant information with regard to the safety, producer quality and risk aspects of goods and services. This will encourage consumers and producers to re-enter the market. Note: "Insider trader" dealings help improve the efficiency of a market by providing an incentive to look for information but it is illegal because it is not fairly available to all!

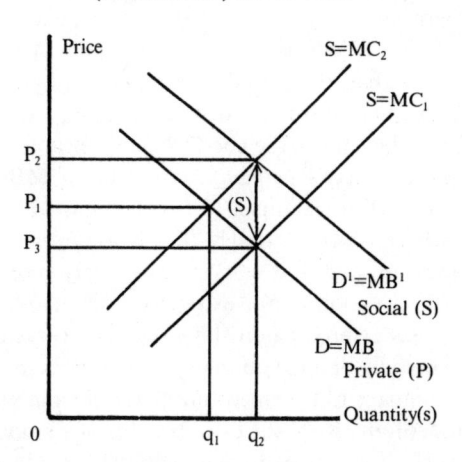

FIG. 14.7
POSITIVE EXTERNALITIES (RAIL SUBSIDY)
(BENEFITS) i.e. D to D^1

FIG. 14.8
NEGATIVE EXTERNALITIES
(COSTS) i.e. MC_1 to MC^2

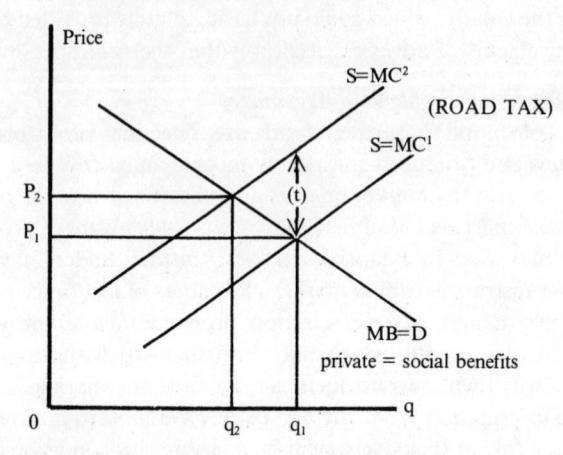

[Graph: Price on vertical axis, q on horizontal axis. Curves labelled $S=MC^2$ (ROAD TAX) and $S=MC^1$, with arrow (t) between them. Demand curve labelled MB=D private = social benefits. Prices P_2 and P_1 marked on vertical axis; quantities q_2 and q_1 marked on horizontal axis.]

(vii) *There are no externalities in consumption or production*

The free market equilibrium assumes all the costs and benefits are private and internal to the market. In reality there are benefits other than those paid for by the consumer. These can be in consumption or production. When I telephone a person the phone call provides benefits which are not paid for directly by the receiver of the call. In production I can benefit from the crop spraying of my neighbouring farmer. There can also be additional costs incurred when others consume or produce. When I smoke cigarettes others suffer from the fumes whilst the production of cement or bricks means others have clear up costs incurred upon them. These extra benefits or costs are external to the market and are known as externalities. Furthermore, external costs (negative benefits) or positive benefits are also known as spillover effects and Figs. 14.7 and 14.8 illustrate. The free market will supply less than the socially optimal quantity of a good providing external benefits. Individual consumers demand only oq_1 at a price of op_1 which reflects only the private benefits of the good to each consumer (see Fig. 14.7). The external benefits push society's demand curve out to MB^1, and the socially optimal output is oq_2. For example, A's vaccination against a contagious disease benefits B, who might have caught the disease from A if A had remained unvaccinated. Conversely, the free market will supply more than the socially optimal quantity of a good with external costs. Adding these negative externalities to the costs of production shifts the MC_1 curve backwards to MC_2 and shows that the socially optimal output is oq_1 rather than oq_2, (see Fig. 14.8). Pollution and other damage to the environment are obvious external costs of free market transactions. Alternatively, the extra benefits of subsidising rail users may take the form of achieving less road congestion. This could be shown as a rail subsidy (S) which shifts MC_2 to MC_1, in Fig. 14.7, and increases rail demand and use from oq_1 to oq_2 as price drops from op_2 to op_3. At the same time road users could be taxed (t), in Fig. 14.8, so reducing road use from oq_1 to oq_2 as price rises from op_1 to op_2.

Dealing with Externalities

The following, A to E, identify methods of dealing with and correcting for externalities:-

A. *Government's tax (T) or subsidise (S)*. As discussed above, governments can discourage production or consumption by taxation aimed at reflecting social costs or can subsidise production or consumption in order to acknowledge and encourage benefits.

B. *Grant Legal Property Rights - Compensation.* The government or the common law can assign to consumers or producers certain legal "rights", i.e. the right to clean air, etc. If these rights are violated by the polluter, the consumer can sue the producer. In theory the compensation claimed should be the same as the tax imposed so pollution reduces by the amount shown in Fig. 14.8. A cheaper, non-legal solution, may be for the polluting company to pay compensation to the victim/s of the pollution. Even if rights are not granted it is alleged that the cheapest solution is to allow those affected by the pollution to meet with the polluter and come to an economic bargaining solution. This means either the polluter pays compensation or those being polluted pay the polluter to stop polluting. Thus the social costs are "internalised" by the market. This is known as the "Coase" solution. However, for this to be a practical solution those being affected have to organise themselves into a force able to take on a large corporation doing the polluting. The risk of expensive legal action together with "free rider" problems on the part of some affected consumers means in practice that consumer groups may not press fully for the optimum solution because of the transaction costs involved.

C. *Direct controls or standards.* Governments have sought to limit pollution and other negative externalities imposed on the individual or society by setting controls on emission of pollution and/or by setting industry standards for pollution and/or behaviour. The former idea applies to toxic chemical wastes and the latter applies to such problems as noise levels, smoke emissions and the behaviour of media advertising, e.g. there are controls on advertising alcoholic drink on the television. These rules and regulations normally apply across an industry or sector and can be enforced by a state-financed regulatory agency.

D. *Using the market to clear up external costs*. This approach used in the U.S.A. is now seen as a serious alternative to the above techniques. As reported in the Economist of 8th September 1990,

"_____ In America some of the more far-sighted green lobbying groups have been helping to devise ways to work with the market, rather than against it. America's new clean-air legislation, based on ideas developed by the Environmental Defence Fund (EDF), sets an absolute cap on emissions of sulphur dioxide and nitrous oxide by power stations. It then gives companies permits to emit a certain amount of the gases each year, and allows them to buy or sell these permits. The aim is to encourage those power stations which can clean up most cheaply to do so, and then make money by selling spare polluting capacity to those for whom cleaning up is expensive.

Alread, this potential new market is attracting a new kind of trader who will help to make it work more efficiently. Mr. John Palmisano, whose company AER*X has been arranging trades in pollution permits under an older, less satisfactory bit of clean-air legislation, looks forward to a big increase in business. He is the only specialised broker in the business. Since the new clean-air bill came before Congress, others have become interested: for instance, Asea Brown Boveri, a European engineering firm, has recently bought Combustion Engineering, the largest manufacturer of scrubbers in America. A growing number of companies are putting together broking skills, engineering expertise and an understanding of environmental regulations. They will then approach companies, offering to cut their emissions and pay for it by selling their spare emission rights. 'My best client is the finance manager,' says Mr. Palmisano. 'Not the pollution-control manager, who is probably an engineer with a strong not-invented-here attitude.'"

However, some economists argue that tradeable licences to pollute act as an entry barrier (cost) for would-be entrants into the industry since incumbents own the licences to pollute. Furthermore, trading companies, rather than governments or taxpayers make profits by selling these licences to those who will still pollute as they come into the industry.

E.   *Government Provision – Cost Benefit Analysis.* In many sectors social benefits far outweigh social costs but the private sector fails to recognise this and so it underinvests in the provision of the goods, e.g. roads, etc. Cost Benefit Analysis (C.B.A.) in such public investment projects identifies and attempts to value social costs and benefits in order that a comprehensive comparison of private and social costs and benefits can be evaluated. Cost Benefit Analysis of the M1 motorway, the Victoria underground line, in London, and the Severn Bridge all provided evidence that the value of discounted social benefits exceeded the private and social costs of construction and operating these large civil engineering projects. This analysis helped governments evaluate and publicly fund major infrastructure projects in the 1970s, although the cutbacks in public investment in the 1980s reduced the importance of C.B.A. The "Channel Tunnel" link between the U.K. and France was privately funded, on the U.K. side, and when opened in 1994 it will be a privately operated venture. Public investment in this project, aided by C.B.A., may have been able to fully appreciate both micro- and macro-social benefits.

Dealing with Externalities — The Cement Production Case

Fig. 14.9 illustrates both private and social costs of pollution caused by a cement works together with marginal clean up costs. The vertical axis measures the costs whilst the horizontal axis at zero shows no pollution and moves to high pollution emission of around 400 units. As pollution increases the marginal cost to the firm increases as machines become more difficult to operate and dirt and pollution affect the neighbourhood, i.e. social pollution costs increase. There are a number of achievable levels of pollution together with remedy policies which could be used. These are outlined:-

1. *The Green Solution* of zero pollution, i.e. output level (a). This is an ideal solution but the cost of clean up is far in excess of the damage to society and the firm. Thus the high clean up costs outweigh any gains in benefits and the resources used to clean up pollution could be used more efficiently, in terms of potential benefits, elsewhere.

2. *The Unregulated and the Social optimum output.*

The unregulated approach to pollution would rely upon the producer to reduce pollution up to the level (b) where the marginal private damage to the firm equals the marginal cost of clean up. However, this level means that the social costs of pollution are ignored. When these are taken into account the optimum level of pollution emission is at level (c), 130 units, which corresponds with both clean up costs and pollution damage of around £25th. At this level of pollution, c, there is around £10th worth of private pollution and £15th worth of social pollution. This is a Pareto optimum but the problem is how best can this level be achieved? The following policies, (i) – (iv), outline a range of solutions.

(i) *Grant Legal Property Rights to those affected.* If those affected could be given the right not to be polluted then they could sue for compensation, ideally up to £15th representing the private pollution caused. However, there are practical problems. Those affected, may rely on others to take action and the legal costs may deter action so that a second best solution between b and c may result.

(ii) *Direct Controls by Government Pollution Agencies.* If the government set standards of pollution emission which can be enforced by imposing fines upon the polluters then in theory the optimum level, c, can be attained. However, if the level of fines is low then the cement works could flout these standards. Furthermore, direct standards of control fail to appreciate that the marginal costs of clean up vary between cement works so there is no financial incentive to clean up for the firm other than the fines imposed.

(iii) *Emission Taxes and Pollution.* This policy attempts to theoretically graduate taxation imposed on the cement works and is equivalent to the difference between the marginal cost to the firm and to society, with respect to pollution caused. It would be equivalent to £15th at c. However, in practice there is the problem of

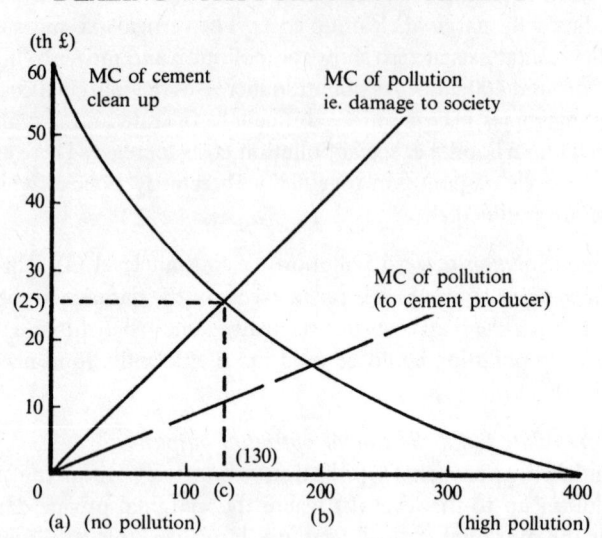

FIG. 14.9
DEALING WITH POLLUTION: CEMENT

(th £)

- 60 — MC of cement clean up
- MC of pollution ie. damage to society
- MC of pollution (to cement producer)
- (25) at intersection
- (130) at c

x-axis: 0, 100 (c), 200 (b), 300, 400
(a) (no pollution) ... (high pollution)

correctly estimating the correct amount of tax for both the cement works and/or the industry. Also the enforcement costs of tax collecting could outweigh any extra benefits gained.

(iv) *Using the Market to Reduce Pollution.* Assume that Fig. 14.9 illustrates the whole cement industry then the market solution would be to allow so much pollution, 130 units at c, and this amount of pollution is rationed between cement works in the industry, i.e. each works is allowed to emit so much pollution. This means low cost clean up cement works are given the same pollution allowances as high cost clean up works. The low cost works can attain their levels of pollution limits and then sell for a profit some of their unused pollution quotas to high cost clean up firms. This means there will be a built-in incentive to clean up since unused pollution rations can be sold for a profit. Furthermore, the bureaucracy costs of tax collection and setting up legally enforceable standards of pollution emission are eliminated. Proponents of this market solution allege there is a built-in incentive to reduce clean up costs. In effect this shifts the MC of cement clean up to the left and so a lower social optimum of pollution is achieved at no extra costs to the community. On the other hand, it is alleged that incumbents who have been granted these emission quotas may well use them as barriers to entry for new would-be cement works.

Efficiency and Equality — The Impact of Taxation on markets

Governments use taxation and subsidies in order to achieve the two conflicting objectives of economic efficiency and equality of income. Income tax policies, designed to reduce inequality of income, and/or regional subsidies, designed to boost employment, are, it is alleged, economically inefficient since they distort prices and ensure that they are never equated to marginal cost, i.e. market forces are not allowed to operate.

FIG. 14.10
PROGRESSIVE, REGRESSIVE & PROPORTIONAL TAXATION

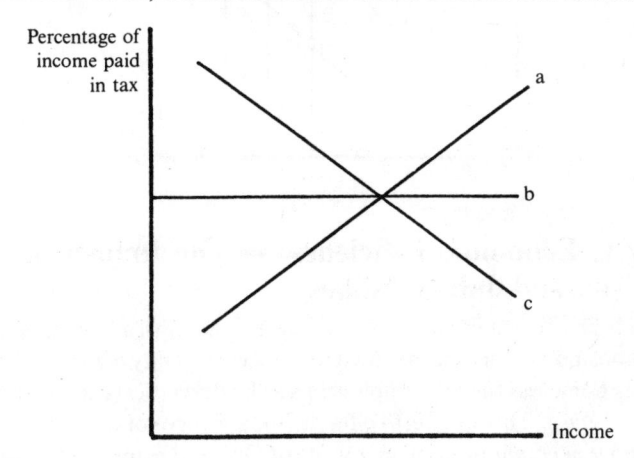

Equality and Progressive Taxation

Taxation policies use the concept of (i) direct/indirect tax and (ii) progressive/regressive tax. Each is explained. A direct tax is one which is directly placed upon income, e.g. P.A.Y.E. Income tax. An indirect tax is one placed upon expenditure, e.g. V.A.T. because this indirectly taxes income. A progressive tax is one where the percentage of tax paid, either directly or indirectly from income, rises whilst a regressive one has the opposite effect. A proportional tax takes a constant proportion of income, e.g. corporation profits tax. These are illustrated in Fig. 14.10 viz. a, b and c. In each case for a, b and c the actual amount of tax paid can still increase; it is the percentage of income the tax represents which defines whether it is progressive, etc. The impact of a progressive, proportional and regressive tax are shown in the Fig. 14.10 as a, b and c respectively.

FIG. 14.11
THE AFFECT ON LABOUR MARKETS OF INCOME TAX AND JOB SUBSIDIES

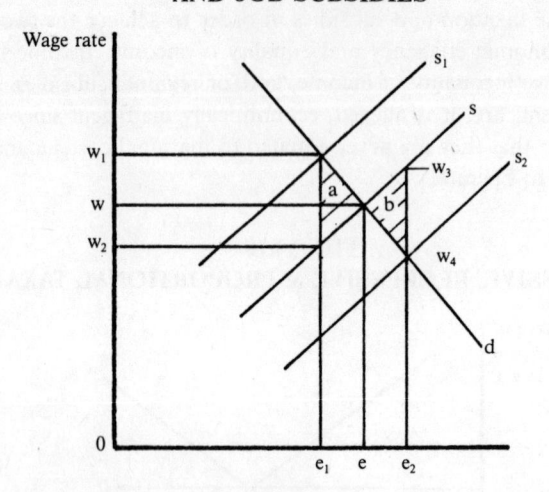

Equality v. Economic Efficiency — The Impact of Income Tax and Job Subsidies

In Fig. 14.11 the efficient use of labour resources is Oe with a free market wage of Ow. The imposition of income tax, used to reduce inequality of income, means the worker takes home less than the employer pays, by the vertical distance between s1 and s (Ow$_1$ - Ow$_2$). This in effect shifts the supply curve of labour to s$_1$ and the employer, now in equilibrium, pays a wage of Ow$_1$ and employs Oe$_1$ labour who receive Ow$_2$ wage. The shaded area, a, represents a waste of resources since the real marginal revenue product at Ow$_1$ exceeds the true marginal cost of labour, Ow$_2$. Subsidising jobs in the regions by means of capital grants leads, it is alleged, to the same thing in reverse. A labour subsidy artificially lowers labour supply cost and moves the supply of labour from s to s$_2$ with the vertical distance between s and s$_2$ representing the subsidy to the employer. In this case, employment increases to Oe$_2$. Here the value of the marginal revenue product is Ow$_4$ but the real marginal cost of labour is Ow$_3$. The shaded area, b, represents the waste of labour resources. If, however, the labour supply had no alternative use (it was inelastic at Oe), the difference between Ow$_4$ and Ow$_3$ would not be a waste. It would be a neutral subsidy in the same way an income tax, under these conditions, would be neutral. Nevertheless, the above attempts to use an income tax or a subsidy in order to achieve less inequality distort and conflict with economic efficiency.

15 GOVERNMENTS & MARKETS — MONOPOLIES — MERGERS

AIMS: To define, explain and discuss
- Monopolists, mergers and efficiency
- Nationalisation and privatisation
- Public choice economics
- Governments and regulation

KEY CONCEPTS

x inefficiency, regulation, conduct and market structure, costs of regulation, unproductive activity, privatisation, cost-benefit analysis, mergers and legislation, second-best theory.

The Economic Justification for Intervention (see Fig. 15.1)

Assuming constant long-run costs (LMC' = LAC') in a competitive industry, the price/output levels are opc/oqc and overall economic efficiency is maximised as price = marginal cost = long-run average cost. If the structure of industry became monopolistic, initially in the form of a cartel, price and output levels change to op_m, oq_m and inefficiency arises in the form of the deadweight loss, triangle a, where price (p_m) exceeds marginal cost. Otherwise the higher price and profits, area b, represent a transfer of resources from consumers to producers and factors of production. The higher price and profits together with lower output under monopolistic conditions provide the theoretical justification for intervention in the market. There are two approaches possible, namely to control or regulate the conduct of the monopolist or to influence the structure of the monopolistic industry by breaking it up into smaller competitive units or by functionally separating its ability to operate in different markets.

A. *Regulation of Monopoly Conduct*
(1) The government, or regulatory body, can induce a competitive price/output level by subsidising costs so that MC = MR at an output/price level consistent with a competitive market structure, i.e. costs fall to LMC_2, LAC_2 and price/output are at opm_2, oqm_2. Even so critics argue that this policy will still create a monopoly profit and the lower price is paid by the tax payer.

FIG. 15.1
COMPETITIVE v MONOPOLISTIC INDUSTRIES

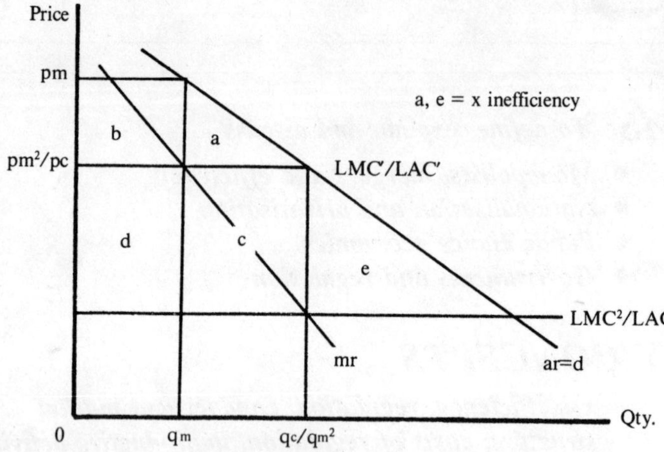
Price
pm
pm²/pc
0
a, e = x inefficiency
b
a
LMC'/LAC'
d
c
e
LMC²/LAC²
mr
ar=d
qm
qc/qm²
Qty.

(2) The government can impose a competitive price/output level or leave the monopolist to set a price and then tax away any excess profits. However, this policy presumes (a) the government knows the competitive price/output level and, anyway, (b) the monopolist can artificially inflate costs so any profits disappear and there is, therefore, nothing to tax.

(3) The government can encourage competitively priced imports into the country so the monopolist has to reduce price and increase output to a more competitive level.

The government can also increase competition by:-

B. *Changing the Structure of the Industry*
(1) The government can encourage new entrants into a monopolistic industry by reducing barriers to entry. This would mean the abolition of patent or copyright laws protecting existing firms, the limiting of advertising expenditure, the outlawing of restrictive practices in both product and factor markets and an insistence upon competitive codes of practice being pursued by the monopolist.

(2) The government can actively encourage overseas imports (see above) as well as attracting overseas capital, i.e. providing other suppliers of the product. A free trade policy within the international economy would also have a similar result.

(3) Where state owned monopolies, e.g. Nationalised Industries exist these should be open to competitive pressures such as (a) privatisation, (b) deregulation and (c) competitive tendering. These policies are discussed later in the chapter under Nationalisation and Privatisation.

Mergers and Economies of Scale

When mergers exist in an industry, so creating multiplant operations, then long-run economies of scale arise which lower costs, i.e. LMC_2/LAC_2 in Fig. 15.1. This leads to price and output levels consistent with competitive markets, i.e. pm_2, qm_2. Monopoly profits are still made (areas c plus d). In this case the gains in profit are achieved through economies so costs reduce. The only inefficiency is that there is a theoretical loss of consumer surplus equivalent to the triangle e. However, the cost reduction, areas d plus c, means that these resources are released and can be used elsewhere in the economy.

U.K. Monopoly and Mergers Policy and Control

Government Regulatory Agencies

1. *Monopolies and Mergers Commission (M.M.C.) (Established 1948)*
The M.M.C. can investigate any local or national dominant firm which has 25% or more of the market. The investigation seeks to establish whether the monopoly operates "against the public interest". A pragmatic approach is adopted and such things as whether there are substitutes available in the market for the public, the level of profits earned to capital employed by the monopolist, the level of technical innovation in the monopolistic industry, as well as potential methods of reducing entry barriers in order to encourage future competition, are investigated. The M.M.C. has reported on over fifty monopoly situations which have covered such things as brick production, film processing, drug pricing, breakfast cereals and the instant coffee market (1991), etc. In 1989 it reported on the U.K. brewing industry and recommended that the industry adopt a more competitive structure by advising that the brewers sell off some of their pubs and also suggesting that "guest" beers be introduced into the brewers' tied houses. Nevertheless, throughout its history the M.M.C. has not generally been overly critical of those monopolies investigated. At the same time, the often inconsistent behaviour of the M.M.C. with respect to merger policy has led some to suggest that in a takeover situation the predatory company should have to show the bid was in the public interest which may be more difficult to prove than merely not being against the public interest.

2. *Restrictive Trade Practices Court (Established 1956)*
This court, together with the Registrar of Restrictive Practices, investigates restrictive practices such as collusive price and restrictive conditions of sale agreements. It assumes these are illegal unless it can be proved they are justified by one of the eight "gateways" which show they may be beneficial to the public interest. These are listed below [(a) to (g)]:-

(a) the agreement is necessary to protect the public against injury;

(b) the agreement ensures that the public receives some specific and substantial benefit which would disappear if the agreement were ended;

(c) the agreement is necessary to enable small firms to compete with large firms;

(d) the agreement is necessary to prevent small firms being exploited by very large customers or suppliers;

(e) the agreement is necessary to maintain the level of employment in particular areas or industries;

(f) the agreement is necessary to maintain exports;

(g) the agreement is necessary to maintain another restriction already approved by the Court.

Even if an agreement satisfies one of these points, it must still be shown that the benefit from it outweighs any general detriment to the public from the agreement as a whole.

The Fair Trading Act 1973 transferred responsibility for the control of restrictive practices to the Director General of Fair Trading, and at the same time brought the provision of services within the same framework of control. As a tidying-up process, the various aspects of the policy were pulled together in the Restrictive Practices Act 1977.

Over 5,000 restrictive practice agreements had been registered by the late 1980s and the vast majority had been outlawed and disbanded. In terms of Fig. 15.1 restrictive practices operate as if they were monopolies, with a price output of opm/oqm, but they have none of the corresponding economies of scale associated with large scale monopolistic production.

Merger Policy — Monopolies and Mergers Act 1973

The strong movement towards market and output concentration in the U.K. since the war has led to a rise in the five firm concentration ratio, CR^5, in manufacturing industries and, recently, the growth of conglomerate holdings. The Monopolies and Mergers Act of 1973 amended the 1965 act and allowed investigation, and hence recommendation to the relevant government minister, with respect to allowing a proposed merger. A merger could be investigated if (i) it leads to an increase in monopoly power (25% or more of the market share) and hence, a reduction in consumer choice, or (ii) where gross assets after the merger exceed £38 million. The onus is on the investigation proving the "guilt" of the merger in terms of it being against the public interest and this in practice is difficult to show. Few large mergers have been prevented. In the event that the M.M.C. concludes, by a greater than two-thirds majority, that the proposed merger is against the public interest, then the merger is not allowed to proceed.

The Rationale for Merger Policy (some views)

(a) The free-trade view is to allow all mergers to take place since the reason why one firm wishes to buy another is that the acquiring firm believes it can run the acquired firm more profitably than its existing owners. This threat of takeover makes all firms operate efficiently and when mergers take place resources move from less profitable to more profitable uses. The implication is that policy should be non-interventionist regardless of likely social or political implications.

(b) The cost-benefit approach is to compare the likely cost gains of a merger and weigh them against the loss of choice and consumer surplus. A horizontal merger would lead to cost savings, in Fig. 15.1, shown as the areas (d + c), due to greater economies of scale. However, competitor pressures might have reduced the price so consumers could lose the area e, in the form of consumer surplus. However, this assumes a non-merged industry could keep costs and prices below opm_2.

(c) The interventionist stance is that mergers should be closely monitored because of the impact on industrial structure and the possibility of regional unemployment resulting from mergers. Furthermore it is argued that pre- and post-merged industries do not show significant profitability changes so the commercial efficiency of mergers has not been proven. Evidence seems to suggest whilst profitability does not result from mergers monopoly, control over markets certainly does.

The Impact of U.K. Merger Policy

During the period from the introduction of the merger policy to the end of 1984, a total of 2,565 proposed mergers was examined by the Mergers Panel as falling within the scope of the policy. Of these proposed mergers, 79 were referred to the M.M.C. for further investigation (and this includes seven cases where two or more bids for a single firm were referred). Amongst those referred to the M.M.C., 23 have been abandoned during the M.M.C. investigations so that the M.M.C. has not finally reported. Of those proposed mergers on which the M.M.C. had reported by 1986, 23 were found to be against the public interest and 32 not against the public interest. Thus the direct impact of the merger policy can be seen to be rather small: only 1 – 2% of all proposed mergers have been stopped.

Consumer Protection Acts

Fair Trading Act 1973
This act created the post of Director General of Fair Trading under whom all competition and consumer law was centralised. Consumer protection was provided under this act in such areas as insurance, hire purchase and house purchase. The Director General could prohibit practices which adversely affect consumers in the market place.

Competition Act 1980
This was designed to stimulate competition and this act was extended to Nationalised Industries. The Director General of Fair Trading could refer price rises and practices of Nationalised Industries to the M.M.C. which was empowered to investigate in order to see whether the Nationalised Industry acted against the public interest.

The Costs of Government Regulation — (Public Choice Economics)

Many argue that excessive government regulation in factor and product markets can be costly because:-

(a) regulators may not know the correct economic standards of output or price and attempts to ascertain these can be expensive and lead to a waste of resources;

(b) legal controls imposed can push up costs of production which mean consumers pay more than they want or should have to pay. Bureaucratic costs also have to be paid by producer and/or consumer (see below);

(c) taxation and subsidies distort factor resource allocation because they provide the wrong price signals to producers, consumers and income earners;

(d) politicians can interfere in markets in order to gain votes. Public choice economics argues that regulation is a product which is bought and sold like any other good. Regulations, e.g. import controls, featherbed home producers at the expense of cheaper import prices for the consumer;

(e) the regulators often rely upon the regulated industry for the information which enables them to supposedly exercise regulatory control. However, this over-dependency by the regulator leads to "regulatory capture" so the regulatory authority is unable to exercise objective control on behalf of the consumer;

(f) the development of Public Choice economics stresses that the bureaucratic cost of regulation outweighs the benefits. This can be shown with a simple diagram (see Fig. 15.2) relating the marginal costs and benefits to the community of control. The optimum level is oq but because the bureaucrat relates his power and salary to the largest level of bureaucratic control the level of control is increased to oq_1. Here the marginal cost of control outweighs the benefits and so there is a waste of resources;

(g) of directly unproductive profit seeking (D.U.P.). This area of economics analyses the ways of profit seeking that do not directly contribute to the output of an economy's goods and services. A government is a monopoly provider of goods, services, taxation, regulation, etc. and within this situation bureaucratic and lobby interests develop because monopoly profits can result from government action.

FIG. 15.2

BUREAUCRATIC AND SOCIAL LEVELS OF CONTROL (D.U.P.)

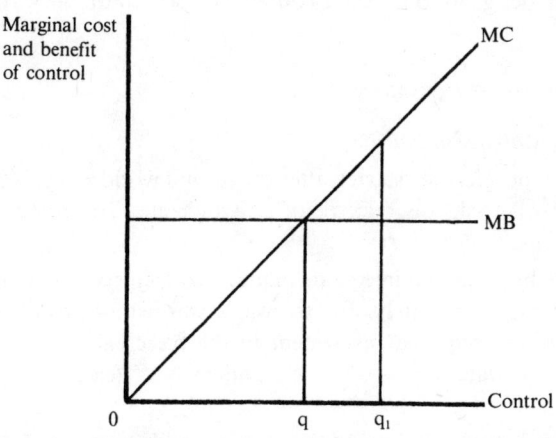

Safety regulations can increase the profits of seat belt manufacturers and tax avoidance schemes provide income for accountants and other professionals. Professional lobbyists sell their services in order to convince government bureaucrats of regulation in certain areas so wasteful costs can arise, e.g. lobbying to encourage governments to place a tariff on an imported good means consumers pay more and producers gain monopoly profits. Many argue that in order to reduce D.U.P. and hence its associated waste, governments should devolve more power to its citizens who are the only impartial or non-biased agency with respect to the general interests of all citizens. This means markets make the decisions and the lobby costs of vested interests would disappear;

(h) since commercial control of monopolies, using regulatory agencies, was seen to be expensive, in particular with respect to Nationalised Industries, it was argued the cheapest course of action would be to introduce competition, i.e. self-regulation by a privatisation process which would loosen up markets. In its most extreme this view argues that governments should reduce **all** artificial entry barriers to an industry, eg. abolish patents and copyrights and, where externalities exist, allow each party to the externality free negotiation rights rather than pursuing a government policy of taxation or regulatory control, i.e. allow markets to determine the outcome (internalise the situation).

Nationalisation, Privatisation and Deregulation

The 1980s saw a radical programme of government action in the industrial sphere. This programme had three policy objectives:-

(i) to privatise nationalised industries and re-regulate where necessary;

(ii) to deregulate controlled industries;
(iii) to subject state agencies to competitive price tender.

These policies were designed to improve competition within the state run sectors of the economy.

1. *Nationalisation and Privatisation*

The Economics of Nationalisation

The nationalisation programme started after the second world war (1945) with the public ownership of coal, gas, electricity and rail, etc. The basic economic rationales for nationalisation were:-

(i) to provide the huge capital injections required to gain economies of scale in key industrial sectors. Immediately after the war it was felt the private sector was unable to generate the required investment in the basic energy and transport industries and only state provision and funding was feasible under these circumstances.

(ii) only by owning monopolies could the state properly regulate their conduct and performance, i.e. non-profit-maximising price and monopoly output levels could be pursued by state owned industries. This would enable the state to pursue non-profit-maximising objectives such as levels of service, equality of opportunity and other social objectives. In terms of Fig. 15.1 any combination of price and output levels could be agreed upon, eg, in particular, opc/oqc so that the maximisation of economic efficiency, with price (p) = marginal cost (mc), was theoretically achieveable. Not only does a p = mc level ensure allocative efficiency but it also stops monopoly exploitation which would result if private enterprise existed.

2. *Problems of Marginal Cost Pricing in Nationalised Industries*

Where industries were nationalised in order to achieve economic efficiency by setting price to marginal cost certain problems were encountered:-

(i) How to define the marginal unit? In order to work out marginal cost, it is necessary to be clear about the units produced. In terms of railway services, is the unit the train, or the carriage, or the extra seat?

(ii) Furthermore it is difficult and expensive to estimate and charge the marginal cost of the last train since there are practical problems of costing fixed and variable costs.

(iii) Many nationalised industries are faced by daily and seasonal fluctuations in demand so making it difficult to identify and charge the actual marginal cost for the good provided, e.g. the electricity industry is a case in point.

(iv) In some industries short- and long-run marginal cost differences exist so there are problems of which one to choose, with respect to pricing policies.

((v) Marginal cost pricing can lead to losses in natural monopoly situations. See below (4)

3. *Nationalisation and Natural Monopolies*

The strongest reason for nationalisation was based on the view that many industries were natural monopolies which needed strict control through state ownership and which thus allowed the state to exploit potential economies of scale. A natural monopoly is one where one firm is so efficient that its costs of production preclude the possibility of competition by other firms. This is because the single firm experiences cost falls over its entire output range. A single firm can produce the total output at a lower unit cost than can two or more firms sharing that industry output amongst them. Thus natural market forces lead to the emergence of one large firm, i.e. a natural monopoly. This is illustrated in Fig. 15.3a. A single firm industry has costs as shown and is producing at oq_1 with costs of oc_1 and a price of p_1. Two firms in the industry could produce oq_2 each, i.e. half oq_1, at a cost of c_2 and price of op_2. These costs and price are higher than those of the single firm. Thus the single firm can produce the total output of oq_1 at a lower price of op_1 which is lower than the cost oc_2 of either of the two potential entrants. In the case of electricity or gas supply such economies of scale exist which was one reason why these industries were nationalised.

4. *Natural Monopolies and Financial Losses*

Allocative efficiency requires that price be set to marginal cost. In the case of a natural monopoly, in Fig. 15.3a, the price/output level of op_3/oq_3 implies a price less than average cost, i.e. a loss for the nationalised industry. This means long term investment will not produce a commercial return on capital employed and

FIG. 15.3a
A NATURAL MONOPOLIST

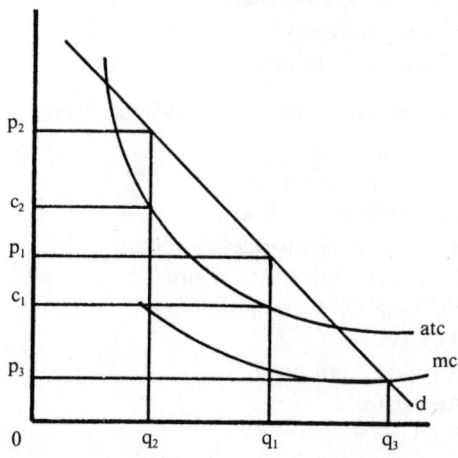

will appear to be commercially uneconomic. The industry is nationalised and the loss paid by the taxpayer.

5. *Other Reasons – Social Justice*
An industry should not only be owned by those who can afford to buy shares but by all in society. Also nationalisation helps maintain national defence interests and by nationalising coal, etc. it helped the government control the economy more easily and establish minimum safety standards underground.

Criticisms of Nationalised Industries — Privatisation

The problem of pricing within nationalised industries led to charges of inadequate and uncertain investment, a poor return on capital, less choice and quality of service, accompanied by strong trades unions with featherbedding and subsidies which wasted taxpayers' money. It was alleged that a more competitive market structure was needed to force costs and prices down. Following the 1979 Conservative Government, a policy of privatisation was pursued whereby state industries were sold off to the public in return for ordinary shares. The list below shows the current position of those industries which were privatised along with existing nationalised industries.

The following nationalised industries remained in the public sector at the end of 1990:

    British Coal
    Post Office
    Girobank (now owned by Alliance & Leicester Building Society (1991))
    British Railways Board
    British Waterways Board
    Scottish Transport Group
    British Shipbuilders (Merchant)
    Civil Aviation Authority
    London Regional Transport

The following industries have been privatised since 1979:

    British Telecom
    British Gas Corporation
    Electricity (England and Wales)
    North of Scotland Hydro-Electric Board
    South of Scotland Electricity Board
    British National Oil Corporation
    British Airways
    British Airports Authority
    British Aerospace
    Water (England and Wales)

British Shipbuilders (Warships)
British Steel Corporation
British Transport Docks Board
National Freight Company
Enterprise Oil
National Bus Company

TABLE 15.1 DEREGULATION

Transport Act (1980)	Long-distance buses. Real fare reduction of 40% 1980–83.
Transport Act (1986)	Urban bus service. Abolition of opticians' monopoly in dispensing and selling spectacles.
Health and Social Security Act (1984)	
Stock Exchange agreement	'Big Bang'. Abolition of solicitors' monopoly on property conveyancing. Charges down 25%.
Financial Services Act (1986)	
Other	Abolition of wage, price, and foreign exchange controls (1979).

Other state owned companies, many of which were initially bought up in order to rescue them from bankruptcy, were also privatised. These were British Aerospace, Cable and Wireless, Amersham International, British Leyland, Britoil, Jaguar Cars, etc.

Deregulation etc.

Initiated by the acts of Parliament, shown in Table 15.1, deregulation was seen as an attempt to reduce local monopoly power and increase competition and, hence,

FIG. 15.3b.
PRIVATISATION AND THE PARETO OPTIMUM

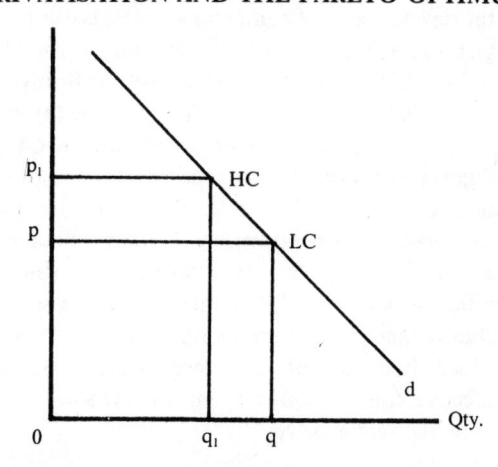

lower prices to consumers whose preferences would, thus, be better appreciated and served. The alleged effects of deregulation are also indicated in note form on the Table.

Privatisation and Pareto Efficiency

A Pareto optimum means that goods are not only produced at least cost but also they are priced and supplied to consumers at least cost, inclusive of normal profits. In terms of Fig. 15.3b this Pareto optimum is achieved when long run costs are minimised at level LC with a price of op. Inefficiency increases costs to HC which also reflect the higher price of op_1. In order to ensure goods are produced at least cost many argue that competition for the ownership of companies, by takeover bids, ensures that efficient firms with costs of LC can buy out the inefficient ones with costs of HC, in order to gain from cost savings and increase profit levels. Privatisation means company shares can be purchased which forces companies to try to achieve lowest cost levels. At the same time competition is required in product markets so prices are reduced in line with cost and, hence, allocative efficiency is guaranteed with a price of op. Competition in product markets, however, requires non-monopolistic structures and competitive pricing practices.

Strictly speaking, privatisation means not only the selling off of Nationalised Industries to the public but also the deregulation or opening up of state monopolies as well as the public tendering of services once carried out by state agencies. These latter two forms of privatisation are supposed to lead to both lowest cost and price levels, i.e. op/LC and output oq. The problem with the privatisation of a Nationalised Industry such as British Telecom is that whilst costs may be forced down to LC this does not guarantee a lower price since British Telecom is still a monopoly supplier able to set price above costs at op_1, i.e. excessive profits can still be made. The same argument applies in the case of British Aerospace which operates in monopolistic market structures. On the other hand, deregulation and the development of competitive markets can go some way to not only reducing costs, because of the ease of entry into the industry, but also to prices falling in line with costs. Hence other methods of ensuring British Telecom reduces prices in line with costs have to be sought. These may be (a) the setting up of a regulatory agency, i.e. "Oftel", to oversee price rises and the quality of consumer services and/or (b) governments introducing the threat of competition by allowing other telecommunications operators to enter the market by franchising British Telecom services to those new operators, e.g. Mercury. Economists thus argue that the key issue is not ownership (i.e. state or privatisation) but rather the degree of market competition which the industry faces. Yarrow's surveys of industrial performance concluded that private firms tend to be more efficient than public sector firms provided both operate in markets facing strong competition. However, when effective competition is absent the evidence is less clear cut and sometimes favours public sector firms.

Regulation: Problems for the 1990s — A summary

1. Regulation, it is alleged, should respond to a particular market failure or weakness, i.e. monopoly, structure, externality, or information problems. The failure should be remedied by a targeted cost effective policy not by a generally interventionist one.

2. Conduct regulation, e.g. OFTEL'S ability to determine the terms on which BT allows Mercury to use its network, often leads to "regulatory capture" and does not solve the problem of the regulated knowing more than the regulator and hence the market. On the other hand, conduct regulation designed to limit environmental externalities, cannot be left to the market. Pollution control on the privatised Water Boards must be effective.

3. Structural regulation such as privatisation designed to encourage competition may not always work. The question is whether competition is both feasible and desirable, i.e. a privatised natural monopoly does not guarantee competition whilst a deregulated taxi service may be possible but not desirable.

4. Structural deregulation and/or privatisation of industry may help market efficiency by (a) encouraging 'yardstick competition' — privatising the water boards means comparative performance can be monitored and so there are incentives to cut costs and (b) franchising or the licensing by competitive tendering of privatised natural monopolies can enable others to cut consumers costs, e.g. franchising British Telecom's operating lines means that both information flow, accountability and competitive practices can improve.

5. Governments should try to minimise regulation and use competition to improve market efficiency. Competition in the E.C. after 1992 should be stimulated in factor and product markets so making further regulation of market power unnecessary. Simple rules on information disclosure and/or private certification and self regulation may be cheaper than excessive bureaucratic regulation. Nevertheless the self regulation of financial services has not been successful. Here regulation should be targeted to improve information flow and improve consumer confidence; especially where a conflict of interest arises, e.g. it is alleged that accountants are often less than critical at audit because they rely upon the company for other financial services. Thus share prices do not always reflect accurately audited market information!

U.K. Competition Policy and the Theory of the Second Best

Attempts to achieve Pareto optimum imply price should equate with marginal cost in all markets. If we attempt to achieve this optimum in one particular market we achieve a Pareto optimum only if price equals marginal cost in all other markets. If price does not equate with marginal cost in the other markets, the

FIG. 15.4
THE THEORY OF THE SECOND BEST

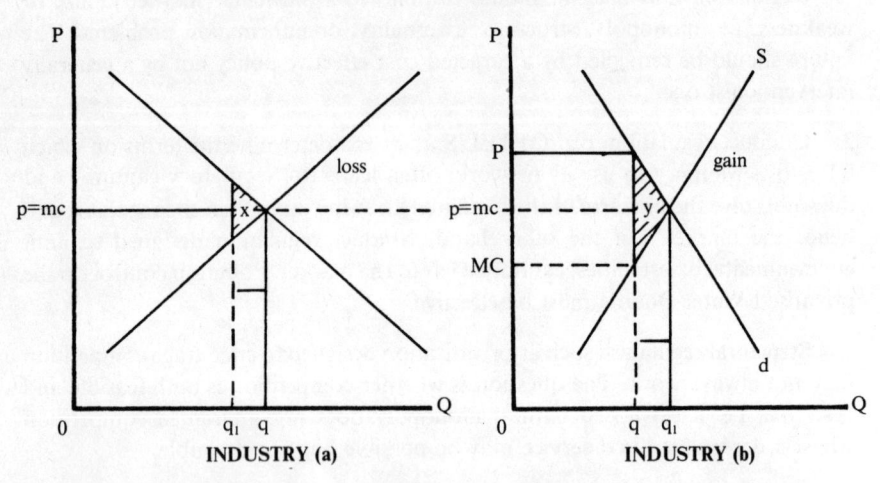

movement towards a Pareto optimum might be better achieved by deliberately moving away from p = mc in one market in order to move price towards marginal cost in another. Thus the loss from moving away from p = mc in market (a), (see Fig. 15.4) might be more than offset by the gain of moving price towards marginal cost in market (b). This is implied by the theory of the second best.

As Fig. 15.4 illustrates, market a shows a competitive market in equilibrium at op/oq, i.e. p = mc, whilst market b shows a monopolistic market at output of oq where price is greater than marginal cost.

If a policy was designed which moved the competitive equilibrium to oq_1, e.g. a tax is imposed, and this enabled industry b to be subsidised in order to move to oq_1, then the shaded loss, shown as triangle x, is less than the gain in welfare shown by the move from oq to oq_1, i.e. the triangle y. Ironically moving away from p = mc in industry (a) moves the economy towards a Pareto optimum as there is a net gain. This theory implies government industrial policy should take these factors into account since U.K. markets are neither wholly competitive nor monopolistic. The theory of the second best implies a pragmatic approach of balancing policy gains against losses in order to move to a Pareto optimum where it is possible that price is never equal to marginal cost.

CHAPTERS 14 and 15 Research

1. Can you identify any local environmental problems or disputes and hence those groups likely to potentially lose or benefit? See for example road congestion problems or chemical pollution.

2. Try to follow national political debate concerning privatisation, the environment and consumer affairs and identify the main economic factors in each particular issue. How far do political motives cloud the issue?

3. Using the Channel Tunnel link (a) draw up a list of costs and benefits to Kent and the U.K. and (b) identify the main gainers and losers and (c) discuss the impact of this project re privatisation, competition, efficiency and nationalisation.

DATA RESPONSE QUESTIONS

Question 1 — Market Structures and Welfare Economics

One way of comparing market structures in terms of benefits and costs is "**area analysis**". If the area under the supply schedule, reflecting successive units of marginal costs, is seen as total costs and the area under the demand schedule reflects total benefits or utility, then by comparing areas judgements can be made in terms of overall net benefits to the community. When social costs and benefits are different from private costs and benefits, adjustments have to be made. The following problems cover specific market problems and illustrate these ideas.

Data 1   Market X (industry)   Market Y (industry)

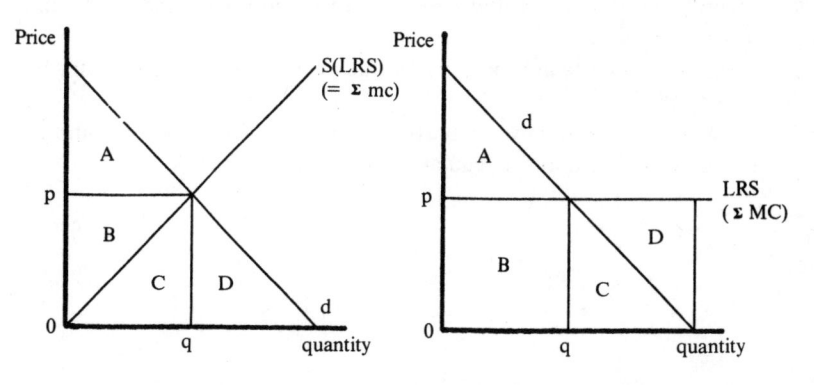

Diagrams X and Y show two **competitive industries** which experience different long run cost conditions. (LRS)

For each market show in turn:-
1. At the price of op show the total consumer benefits, costs and hence **net benefits** to the community.
2. Why does industry X provide a conclusion re Q1. at variance with the theory of competitive markets?
3. If in industry Y zero prices were charged, because it was felt it was producing a "public good", show the total benefits, costs and hence net benefits if any. Compare this result to the net benefits of op price and comment. What other factors should be borne in mind regarding public goods?

Question 2 — The Social Costs of Monopoly

Data II

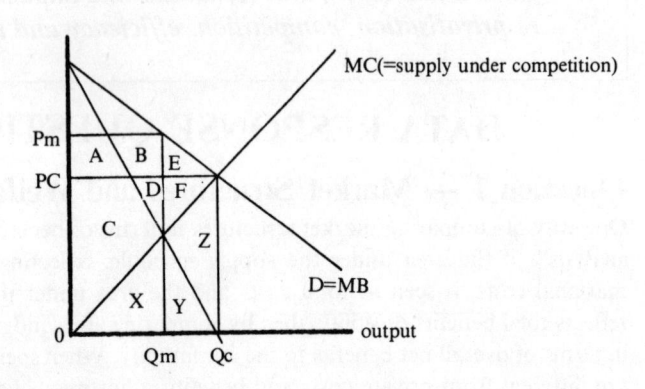

Note: Competitive Equilibrium Qc Pc
Monopoly Equilibrium Qm Pm.

1. Identify the total costs and benefits and hence net benefits of the industry when competitive.
2. Identify total costs and benefits and hence net gains if the industry became monopolistic.
3. Comparing the results you have obtained in questions 1 and 2, could you use this as a justification for regulating monopoly power?

Question 3 — The Impact of Subsidies and Tax on Markets

Data III

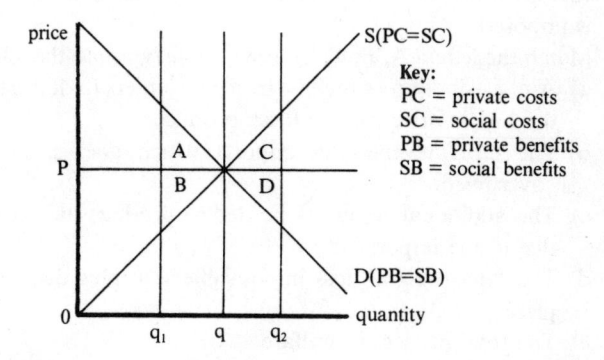

[Diagram: price vs quantity. Upward-sloping S(PC=SC) curve and downward-sloping D(PB=SB) curve intersect at price P, quantity q. Areas A and C above equilibrium price line; B and D below. Quantities q_1 and q_2 marked either side of q.]

Key:
PC = private costs
SC = social costs
PB = private benefits
SB = social benefits

The free market equilibrium in the market is op/oq but a tax on the good reduces the amount bought and sold to oq1 whilst a subsidy increases it to oq2.

1. Use "area" analysis to show that A + B are net losses to the community when a **tax** is imposed on a good **or**, e.g. on a free market wage.
2. Use area analysis to show that C + D are net losses to the community when a subsidy is given on a good.
3. Under what conditions are social costs and benefits not the same as private costs and benefits? Give examples.
4. Use the diagram to show that under certain circumstances areas A + B and C + D may be net gains to the community.

Question 4 — The Welfare Effects of a Tariff

Data V

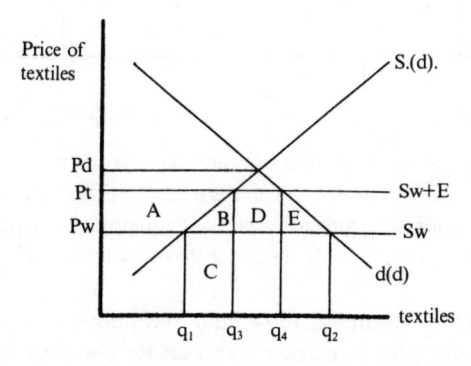

[Diagram: Price of textiles vs textiles. Domestic supply S.(d) and domestic demand d(d) curves. Horizontal lines at Pd, Pt, Pw. World supply Sw and Sw+E (with tariff). Areas A, B, C, D, E marked. Quantities q_1, q_3, q_4, q_2 on horizontal axis.]

A country produces its own textiles in the absence of trade. World imports are allowed in at Pw but a tariff is eventually placed upon the world price.

224 Governments & Markets – Monopolies – Mergers

1. Identify the domestic price before world trade.
2. Identify the world price before and after the tariff is imposed.
3. Identify home production and hence imports both before and after the tariff is imposed.
4. Match the letters A, B, C, D, E, in the diagram to the following statements:-
   a) A redistribution of income from consumers to domestic producers due to the higher price paid to these producers.
   b) The tariff revenue on imports which goes from consumers to the government.
   c) The additional resources needed to produce the extra output of textiles due to the import duty.
   d) The "deadweight" loss in consumers surplus due to the higher import price.
   e) The total net loss in welfare.
5. Show how a voluntary export restraint policy (VER) can have the same effect as a tariff.

Question 5 — Public Transport (x) versus Private Car Use (y)

Data VI

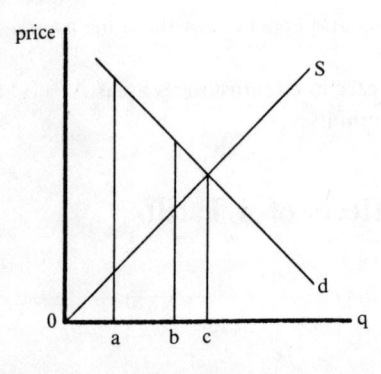

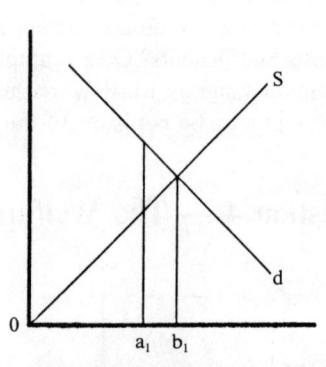

No. of trips/volume of traffic

In a city the public transport system operates as a profit maximising monopolist and its outputs oa. Private motor car use is a competitive market and operates at ob_1 output. It is proposed to subsidise public transport so output increases to ob. This subsidy will have the effect of reducing private motor car demand and hence output to oa_1.

1. Use the above diagram to show that the above policy will distort the allocation of resources in market y and create a welfare loss in y.
2. Compare the welfare gains and losses in both market x and y and show that overall net benefits increase from such a policy.

DATA RESPONSE QUESTIONS

Question 1 — A Liberalised Coal Market

The case for liberalization begins from the argument that there is no obvious economic reason for centralizing the British coal industry in one corporation. The industry is not a natural monopoly, where efficiency dictates that there should be only one supplier. Parts of some of the other fuel industries do have natural monopoly elements — for instance, long distance transmission and local distribution networks for electricity and gas. In such circumstances, there is a case for regulation (of which state ownership is one example) so that consumers are not exploited. But coal is a naturally competitive industry. Coal deposits are dispersed by nature, they vary in terms of size, quality and capital requirements and the natural state of the industry is one in which there are competing suppliers, though efficiency considerations would probably prevent there being separate ownership of each deposit. The essence of liberalization is increased competition. It must therefore be distinguished clearly from some of the privatization practised by the present government, which has involved no liberalization at all but the mere transfer of monopolies from public to private sector. Privatization British Gas-style is little, if any, advance on continued nationalized ownership.

Source: Lloyds Bank Review, April 1987.

1. Explain what is meant by natural monopoly and say why efficiency dictates that there should be only one supplier. Give examples.
2. Use economic analysis to show the impact of a liberalisation policy upon the National Coal Board.
3. Explain what is meant by the last two sentences.

Question 2 — Peak Load Pricing

This passage discusses the problem of intensive road and bridge use which gives rise to the 'peak load' pricing problem.

In April 1986 I* proposed, in a letter to *The Times*, the above kind of 'peak-load pricing' solution to the problem of congestion of bridges and tunnels. Journalists on local newspapers in Cardiff, Newport and Bristol gave the story some prominence, because of the local news value of anything to do with the Severn bridge, which is severely congested at peak times and is of great economic importance as the main road link between the industrial areas of South Wales and the rest of the country. At present there is a toll of 20p for cars and 40p for lorries which is charged at all times of the day and night. The bridge administrators essentially see the toll as a way of raising revenue to cover costs, including costs of toll collection, maintenance and interest on the debt incurred to finance the construction of the bridge. In an interview with a journalist I suggested that the toll should be abolished off-peak, and raised at peak-times to achieve significant reductions in congestion, with a substantially higher charge for heavy lorries (essentially, of course, I had the analysis of the previous sections in mind). Somehow the latter proposal was translated into a specific recommendation of a £2 toll for cars and a £10 toll for lorries — without knowing the precise demand and cost curves, of course, I had not been able to specify numbers, but journalists like the shock value of figures of this kind.

*Prof. G. Rees, Cardiff University, U.K.

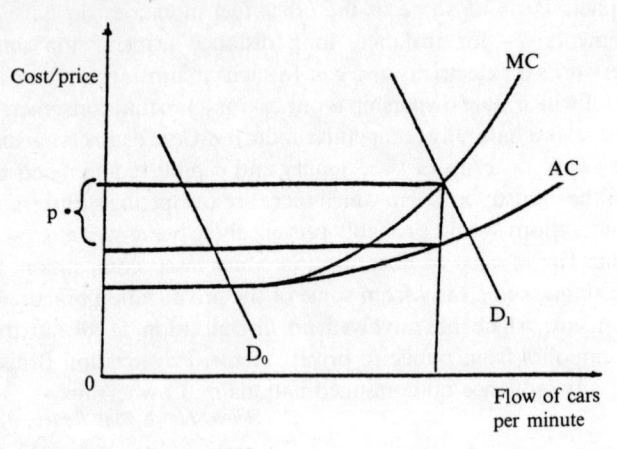

Source: Economic Review, January 1987.

1. Relate the passage to the diagram showing such things as the proposed toll, peak demand, social costs etc., economic efficiency etc.
2. How would bridge users, economists and administrators view the toll?
3. Who should pay for roads and bridges within the transport system? Why?

16 OPTIMISING BEHAVIOUR — DECISION THEORY

AIMS: *To define, explain and discuss*
- *Economic optimising behaviour*
- *Decisions taken by consumer, factors and producers*
- *Economic applications of decision theory*

KEY CONCEPTS
Utility, indifference analysis, budget line, Income Substitution effects, inferior goods, Giffen goods, isocost, isoquant, price lines, normal goods.

Consumer Behaviour

1. *Marginal Utility (M.U.) and Demand*

Demand Theory assumes that consumers allocate their incomes so they maximise total utility, satisfaction or benefits from their outlay. This means consumers relate the utility derived from each extra unit purchased of a good to the price of the good. Maximum satisfaction or benefit is achieved when the ratio of marginal utility (M.U.) to price for each good is equal, i.e.

$$\frac{\text{MU of good x}}{\text{price of x}} = \frac{\text{MU of good y}}{\text{price of y}} = \frac{\text{MU of good z}}{\text{price of z}}$$

TABLE 16.1

Example

Kg consumed	Goods Price	x £4	y £2	z £1
1		36	30	32
2		[24]	22	28
3		30	16	20
4		18	[12]	14
5		16	10	8
6		10	4	[6]
7		6	2	4

Table 16.1 shows the marginal utilities derived from consuming extra units of goods x, y and z given the prices of each. Using the above formula, the best combination for the consumer will be when the MU/P ratios are equal, i.e. $\frac{24}{4} = \frac{12}{2} = \frac{6}{1}$ or a consumption of 2 units of x, 4 of y and 6 of z. If, for example, the price of x increased to 6, these ratios can only be maintained by the consumer by reducing the consumption of x to 1 unit, i.e. $\frac{36}{6} = \frac{6}{1}$ which

is the same ratio as for y and z. This shows that as the price of x increases from 4 to 6, consumption of x reduces from 2 to 1 and hence the downward sloping demand schedule is derived.

FIG. 16.1
INDIFFERENCE CURVES (Map)

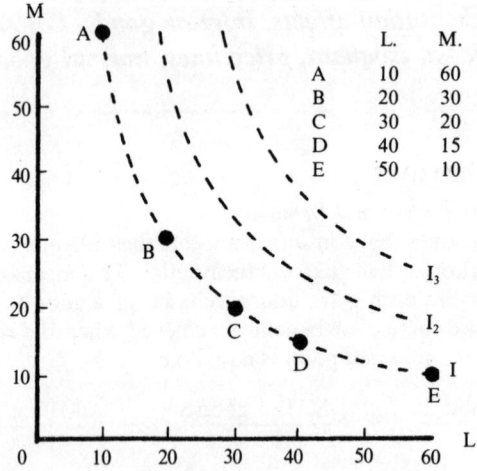

	L.	M.
A	10	60
B	20	30
C	30	20
D	40	15
E	50	10

2. Indifference Curve Analysis (ICA)

ICA relates the tastes, incomes and relative price of goods in order to illustrate the rational consumers' buying behaviour in terms of maximising utility or benefit. An indifference curve shows the different combinations, A to E, see Fig. 16.1, of goods L and M which give exactly the same total utility. Indifference curves, concave to the origin, slope downwards indicating that as more of one good is consumed its opportunity cost increases and this reflects the rate of substitution between each good. Different shaped curves reflect different preferences of tastes between each bundle of goods, i.e. a flatter indifference curve would show that the consumer prefers more L for any given amount of M foregone. Fig. 16.1 shows the indifference curve I for goods L and M and a decrease or increase in overall satisfaction levels would be indicated by an indifference curve which is closer or

FIG. 16.2
BUDGET OR PRICE LINE

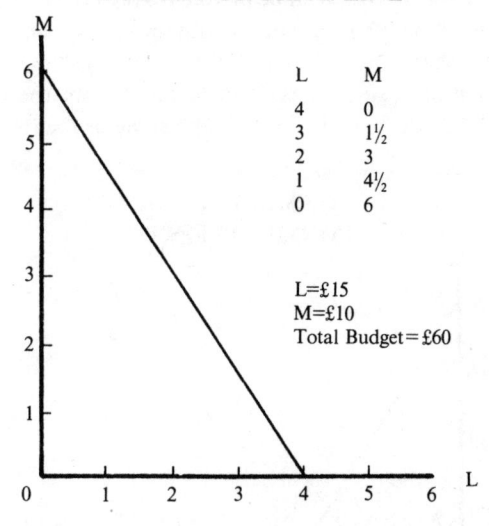

L	M
4	0
3	1½
2	3
1	4½
0	6

L=£15
M=£10
Total Budget=£60

FIG. 16.3
INDIFFERENCE CURVE EQUILIBRIUM

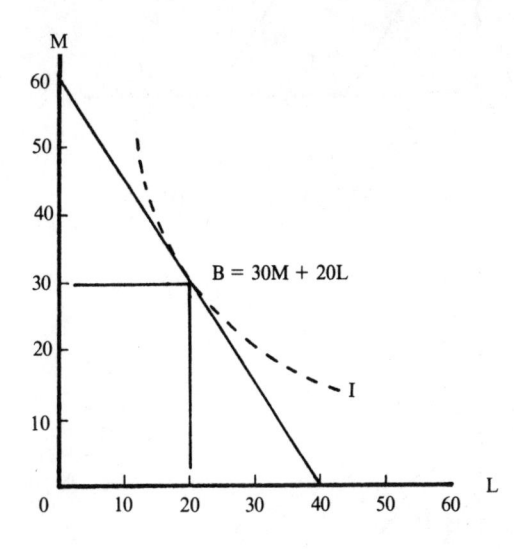

B = 30M + 20L

further from the origin zero. Indifference curves I_1 and I_2 give an indifference map showing increasing levels of utility as the indifference curves shift from the origin. Whilst indifference curves show consumers' tastes, the actual amount of L and M consumed, will depend upon the relative price of each good which is given by the

230 Optimising Behaviour – Decision Theory

total income or budget of the consumer. Given a budget of £60 and relative prices of £15 for L and £10 for M, these can be plotted on the budget or price line shown in Fig. 16.2. Putting the indifference curve I with the budget line in Fig. 16.3, we see that B is the best combination of L and M for the consumer, i.e. it maximises satisfaction, given prices, since it is furthest away from the origin. Here the marginal rate of substitution of L for M is the same as the ratio of their prices.

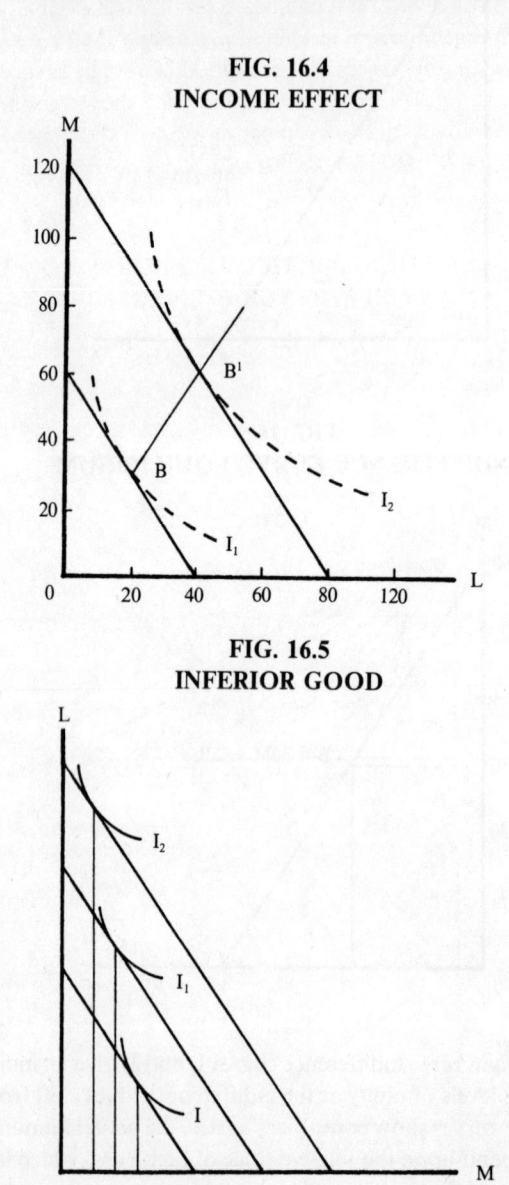

FIG. 16.4
INCOME EFFECT

FIG. 16.5
INFERIOR GOOD

Applications and Predicted Behaviour

a) *A Rise or Fall in Income – Income Effect*

With a normal good, as consumers' incomes rise or fall, the budget line shifts parallel to the origin as Fig. 16.4 shows with I_1 to I_2, and the optimum combination of L and M consumed increases as B moves to B^1. Thus the consumer buys an extra 30 of M and extra 20 of L. If income falls or all prices double, we move from the outer to inner budget line and indifference schedule I_1 where less is bought of each. Under certain circumstances less of a good is bought as income rises, (see Chapter 4). These are inferior goods and as Fig. 16.5 shows, good M behaves in this way. As budgets increase, the consumer moves to indifference schedules I_1 to I_2 which shows less of M purchased.

FIG. 16.6
CONSTRUCTING THE DEMAND CURVE FROM INDIFFERENCE CURVES

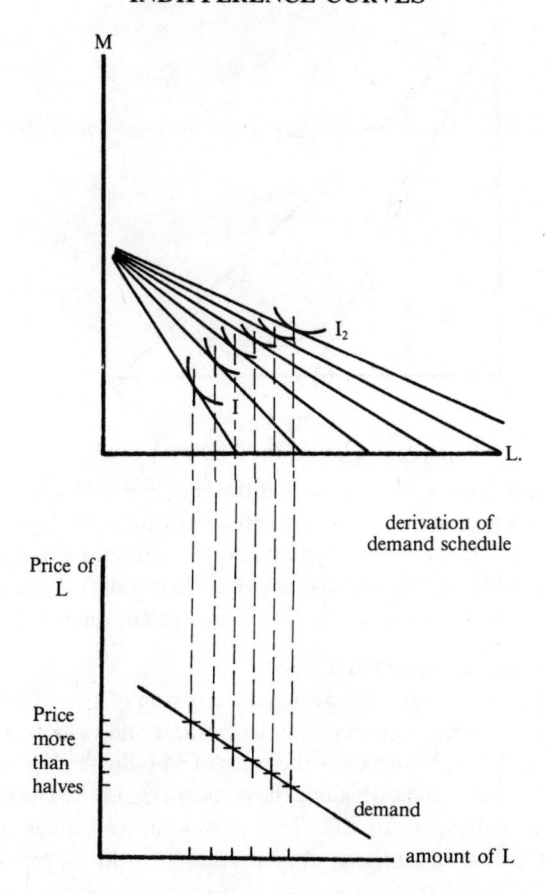

232 Optimising Behaviour – Decision Theory

b) *A Change in the Relative Price of a Good (Substitution Effect)*
If good L becomes cheaper than M, then the price line pivots on the L axis so more of L can be bought with the same income. This is shown in Fig. 16.6.. and as the price line pivots the consumer moves onto higher indifference schedules and buys more of L. If this fall in price is plotted against a quantity of M bought, see Fig. 16.6, then the normal downward sloping demand curve is derived. Fig. 16.7 shows an unorthodox good where the rise in price from OS to OR leads to an increase in demand. These may be goods which have a 'snob' appeal or where speculative demand conditions apply. See Chapter 4 on 'perverse demand' behaviour.

FIG. 16.7
UNORTHODOX GOOD

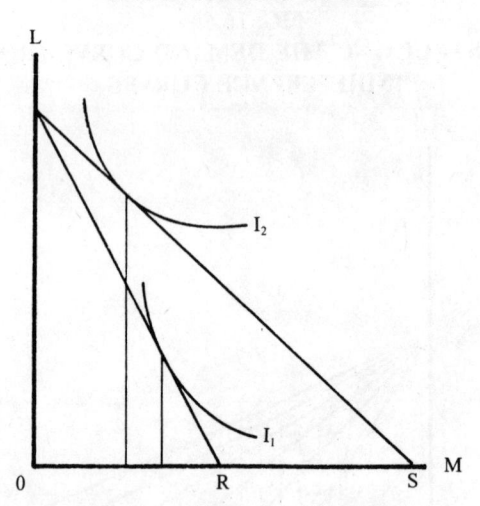

c) *Substitutes and Complements*
Figs. 16.8 and 16.9 show the typical indifference curve shapes of substitutes and complements where the rate of transformation varies. In Fig. 16.8 as the price of b falls, only more of the cheaper good is bought. Less of a is bought so a is a substitute for b. In Fig. 16.9 as the price of one falls the amount of both a and b purchased increases so indicating they are complementary goods.

d) *Income and Substitution Effects*
A fall in the price of a good will increase consumption of a good because in most cases the incomes and substitution effects are positive and vice versa for a good in the event of a price rise. In this case, the price of M falls, see Fig. 16.10. and the price of all other goods are shown along the vertical axis, i.e. R. The price of M falls so the price line RB pivots to RC. This moves the consumer onto a higher indifference curve I to I2 and overall consumption of M increases from 1 to 3

FIG. 16.8
SUBSTITUTES (Cheaper b, more b less a)

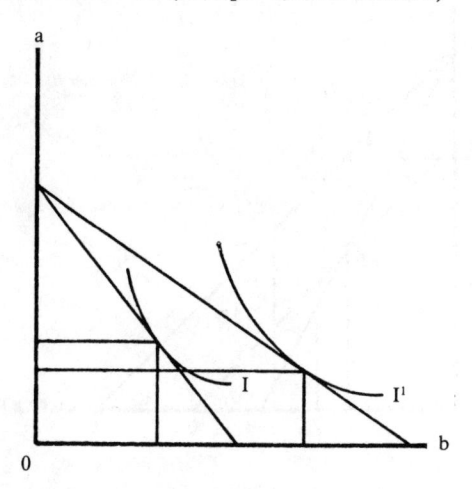

FIG. 16.9
COMPLEMENTS (Cheaper b, more of each)

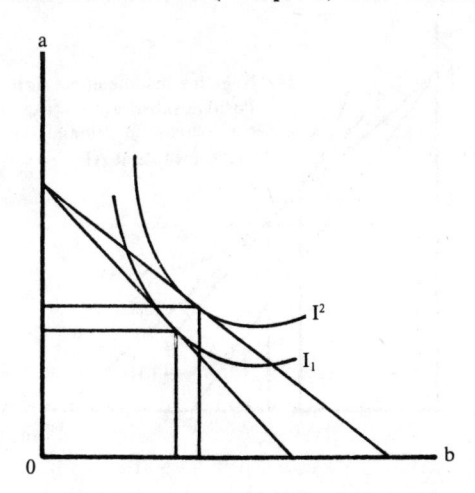

along the horizontal axis. If we now reduce the consumer's real income to the original level, moving the budget line parallel back to I as shown by $R^1 C^1$ it is possible to split up the change of demand from 1 to 3. There is a substitution effect in favour of the cheaper good measured from 1 to 2. This is because real income is the same as before but the price of M has fallen. This means that the change from 2 to 3 is the income effect, i.e. more of M is purchased because the

FIG. 16.10
INCOME/SUBSTITUTION EFFECT

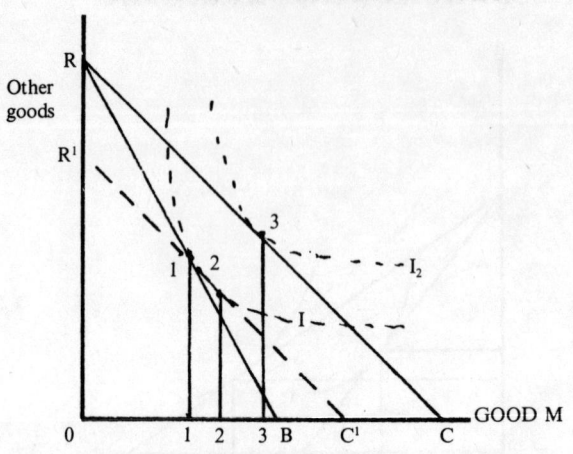

FIG. 16.11
BEHAVIOUR OF A GIFFEN GOOD (Inferior Good)

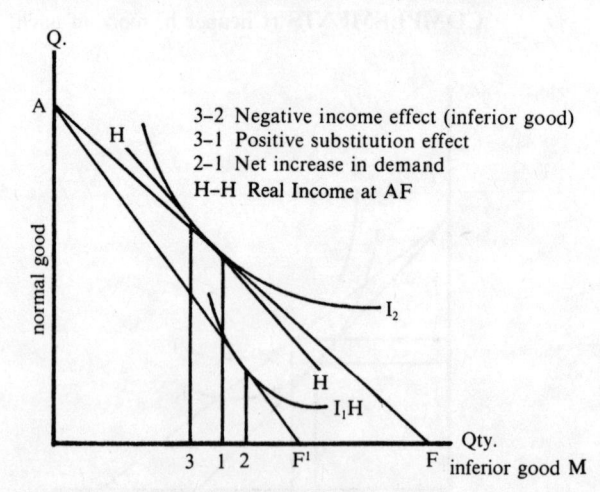

3-2 Negative income effect (inferior good)
3-1 Positive substitution effect
2-1 Net increase in demand
H-H Real Income at AF

consumer experiences a rise in real income due to the fall in the price of M. A rise in the price of M will reduce demand for the same reasons. In the case of a Giffen good, a fall in the price of M will have led to a reduction in demand for M or vice versa. This is because the income effect works in the opposite direction, it is negative, and this swamps the substitution effect which still works in favour of the cheaper good. When prices rise the perverse behaviour of the income effect once again outweighs the positive substitution effect. Fig. 16.11 shows this behaviour

FIG. 16.12
WORK OR LEISURE

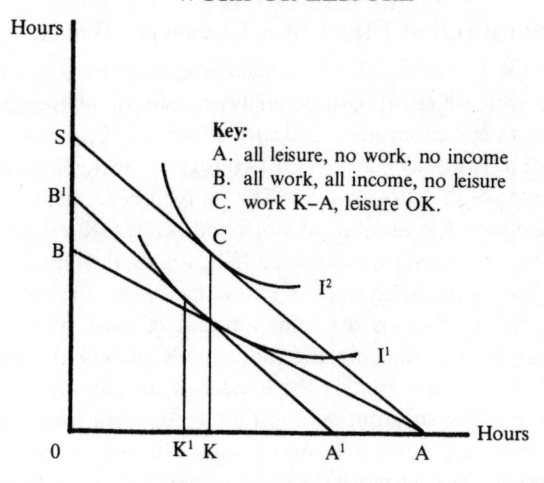

Hours

Key:
A. all leisure, no work, no income
B. all work, all income, no leisure
C. work K-A, leisure OK.

I^2
I^1

0   K^1 K A^1 A   Hours

FIG. 16.13
SUPPLY OF EFFORT

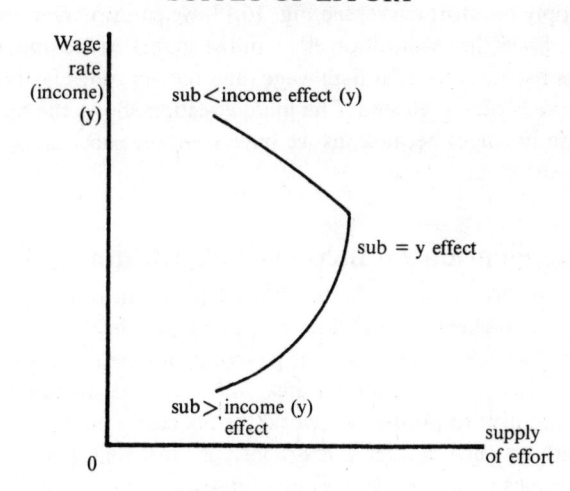

Wage rate (income) (y)

sub < income effect (y)

sub = y effect

sub > income (y) effect

supply of effort

for an inferior good. When price rises from AF to A^1F^1 there is a net increase in demand from position 1 to 2. The substitution effect from 1 to 3 reduces the quantity of the inferior good demanded. As the good is inferior the income effect from 3 to 2 increases the amount of the inferior good demanded. For a Giffin good the income effect dominates so 2 is to the right of 1.

Application — Factor Markets

The Income Substitution Effect of a Change in Wages

The impact of a rise in wages due to an increase in wage rates or a cut in income tax, designed to increase effort, can be analysed using indifference analysis, see Fig. 16.12. A person can either work and earn all income, B, or not work and have more leisure, A. The trade off between the two is given by the slope of the line AB which shows the price of work (wages). The indifference schedule I_1, shows the current preference with KA amount of work and hence OK leisure consumed. If now the wage rate increases, or income tax falls, to AS, then more can be earned by working, i.e. the opportunity cost of leisure has risen. The indifference curve I2 now touches SA so there is the same amount of work and leisure time as before, i.e. KA, OK. By reducing the individual's present income to the old income SA to B^1A^1, we can analyse the impact of the income and substitution effect of a wage rise. The substitution effect increases work from AK to A^1K^1 as leisure becomes more expensive in terms of work. This means we substitute work for leisure. However, since we work the same amount as before, the income effect exactly offsets the substitution effect and is equal to K^1K. Evidence regarding the impact of cutting income tax in the U.K. often confirms this analysis. Applying this to the supply of effort curve, see Fig. 16.13, we can say the normal curve of labour supply shows the substitution effect outweighing the income effect so more work as wages rise. However, at high wage rates the opposite effect occurs so less work and leisure is now preferred. The middle section shows the same supply of effort for a rise in wages because, as we have seen, the substitution and income effects exactly offset each other.

General Application of Income/Substitution Effect

Several years ago Professor Art Laffer of the USA pointed out that tax revenue would be zero both when tax rates were zero and when they were 100 per cent. In the former case they are zero because the government does not wish to collect any tax; in the latter case they are zero because when tax rates are 100 per cent there would be no incentive to produce or work, the tax base would be zero and so tax revenue would be zero. Laffer's main insight was that between these two unrealistic extremes there must be a point of maximum tax revenue, as illustrated in Fig. 16.14, i.e. since revenue is positive between the extremes there will be some tax rate at which tax revenue is maximised.

Economists are in broad agreement that Laffer must be almost tautologically correct; the main controversy is about the shape of the curve, which in practice may be quite complex. The curve itself reflects the disincentive effects of taxation. In the lower reaches of the curve, revenue rises when tax rates are raised. This could reflect at least two possibilities. First, the income effect could dominate the

FIG. 16.14
UK 'LAFFER CURVE'

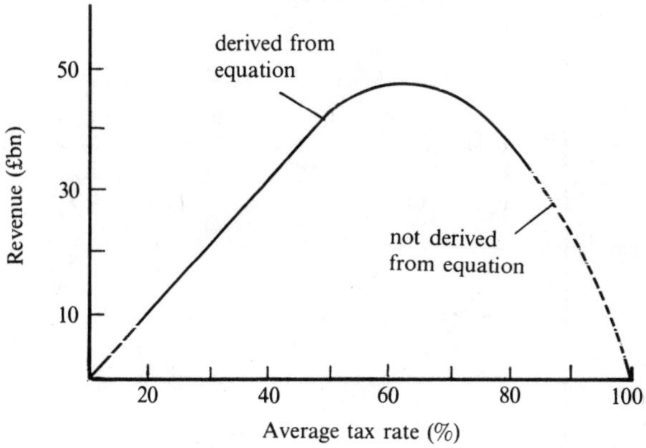
Revenue (£bn)
50
30
10
derived from
equation
not derived
from equation
20
40
60
80
100
Average tax rate (%)

substitution effect so that higher tax rates increase the taxable base by injecting a new incentive effect into working behaviour. Secondly, the substitution effect could dominate the income effect so that higher tax rates inject a new disincentive effect which reduces the taxable base. However, as long as the marginal percentage reduction in the taxable base is less than the marginal percentage increase in the tax rate, revenue will rise. At the peak of the curve, the percentage reduction in the taxable base is exactly equal to the percentage increase in the tax rate. To the right of the peak, revenue begins to fall, since higher tax rates generate a percentage reduction in the taxable base via disincentive effects that is greater than the percentage increase in tax rates.

This does not of course imply that governments should seek to maximise tax revenue by aiming for the peak of the 'Laffer curve', for this can be achieved only by generating disincentive effects, perhaps on a massive scale. Even if higher taxation made people work harder, it obviously would not follow that the authorities should raise taxation, since such a policy ignores the value that people attach to leisure. Furthermore, the tax system has distributional objectives which must be entered into policy calculations. Nevertheless, it is possible to calculate from the 'Laffer curve' the implicit trade-off between disincentive effects and tax revenue as is illustrated.

Producers Optimising Behaviour: Isoquants and Isocosts

In the long run a business can vary factor proportions in order to minimise costs for any given level of output. An isoquant shows the firm's alternative methods, a to d in Fig. 16.15, of producing a given output level of 23 units. The shape of the isoquant reflects a diminishing rate of substitution, i.e. from c to d it requires one less unit of capital but three more units of labour. The isoquant is similar to an

238 *Optimising Behaviour – Decision Theory*

**FIG. 16.15
ISOQUANTS**

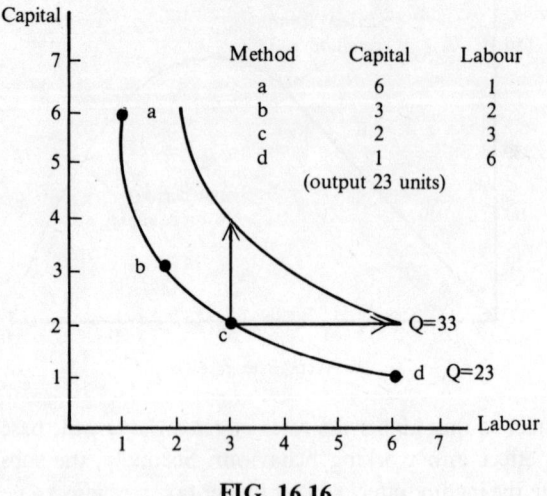

Method	Capital	Labour
a	6	1
b	3	2
c	2	3
d	1	6

(output 23 units)

**FIG. 16.16
ISOCOSTS**

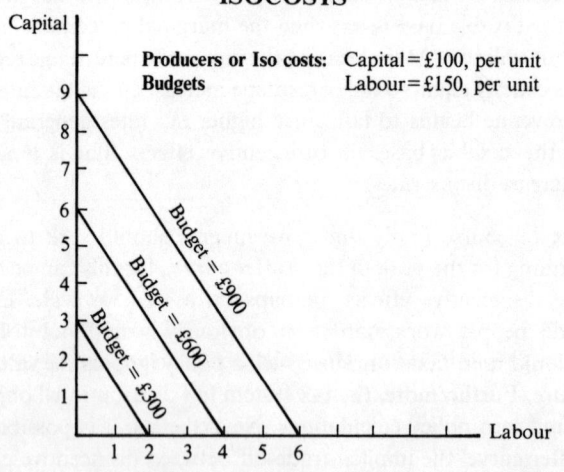

Producers or Iso costs: Capital = £100, per unit
Budgets Labour = £150, per unit

indifference curve but instead of showing equal utility it shows equal output. An isoquant map shows a set of isoquants for different output levels, i.e. 23, 33. Furthermore the increase from 23 to 33, around 50% more output, can only be achieved (with fixed factors of 3 labour or 2 capital) at a diminishing rate. In both cases the arrows in Fig. 16.15 show for each fixed factor twice as much variable factor is needed to increase output by 50%, i.e. 2 to 4 and 3 to 6.

FIG. 16.17
THE LEAST COST COMBINATION OF e

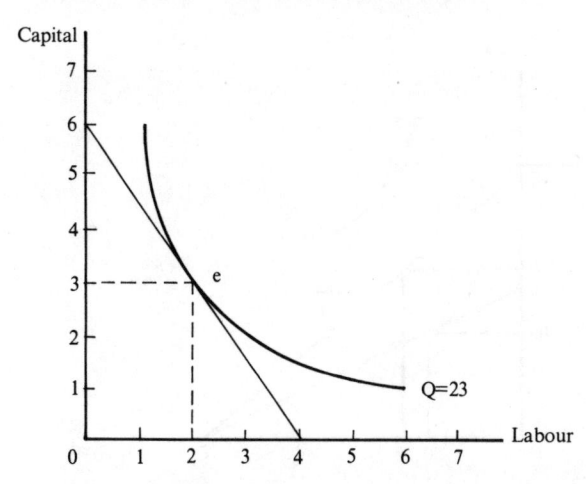

Isocosts. An isocost line shows alternative factor combinations that can be purchased for a given outlay, i.e. the producer's budget. If labour costs £150 and capital £100 a unit, then with a budget of £600 either 6 capital or 4 units of labour or some other combination can be purchased as shown in Fig. 16.16. If the budget halves or doubles the line moves towards or from the origin as shown. Putting both isoquant and isocost together, in Fig. 16.17, the least cost combination for 23 units is shown at e where both just touch. If the total cost of 23 units is £600 and 3 units of capital and 2 units of labour are employed, then the unit cost is $\frac{£600}{23 \text{ units}}$, i.e. around £26 each.

Application (1) Capital (machinery) and Labour in the Construction Industry

In Fig. 16.18 the current building programme of 10 houses minimises costs when £100,000 worth of capital and £50,000 worth of labour units are employed. In the long run the cost of capital decreases and this shifts the capital to labour ratio from AC to BC. The relative decline in the cost of capital means that the firm is able to produce 15 houses, in the long run and proportionately employs more capital as well as more labour because of the income effect derived from cheaper capital costs. The rise in capital use to £170,000 is due both to income and substitution effect whilst extra workers are employed due to the income effect as outlined. The same analysis applies if the price of capital had risen, i.e. BC had moved to AC.

FIG. 16.18
PRICE CHANGES AND FACTOR DEMAND

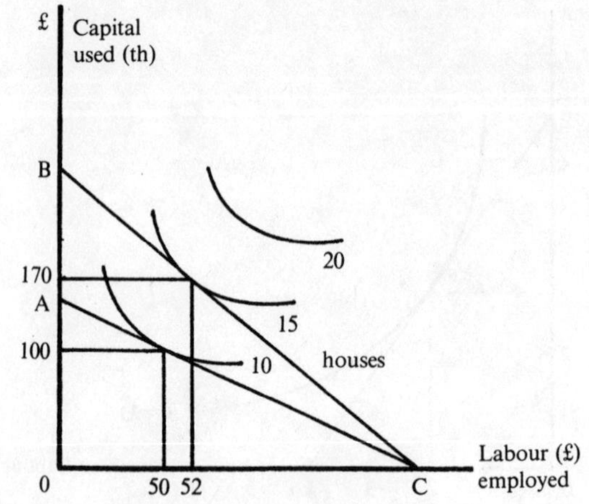
£
Capital
used (th)
B
170
A
100
0
50 52
C
20
15
10
houses
Labour (£)
employed

FIG. 16.19
HOUSING SUBSIDIES?

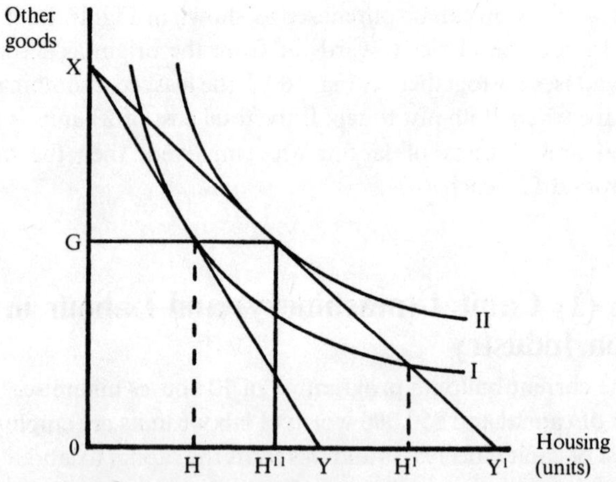
Other
goods
X
G
0
H
H''
Y
H'
Y'
II
I
Housing
(units)

Application (2) Housing Subsidies?

Housing subsidies can be given in a variety of forms such as tax relief on mortgage payments and/or by subsidised council housing. The efficiency of such subsidy policies can be analysed using Fig. 16.19. The original housing price line is XY which, when reduced by a subsidy, pivots to XY^1. The subsidy can be based upon providing some amount of council housing, i.e. OH^1 which is based upon the need of the community or by leaving the subsidised mortgage owner to buy houses based upon individual wants, as given by OH^{11}. **Note:** The original amount of other goods and housing units consumed are OG/OH. Using indifference analysis it can be seen OH^1 housing units leaves the user on the same indifference curve I as before, since other goods have been sacrificed. The mortgage subsidy moves the house user to a new higher indifference curve II which improves the situation because more housing is not paid for by consuming fewer of other goods, i.e. overall efficiency (welfare) is improved. However, this analysis ignores the social problems of insufficient housing for the community since OH^{11} may still be inadequate housing provision since there may be problems of homelessness, social delinquency and ill health, etc,

DATA RESPONSE QUESTIONS

Question 1

In the diagram below the curves, labelled 100 and 200, show the combinations of capital and labour which a firm requires in order to produce 100 and 200 units of output respectively. The parallel straight lines show combinations of capital and labour that can be hired by specified money outlays.

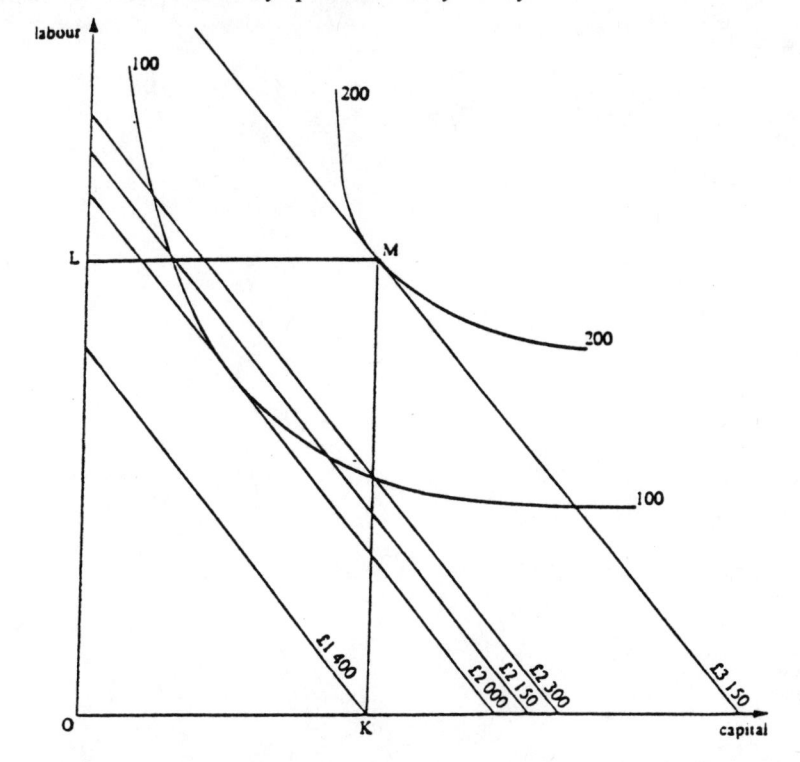

In the short run capital is in fixed supply and the firm is in equilibrium at M, producing 200 units at a cost of £3,150. There is a fall in demand and the firm decides to reduce output to 100 units. At this level of output its costs in the short run will be

A £1,400
B £2,000
C £2,150
D £2,300
E £3,150

In the long run the costs associated with the new level of output of 100 will be:-
1. £1,400
2. £2,000
3. £3,150
4. £2,300

BASIC MATHEMATICAL & STATISTICAL CONCEPTS

AIMS: To define, explain and discuss
- Statistical concepts and their use in economics

KEY CONCEPTS
Graphs, trends, indices, tables, histograms, stocks, flows, marginals, regression and correlation, discounting techniques.

Statistics — Descriptive

The following provide a selection of simple statistical and quantitative concepts which may be useful when answering data response questions. They do *not* provide a comprehensive treatment and students are advised to refer to the standard texts on statistics and mathematics.

Averages

1. *Averages:- The Mean*

TABLE 17.1
SCHOOLS AND COSTS 1986/87

Authority	Pupil : Teacher Ratio Secondary Schools	Secondary School Unit Cost per Pupil (£)
1. Barnet	19.9	1305.5
2. Brent	11.2	1807.9
3. Enfield	14.9	1220.9
4. Hertfordshire	15.0	1213.1

Source: T.E.S., 31/10/86.

Most people use the "mean" when they calculate an average. This is calculated by dividing, as in the case of unit cost per secondary school pupil, the total costs by the number of pupils. Again the pupil:teacher ratio is calculated in the same way; by dividing the total number of teachers in an authority by the total number of secondary school children. It is simple to work out and easy to understand. In economics it is used to calculate average cost and average revenue etc.

Question on Table 17.1. Comment on the cost-effectiveness of secondary school education between the four authorities.

2. *Averages:- Median and Mode and Frequency Distributions*
Often the mean is used in Income analysis to calculate average or "per-capita" income in a country. However, as with all mean average figures, it fails to take account of the overall distribution of income, so this average can sometimes be misleading and unrealistic. In order to give a better indication of average incomes the "median" can be used. The median is the value of the middle item between the lowest and highest value and would therefore indicate more accurately, for example, the representative income in the country. The mode is another measure of the average and is the most common or most frequently occurring value in the distribution.

FREQUENCY DISTRIBUTIONS show the overall behaviour of the variable and indicates whether the pattern is "skewed" or "normal" in its behaviour.

FIG. 17.1

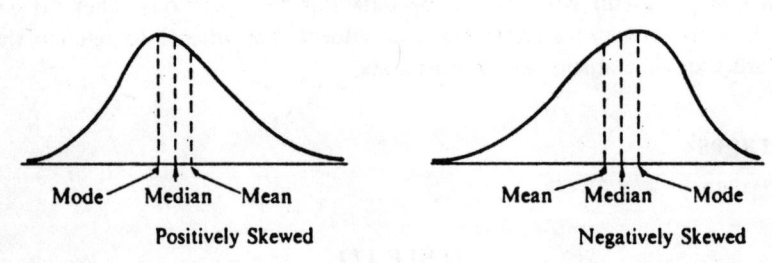

Mode — Median — Mean
Positively Skewed

Mean — Median — Mode
Negatively Skewed

SKEWED DISTRIBUTIONS see Fig. 17.1
A frequency distribution is positively skewed if the right tail is longer, ie. mean > median > mode. A distribution is negatively skewed if the left tail is longer or mode > median > mean.

FIG. 17.2

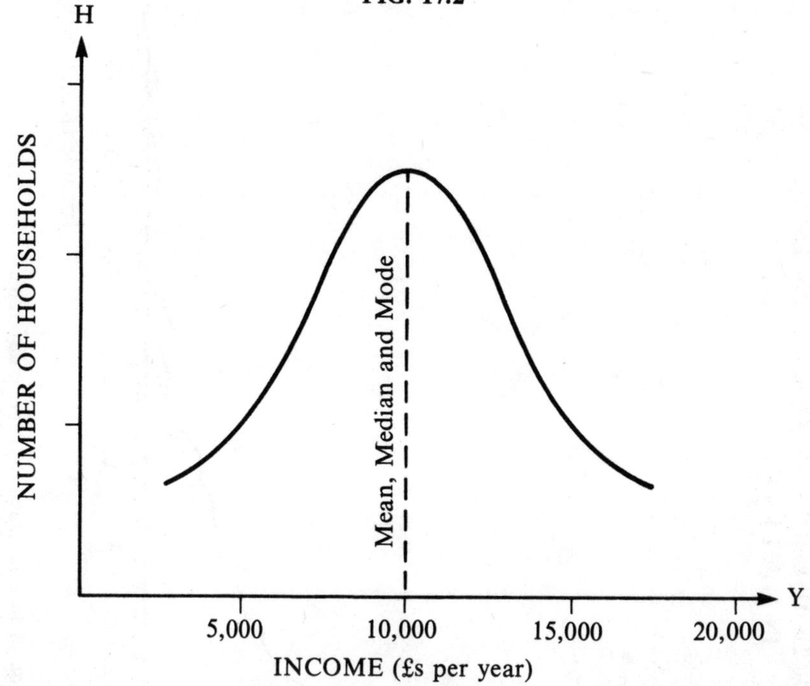
H
NUMBER OF HOUSEHOLDS
Mean, Median and Mode
Y
5,000
10,000
15,000
20,000
INCOME (£s per year)

A perfectly normal distribution of income; the mean, median and mode coincide.

In a perfectly normal distribution of income, see Fig. 17.2, referred to as a "bell" curve the mean, median and mode would be the same, ie. £10,000 and if everyone earned the same, ie. £10,000, the distribution would be a single line perpendicular to £10,000 on the Y axis. However, in the real world, income distribution is usually lopsided and in the case of Fig. 17.3 the U.K. distribution in 1979 indicates a 'skewed' distribution with each average different. Again Fig. 17.4 shows the frequency distributions, in percentage terms, for manual male and female G.B. employees in 1984 which indicate different overall income distributions.

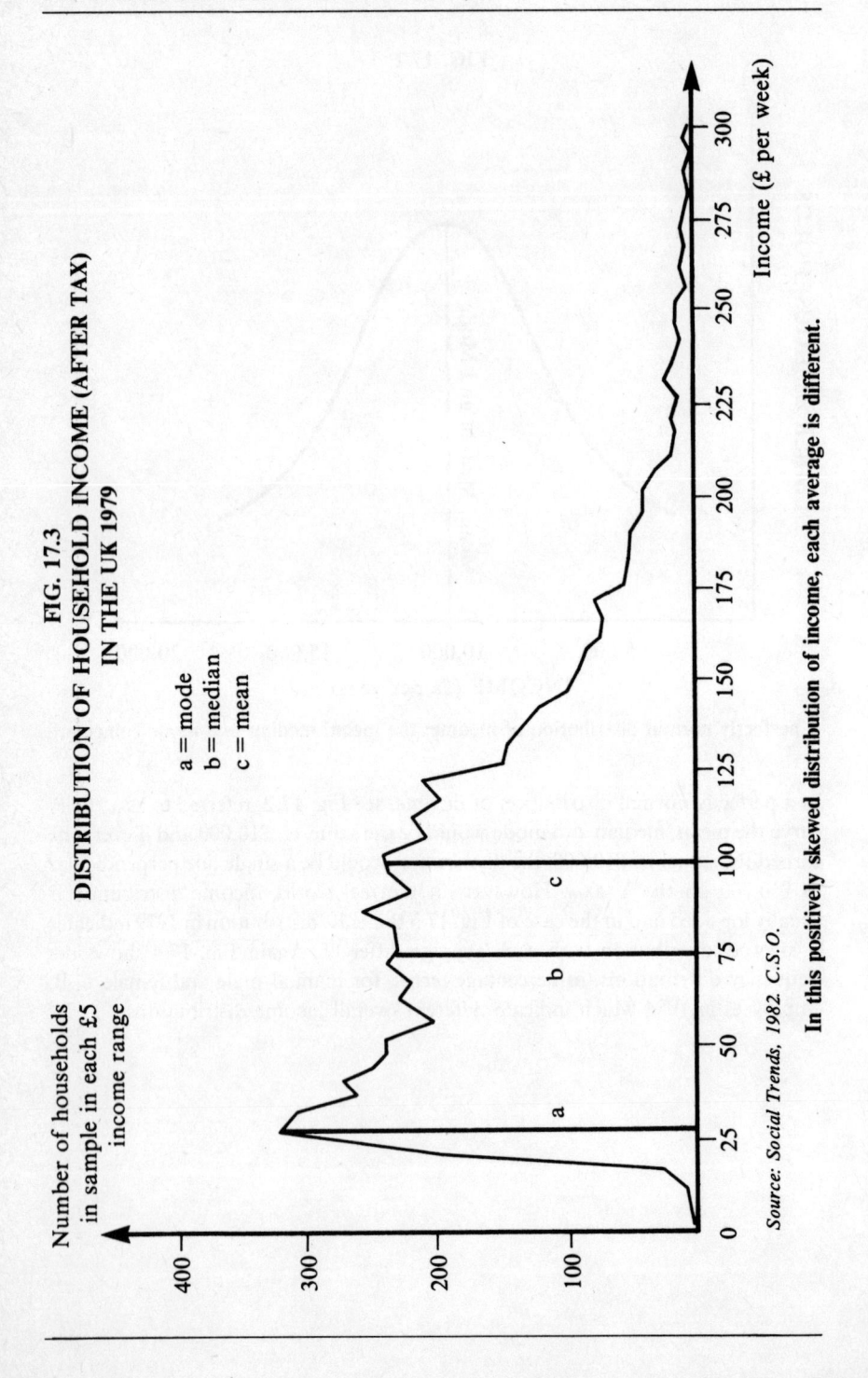

FIG. 17.3
DISTRIBUTION OF HOUSEHOLD INCOME (AFTER TAX) IN THE UK 1979

a = mode
b = median
c = mean

Source: Social Trends, 1982. C.S.O.

In this positively skewed distribution of income, each average is different.

Fig. 17.4 shows the frequency distribution in percentage terms, for manual employees, male and female, in 1984. This illustrates how frequency distributions can vary and in both cases the distributions are positively skewed with most workers earning low wages.

FIG. 17.4
DISTRIBUTION OF GROSS WEEKLY EARNINGS[1], APRIL 1984
Great Britain
Estimated percentage with gross weekly earnings in £5 earnings groups

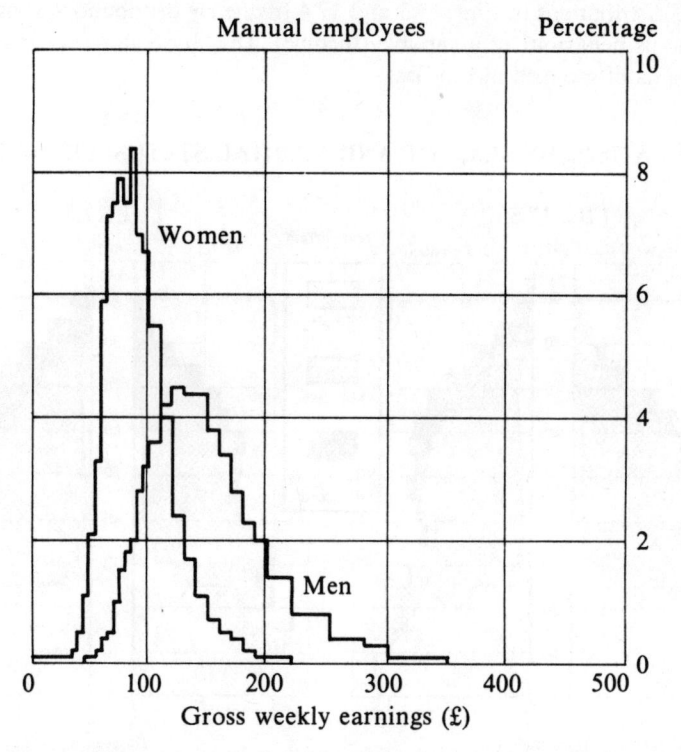

Manual employees   Percentage

Gross weekly earnings (£)

[1]Of full-time employees on adult rates whose pay for the survey pay-period was not affected by absence.

Source: New Earnings Survey, Department of Employment, Social Trends 1986 C.S.O.

MANUAL INCOME DISTRIBUTION, G.B., APRIL 1984

Question on Fig. 17.4. Comment on the distributions of male and female earnings in 1984.

248 Basic Mathematical & Statistical Concepts

Graphs and Charts

Graphs and charts are simple devices which help illustrate economic theory, data, and findings. A familiarity with the main types are essential when answering data response questions.

(i) Histograms

These relate the value of discrete or grouped data, along the horizontal axis, to the number of observations or frequency, along the vertical axis. A typical example is the "Population Pyramids" of Figs. 17.5 and 17.6, where frequency is along the horizontal axis and the variable (age) is along the vertical axis. Also, the income distributions in Figs. 17.3 and 17.4 frequency distributions showing the continuous behaviour of a variable (Income). They have all been derived from histograms of grouped income data.

POPULATION: BY SEX, AGE AND MARITAL STATUS, 1971 AND 1981

FIG. 17.5 **FIG. 17.6**

Great Britain

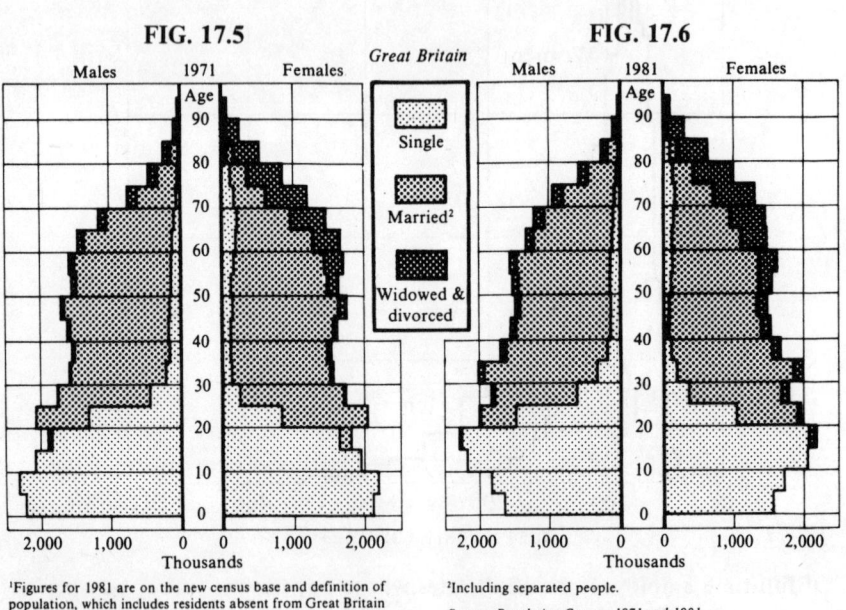

[1]Figures for 1981 are on the new census base and definition of population, which includes residents absent from Great Britain and excludes overseas visitors. The reverse was the case in 1971.
Source: Social Trends, 1986. C.S.O.

[2]Including separated people.
Source: Population Census, 1971 and 1981.
Office of Population Censuses and Surveys.

Frequency Distributions of GB Population

Note: Frequency or numbers are along horizontal axis and class intervals are on vertical axis.

Question on Figs. 17.5, 17.6. Comment on the changing structure of the GB population between 1971 and 1981. Discuss their economic significance.

(ii) Bar Charts

Bar charts represent data by a series of bars which visually indicate the scale of the variables. Figs. 17.7 and 17.8 illustrate their use in economics.

FIG. 17.7

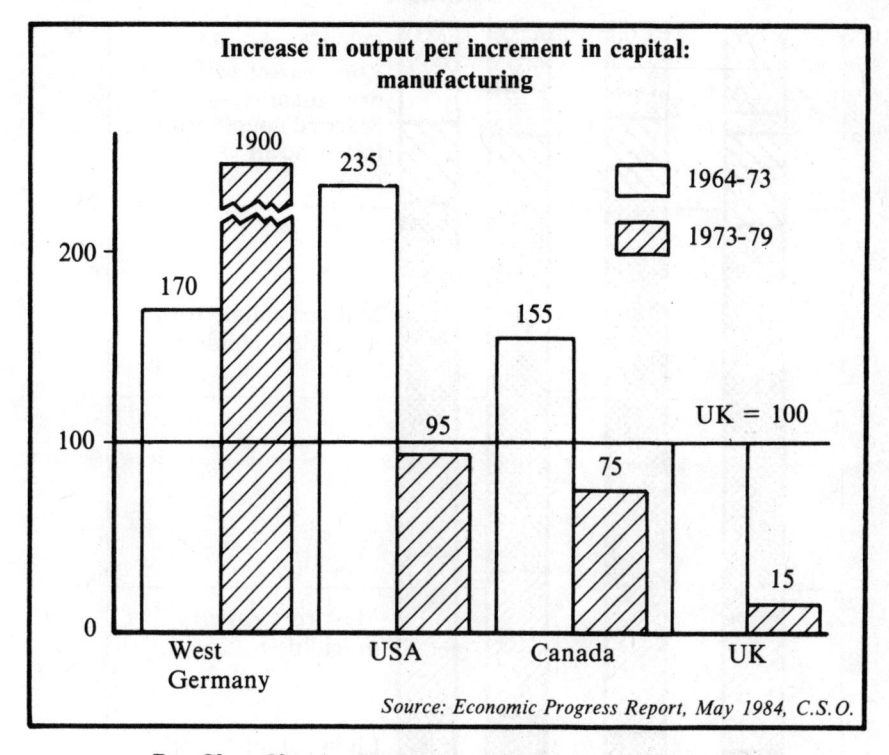

Increase in output per increment in capital: manufacturing

- 1964-73
- 1973-79

West Germany: 170, 1900
USA: 235, 95
Canada: 155, 75
UK: 100, 15

UK = 100

Source: Economic Progress Report, May 1984, C.S.O.

Bar Chart Showing International Productivity of Capital

Fig. 17.7 comparison over time/between country — CAPITAL OUTPUT.

Question on Fig. 17.7. Which country has experienced the largest fall in manufacturing capital productivity? Can you explain why this has happened?

FIG. 17.8
PEOPLE IN HOUSEHOLDS[1]: BY TYPE OF HOUSEHOLD AND FAMILY IN WHICH THEY LIVE

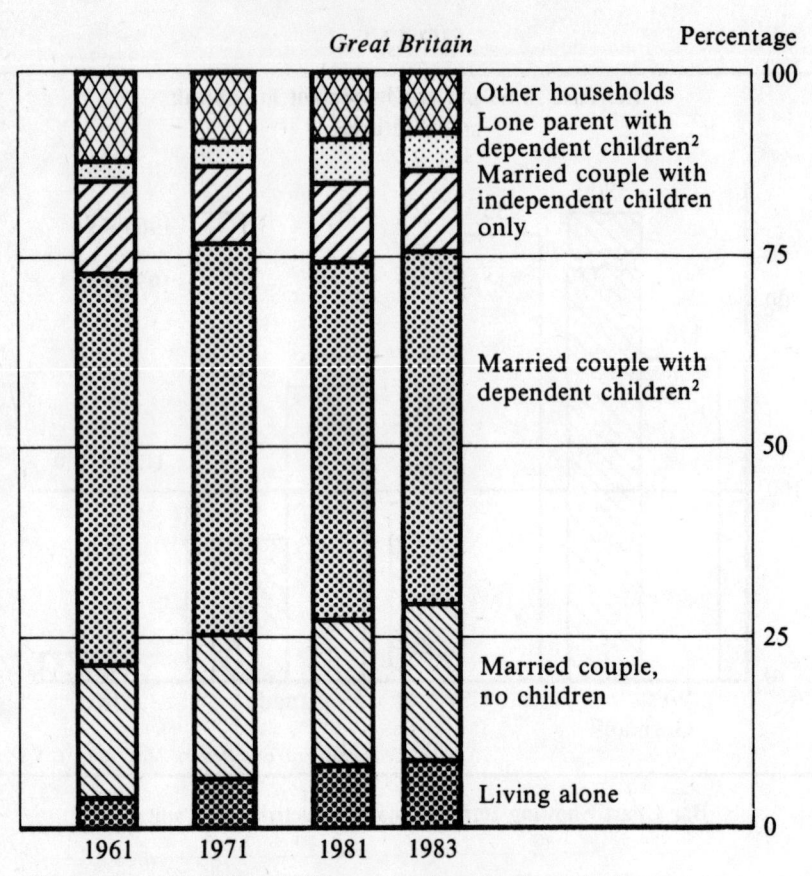

Great Britain   Percentage

Other households
Lone parent with dependent children[2]
Married couple with independent children only

Married couple with dependent children[2]

Married couple, no children

Living alone

1961   1971   1981   1983

[1] The data for 1961, 1971, and 1981 are taken from the Population Censuses for those years; the 1983 data are from the General Household Survey.
[2] These family types may also include independent children.

Source: Office of Population Censuses and Surveys, C.S.O.

Question on Fig. 17.8. Describe how the household unit has changed in GB from 1961 to 1983. What are the economic implications of these changes?

FIG. 17.9
COMPARISON OF SECTOR SHARES OF GDP OVER TIME

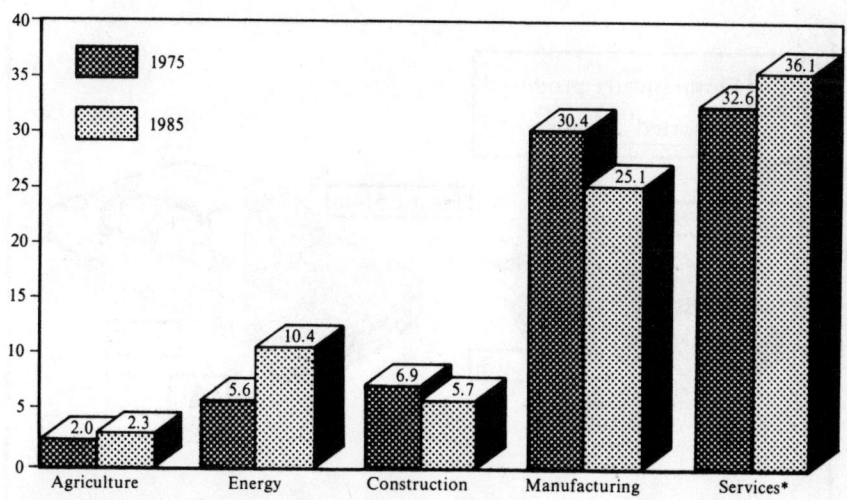

[Bar chart comparing 1975 and 1985 sector shares of GDP:
- Agriculture: 1975 = 2.0, 1985 = 2.3
- Energy: 1975 = 5.6, 1985 = 10.4
- Construction: 1975 = 6.9, 1985 = 5.7
- Manufacturing: 1975 = 30.4, 1985 = 25.1
- Services*: 1975 = 32.6, 1985 = 36.1]

*Excluding national and local government, education and health
Source: UK National Accounts, HMSO and CSO data.

Question on Fig. 17.9. Discuss the significance of the changing industrial shares of GDP as shown in the bar chart.

(iii) *Pictograms*

This form of visual presentation involves the use of pictures to present data. Fig. 17.10 illustrates.

252 Basic Mathematical & Statistical Concepts

FIG. 17.10
GROWTH IN IMPORT PENETRATION IN THE UK CAR MARKET

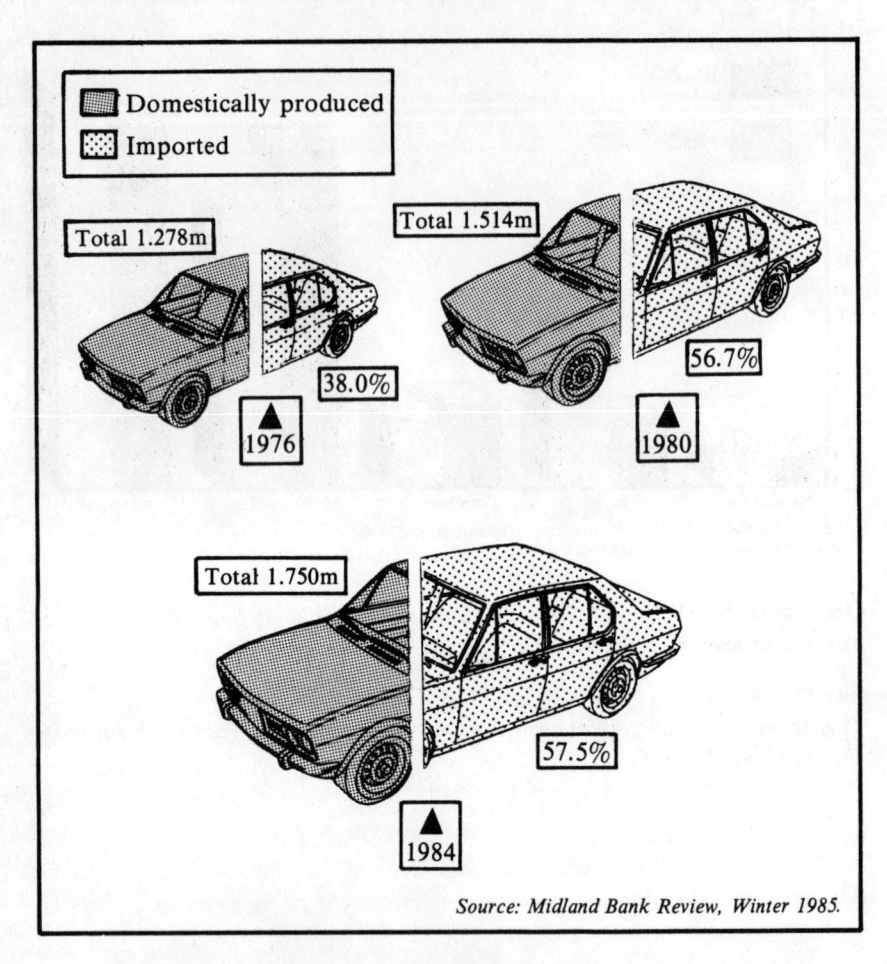

- Domestically produced
- Imported

Total 1.278m
38.0%
▲ 1976

Total 1.514m
56.7%
▲ 1980

Total 1.750m
57.5%
▲ 1984

Source: Midland Bank Review, Winter 1985.

Pictogram showing import penetration in UK car market (new cars)

Question on Fig. 17.10. Describe and comment on the UK new car market between 1976 and 1984.

(iv) *Pie Charts*
This is a circle, divided by radial lines, into sections, so that each one is proportional to the size of the figure represented. It therefore shows the sizes of component figures in proportion to each other and to the overall total. Fig. 17.11 illustrates.

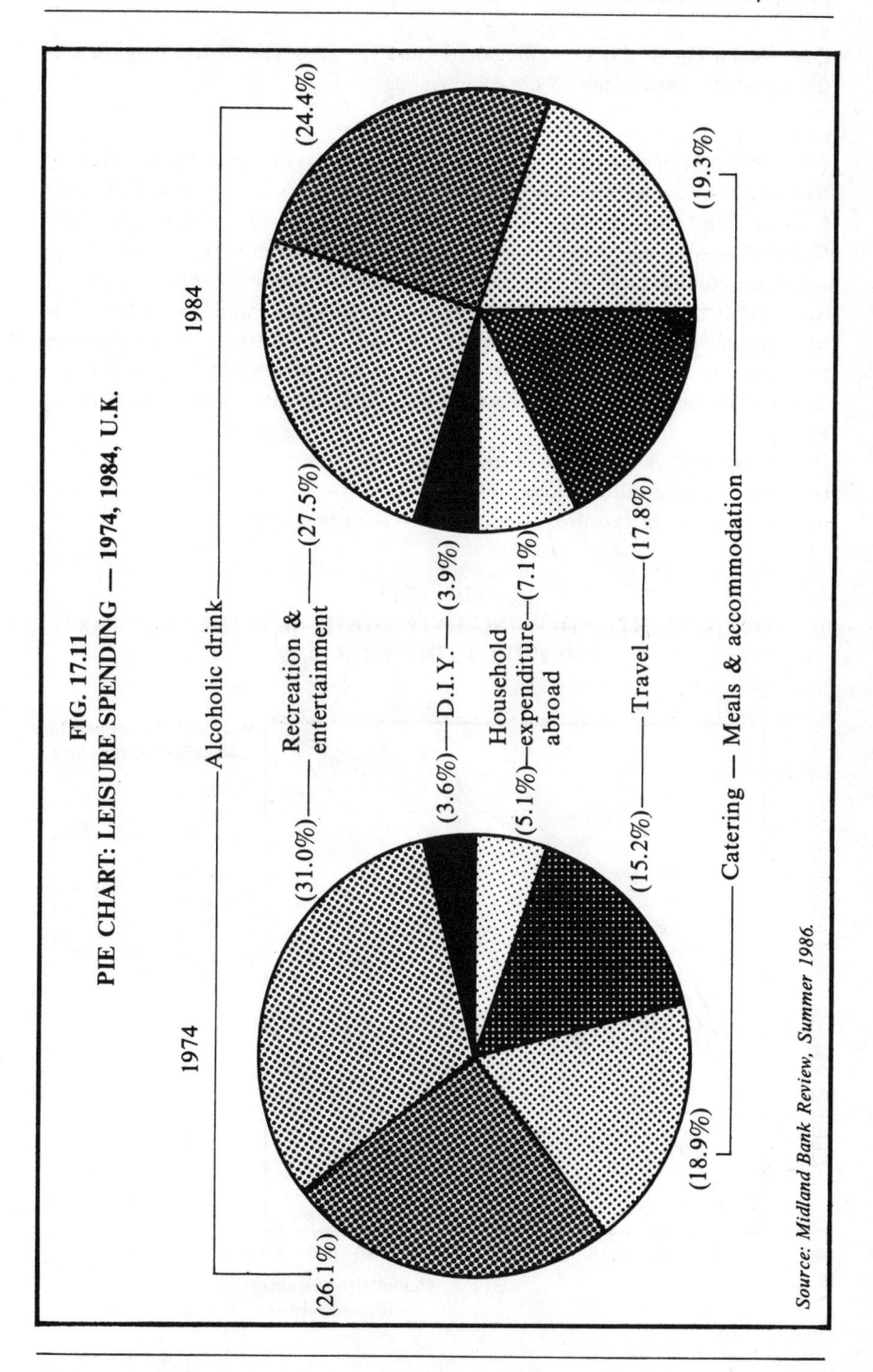

FIG. 17.11
PIE CHART: LEISURE SPENDING — 1974, 1984, U.K.

1984

Alcoholic drink —— (24.4%)
Recreation & entertainment —— (27.5%) ... (19.3%)
D.I.Y. —— (3.9%)
Household expenditure abroad —— (7.1%)
Travel —— (17.8%)
Catering — Meals & accommodation

1974

(31.0%)
(3.6%)
(5.1%)
(15.2%)
(18.9%)
(26.1%)

Source: Midland Bank Review, Summer 1986.

254 Basic Mathematical & Statistical Concepts

Question on Fig. 17.11. Describe how leisure spending has changed and outline the economic importance of the main trends.

(v) *Lorenz Curves*

The derivation of frequency distributions is based upon actual income received by householders. Another way of presenting this information is by a LORENZ CURVE. This indicates how far the actual distribution of income etc. deviates from a perfectly equal distribution. It is derived by calculating, in percentage terms, the cumulative change in both income and frequency variables. The further the curve is from the centre line the greater the inequality and vice versa. In the hypothetical Lorenz Curve, Fig. 17.12, around 10% of pre-tax income earners receive 40% of income which illustrates how unequal income distribution often is. Lorenz Curves can be used to illustrate inequalities in other areas of economics, eg.

(i) Industrial concentration of output etc., over time etc.
(ii) Industrial output and costs (efficiency).
(iii) The impact of taxation on incomes — see Fig. 17.12.

FIG. 17.12
LORENZ CURVE SHOWING HYPOTHETICAL PRE & POST TAX DISTRIBUTION OF INCOME

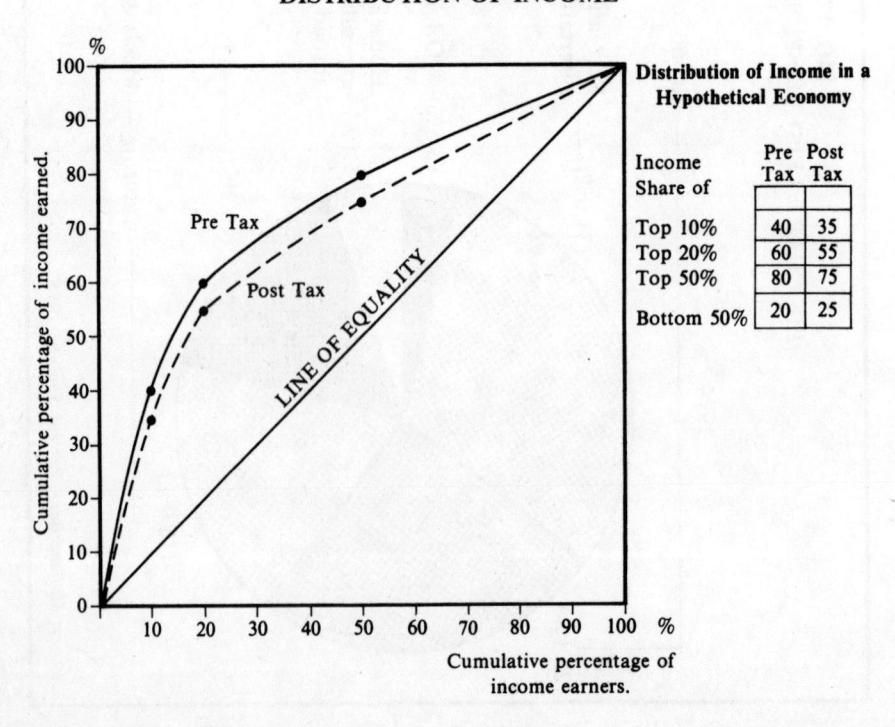

Distribution of Income in a Hypothetical Economy

Income Share of	Pre Tax	Post Tax
Top 10%	40	35
Top 20%	60	55
Top 50%	80	75
Bottom 50%	20	25

Basic Mathematical & Statistical Concepts 255

Time Series Graphs

Whilst it is possible to present time series data in a table it is normally easier to identify the main findings in a graphical form. Much of economics is concerned with analysing behaviour over time and so these graphics are used in demand, output, income, distribution and trade cycle analysis etc. Time Series graphs can be used with index numbers to show up "real" changes — Fig. 17.13 illustrates and shows three components of a time series graph, in 'real' terms.

FIG. 17.13
REAL CHANGES IN MOTOR VEHICLE EXPENDITURE AND TOTAL CONSUMERS' EXPENDITURE

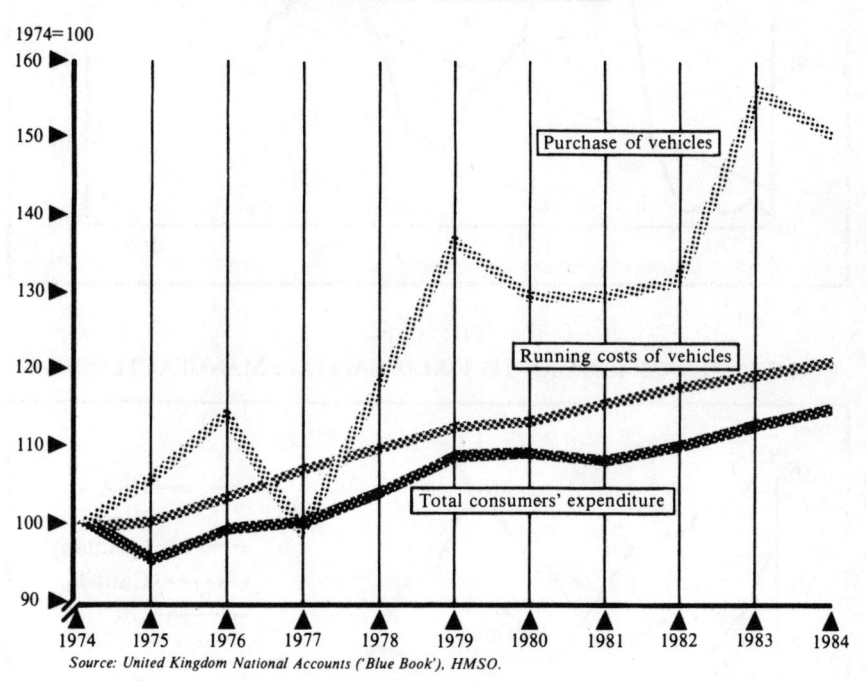

Source: United Kingdom National Accounts ('Blue Book'), HMSO.

Time Series Graphs. Motor Vehicle Expenditure (index numbers)

Time Series graphs can indicate the overall trend within the series and other graphs can break total values into component items or show comparisons between countries etc. See Figs. 17.13 to 17.17.

Question on Fig. 17.13. Comment upon the behaviour of the three variables illustrated in Fig. 17.13. What is the significance of 1974 = 100?

FIG. 17.14
TIME SERIES GRAPHS. REAL HOUSE PRICES
(INDEX NUMBERS — TRENDS)

Source: CSO Economic Trends and BSA Bulletin, July 1986.

1980 - 100

1956 - 85 Trend

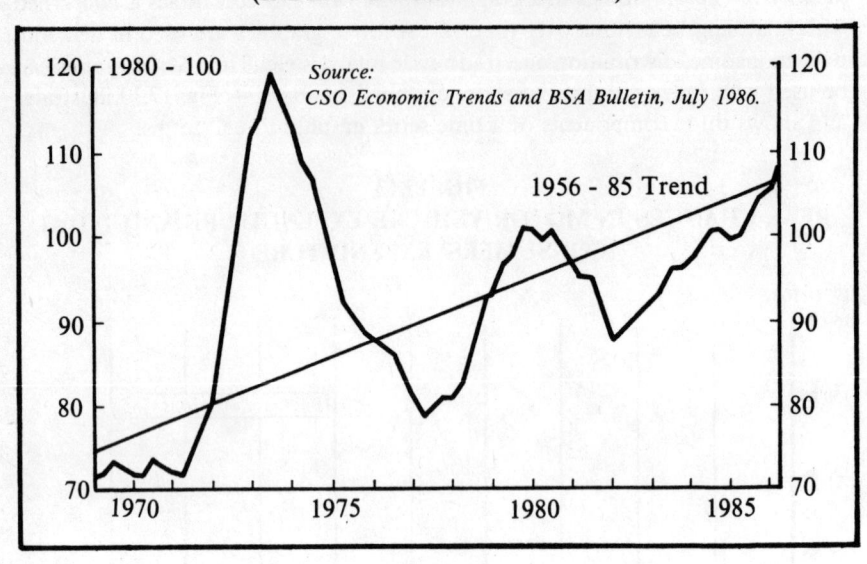

FIG. 17.15
NET RATES OF RETURN TO FIXED CAPITAL: MANUFACTURING

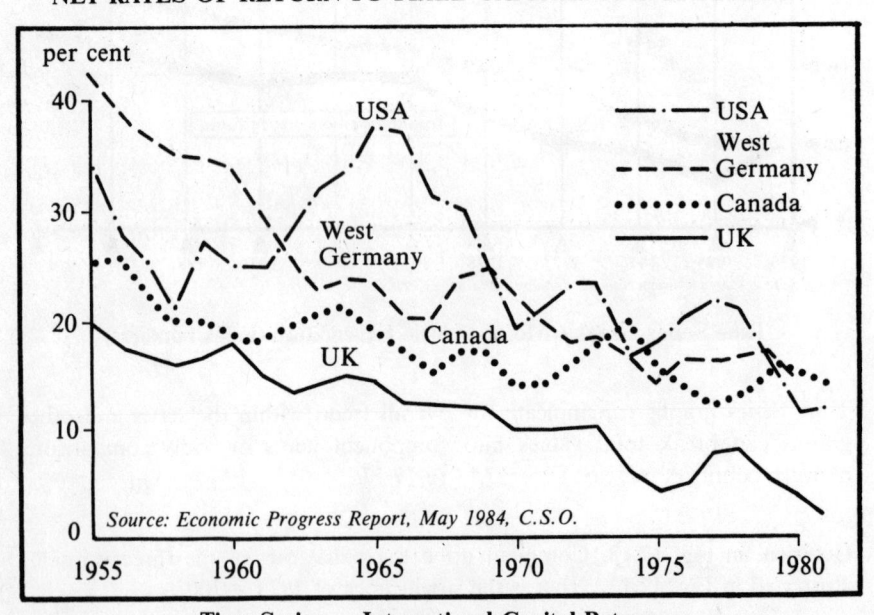

Source: Economic Progress Report, May 1984, C.S.O.

Time Series — International Capital Returns

Fig. 17.14 also uses the notion of index numbers to obtain a "real" trend line which helps show up cyclical or seasonal variation over time. This trend could then be 'extrapolated' or projected into the future so that predictions could be made. Interpolation is when a trend is predicted *between* known values. Fig. 17.16 shows four separate trends on one diagram.

Question to Fig. 17.14. Describe and account for the 1956–85 trend in real house prices.

Question to Fig. 17.15. Explain the term "net rates of return" and describe and comment on the overall trend shown.

Lastly, Fig. 17.16 shows how time series graphs can be used to show the components of an overall trend; in this case passenger transport. However, the same idea could be used to compare components of aggregate demand such as consumer spending (C), investment spending (I) etc.

FIG. 17.16
PASSENGER TRANSPORT BY MODE 1954:1984

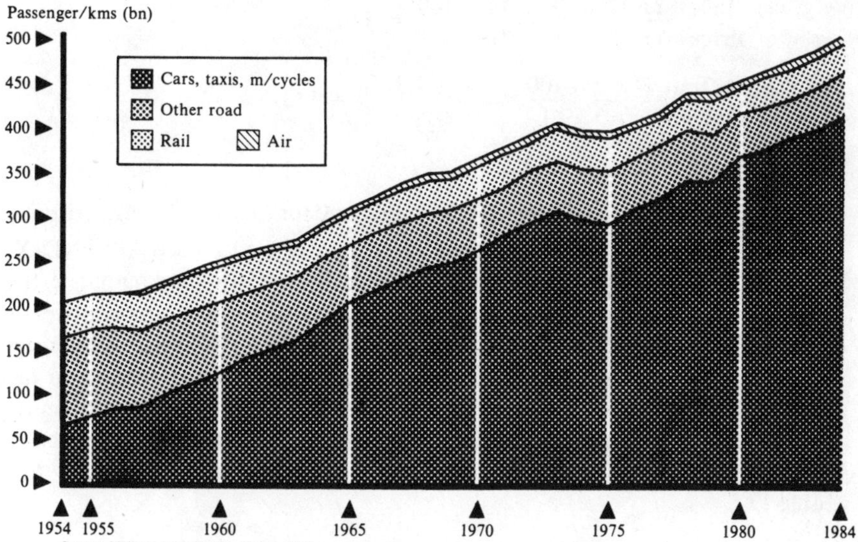
Passenger/kms (bn)
500
450
400
350
300
250
200
150
100
50
0
Cars, taxis, m/cycles
Other road
Rail
Air
1954
1955
1960
1965
1970
1975
1980
1984

Source: Midland Bank Review, Winter 1985.

Time Series — Passenger Transport

Question to Fig. 17.16. Comment on the changing passenger modes of transport 1954–84.

Finally, many time series graphs are *"seasonally adjusted"*. All this means is that where regular, predictable, seasonable variations exist, then these can be calculated and eliminated from actual figures to give the overall trend figure.

Index Numbers

Index Numbers are simple and easy to understand numbers which attempt to relate the change in a number of variables through one number called the base year number and represented by 100. In Table 17.2 the price of oranges (current money prices) is reduced to a simple price relative and shown as an index of price compared to the original year 1, ie. the base year. See (a).

TABLE 17.2

Years	Output of Oranges	Price of Oranges	Index of output	(Price Relative) Index of Prices
1	10,000	10	111	100
2	12,000	11	133	110
3	9,000	15	100	150

(a) Price Index — Year 1 = 100 Base weighted (Laspeyres)
(b) Output Index — Year 3 = 100 Current weighted (Paasche)

e.g. (a) $\dfrac{\text{Price Yr.2} \times 100}{\text{Price Yr.1}} = \dfrac{11 \times 100}{10} = 110$,

(b) $\dfrac{\text{Output Yr.2} \times 100}{\text{Output Yr.3}} \cdot \dfrac{1}{1} = \dfrac{133 \times 100}{100} = 133$

Economic data often show "base" weighted and/or "current" weighted price and output indices, so carefully note which one is used — see APPENDIX. Table 17.2 indicates at a glance the overall behaviour of price and output, ie. the Trend. Whilst this analysis is sufficient when using one product, *overall* prices or output calculations have to incorporate appropriate "weights" in order to reflect the significance of say oranges within the household budget (prices) or in the *overall* output of an economy. Weights are thus given so as to provide more realistic analysis. A simple example incorporating the price of oranges and apples in Year 1 and 2 gives a weighted fruit price index, using the base year 1. See Table 17.3.

TABLE 17.3

Product	Price Yr.1	Price Yr.2	Weight =	Yr.1	Yr.2
Oranges	10	11	×4	40	44
Apples	6	12	×6	36	72
Yr.1 =100	16	23		10	76	116

Unweighted Fruit Index (Base Yr.1 = 100) (Laspeyres) $\left(\begin{array}{c}\text{less accurate}\\ \text{than weighted.}\end{array}\right)$
$$\frac{\text{Price of Oranges + Apples Yr.2}}{\text{Price of Oranges + Apples Yr.1}} \times 100 = \frac{23}{16} \times 100 = 144$$

Weighted Fruit Index (Base Yr.1 = 100) (Laspeyres)
$$\frac{\text{Weighted Price of Oranges/Apples Yr.2}}{\text{Weighted Price of Oranges/Apples Yr.1}} \times 100 = \frac{116}{76} \times 100 = 153$$

Table 17.4 and 17.5 show how index numbers can be used to indicate the extent of inflation and purchasing power. In 17.4 the base years are periodically changed, e.g. 1889=100, 1900=100 etc., so realistic and representative baskets of goods are updated. The table thus indicates the changing purchasing power of the £ over the short and long term.

TABLE 17.4
Purchasing power of the £ UK taking value as equivalent to 100p in various years

Year													
1889	100												
1900	100	100											
1913	92.9	92.9	100										
1929	56.5	56.5	61.0	100									
1939	55.3	55.3	63.6	97.9	100								
1949	29.5	29.5	31.8	52.3	53.4	100							
1959	21.0	21.0	22.3	37.1	37.3	71.0	100						
1969	14.9	14.9	16.1	26.4	27.0	50.6	71.3	100					
1979	4.6	4.6	4.9	8.1	8.3	15.5	21.9	30.7	100				
1983	3.1	3.1	3.3	5.4	5.5	10.4	15.0	20.5	66.7	100			
1984	2.9	2.9	3.1	5.2	5.3	10.0	13.9	19.5	63.5	95.3	100		
1985	2.7	2.7	3.0	4.9	5.0	9.3	13.1	18.4	59.9	89.8	94.3	100	
1986	2.7	2.7	2.9	4.7	4.8	9.0	12.7	17.8	57.9	86.8	91.2	96.7	100
1987	2.6	2.6	2.7	4.5	4.6	8.6	12.2	17.1	55.6	83.4	87.5	92.8	96.0	100
1988	2.4	2.4	2.6	4.3	4.4	8.2	11.6	16.3	53.0	79.5	83.4	88.5	91.5	95.3	100
1989	2.3	2.3	2.4	4.0	4.1	7.6	10.8	15.1	49.2	73.7	77.4	82.1	84.9	88.5	92.8	100

Note: Moving Base Years.

TABLE 17.5

Prices and indices	1979	1984	1989
Retail prices	100	157.4	203.3
of which food	100	142.8	171.4
Input prices (8)	100	147.0	154.4
Average price of new dwellings on mortgage	100	150.3	352.0
Import prices	100	154.2	168.0
Export prices	100	154.7	164.8
Terms of trade (9)	100	100.2	98.1

(1979=100)

Actual prices (end year)		1979	1984	1989
Bread	standard loaf	30p	39.4p	49p
Milk	pint	15p	22p	29p
Tea	125g	21p	53p	47p
Quarterly rail season ticket	Woking–Waterloo	£128.00	£226.00	£338.70
Petrol	one gallon of 4 star	£1.20	£1.89	£1.82
British Leyland Mini	1,000cc	£2,829	£3,298	£4,554
Newspaper	Daily Mail	10p	20p	25p

Source: *The UK Economy in Figures 1990 – Lloyds Bank 1990.*

260 Basic Mathematical & Statistical Concepts

Question on Table 17.5. Identify periods in the UK when the purchasing power of the £ *rose* and *fell* most rapidly.

Table 17.5 shows actual prices and price indices for a number of items. Price indices are 1979=100 and allow quick and simple comparisons of inflation rates to be made. Actual prices can be changed to indices form using base prices, e.g. 1979=100 (Laspeyres) or current prices, e.g. 1989=100 (Paasche). This is a useful exercise and so a price index based on milk prices for 1979=100 would be for

$$1984 = \frac{22p}{15p} \times \frac{100}{1} = 147$$

Task. Work out base and current price indices for tea between 1979 and 1989.

Logarithmic Scales
On a normal axis the distance between 0, 1, 2, 3 etc. would be the same whereas on a log scale there is equal distance between 0.1, 1.0, 10, ie. in absolute terms these figures increase in each case by a factor of 10. Hence log scales are designed to show the rate of growth of the variables rather than its absolute change. The example below linking days lost to plant size use log scales on both axis and show how both these scale increases are closely related. To show the same information on normal scales would not be possible. Log scales are useful when showing compound rates of growth of say population or capital values.

FIG. 17.17
STRIKES IN THE UK (1971-3)

Strikes and plant size

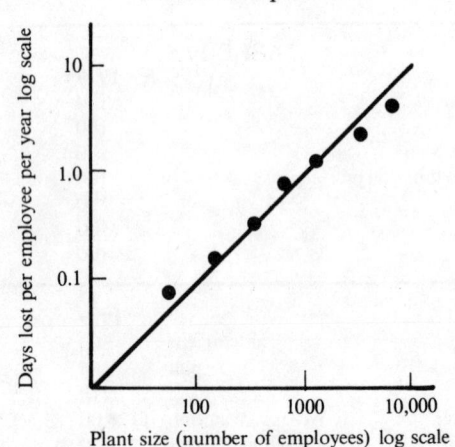

Source: Lloyds Bank Economic Bulletin, March 1979.

STATISTICAL APPENDIX

ARITHMETIC MEAN and STANDARD DEVIATION

$$x = \frac{\Sigma fx}{\Sigma f} \qquad s = \sqrt{\frac{\Sigma fx^2}{\Sigma f} - \frac{(\Sigma fx)^2}{(\Sigma f)^2}}$$

QUARTILE DEVIATION $= \dfrac{Q_3 - Q_1}{2}$

SKEWNESS Quartile measure $= \dfrac{Q_3 + Q_1 - 2 \text{ (Median)}}{Q_3 - Q_1}$

Pearson measure $= \dfrac{3(x - \text{Median})}{s}$

COEFFICIENT OF VARIATION $= \dfrac{100s}{x}$

SPEARMAN RANK CORRELATION COEFFICIENT

$$rs = 1 - \frac{6\Sigma d^2}{n^2(n-1)}$$

PRODUCT MOMENT CORRELATION COEFFICIENT

$$r = \frac{n\Sigma xy - \Sigma x \Sigma y}{\sqrt{(n\Sigma x^2 - (\Sigma x)^2)(n\Sigma y^2 - (\Sigma y)^2)}}$$

REGRESSION. Regression line of Y on X: $Y = a + bX$

$$b = \frac{n\Sigma xY - \Sigma x \Sigma Y}{n\Sigma x^2 - (\Sigma x)^2} \qquad a = \frac{\Sigma Y}{n} - \frac{b\Sigma x}{n}$$

STANDARD ERROR OF A SAMPLE MEAN

$$= \frac{\delta}{\sqrt{n}} \quad \text{or} \quad \frac{s}{\sqrt{n}} \quad \text{when is unknown.}$$

STANDARD ERROR OF A SAMPLE PROPORTION

$$= \sqrt{\frac{\pi(1-\pi)}{n}} \quad \text{or} \quad \sqrt{\frac{p(1-p)}{n}} \quad \text{when } \pi \text{ is unknown.}$$

INDEX NUMBERS

Σw_I where w = Weight; I = Price relative

		Price	Quantity
Base	; Laspeyres	$\dfrac{\Sigma P_n Q_o}{\Sigma P_o Q_o} \times 100$	$\dfrac{\Sigma P_o Q_n}{\Sigma P_o Q_o} \times 100$
Current	: Paasche	$\dfrac{\Sigma P_n Q_n}{\Sigma P_o Q_n} \times 100$	$\dfrac{\Sigma P_n Q_n}{\Sigma P_n Q_o} \times 100$

COMPOUND INTEREST $P_n = P_o(1+i)^n$

Present value of an annuity: $a_n = \dfrac{1 - (1+i)^{-n}}{i}$

Sinking fund or future value of an annuity: $S_n = \dfrac{(1+i)^n - 1}{i}$

DISCOUNTED VALUES

$$\frac{A_1}{(1+r)} + \frac{A_2}{(1+r)^2} + \frac{A_3}{(1+r)^3} + \cdots\cdots \frac{A_n}{(1+r)^n}$$

18. BASIC MATHEMATICAL CONCEPTS: USE IN ECONOMICS

AIMS: To define, explain and discuss
- Basic mathematical concepts and their use in economics
- Discounting and compounding and investment economics

KEY CONCEPTS
Variables, models, linear expressions, co-ordinates solving problems, regression and correlation, slopes and trends, marginals and totals, stocks and flows.

Variable — Symbols and Functions

A variable is a quantity that can take various numerical values either positive (+) or negative (−). The price of potatoes is a variable as is the amount of potatoes bought or sold. These variables can be expressed in symbolic, or shorthand form, e.g. P_p, Qdp (price and quantity demanded of potatoes) and put into a function which relates which one affects the other, e.g. $Qdp = f(P_p, Y, T......)$ This says the demand for potatoes (f) depends upon the price of potatoes, income, taste, etc.

Linear Functions and Hypotheses (models)

A linear function is one which when plotted on a graph appears as a straight line. One example is $C = .5Y$ where consumer spending is related to income, i.e. consumption is always a half of income. A more developed expression or testable hypotheses would be $C = 10 + .5Y$ which says that for any level of income, consumption will be half of income plus 10 units. In mathematics the 10 is a constant and .5 is a coefficient which shows how consumption depends upon income. This gives the standard linear expression $y = a + bx$ where for $C = 10 + .5Y$, $a = 10$, $b = .5$, $Y = C$, $Y = x$. In its simplest $C = 10 + .5Y$ is a model predicting how aggregate demand will vary with income. In macro-economics the 10 would be autonomous expenditure and the .5Y would be induced, i.e. dependent, expenditure. The linear function $C = .5Y$ is shown in Fig. 18.1.

Non-Linear Functions, e.g. total revenue and cost

These take the form of $Y = a + bx^2$ and on a graph appear as a curved line. In economics, non-linear expressions are usual in describing how total revenue (TR), total cost (TC) and profit vary for an industry or a monopolist, etc. The rate of change of a function (TR or TC) is obtained by differentiating $Y = a + bx^2$ by the quantity change and this shows how marginal revenue or marginal costs change. This analysis is not usual in A level courses. However, it can be used to show that the marginal revenue curve, facing a monopolist, has twice the slope of average revenue where $ar = d =$ price under monopolistic conditions. The steps are as follows:-

(i) A downward sloping demand curve (facing the monopolist) has the function price $= a - bq$ where a is a constant, b is the gradient and q is the quantity demanded.

(ii) Total revenue (to the monopolist) is p x q so multiply price $= a - bq$ by q to give total revenue. This will be $TR = aq - bq^2$. This would be a non-linear expression and shown as a curve.

(iii) Take the first differential of this function and obtain the marginal revenue, i.e. $MR = \dfrac{dTR}{dq} = a - 2bq$ (straight line).

(iv) Thus $MR = 2bq$ which is twice the slope of ar or price which $= a - bq$, or ar falls at half the rate of MR — see Chapter 8 on Monopoly.

FIG. 18.1
A SIMPLE LINEAR FUNCTION   C = .5Y

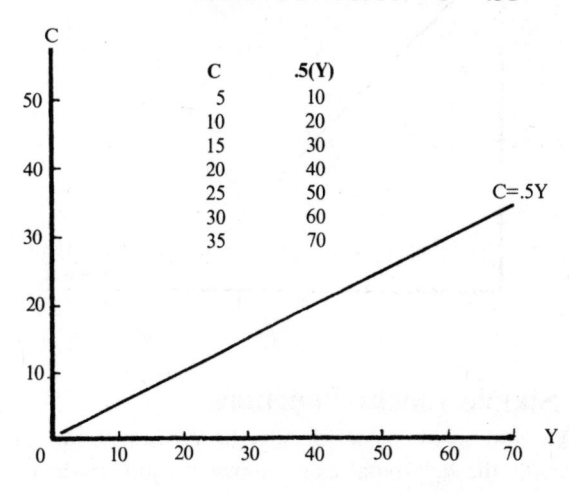

C	.5(Y)
5	10
10	20
15	30
20	40
25	50
30	60
35	70

FIG. 18.2
PLOTTING THE SUPPLY FUNCTION

Price (£)	Supply (q)	Price £
	3	1
	5	2
	7	3

$S = 1 + 2p$

Normal Cartesian graph shows $(y = 1 + 2x)$

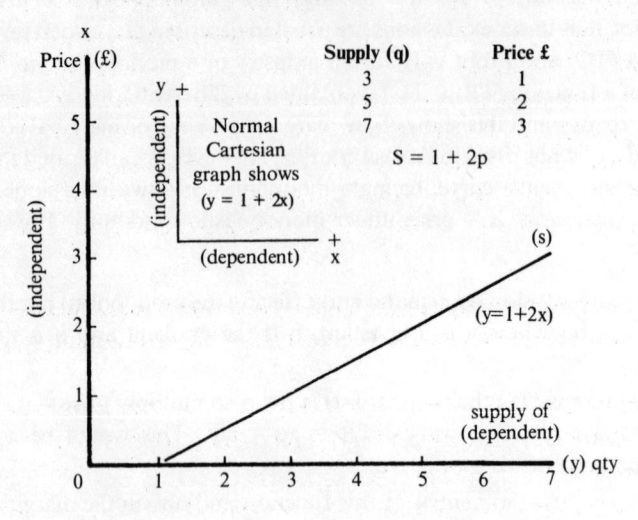

$(y = 1 + 2x)$

supply of (dependent) (y) qty

FIG. 18.3
PLOTTING THE DEMAND FUNCTION

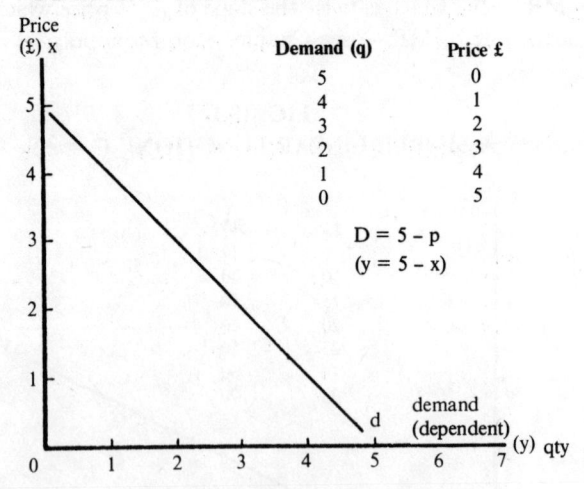

Price (£) x	Demand (q)	Price £
	5	0
	4	1
	3	2
	2	3
	1	4
	0	5

$D = 5 - p$
$(y = 5 - x)$

demand (dependent) (y) qty

Graphing Simple Linear Functions

Graphs quickly and easily show visually the relationship of one variable to another. Normally the horizontal axis x shows the independent variable whilst the vertical axis y shows the dependent one, i.e. $y = f(x)$ says y depends upon the behaviour of x. This is referred to as a Cartesian graph or relationship, as shown in Fig. 18.1. In the original relationship consumption y depends upon income level x. Suppose C = .5Y then, by assigning values to income, we can calculate the consumption and plot the resulting values as shown in Fig. 18.1. If a function was y = 1 + 2x, then y and x are directly related, e.g. this could be a supply function where supply (s) or y increased as price rose, i.e. 1 + 2x. So quantity supplied (y) is now the dependent variable whilst price (x) is independent. In the previous example C = .5Y, consumption, the dependent variable, was plotted on the y vertical axis but in the supply function y, the quantity supplied or dependent variable, is plotted on the horizontal axis x. This is because Alfred Marshall, the economist who developed these ideas, plotted supply along the horizontal x axis and this has been the accepted method ever since. Thus the supply function of quantity s = 1 + 2P is graphed with quantity supplied as the dependent variable which is plotted on the horizontal y axis as shown in Fig. 18.2. At the same time the demand function D = 5 - P, see Fig. 18.3, is similarly plotted.

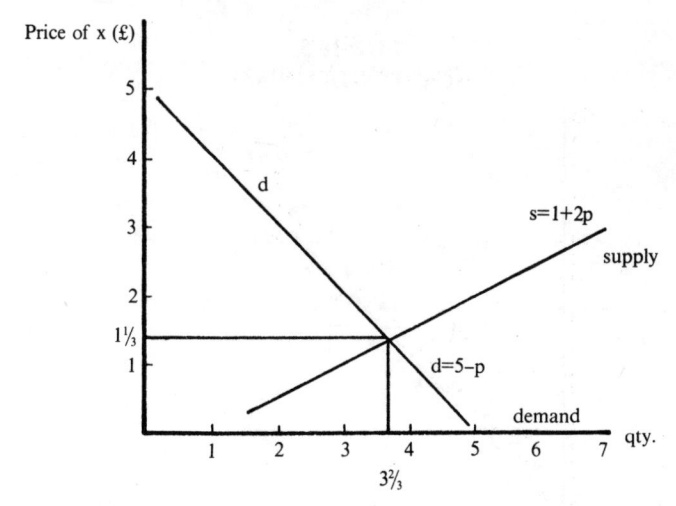

FIG. 18.4
THE MARKET SOLUTION

Problem Solving

The two expressions plotted in Figs. 18.2 and 18.3 illustrate supply and demand functions. This means there will be an equilibrium price and quantity which can be calculated either by solving the equations, see below, or by plotting these functions as is done in Fig. 18.4.

Solving the Equations.
  (i) $S = 1 + 2P$
  (ii) $D = 5 - P$
in equilibrium (i) = (ii) or $D = S$
  so $1 + 2P = 5 - P$
moving numbers and P to opposite sides gives
  $3P = 5 - 1$
  so $P = 1\frac{1}{3}$ which equals equilibrium price
to obtain equivalent output substitute $P = 1\frac{1}{3}$ into
  $S = 1 + 2P$ so $1 + 2 \times 1\frac{1}{3} = S = 3\frac{2}{3}$ in equilibrium.

So quantity = $3\frac{2}{3}$ and price = $1\frac{1}{3}$. This can be checked with reference to Fig. 18.4.

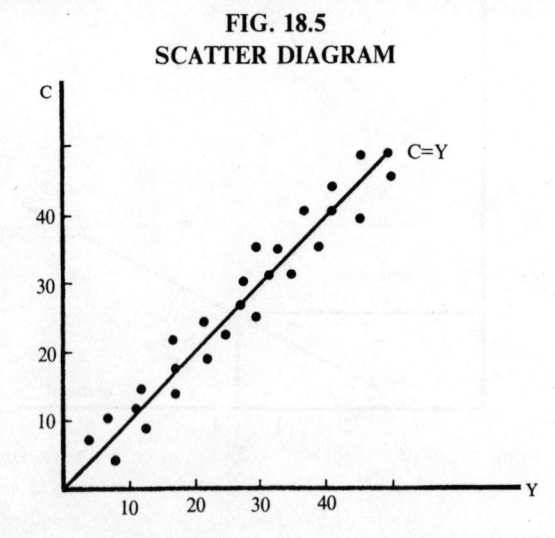

FIG. 18.5
SCATTER DIAGRAM

Correlation and Regression

Correlation is where there is a connection between two variables as shown in the Scatter diagram in Fig. 18.5 and where, by drawing a straight line, a correlation of a relationship indicates how the two variables are related. In this case they are positively related as they move together. The extent of this correlation can be determined by regressing expenditure (C) on income using the least squares method to obtain a regression equation $C = Y$, which says for any given level of income we consume the full amount of income. Correlation outlines the overall relationship whilst regression presents it in a testable, causal form.

FIG. 18.6
SLOPES AND TRENDS

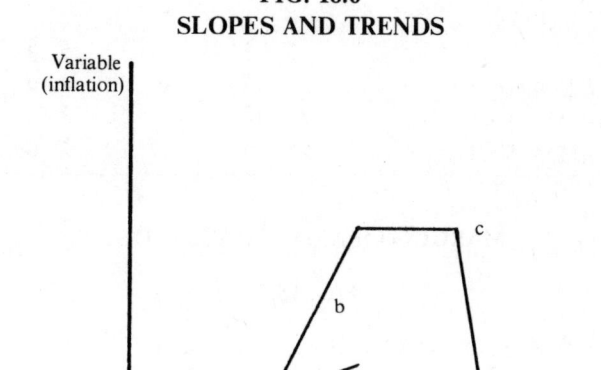

Slopes and Trends (see Fig. 18.6)

The slopes a, b, c and d show different rates and trends over time. Slope a and b are upward while d is downward and c neither rises nor falls as a trend line. Although a shows an upward trend it does not rise as fast as d and though d falls it does so at a faster rate than a or b increase. Using a, b and c as inflation rates, we see that both a and b show rising trends whilst c shows zero inflation which means that prices have stopped rising. If prices fall as in d, we see that inflation becomes negative, i.e. they decrease from the levels attained at c.

Marginals and Totals

Marginal changes, e.g. mc, mr, show the difference between successive totals, e.g. TC, TR. The marginal utility of the 4th unit consumed is the difference between the total utility of the 3rd and 4th unit. If these are illustrated in Table 18.1 you notice that it is always possible to add up successive marginals in order to obtain total utility, i.e. the total utility of the four units is equal to $5 + 4 + 3 + 2 = 14$.

TABLE 18.1

Units Consumed/produced	Total Utility/Cost	Marginal Utility/Cost
0	0 0	
1	5 3	5 3
2	9 7	4 4
3	12 12	3 5
4 etc.	14 18	2 6

MARGINALS AND TOTALS (COST)

FIG. 18.7

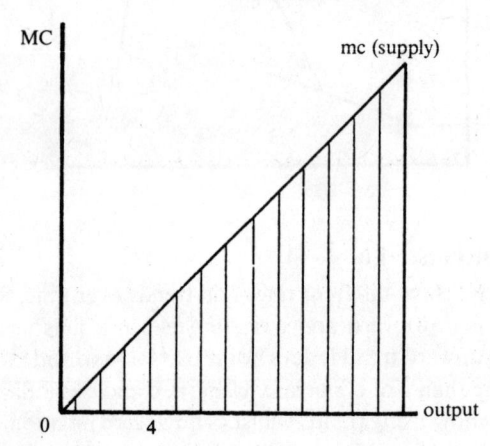

FIG. 18.8 (UTILITY)

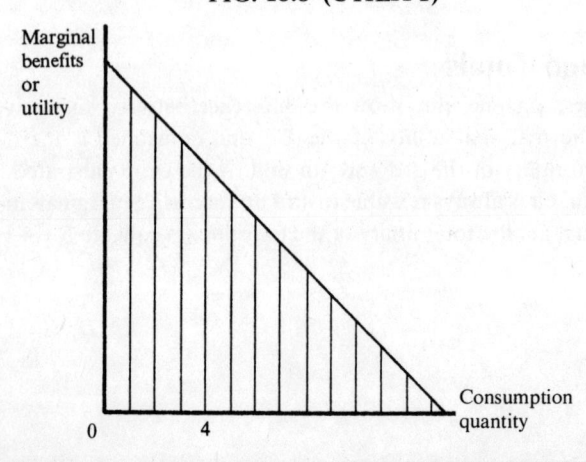

This means, using Fig. 18.8, that the sum of the marginals under the marginal utility or marginal benefit line when added up, give the total value of utility or benefits under the demand curve, as discussed in Area Analysis in the Problem Sections. See Chapter 14. The same analysis means that the area under the cost curve in Fig. 18.7 is the same as the total costs for any level of output, i.e. for 4 units of production total cost is the same as the sum of the marginals, i.e. $3+4\ldots=18$.

Stocks and Flows

A stock is the total amount of a quantity at any one time whereas a flow represents a net addition or reduction in stock over a period of time. The amount of water in a bath is a stock whilst water coming in from the tap or leaving down the plug hole is a flow which can therefore be positive or negative. If the flow in and out are equivalent, the stock remains unchanged. In economics the stock of second hand houses in price terms influences the flow of new houses built, whilst the value of second hand cars (stock) is influenced by the price of the flow of new cars coming onto the market. Economic growth is represented as a flow of goods and services produced over a year and this is made possible by the total stock of capital goods in an economy which gradually increases as the flow of new investment goods are used by industry.

(COMPOUNDING AND DISCOUNTING INVESTMENT ANALYSIS — Examples from Tables (1) to (4) — (See Chapter 13).)

The economics of investment analysis often require calculations to be made concerning the capitalisation of an income stream over time as well as the yield, interest or discount rate on a capital project. This can apply in the profit motivated private sector and the public sector with, for example, Cost-Benefit Analysis. It is useful to both understand the idea of compounding and discounting and be able to calculate and use appropriate tables to solve quantitative problems. See the Table 18.2 and specific examples, below. The idea of compound interest shows how a sum of money invested now and in the future grows over time and therefore it shows the value of savings and how the interest rate affects the principal invested. See specific examples (1) and (3).

The use of discount factors in investment analysis illustrate the idea that a sum of money received in the future foregoes interest and is less valuable than a sum held today which could earn interest. In a sense it illustrates the fact that future income received foregoes interest and thus has an opportunity cost. This foregone income will depend upon the rate of interest and the time period as well as the actual amount of money involved. Therefore the discount factors, given by the formula shown for the Discount factors in the table, incorporates a "weighting" which will depend on the interest and time involved. See (2). Discounted Cash Flow (DCF) analysis applies this reasoning using the Net Present Value (NPV) and Internal Rate of Return (IRR) or yield techniques.

The NPV technique of investment appraisal discounts the future income stream on a capital investment using a given rate of interest and this discounted income is subtracted from the Capital Cost to give the Net Present Value. If this is positive the investment is worthwhile and if negative the project may be abandoned. This can thus be used to compare and rank alternative capital projects where the same discount rate is applied. This often happens in large multinational companies. As higher discount rates are applied the NPV of a project reduces to zero until the discounted income stream equals the capital cost or value. This rate of interest is the yield or the internal rate of return (IRR). When companies seek to maximise the profit yield the IRR technique will be preferred to the NPV. Specific example (4) below applies both NPV and IRR. Here the constant stream of income is known as an annuity and the principle is the same as above. In this case a property company would see the purchase of the lease as the capital cost and this provides a constant stream of rental income to be discounted; in this case at 20%. If the discount factor had been 25% the NPV would have been negative, as it would if the rental had only been received over say four years, i.e. £300 − 259 = −£41.

Specific Examples — see tables over

(1) *Compound Interest*

Uses 1) Compound Interest. Enables calculations to be made regarding the future value of a present investment. So £100 invested today at 15% interest will be worth £100 × 2.31306 or £231.31 after six years.

(2) *Discount Factors*

Uses 2) Discount Values. Enables calculations to be made regarding the present value of a sum of money received in the future. So £100 to be paid in 6 years time at an interest rate of 15% over the period is now worth £100 × .432 or £43.20.

(3) *Future Value of an Annuity*

Uses: Enables calculations to be made regarding the future value of a constant "investment" sum paid annually. So £100 annually invested over six years at 10% interest will be worth £100 p.a. × 7.72 or £772.

(4) *Present Value of an Annuity*

Uses: Enables calculations to be made regarding the present value of a constant annual income paid in the future. So £100 a year paid as rental income over the next six years at 20% will have a present or current capitalised value of £100 p.a. × 3.32 = £332. If the investment cost £300 to buy the NPV will be £332 − £300 = i.e. £32. i.e. the capital investment is worthwhile. If the investment cost £332 the IRR will be 20%, i.e. £332 − £332 = 0.

TABLE 18.2 (1–4)
COMPOUND AND DISCOUNT TABLES

(1) Compound Interest $P_n = P_o(1+i)^n$

Year	5%	10%	15%	20%
0	1.00000	1.00000	1.00000	1.00000
1	1.05000	1.10000	1.15000	1.20000
2	1.10250	1.21000	1.32250	1.44000
3	1.15763	1.33100	1.52088	1.72800
4	1.21551	1.46410	1.74901	2.07360
5	1.27628	1.61051	2.01136	2.48832
6	1.34010	1.77156	**2.31306**	2.98598

(2) Discount Factors = $P_o \left(\frac{1}{1+i}\right)^n$

Year	5%	10%	15%	20%
0	1.00000	1.00000	1.00000	1.00000
1	0.95238	0.90909	0.86957	0.83333
2	0.90703	0.82645	0.75614	0.69444
3	0.86384	0.75131	0.65752	0.57870
4	0.82270	0.68301	0.57175	0.48225
5	0.78353	0.62092	0.49718	0.40188
6	0.74622	0.56447	**0.43233**	0.33490

(3) $S_{\overline{n}|}$ = Future Value of an Annuity, eg. Insurance Policy, Sinking Fund

Year	5%	10%	15%	20%
1	1.00000	1.00000	1.00000	1.00000
2	2.05000	2.10000	2.15000	2.20000
3	3.15250	3.31000	3.47250	3.64000
4	4.31013	4.46410	4.99338	5.36800
5	5.52563	6.10510	6.74238	7.44160
6	6.80191	**7.71561**	8.75374	9.92992

(4) $a_{\overline{n}|}$ = Present Value of an Annuity, eg. Capitalisation of future rental income

Year	5%	10%	15%	20%
1	0.95238	0.90909	0.86957	0.83333
2	1.85941	1.73554	1.62571	1.52778
3	2.72325	2.48685	2.28323	2.10648
4	3.54595	3.16987	2.85498	2.58873
5	4.32948	3.79079	3.35216	2.99061
6	5.07569	4.35526	3.78448	**3.32551**

Note: (4) is the cumulative summation of (2).

MULTIPLE CHOICE QUESTIONS

1. "Economic goods are scarce goods."
   The meaning of the word "scarce" in this quotation is that:
   a) There are very few of these goods.
   b) There are insufficient goods to meet effective demand.
   c) The goods are limited in supply.
   d) There are not enough goods to meet all our wants.
   e) The goods are insufficient to meet all our physical needs.

2. In economics, an "inferior good" means a commodity
   a) for which there is no demand;
   b) which is produced in large quantities;
   c) made of shoddy materials;
   d) which is a poor substitute;
   e) for which demand may fall as income rises.

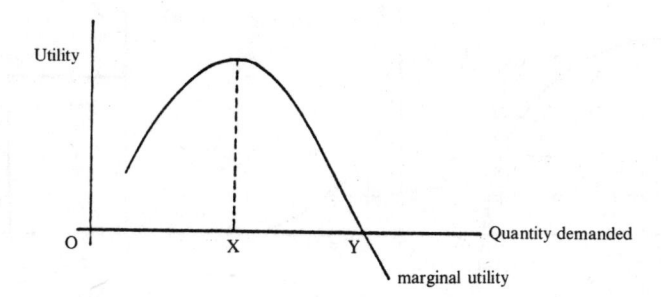

3. The diagram shows that:-
   a) marginal utility exceeds total utility when more than OY units are consumed.
   b) marginal utility becomes negative as soon as OX units have been purchased.
   c) diminishing marginal utility applies only after OY units have been purchased.
   d) total utility rises until OY units have been purchased.

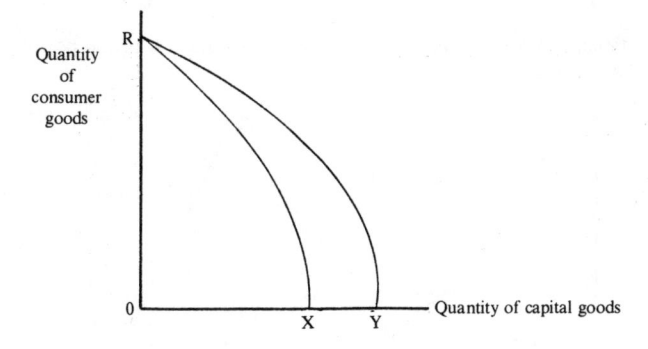

274 Multiple Choice Questions

4. The diagram above illustrates two production possibility boundaries for an economy. The shift in the production possibility boundary from RX to RY may reflect:-
   a) a rise in productivity in the capital goods industries.
   b) a fall in the government's growth target.
   c) a decrease in the opportunity cost of producing consumer goods.
   d) unemployment in the capital goods industries.

5. Which one of the following conditions defines economic efficiency in production?
   a) Most firms are maximising profits.
   b) All factors of production are fully employed.
   c) All firms are using the most advanced technology.
   d) There are no further opportunities for substituting capital for labour.
   e) Output of any one good cannot be increased without reducing the output of some other good.

6. Which one of the production possibility curves below is/are consistent with the statement that "scarce resources have alternative uses"?

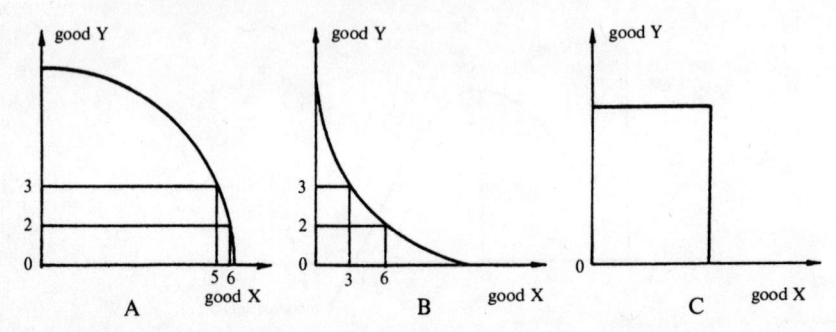

7. An economy has 100 units of capital and 200 units of labour. It produces two goods, X and Y, which require units of capital and labour per unit of output as shown in the table below.

	capital	labour
X	4	3
Y	2	4

   a) Which one of the diagrams (i)/(ii) represents the production possibility frontier of the economy?

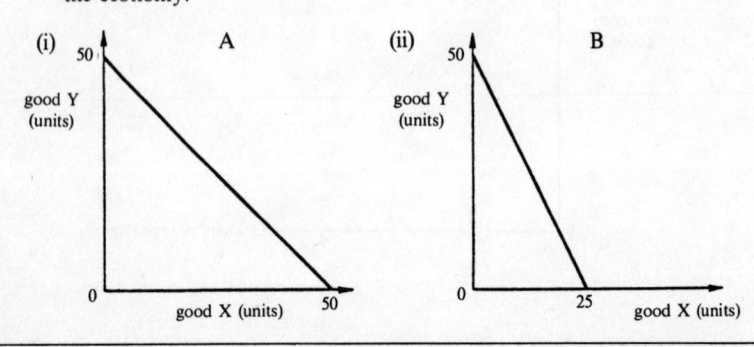

Multiple Choice Questions

8. Which of the following sentences best describes the operation of the law of diminishing returns?
   a) As the consumption of a good increases, total satisfaction rises but at a diminishing rate.
   b) As more of a variable factor is added to a fixed factor, total product rises but at a diminishing rate.
   c) As all factors are increased in proportion, total product rises but at a diminishing rate.
   d) As more of a variable factor is added to a fixed factor, the marginal cost of production diminishes.
   e) As all factors are increased in proportion, the marginal cost of production decreases.

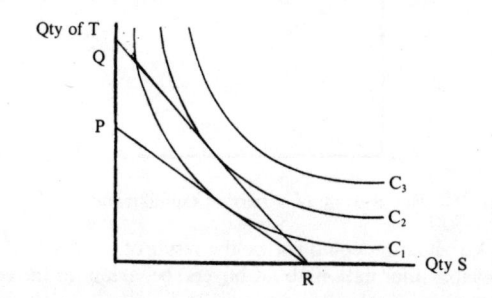

9. The diagram above shows an indifference map of the relationship between two goods S and T. The shift in the budget constraint line from RP to RQ in the diagram would be consistent with
   a) a decrease in the money income of the consumer.
   b) an increase in the price of good T.
   c) an increase in the price of good S.
   d) a rise in the price of good T.
   e) none of the above.

10. The following is a normative economic statement. True or false.
    "A tax increase pushes up supply price and is inflationary in its impact."

Market Analysis

Demand/Supply Schedule in a Market

Price	Demand	Supply
12	120	300
11	140	260
10	160	220
9	180	180
8	200	140

11. Use the above schedule to answer:-
    (i) If a tax of 3p is imposed, the new equilibrium price is:-

a) 12p; b) 11p; c) 10p; d) 9p; e) 8p.
(ii) Demand is inelastic within the price range:-
a) 11–12p; b) 10–11p; c) 9–10p; d) 8–9p; e) 8–12p.
(iii) If demand increased by 60 at all prices the new equilibrium will be:-
a) 8p; b) 10p; c) 11p; d) 12p.

Data

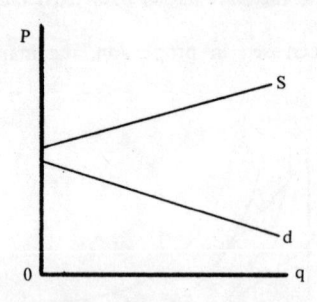

The absence of a market equilibrium

12. The above market situation could **not** be the result of:-
    a) A lack of reliable information about buyers' behaviour in the market.
    b) The existence of "free-riders" in the market.
    c) Buyers distrusting the information which price imparts regarding the quality of the product.
    d) Cheap imports from abroad.
    e) Government advertising stressing that the good was an economic bad.
    f) Uncertainty about future demand in the market.
    g) Monopoly power.

13. Two goods, X and Y, are complementary goods. Column T_1 of the table below shows the market situation at time period 1 and column T_2 shows the situation following an increase in the price of good Y.

	T_1	T_2
price of good X	10	10
quantity demanded	50	40
price of good Y	20	30
quantity demanded	80	60

The value of the cross elasticity of demand for good X lies between:-
a) –1.7 and –2.6.
b) –0.8 and –1.3.
c) –0.3 and –0.8.
d) +0.3 and + 0.6.
e) +1.7 and +2.6.
f) –1.7 and +2.6.

Multiple Choice Questions 277

14. There is movement along a demand curve when:
    a) income rises;
    b) the population increases;
    c) price falls;
    d) supply increases and the price of competitive goods changes;
    e) there are changes in people's tastes.

15. Each of the following affects the supply of potatoes except:
    a) the cost of fertiliser;
    b) the wages of farm labourers;
    c) the price of agricultural land;
    d) the popularity of chips;
    e) an attack of Colorado Beetle.

16. The movement of the demand curve from DD to D_1D_1 might be attributable to: See Fig. 1.
    a) a switch in demand to a substitute;
    b) anticipation of an increase in VAT on the good;
    c) a rise in the price of a complementary good;
    d) a change in consumer tastes away from the good;
    e) a fall in price of the good.

    Fig. 1

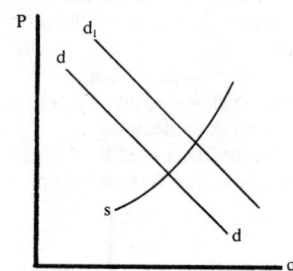

17. Using the diagram in question 16, a normal supply curve is now introduced, how would the change in demand affect equilibrium price?
    a) It would rise.
    b) It would fall.
    c) It would not change.
    d) It would double.
    e) It might rise or fall.

    Fig. 2

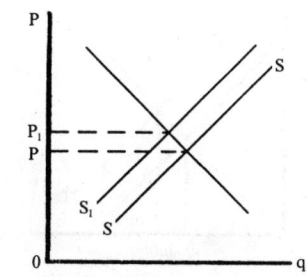

278 Multiple Choice Questions

18. The movement of the supply curve from SS to S_1D_1 might be attributable to: See Fig. 2.
   a) a bumper harvest;
   b) a fall in the costs of production;
   c) the granting of a subsidy to producers;
   d) the imposition of a tax on the commodity;
   e) the Government declares a statutory price of OP_1.

19. Products X and Y are both produced in Perfectly Competitive product markets using unskilled labour obtained from a Perfectly Competitive labour market.
   X has an income elasticity of demand = –0.5
   Y has an income elasticity of demand = 0.5.
   Firms produce either product X or Y, and initially all firms within each industry are at a long run equilibrium.
   Over the next year there occurs an increase of 20% in the average consumer disposable income.
   a) What term would be used to describe good X?
   b) Calculate how the change in income will affect the demand for each good.
   c) Describe, with the help of relevant diagrams, the changes which will occur over time in the above product and factor markets.
   d) Why might a problem occur if labour were occupationally immobile?

20. For each of the following questions, choose one option (A, B, C, D or E) which correctly describes the condition illustrated by the graphs (1 to 5). Each option may be used once, or not at all.
   a) A rise in the quantity supplied caused by a rise in price
   b) A rise in price caused by a fall in supply
   c) A fall in price caused by a fall in demand
   d) A rise in the quantity demanded caused by a fall in price
   e) Constant price but changes in demand and supply

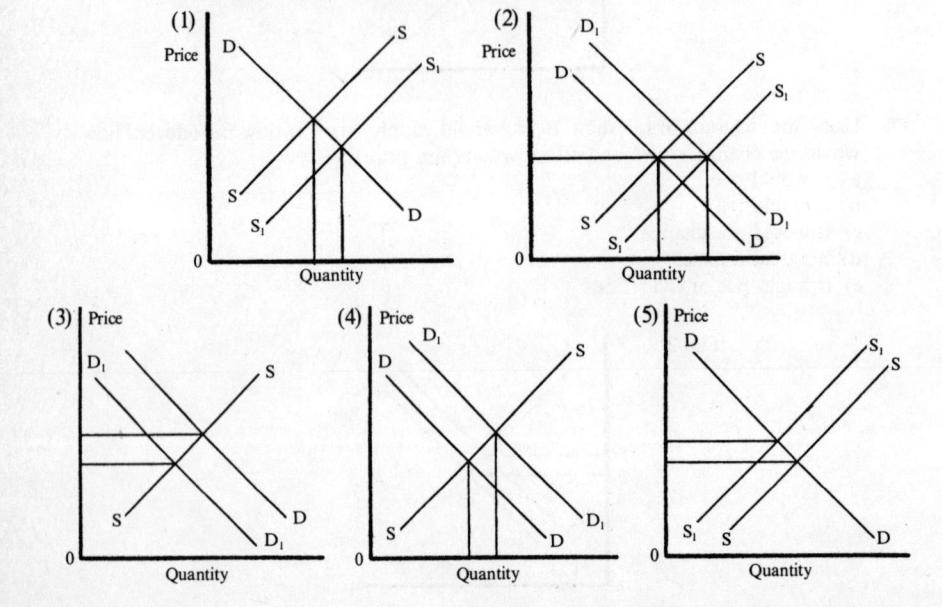

Comparing Agricultural Support Policies

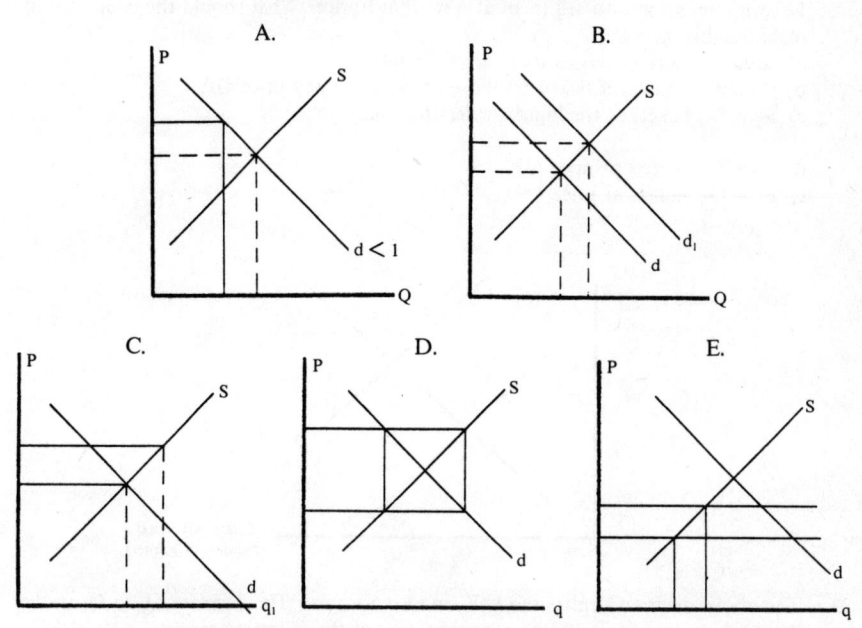

A. B. C. D. E.

21. The diagrams above illustrate the market situation for government policies designed to boost the incomes of producers of certain agricultural commodities.
    a) Match the diagrams A to E to the statements (i) to (v).
       (i) Advertising campaigns stressing the nutritional value of certain products.
       (ii) The imposition of quotas on domestic producers with the intention of restricting quantities produced.
       (iii) Intervention purchasing to ensure that producers receive minimum prices above free market levels.
       (iv) A per unit subsidy on a target price set above equilibrium.
       (v) A deficiency payment scheme whereby producers receive a subsidy equivalent to the difference between the cheap imported price and a higher guaranteed home price below the equilibrium price.
    b) Compare the impact of each policy upon producers, consumers and taxpayers.

22. The diagram below shows the price that successive salmon fishermen would be willing to pay for a ticket to fish a river.

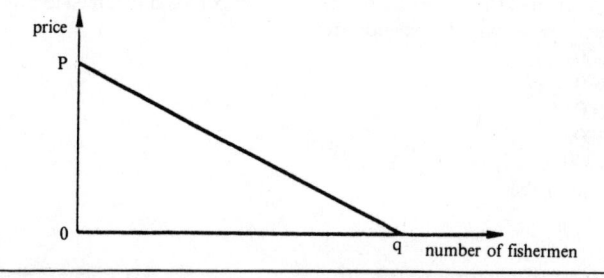

280 Multiple Choice Questions

The owner intends to state publicly the number of tickets to be sold (No Price Discrimination) and to sell them at a standard price. What should the owner do to maximise his income?
a) issue as many tickets as there are fishermen;
b) restrict the issue of tickets to those prepared to pay price OP;
c) issue $\frac{Oq}{2}$ tickets at the highest price they will fetch;
d) issue Oq tickets at price OP;
e) issue $\frac{Oq}{2}$ tickets at price OP.

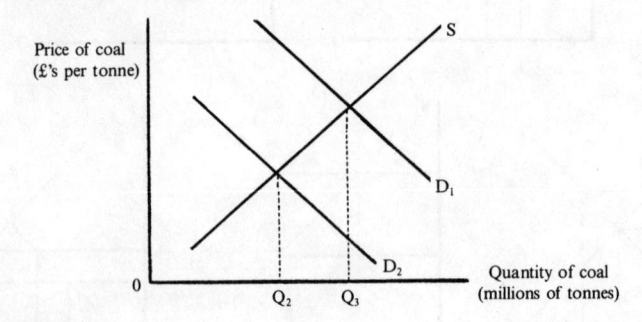

23. The above diagram depicts the U.K. market for coal. The decrease Q_1 to Q_2 in the equilibrium quantity could be caused by any of the following except:-
a) a decrease in the world price of oil;
b) an increase in the amount of electricity generated by nuclear power;
c) increased production of natural gas from the North Sea;
d) a reduction in the number of mines producing coal.

24. The figures in the table below relate to the demand and supply schedules for a good.

price per kg (p)	amount demanded (thousand kg)	amount supplied (thousand kg)
30	1	12
25	2	9
20	3	7
15	5	5
10	7	3
5	10	1

The government imposed a fixed price of 25p per kg and agreed to buy up any unsold produce. What was its expenditure?
a) £200
b) £600
c) £800
d) £1000
e) £1400
f) none of these.

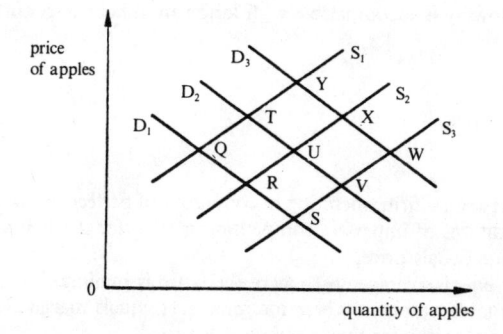

25. The above demand and supply schedules relate to the demand and supply for home produced apples, currently in equilibrium with a price of V.
Identify the new price, in each case from V when the following occur:-
a) cheap imported apples flood the market;
b) intensive TV advertising for home produced apples;
c) a house building programme using apple orchards;
d) a new highly productive strain of apple trees introduced.

26. A profit maximising firm sells its output in two separate markets, X and Y. In market X, in which it enjoys monopoly power, it sells 200 units at £40 per unit. In market Y, which is a perfectly competitive market, it sells 300 units at the prevailing market price. The firm's total output of 500 units is the output which minimises its average costs at £20.
What is the firm's profit?
a) £2000 in each market
b) £2000 overall
c) negative in market Y
d) £4000 overall
e) £6000 overall

27. Which is the best definition of the marginal firm?
a) The most efficient firm in the industry.
b) The firm with the largest profit.
c) The firm with lowest costs.
d) The firm which equates its marginal costs with marginal revenue.
e) The firm which makes only normal profit.

28. If a monopolist charged a price which maximised profit
a) The price would equal the cost of the last unit produced.
b) Total revenue would be at a maximum.
c) Production would take place at an optimum level of output.
d) The revenue received from the last unit produced would equal the cost of producing that unit.
e) All economies of scale would be gained by the monopolist.

29. Which of the following is incompatible with long run abnormal profit?
    a) Monopoly
    b) Oligopoly
    c) Duopoly
    d) Perfect competition
    e) Monopsony

30. One difference between a firm operating in conditions of perfect competition and one operating in conditions of imperfect competition is that, for the latter only.
    a) average revenue equals price;
    b) marginal cost equals average cost where the latter is minimal;
    c) the most profitable output is where marginal cost equals marginal revenue;
    d) marginal revenue is greater than average revenue;
    e) marginal revenue is not equal to price.

COSTS, BEHAVIOUR OF FIRMS etc.

31.

Price	Sales	Total Cost of Production*
14	40	500
13	60	520
12	80	560
11	100	610
10	120	650
9	140	710

*including normal profit.

Assuming that the firm described in the table relates output and price at the profit maximising level, it can be deduced that the firm:
a) Is using full cost pricing.
b) Must be a price taker.
c) Is operating in a perfectly competitive market.
d) Is experiencing constantly decreasing returns to scale.
e) Is producing at less than the optimum scale of production.

32. If a firm's current output is being produced under conditions of diminishing returns, which of the following will be true?
a) The marginal product of labour exceeds its average product.
b) Marginal costs are declining.
c) Average fixed and average variable costs are both falling.
d) Average total costs are rising.
e) The firm will have to raise its selling prices.

33. The following table gives marginal cost and marginal revenue for a firm producing home attic extensions.

Output	Marg Cost	Marg Rev	Aver Cost	Aver Rev	Total Cost	Total Rev
1	5000	7500				
2	4500	6000				
3	3500	4000				
4	2000	2500				

Complete the other columns.

34. Which is the most profitable output for the firm?
a) 1   b) 2   c) 3   d) 4   e) More than this

35. A builder could build 10 or 11 houses on a plot of land. If he builds 10 houses they would cost him £12,000 each to build and he could sell them for £13,650 each. If he builds 11 houses they would cost him £11,250 each to build and he could sell them for £12,750 each.
a) What would be the marginal cost of the eleventh house?
   i) £5250   ii) £96000   iii) £101250   iv) £750   v) £1500

b) What would be the marginal revenue from the eleventh house?
   i) £114750   ii) £109200   iii) £2400   iv) £5500   v) £1650
c) It is worth his while building the eleventh house. True/false.

36. The main difference between the oligopolistic market and that of monopolistic competition is that under oligopoly:
    a) There is no competition through advertising.
    b) There is product differentiation.
    c) There are few sellers, each with a sizeable proportion of the market.
    d) The firms will earn super-normal profits.
    e) The firms can aim at profit maximisation.

37. Where a few large firms dominate the market, barriers to the entry of other firms into the market are not uncommon. One of the following is **unlikely** to be applied:
    a) Existing firms restrict the new entrant's share of the market by increasing the number of similar but differentiated products made by each firm.
    b) 'Fighting Companies' can be established specially to undercut the new entrant in its market.
    c) Existing firms can increase the strength of their advertising.
    d) Existing firms can erect legal barriers to the entry of potential competitors.
    e) Where economies of scale exist the individual firm may be large enough to ensure lower unit costs than the necessarily small new entrant, and the cost differential will be a barrier.

38. An oligopolist
    a) Needs to consider how competitors will react to any price change.
    b) Is not concerned with competitors since there are so few of them.
    c) Must always attempt to maximise profits or be eliminated.
    d) Does not have to be concerned about either marginal or average cost.

39. If all sellers in a market are known to be charging the same price which one of the following statements about market structure and behaviour is correct?
    a) The market is perfectly competitive.
    b) The market is perfectly oligopolistic.
    c) The price is determined collusively.
    d) The price is set by a price leader.
    e) Any of the above statements is correct because uniform prices may emerge from several different market situations.

40. Which of the following conditions are necessary for price discrimination to be possible and profitable?
    a) Imperfect competition, including monopoly, exists in the market.
    b) The market is capable of division into different price elasticities of demand.
    c) Costs of maintaining market divisions are low in relation to benefits arising from elasticity differences.
    d) There are different costs for supplying different markets.

Units of output	Marginal Costs (£s)			
	a	b	c	d
1	1	2	4	8
2	4	3	5	10
3	5	4	8	12
4	6	5	10	14
5	8	6	12	16

41. The table above shows the marginal cost schedules of four profit-maximising firms, a, b, c, and d, within a competitive industry.
    a) What is their (combined) elasticity of supply in the market for an increase in price from £3 to £4?
       (i)   2.5
       (ii) 2.0
       (iii) 0.5
       (iv) 0.4
       (v)   None of these.
    b) The average cost of producing 4 units of firm d is
       (i)   13
       (ii) 11
       (iii) 10
       (iv) None of these.

42. The questions (a) and (b) are based upon the following diagram which shows the Total Revenue and Total Cost curves of an individual firm.

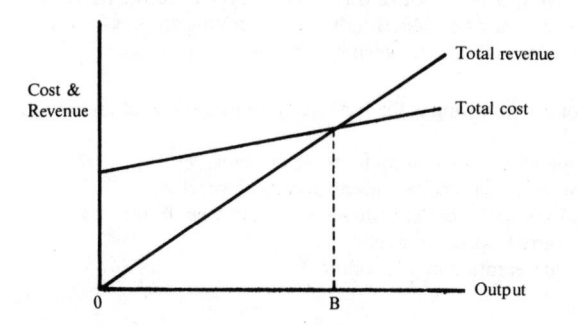

    a) Which of the following statements are correct?
       (i)   Variable costs per unit will be constant over the range of output shown.
       (ii) Marginal revenue will be less than price.
       (iii) OB represents the maximum profit output.

286 Multiple Choice Questions

b) If fixed costs, in the above, were £100 and selling price £1 and variable unit cost 50p, calculate:-
  (i) the break even output;
  (ii) output when profits are £50, £150?

43. Which one of the following measures is specifically designed to deal with divergences between private and social costs?
  a) the imposition of toll charges on road bridges;
  b) equal pay legislation
  c) minimum wage legislation
  d) the introduction of full cost fees for university students from overseas;
  e) the introduction of 'bus only' lanes in city centres.

44.

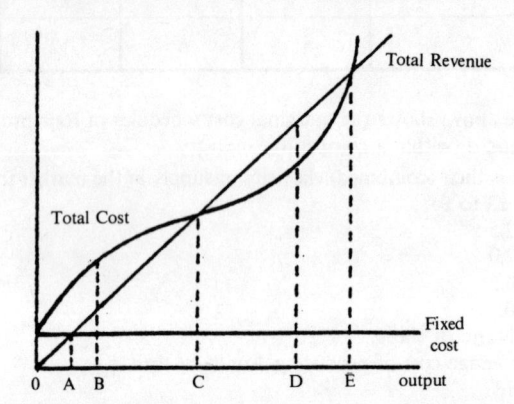

The above diagram shows the cost and revenue situation of a firm.

If the firm increases output from OD to OE which of the following is incorrect. (use above diagram)
  a) The firm moves to the long run perfectly competitive output level.
  b) The firm is a member of a price fixing cartel.
  c) The firm is a profit maximising monopolist in equilibrium.
  d) The firm is a nationalised industry attempting to break even.
  e) None of the above statements is incorrect.

45. Which of the following is the least likely characteristic of an oligopolistic situation in industry?
  a) Co-operation, overt or tacit, between firms.
  b) Competition in service and/or quality of product.
  c) The domination of the industry by a few large firms.
  d) "Cut-throat" price competition.
  e) Some differentiation of product.

46. The table shows hypothetically how motor car costs behave as output increases.

Output per Year	Index of Unit Average Costs (Cars)
100,000	100
250,000	83
500,000	74
1,000,000	70
2,000,000	66

Which of the following are/is true:-
a) The table illustrates economies of scale.
b) Doubling output can lead to costs falling by 30%.
c) Motor car costs fall at a linear rate as output increases.

Directions Summarized (see Q's 47–57)				
A	B	C	D	E
1, 2 3 correct	1, 2 only	2, 3 only	1 only	3 only

47. Which of the following statements about price, marginal revenue and marginal cost is/are true?
    a) Under conditions of perfect competition profits are maximised when price equals marginal revenue equals.
    b) Under imperfect competition marginal cost equals marginal revenue when profits are maximised.
    c) Under imperfect competition price equals average revenue.

48. The practice of "charging what the traffic will bear" is:
    a) A form of discriminating monopoly.
    b) A policy confined to telephone calls.
    c) Adopted when fixed cost is spread over the greatest quantity of output.

49. A monopolist, incurring fixed costs but with zero variable costs, maximises his total profit at a level of output at which
    a) Marginal revenue is positive.
    b) Point elasticity of demand is positive approaching unity.
    c) Total revenue is maximised.

50. In the long run, a profit maximising firm under conditions of perfect competition produces an output at which
    a) Average revenue equals marginal cost.
    b) Average cost equals marginal revenue.
    c) Average revenue equals average cost.

51. When marginal costs are below average costs at a given output, one can deduce that, if output increases

a) Variable costs may fall.
b) Average costs will fall.
c) The firm is at optimum size.

52. Which of the following is/are necessary for the charging of discriminatory prices by a profit maximising monopolist?
    a) Some markets cost more to supply than others.
    b) Markets are spread over the whole world.
    c) Different markets have different price elasticities of demand.

53. Which of the following prevent(s) markets being perfect?
    a) Advertisers claiming special characteristics of goods.
    b) The number of producers being small.
    c) Government action to subsidise some producers.

54. The following graph indicates the impact of social marginal benefits on the market for Underground Travel, eg. London Transport.

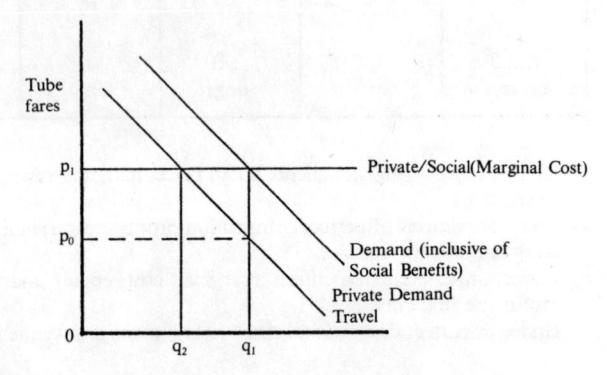

Which of the following statements is/are implied by the diagram:-
a) Social costs are zero whilst social benefits are positive.
b) Economic efficiency is achieved with a subsidy of $OP_1 OP_0$.
c) In order to achieve economic efficiency taxpayers will have to subsidise a loss $(OP_1-OP_0) \times OQ_0$.

55. A profit maximising firm in monopolistic competition making normal profit will produce at the output where price is equal to:
    a) Average cost
    b) Marginal cost
    c) Marginal revenue.

56. The following diagram illustrates the cost and revenue conditions facing a firm.

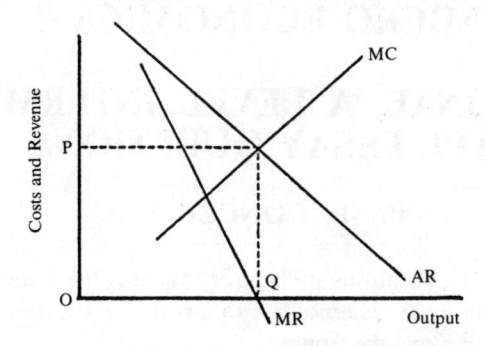

Which of the following statements is/are true of output OQ in the above diagram?
a) Price elasticity of demand is unity.
b) Marginal cost pricing is being implemented.
c) Maximum profits are being made.

57. An unregulated profit maximising monopolist will produce at the output which:-
a) Accords with the monopolies commissions recommendations to earn only normal profit.
b) Maximises the optimum output.
c) Is at a point where price is above marginal revenue.

III BASIC CONCEPTS IN MICRO ECONOMICS

PROFESSIONAL, 'A' LEVEL, INTERMEDIATE TYPE ESSAY QUESTIONS

BASIC CONCEPTS

1. What is a production possibility frontier? What is the meaning of
   (i) a movement from underneath it to a point on the frontier, and
   (ii) a movement along the frontier?
2. Under what conditions might a market not reach a stable equilibrium? Outline the measures which might be used to introduce stability?
3. Explain how a consumer reaches an equilibrium at which he gains the maximum possible satisfaction from the consumption of goods and services?
4. What is meant by economic efficiency in the case of a single firm? What criteria could be used to estimate the extent to which a firm was economically efficient?
5. Describe the main features of a command economy and assess its overall advantages and disadvantages.
6. Discuss and illustrate the relevance of total and marginal utility with respect to the determination of consumer demand in the cases of water and gold.
7. 'The main weakness of microeconomic analysis is in the widespread use of the "other things being equal" or ceterus paribus assumption.' Discuss.
8. Discuss the purpose of economic theory? Discuss if it is necessary for consumers, firms or governments to have an economic theory in order to make rational decisions?
9. (a) Discuss the term 'economic efficiency'?
   (b) How far does the price mechanism ensure that resources are allocated efficiently?

MARKET ANALYSIS

10. Outline and discuss
    (a) The significance of income elasticity of demand to (i) car telephone producers and (ii) potato farmers.
    (b) Apply the idea of cross elasticity of demand to the Post Office when considering higher postal rates.

11. How far do market forces determine the provision of:
    (a) housing;
    (b) health care;
    (c) teachers?
12. What economic factors determine the relative strength of trades union bargaining power in the cases of agricultural workers, ambulance workers, school teachers and elasticity supply workers? Is it likely that trades unions can improve the level of wages in an industry or occupation beyond what the level would be in the free market?

FACTOR INCOMES

13. Discuss the relationship between economic rent and the elasticity of supply of factors of production.
14. What determines land values? Assess the economic arguments for taxing increases in land values.
15. What are the main causes of labour immobility in the United Kingdom? How might the government seek to improve the mobility of labour?
16. What is meant by the 'marginal productivity theory' of wages? Evaluate the validity of this theory in explaining wage levels in a developed economy.
17. 'In order to have the optimum allocation of capital, it should earn the same rate of return in all its uses.' Discuss.

BUSINESS ORGANISATIONS

18. Explain why a firm might wish to grow. Examine the advantages and disadvantages for the consumer of such growth.
19. With reference to current (1992) examples, discuss the factors that influence the location of firms.
20. Discuss the view that it is the existence of barriers to entry rather than the number of producers in an industry which is the main cause of concern to the economist.
21. To what extent can the economic efficiency of an industry be affected by the existence of scale economies. Discuss whether or not the economic efficiency of the water and electricity supply industries is likely to be improved by privatisation.

THEORY OF THE FIRM

22. Outline and assess the relevance of average and marginal costs for the determination of prices in the short and in the long run.
23. Outline how might an individual businessman react to a rise in the general level of interest rates?

24. Discuss the economic factors which (a) encourage, and (b) discourage the development of monopolies.
25. Discuss some of the reasons for any *one* nationalised industry making persistent financial losses, and discuss whether such losses should be eliminated.
26. What factors influence the extent of any change in the sales revenue of a firm following its decision to increase supply?
27. Explain the determinants of the firm's average cost curve in (a) the short run, and (b) the long run.
28. 'Price can only temporarily differ from average cost.' Discuss.

MICRO-ECONOMIC POLICY

29. Describe briefly what are 'externalities'. How and why might taxes and subsidies be used to regulate externalities?
30. Outline and discuss the economic arguments for and against the imposition of high taxes to deter cigarette smoking.
31. Explain why a divergence between the private and social costs of road travel may result in congestion. Discuss the economic policies which might be employed to reduce road congestion.
32. 'As with all externalities, the proper way to treat them is to make those who cause environmental damage pay for it.' Explain and discuss.
33. Why and how do governments intervene to regulate the prices of agricultural products?
34. 'Pollution of the environment is viewed by economists as an external cost.' Explain this statement and discuss possible economic solutions to the problem of controlling pollution.
35. With reference to recent experience, discuss the economic arguments for and against privatisation.
36. Some have estimated that road congestion costs the economy £15 billion annually. Define what is meant by 'cost' and suggest what items might comprise congestion costs. What economic policies can be taken to deal with congestion?
37. Discuss whether the acceptability of the findings of the theory of the firm depend on the acceptability of profit maximisation as the motivating force?
38. "Monopoly is neither good nor bad, but can be either." Discuss.
39. Describe what is meant by profit and discuss the view that profit is always the best guide to resource allocation.
40. Under what conditions would a profit maximising producer gain from a policy of price discrimination?
41. Distinguish carefully between fixed and variable costs. To what extent are the price and output decisions of a firm affected by the existence of fixed costs?

BIBLIOGRAPHY OF MICRO ECONOMICS & GENERAL WORKS

General
Begg, *et al., Economics (2nd Ed.),* McGraw Hill.
Dunnett, A., *Understanding the Economy,* Longman.
Heathfield, D., *Modern Economics,* Philip Allan.
Heilbroner, L. and Thurow, L., *The Economic Problem,* Prentice-Hall.
Heilbroner, L. and Thurow, L., *Economics Explained,* Prentice-Hall.
Lipsey, R.G., *An Introduction to Positive Economics,* Weidenfeld & Nicolson.
Lipsey and Harbury, *First Principles of Economics,* Weidenfeld and Nicolson.
Manchester Economics Project, *Understanding Economics,* Ginn.
Maunder, P. *et al., Economics Explained,* Collins.
McCormick, B.J. *et al., Introducing Economics,* Penguin.
Pennant, R., and Emmott, B., *The Pocket Economist,* Martin Robertson and *The Economist.*
Proctor, N., *Essential Concepts in Macro-Economics,* Checkmate.
Samuelson, P.A., and Nordhaus, W.D., *Economics (Ed. 12),* McGraw-Hill.
Stanlake, G.F., *Introductory Economics,* Longman.
Walker, G., *Data Response for Economics,* Checkmate.
Wonnacott, P. and Wonnacott, R., *Economics,* McGraw-Hill KogaKusha.

UK economy
Annual Abstract of Statistics, HMSO
CSO, *Economic Trends,* HMSO
CSO, *Financial Statistics,* HMSO
CSO, *Monthly Digest of Statistics,* HMSO
Department of Trade and Industry, *Employment Gazette,* HMSO
Lloyds Bank Profile of Britain 1990.

Advanced texts
Atkinson, A.B., *The Economics of Inequality,* Oxford University Press.
Baumol, W.J., *Economic Theory and Operations Analysis,* Prentice-Hall.
Black, J., *The Economics of Modern Britain,* Martin Robertson.
Brown, C.V. and Jackson, P.M., *Public Sector Economics,* Martin Robertson.
Cole, C.L., *Microeconomics,* Harcourt Brace Jovanovich.
Galbraith, J.K., *The Affluent Society,* Pelican.
Galbraith, J.K., *Economics and the Public Purpose,* Pelican.

Galbraith, J.K., *The New Industrial State*, Pelican.
Grant, R.M. and Shaw, G.K. (eds), *Current Issues in Economic Policy*, Philip Allan.
Green W., and Clough, D., *Regional Problems and Policies*, Holt, Rinehart & Wilson.
Hartley, K., *Problems of Economic Policy*, Allen & Unwin.
Haverman, R.H., *The Economics of the Public Sector*, Wiley.
Jones, H., *An Introduction to Modern Theories of Economic Growth*, Nelson.
Koplin, H.T., *Microeconomic Analysis*, Harper & Row.
Laidler, D., *Microeconomics*, Philip Allan.
Levacic, Rosalind, *Economic Policy Making*, Wheatsheaf Books.
Lancaster, K., *An Introduction to Modern Micro-economics*, Rand McNally.
Mishan, E.J., *The Economic Growth Debate: An Assessment*, Allen & Unwin.
Pearce, D.W., *Cost-Benefit Analysis*, Macmillan.
Pearce, D.W., *Environmental Economics*, Longman.
Prest, A.R., and Coppock, D.J. (eds.) *The UK Economy: A Manual of Applied Economics*, Weidenfeld & Nicolson.
Prest, A.R. and Barr, N.A., *Public Finance in Theory and Practice*, Weidenfeld & Nicolson.
Price, C.M., *Welfare Economics in Theory and Practice*, Macmillan.
Ryan, W.J.L. and Pearce, D.W., *Price Theory*, Macmillan.

SELECT MICRO-ECONOMIC GLOSSARY

A

Absolute advantage (in international trade) The ability of Country A to produce a commodity more efficiently (i.e. with lower costs) than Country B. Country B may still have the *comparative advantage*.

Administered prices (or **rigid prices**) To describe prices that are not "flexible". Administered prices are set by imperfectly competitive firms.

Arbitrage The buying of a currency or other commodity in one market and selling it in another market at a higher price. Arbitrage is an important force in eliminating the price discrepancy, thereby making markets function efficiently.

Asset A property or intangible right that has economic value. Important examples are plant, equipment, land, patents, copyrights, goodwill, and financial assets such as money or bonds.

Allocative efficiency An economic outcome in which no reorganization or trade could occur which would make all individuals better off (sometimes stated as "you can't make anyone better off without making someone else worse off"). Under certain limited conditions, perfect competition leads to allocative efficiency. Also called *Pareto efficiency*.

Average cost curve, long-run The minimum average cost of producing a commodity, for each level of output, assuming technology and input prices are given. The producer is free to choose plant of optimal size.

Average cost curve, short run The minimum average cost of producing a commodity, for each level of output, using the given state of technology and input prices and existing plant.

Balance sheet A statement of a firm's financial position as of a given date, listing *assets* in one column, *liabilities* plus *net worth* in the other. The two columns balance because net worth is defined as assets minus liabilities.

Barriers to competition Factors that reduce the amount of competition or the number of producers in an industry, thereby allowing greater economic concentration to occur. Important examples are legal barriers, regulation, and product differentiation.

Barter The exchange of one good for another, without using money.

Black market A market in which goods are sold above the legal price.

Budget line On a diagram whose axes measure physical quantities of two goods, the line which shows all the possible combinations of those two goods that a consumer could just purchase with a given income or budget, and with given prices for the two goods.

C

Capital (capital goods, capital equipment) (1) Capital includes those durable, manufactured inputs to production (i.e. machinery, tools and equipment, buildings, stocks of partly or wholly finished goods). (2) In accounting and finance, "capital" means the total amount of money subscribed by the shareholder-owners of a corporation, in return for which they receive shares of the company's stock/shares.

Capital gains The rise in value of a capital asset. Capital gains are "realized" only when the asset is sold. The gain is then the difference between the sales price and the purchase price of the asset, i.e. profit.

Capital-output ratio In economic growth theory, the ratio of the total capital stock to annual GNP, i.e. 3:1.

Capitalism An economic system in which most property (land and capital) is privately owned. In an economy, private markets, with little government intervention, are instruments used to allocate resources.

Capitalization of assets The process of establishing a money value for assets by calculating the present value of the expected future net income those assets will yield.

Cartel An association of producers in a given industry whose purpose is to restrict or bar competition in the industry. They do this by colluding on the prices, by dividing markets, or by engaging in other such practices.

"Ceteris paribus" "Other things equal" — the assumption that factors *other than price* which influence demand (such as consumer incomes and tastes) are held constant, etc.

Coase theorem A view (not actually a theorem) put forth by Coase that externalities or economic inefficiencies will be corrected by bargaining between the affected parties, i.e. internalised.

Cobweb theorem A dynamic model of supply and demand in which adaptive (or non-rational) expectations lead to perpetual oscillations in prices. Sometimes thought to apply to agricultural markets, e.g. Hog cycle.

Collective bargaining The process of negotiations between a group of workers (usually a union) and their employer.

Collective goods vs. market goods Goods are divided into collective or market depending upon whether they are allocated by political decisions or *public choice* (in which case they are collective goods); or by decentralized supply and demand (in which case they are market goods). A modern economy contains a mixture of the two allocative mechanisms, i.e. mixed economy.

Collusion Agreement between different firms to co-operate by raising prices, dividing markets, or otherwise restraining competition, often illegal.

Command economy The economic organization where key economic functions — *How, What,* and *For Whom* — are principally made by government directive, e.g. a "planned economy."

Comparative advantage The law of comparative advantage says that a nation or individual should specialize in producing, trade or export those commodities which it can produce at *relatively* lower costs, so specialization takes place.

Competition, imperfect The condition in which at least one seller is large enough to affect the market price, so *competition* does not operate. Imperfect competition refers to any kind of imperfection — pure *monopoly, oligopoly,* or *monopolistic competition.*

Competitive market A market where there are so large a number of buyers and sellers of a good that no one is large enough to influence the market price.

Complements Two goods which go together in the eyes of consumers (e.g. shoes). Goods are substitutes when they compete with each other.

Compound interest Interest computed on the sum of all past interest earned as well as on the principal. For example, suppose £100 (the principal) is deposited in an account earning 10 percent interest compounded annually. At the end of year 1, interest of £10 is earned. At the end of year 2, the interest payment is £11. £10 on the original principal and £1 on the interest.

Concentration ratio The percentage of an industry's total output or shipments accounted for by the largest firms, typically the largest five.

Conglomerate A large corporation producing and selling a variety of unrelated goods.

Consumer Surplus The triangular area on the demand curve which shows the difference between what consumers will pay and what they have to pay.

Cost Benefit Analysis A technique used in welfare economics which takes into account social costs and social benefits. Used on M1, Victoria Line etc.

D

Diminishing marginal utility, law of The law which says that as more and more of any one commodity is consumed, so its marginal utility declines.

Diminishing returns, law of The law of production stating that the incremental output from successive increases in an input will eventually diminish. Inputs, such as land, are held constant.

Disinvestment This arises when gross investment is insufficient to cover *depreciation,* so that net investment is negative.

Division of labour A method of organizing production where each worker specializes in one stage, perhaps a tiny one, of production.

E

Economies of scale A situation in which the average cost of production declines when plant size and output is increased.

Economies of scope Economies of producing multiple goods or services. Thus economies of scope exist if it is cheaper to produce both good X and good Y together rather than separately.

Economic Rent A payment made to a factor of production in excess of what is necessary to keep in its present position. Sometimes known as producer's surplus, see Ricardo.

Elasticity of Demand Refers to price elasticity of demand but there is also cross elasticity of demand and income elasticity of demand.

Simple Definitions:-

Price Elasticity of Demand $\quad \dfrac{\% \text{ Change in Q}}{\% \text{ Change in P}}$

Cross Elasticity of Demand $\quad \dfrac{\% \text{ Change in QA}}{\% \text{ Change in PB}}$

Income Elasticity of Demand $\quad \dfrac{\% \text{ Change in Q}}{\% \text{ Change in Y}}$

Engel's Laws Recent studies show that with higher incomes, more is spent absolutely — but less relatively — on food; and more is devoted, both absolutely and relatively, e.g. education.

Equilibrium The state in which the forces operating are in balance so that there is no tendency for change.

Equity capital Funds supplied by the owner of a business. Such an investment yields a share in the ownership along with the risk of loss as well as the chance of profit, e.g. shares.

Expectations Views or beliefs about uncertain variables (such as future interest rates, prices, or tax rates). Expectations are said to be rational if they are on average correct and use all available information. Expectations are adaptive if people assume the future will be pretty much like the past, but adapt their expectations if they have made errors in the past.

External diseconomies A firm's actions that impose uncompensated costs on other parties. Factories that cause smoke and fumes harm public health, yet the injured parties are not paid for the damages. This pollution is an external diseconomy.

External economies Economies that occur if a firm's operations yield positive benefits to others without them paying.

Excess Capacity Criticism of monopolistic competition where equilibrium is not at the lowest point of the average cost curve.

Externalities An activity that affects others for better or worse, without those others paying or being paid. Externalities exist when private costs or benefits do not equal social costs or benefits.

F

Factors of production Productive inputs: the machinery, equipment, tools, labour services, land, and raw materials needed to produce commodities or services.

Final good A good that is produced for final use and not for further manufacture.

Firm (business unit) The basic, private producing unit in a capitalist or mixed economy. It hires labour and buys other inputs and sells goods.

Fiscal policy A government's programme with respect to (a) the purchase of goods and services and spending on transfer payments, and (b) the amount and type of tax rates.

Free goods Those goods that are not *economic goods*. They exist in sufficient quantities, so that they need not be rationed out among those wishing to use them. Thus, their market price is zero, e.g. sand in desert.

Free trade A policy where the state does not intervene in trading between nations — by tariffs, quotas, etc.

G

Game theory Theory seeking to draw a parallel between the behaviour of participants in a game of chance (such as poker) or strategy (such as chess) and behaviour of firms or people in small groups, particularly in *oligopolies*.

Gross national product The value, at current market prices, of all final goods and services produced within some period by a nation, without any deduction for depreciation of capital goods.

Giffen Good A good whose demand rises as price rises. This is caused by the negative income effect being greater than the positive substitution effect, e.g. bread possibly.

I

Imperfect competitor Any firm that buys or sells a good in large enough quantities to be able to affect price of that good in the trade.

Incidence The ultimate economic burden of a tax as opposed to the legal requirement for payment. Thus a sales tax may be paid by a retailer, but it is likely that the incidence is upon the consumer. The exact incidence of a tax depends on the price elasticities of supply and demand.

Income effect of a price change Change in the amount demanded of a commodity because the change in its price has the effect of raising or lowering a consumer's real income.

Indifference Curve A curve which shows the various combinations of two goods so that the consumer is indifferent between any combination on the curve. The further the indifference curve is from the x and y axes, the higher the level of satisfaction.

Integration Vertical integration is the combination in a single firm of two or more *different* stages. Horizontal integration is the combination in a firm of different units which operate at *the same* stage of production.

Inefficiency Exists in the model of monopolistic competition, since the actual output from given inputs is less than the maximum level obtainable.

Inferior Good A good where consumption falls as income rises due to its inferior nature, e.g. cigarettes.

Isocost Curve A line showing the various combinations of any two inputs that can be bought for the same amount of money.
Isoquant An isoquant shows the various combinations of any two factors of production which yield the same level of output.

K
Keynesian economics The body of thought developed by John Maynard Keynes culminating in his *General Theory*. The central theme was that (primarily because of sticky wages) a capitalist system does not automatically tend towards a full-employment equilibrium. The resulting "underemployment equilibrium" could be cured by fiscal or monetary policies to raise *aggregate demand* and *reduce unemployment*.
Kinked Demand Curve In oligopolistic markets because competitors would not follow price increase but would match price reduction. This causes an elastic demand curve above the prevailing price and an inelastic demand curve below it.

L
Labour supply The number of workers available to an economy. The principal determinants of labour supply are population, wages, social traditions and participation rates.
Land One of the three basic *factors of production* (along with labour and capital). It includes land used for agricultural or industrial purposes, as well as natural resources taken from above or below the soil, e.g. oil.
Least-cost rule The rule that the cost of producing a specific level of output is at its minimum when the ratio of the *marginal-revenue-product* of each input (to price of that input) is the same for all inputs, etc.
Limited liability Enjoyed by shareholders of a corporation so, if that corporation runs into financial trouble, their loss is limited to their original financial outlay. Shareholders have no further responsibility for the debts of the corporation.
Laffer Curve A diagrammatical exposition which shows that tax yields will fall at certain tax rates because it discourages high taxpayers from working.
Lorenz Curve A method used in the calculation of measures of inequality. If we had complete equality the Lorenz curve would have a straight line of 45°, see Stat. section.

M
Malthus Theory of Population A gloomy prediction by T.R. Malthus who stated that food production could only rise arithmetically 1 2 3 4 ......, while population would grow geometrically 1 2 4 8 ...... so poverty ensues.
Marginal Productivity Theory The theory which stages that a profit maximising employer will employ workers up to the point where the marginal revenue product of the last worker is equal to his marginal cost.
Marginal utility The extra utility derived from the consumption of one extra unit of a good.

Monopsony A monopoly is where there is one seller, a monopsony is where there is one buyer. Used in the labour market where there is one company in a town and villages.

Model A formal framework for representing the basic features of a complex system by a few central relationships. Models take the form of graphs, or mathematical equations.

Monopolistic competition A market structure with a large number of sellers who are supplying goods that are close, but not perfect substitutes. Each firm can exercise some effect on its price in the market.

Monopoly A market structure in which a commodity is supplied by only one firm.

N

Natural monopoly A firm or industry whose average cost per unit of production falls sharply over the entire range of its output. Thus a single firm, a monopoly, can supply the industry output more efficiently than multiple firms.

Normative vs. positive economics Normative economics considers "what ought to be" — value judgments, or goals of public policy. Positive economics, by contrast, is the analysis of facts and data: "the way things are," i.e. scientific.

O

Oligopoly Imperfect competition in which an industry is dominated by a small number of suppliers of similar size.

Opportunity Cost The opportunity cost is the alternative foregone. Economics is concerned with the allocation of scarce resources. If resources are allocated to Project X, they cannot be used for Project Y.

P

Partnership An association of two or more persons to conduct a business but not in corporate form. Thus they do not enjoy *limited liability*. If a partnership fails, one partner may be responsible for *all* its debts if the other partner cannot pay his or her share. Also sleeping partnerships.

Product differentiation The existence of characteristics that make similar goods less than perfect substitutes. Thus locational differences make the petrol sold at separate points imperfect substitutes.

Production function A relation specifying the amount of output that can be achieved with given inputs. Applies to a firm or, as an aggregate production function, to the economy.

Production-possibility frontier A graph showing the goods that can be produced by an economy. In a frequently cited simple case, the choice is reduced to two goods, guns and butter. Points outside the p–p frontier are unattainable. Points inside it would be inefficient since resources are not being fully employed.

Public choice Branch of economics and political science dealing with the way that governments choose. The theory of how democratic systems, under pressure from the desire of politicians to be re-elected, choose among alternative programmes.

Public good A public good is a product or provision which if supplied to one person can be made available to others at no extra cost, e.g. street lighting.

Q

Quantity Theory of Money MV = PT, i.e. M is the quantity of money in circulation, V is Velocity of circulation, P is the general price level and T is transactions demand. If V and T are constant it implies that the price level (inflation) can be controlled by manipulating the money supply, as monetarists believe.

R

Regressive Tax Unlike progressive taxes, the more you earn, the more percentage you pay, a regressive tax is paid regardless of means, e.g. poll tax.

Rate of return (or return) on capital The yield on an investment or on a capital good. Thus, an investment costing £100 and yielding £10 annually has a 10 percent rate of return.

Real GNP GNP adjusted for price change. Real GNP equals nominal GNP divided by the GNP deflator.

Real interest rate The interest rate measured in terms of goods or services rather than money. It is thus equal to the money (or nominal) interest rate less the rate of inflation.

Real wages The purchasing power of a worker's wages. Measured by the ratio of the money wage rate to the retail price index.

Regulation Government laws or rules designed to change the behaviour of firms. The major kinds are economic regulation (which affects the prices, entry, or service of a single industry), and social regulation. The latter attempts to correct externalities that prevail across a number of industries, e.g. water pollution).

Rent, economic This term was applied by Ricardo to income obtained from ownership of land. The total supply of land available in a nation or in the world is fixed, and the return paid to the landowner is rent. The term is often extended to the return paid to any factor in fixed supply.

Resource allocation The way in which an economy distributes its resources (its factors of production) among the occupations in which they could be used, so as to produce an output.

Retained earnings The corporation's profit (net income) not paid out as dividends. dividends).

Returns to scale The rate at which output increases as all inputs are increased together. For example, if all the inputs double and output is exactly doubled, that process is said to exhibit *constant returns to scale*. If, however, output grows by only 60 percent when all inputs are doubled, the process shows *decreasing returns to scale*; if output more than doubles, the process is an *increasing returns to scale* technology.

S
Scarcity The principle that most things that people want are available only in limited supply (the exception being *free goods*). Goods are generally scarce and must therefore somehow be rationed, whether by price or some other means.
Separation or divorce of ownership and control A characteristic of large corporations: They are owned by their shareholders but operated and controlled by their professional managers.
Short run Period in which all factors cannot adjust fully. In microeconomics, the capital stock and other "fixed" inputs do not adjust in the short run, and entry is not free in the short run.
Shutdown price (or point, or rule) In the theory of the firm, the point where market price is so low that the firm's losses per period just equal its fixed costs. Thus it might just as well shut down. The shutdown point comes at the point where the market price is just sufficient to cover average variable cost.
Single-land-tax A nineteenth-century movement, originated by Henry George. The "single tax" was to be a tax on economic rent earned from land ownership due to inelastic supply.
Substitution effect (of a price change) The tendency of consumers is to consume more of a good when its price falls (to "substitute" in favour of that good), and to consume less of the good when its price increases (to "substitute" away from that good).
Supply and demand, law of The "law" that says that (under perfect competition) market price will move to the level at which the quantity purchased equals the quantity sold.

T
Terms of trade A price index which relates the price of exports and the price of imports. If the terms of trade go against a country it means they must sell more exports to buy the same volume of imports, vice versa if it is favourable.
Transfer Earnings The minimum payment required by a factor of production to stop it moving to its next best use, i.e. same as the opportunity cost.

V
Variable Cost Costs which vary according to the level of production, e.g. raw materials. Total Variable Cost = Total Cost − Fixed Cost.

Y
Yield Interest rate or *rate of return* on an asset.

INDEX

A

Abnormal profit 102, 119, 123-124, 141
Absolute advantage 22-23
Accounting costs 39
Adverse selection 56, 199
Age distribution of population 29
Agriculture and elasticity 74, 94
   (see also Cobweb theorem)
Allocative efficiency 12, 194
   — under monopoly — see Ch.15
Areas under curves 271-272
Area analysis 221-225
Articles of Association 36
Assumptions in Economics 1-2, 102, 150
Averages 243-244
Average (total) cost 103
Average fixed cost (AFC) 103
Average product (AP) 15, 27
Average revenue (AR) 118
Average variable cost (AVC) 103

B

Balance sheets 38
Barriers to entry 125-126, 173
Baumol, W. 149, 151
Behavioural theories of the firm 150
Benefit-Cost analysis, see Cost-Benefit analysis
Beveridge Curve 173
Black Markets 73
Budget Line 229 et seq
Buffer stocks 74
Business organisations 34-37
   — owners versus controllers 148-149

C

Capital 17-18, 41, 181-182
   — goods 4
   — sources of 42, 249
   — demand for 184-186
   — returns 256
   — applications 187-188
   — present value of 182-184
   — price of 186
   — supply of 181, 185
   — employed by business 38
   — yield or rental value 184
   — analysis, compound, discount 270-272
Capital/Output rates, selected 249
Cartels 123, 142-144
Central Planning 4-5
Ceterus paribus 2, 61, 69
Choice, basic need for 4-5
Circular flow diagram 6
Coase 201, see also Property Rights
Cobweb theorem 95-96
Collusion 138-139, 141-142
Collectivist Economic System 7
Collective goods 8
Command economies 7

Companies, major UK 47
Comparative advantage 23-24
Competition policy, see Ch.15
Complements in demand 70
Composite demand 71
Compound analysis, table, 270-272
Concentration ratios 45, 210
Conglomerate mergers 47,
   see Lateral integration
Consumer Equilibrium 230-232
Consumer surplus 66, 195
Contestable markets 151
Correlation, statistical 266
Cost-benefit analysis 202, 211
Costs Types, behaviour 102-103, 106
   — long run, 109, 121
   — very long run 122
   — saucer shaped 140
   — constant 13
   — short run 121
   — minimisation 18
   — and market structures 109
Costs and economic efficiency, see Ch.14
Cost of production
   — long run 107, 120-121
   — private and social, see Externalities
   — see also Opportunity Cost
Cross elasticity of demand 90-91
Cyert and March 150

D

Debentures (loans) 38, 41
Debt 42-43, see Gearing ratio
Decreasing returns to scale 108-109
Demand Curves
   — and time 72-73
   — arc elasticity 87
   — composite 71
   — cross elasticity 90-91
   — derived 154
   — determinants of 67-69
   — elasticity of 85-87
   — equation 264
   — for a factor of production 154, 156-157
   — speculative, snob 77-78
   — surplus, shortage 63-64
Demand and Indifference curves 231
   — and marginal utility 65, 227
   — downward sloping 62
Demand intersection with supply 64-66
Demand and elasticity 85-87
Demand and monopoly 123-124
Demand and revenue 86
Demand, determinants of 87-88
Demand
   — for a factor of production 154-156
   — for an industry 156-157
   — graphical representation of elasticity 86
   — equation and representation 264
Demand for money 76

Demand schedule 62–64
Demographic factors, see Population
Dependent population (ratio) 26
Depreciation of capital 38, 182
Deregulation 217
Derived demand 154
Diminishing Returns, see law of
Discounted cash flow 183–184, 270–272
— table of factors 272
Discriminating monopoly,
  see Price discrimination
Discrimination, wage 173–174
Diseconomies of scale 110
Division of labour 24–25
  (see also Specialisation)
Divorce of ownership from control 148
Duopoly 60

E

Economic efficiency, see Efficiency economic
Economic man 3
Economic Problem 4–5
Economic Rent 163–164, 176
Economic resources 4
Economic statistics, Ch.17
Economic systems 4–5
Economic theory, nature of 2–3
Economies of scale 107
  internal to firm 109
  external to firm 110
Efficiency
  allocative/economic 12–13, 193
  technical/cost 12–13, 193
  and monopoly 196
  and privatisation 217–218
  market 194–195
Elasticity, see Demand, elasticity of,
  supply, elasticity of
Elasticity, applications of 94–96
Entitlements and poverty, (SEN et alia) 28
Entrepreneur 18
Entry, see Barriers to Entry
Envelope Curve 108–109
Equilibrium
  — quantity bought and sold 63
  — attainment of 64
  — changes in 67–74
  — in factor markets 155
  — under monopolistic
    competition 127–128
  — under monopoly 123–124
  — under perfect competition 119–121
  — in the long run 121
Equities, see ordinary shares
Equity versus efficiency 205
Expectations 68
External Economies of Scale, see Economies
  of Scale
Externalities 9, 200–207
  — dealing with externalities 203–204

F

Factor markets 151–152
  and goods markets 76–77

Factor mobility 161
— short and long run 153
Factor prices 153
— in perfect markets 151–152
— under monopoly/monopsony 158–159
Factors of production 17–18
Financial Economies of Scale 109
Fixed Costs 103
Flow of funds 41
Footloose industries 50
Free goods 4
Free market economies 5
Free Rider problem 197
Freedom of entry and exit 117, 152
  see also Barriers to Entry and
    Contestable markets
Friedman, M. 150
Futures markets 61

G

Game theory 142–143
Galbraith 150
Gearing ratio 43–44
George, H. 165
Giffen goods 2, 78, 234
Government Intervention 73–74, 178
  see also market failure
Government policy
— and monopoly output 207, 209–210
— and regional problem 152–153
— and price controls 73–74, 75
Graphs, see Ch.17
Gross National Product (GNP) 19–21
Gross Domestic Fixed Capital Formation
  (GDFCF) 182

H

Hayek von 195
Histogram 248
Homogeneous products 117
— factors 152
Horizontal integration 47
Housing subsidies 240–241

I

Imports and markets 74
Incidence of taxation 92
Income distribution UK 246
— Differences 52–53
Income and substitution effects 77–78, 232,
  242
— in factor markets 235–237
Income elasticity of demand 90–91
Increasing returns to scale,
  see Diminishing returns
Index Numbers 258–259
Indifference Curves 228–230
— applications of 231–235
Industry demand for a factor 155–156
Inferior goods 230–231,
  see also Perverse demand

306 Index

Information assymetry 199
— uncertainty, see Cobweb theory
Input/Output Analysis 20–21
Integration, see Horizontal, Vertical and Lateral (mergers)
Interest rates 185–189
Investment decisions 183, 186
Isocosts 238
Isoquants 238

J

Joint demand 70
Joint stock companies 35–36
Joint supply 172
Judgements, value 1

K

Keynes, policy 1, 8
Kinked demand curve 140

L

Labour markets 155–6
— and Trades Unions 171
— non clearing 172
— and strikes 261
— non competitive 166
— in UK 19, 175
— and mobility 51–52
— competitive versus monopsonist 166
Laffer curve 236–237
Lags, time, see Cobweb theory
Land, as a factor 17, 176–178
(see also Economic Rent)
Lateral Integration 47
Law of Diminishing Returns 11, 14–15
Law of Variable proportions 14–15
Learning Economics 110
Least Cost Combination 239
Limit Pricing Barriers 126
Loanable funds theory 189
Location of Industry 49–53
— Government Policy 53–54
— Quotient, Concentration quotient 52–53
Long Run Average Total Cost (LRATC) 111, 121–2
Long Run Equilibrium
— under monopolistic competition 127
— under monopoly 124
— under perfect competition 120
Lorenz curve 254

M

Malthus, T. 26
— neo Malthusians 27
Managerial Economies of Scale 109
Manpower 17
Marginal Cost 105
Marginal Cost Pricing 214
Marginal Efficiency of Capital (MEC)
(see Marginal Value Product of Capital) (MVPK)

Marginal Physical Product (MPP) 154
Marginal product 27
Marginal productivity theory 154–155
Marginal Revenue 105
Marginal Revenue Product (MRP) 154, 175, 184–185
Marginal Value Product of Capital (MVPK) 184–186
Marginal Utility 65, 227
Marginals and totals (area analysis) 267
Market, definitions 60
— characteristics 61–62
— clearing price 64
— demand 61–62
— supply 63, 69–70
— Economies, features 4–5
— Change over time 72–73
— free, advantages 195
— product and factor link 76–77
— equilibrium 63–64
— non clearing labour 172
— drawbacks 75, 195–196
— and time 72
— Quotas and subsidies 74
Market structures and costs, 112–113
Marshall, A. 3, 164
Mathematics and Economics, see Ch.18
Maximum Price Ceilings 73
Memorandum of Association 36
Mergers 45, 47, 211
Merit, demerit goods 9, 197
Method of Economics 12
Micro-economics and macro 3
— policy and markets, see Ch.14
Minimum efficient scale (MES) 45, 108
Minimum, maximum prices 73
Mixed Economies 7–8
Monopolies and Mergers Commission 209–210
Monopolistic Competition 127–128, 193–194
Monopoly 123–126
— allocative inefficiency under 196
— compared to perfect competition 207–208
— discriminating 128–131
— natural 214
— profits under 124
Monopsony 123
Monopsonistic factor markets 166
— labour markets 158
Moral Hazard 56

N

Nationalisation 37, 214
— and natural monopoly 215
— versus privatisation 216
Natural monopoly 214
Net Present Value 183–184
see Discounted Cash Flow
Non Pecuniary advantages 161
Normative Statements
Normal profit 102, 119, 124, 141

O

Office of Fair Trading 210
Oligopoly, characteristics 137
 — cost curves 140
 — demand curves 139
 — interdependency 142
Opportunity Cost 11–12, 164
Optimum Output 193
 — and second best 219–221
 — and perfect competition 117–122
Optimum population 126
Ordinary shares 42
Output decisions 111
 — of UK Economy 20, 251
 — effect of tax upon 92–93
 — for profit maximising 105

P

Pareto, V. (optimum) 163–164, 193, 197, 203, 217–218
Partnership 35
Patents, see Barriers to Entry
Per Capita, measure of output 13
Perfect competition 117–122
 — and monopoly compared 193–194
 — assumptions of 117–118
 — in factor markets 152
Performance Ratios 39–40
Perishable goods markets, behaviour 63–65
Perverse Demand 78
Pollution, policy 201–202
 — private and social optimum 203–204
Population, determinants of 26
 — Age distribution 29, 248–250
 — of the UK 25
 — Optimal 27
 — Poverty and entitlements 28
Positional goods 4
Predictions in Economics 2–3
Price, Determination 63
 — changes 65–68, 70–74
 — equilibrium 64
 — discrimination 128–131
 — functions of 6
Price Index Numbers 258–260
Prisoners Dilemma 142
Privatisation 213, 216–218
Production Costs, long, short term 107
Production Possibility Curve 11–12
Production (Technical) Economies of Scale 109
Profit 38
 — role of profit 39, 185
 — normal, abnormal 102, 119, 124, 141
 — and loss accounts 39
 — maximising objective 102, 149, 164
Profitability 39
Property Rights 201
Proprietorships 34–35
Public goods 8, 197
Public Corporations 37
Public Choice Economics 212
Purchasing power of money 259

Q

Quantification of economic models, see Ch. 18
Quasi-Rent 164
Queues 73

R

Rate of return on capital 39
Regional policy 51
 see also Location of Industry
Regressive taxes 205
Regulations in Economics 201, 203, 207, 212, 217, 219
Regulatory Capture 212
Resource Allocation 3–7
Restrictive Practices Court 209
Retail Price Index (RPI) 259–260
Ricardo, D. 176, 184
Risk 54–56
 — and capital 187, 198

S

Sales Maximisation, see Baumol W.
Satisficing theory of behaviour 128, 150
Scale, returns to, 110, see Economies of
Scarcity problem 3–4
Schumpeter, J. 126
Scope of Economics 15
Second best, theory of 219–220
Sen, A. and Drèze, J. 28
Shares, company 41–42
Short run cost curves 120–121
Shut down rule 111
Simon, H. 150
Small firms 48–49
Smith, A. 22
Snob appeal 78, 232
Social Costs and Benefits, see Externalities
Specialisation 22, 24–25
 see also Division of Labour
Statistical analysis, see Ch. 17
 — appendix 260
Sticky or stable prices, oligopoly 139–140
Stocks and flows 269
Strategic entry deterrence 126, 142–143
Strikes, UK, 1971–3, 261
Subsidies, negative taxes 93–94
Substitutes 71, 233
Substitution
 — among factors of production 156–157
 — effect of price change 77–78, 232
Supply 63, 69–70
 — and time 73
 — determinants of 69–70
 — joint 72
 — of factors of production 160–162
Supply Curves 64–70
 — and demand intersection 64
 — elasticity of 88–90
 — of factors of production 160–163
 — graphical interpretation 89, 264
 — equation 265–266
 — of effort 235

T

Takeovers, method and reasons 45–46
Taxation, Taxes
— specific, advalorum 94
— progressive, regressive, proportional 205
— of labour 206, 236–237
— of Economic Rent 164, 165
— Incidence of 93
— neutral, non neutral 165
Technical (Production) Economies of Scale 109
Theory of Income Distribution, see Ch.11–13
Time and demand 72, 87
— and elasticity of supply 88
— and markets (futures) 61, 72
Time lags, Cobweb theory 95–96
Total Cost 105
Total Fixed Cost 105
Total Product Curve 15–16
Total Revenue 85, 105–106
Total Utility, 65, 267–268
   see also marginal utility
Total Variable Cost 103
Trades Union, role of 170–171
— impact of 171–172
Transfer payments 163–164
Trends 267

U

Uncertainty, see Risk
Unit Cost 103
Urban land, use and values 176–177
Utility
— law of diminishing marginal 65–66
— marginal 65–66, 227, 228

V

Value added analysis 20
Value of marginal product (VMP) 158–159
Value of marginal product of capital (VMPK) 184–186
Variable costs 103
Variable factor 15–16
Variables 262
Vertical mergers 47

W

Wages, and trade unions 171
— determinants of rates 156–160
— in imperfect markets 158, 166
— discrimination 173–174
— disequilibrium (non-clearing markets) 172
Wants, unlimited 3–4
Weights for index numbers 258
Welfare Economics, see Ch.13, 14
Working capital 41–42

X

X-inefficiency 207–208

Z

Zero elasticity of demand 86–87
Zero elasticity of supply 89
Zero opportunity cost 164